WESTERN POLITICAL THEORY

PART 1

ANCIENT AND MEDIEVAL

HARCOURT BRACE JOVANOVICH, INC.

New York • Chicago • San Francisco • Atlanta

WESTERN POLITICAL THEORY

PART 1

ANCIENT AND MEDIEVAL

LEE CAMERON McDONALD
Pomona College

ISBN: 0-15-595297-8

Library of Congress Catalog Card Number: 68–19235

Printed in the United States of America

Acknowledgments

APPLETON-CENTURY-CROFTS—for excerpts from *The Statesman's Book of John of Salisbury,* translated by John Dickinson. Copyright by Alfred A. Knopf, Inc., 1927. Copyright, 1955, by Lindsay Rogers. Reprinted by permission of Appleton-Century-Crofts, Division of Meredith Corporation.

BARNES & NOBLE, INC.—for excerpts from Thomas Aquinas, *De regimine principum* in *Selected Political Writings,* tr. by J. G. Dawson; ed. by A. P. D'Entreves, 1959.

BENZIGER BROTHERS, INC.—for excerpts from Thomas Aquinas, *Summa Theologica,* English Dominican tr., copyright 1947 by Benziger Brothers, Inc.

BASIL BLACKWELL & MOTT LTD.—for excerpts from Thomas Aquinas, *De regimine principum* in *Selected Political Writings,* tr. by J. G. Dawson; ed. by A. P. D'Entreves, 1959. For excerpts from Dante, *The Divine Comedy,* tr. by Geoffrey L. Bickersteth, 1965.

THE BOBBS-MERRILL COMPANY, INC.—for excerpts from David Hume: *Political Essays,* edited by Charles W. Hendel, copyright © 1953, by The Liberal Arts Press, Inc., reprinted by permission of the Liberal Arts Press Division of The Bobbs-Merrill Company, Inc.

BURNS & OATES LTD.—for excerpts from Thomas Aquinas, *Summa Theologica,* English Dominican tr., 1947.

CAMBRIDGE UNIVERSITY PRESS—for excerpts from Robert Tucker, *Philosophy and Myth in Karl Marx,* 1961.

CLARENDON PRESS, OXFORD—for excerpts from *The Dialogues of Plato,* 4th ed., tr. by Benjamin Jowett, 1953, by permission of the Clarendon Press, Oxford. For excerpts from Plato, *The Republic,* tr. by F. M. Cornford, 1945, by permission of the Clarendon

Press, Oxford. For excerpts from *Nicomachean Ethics* in *The Works of Aristotle,* tr. and ed. by W. D. Ross, Vol. 9, 1925, by permission of the Clarendon Press, Oxford. For excerpts from Aristotle, *Politics,* tr. by Ernest Barker, 1958, by permission of the Clarendon Press, Oxford.

J. M. DENT & SONS LTD.—for excerpts from Plato, *Parmenides, Thaeitetos, Sophist, Statesman,* tr. by John Warrington, Everyman's Library Edition, 1961. For excerpts from Thomas Aquinas, *Selected Writings,* ed. by M. C. D'Arcy, Everyman's Library Edition, 1950, © revisions J. M. Dent & Sons Ltd. 1964. For excerpts from Thomas Hobbes, *Leviathan,* ed. by A. D. Lindsay, Everyman's Library Edition, 1950. For excerpts from John Locke, *Second Treatise* in *Two Treatises of Civil Government,* ed. by William S. Carpenter, Everyman's Library Edition, 1924.

E. P. DUTTON & CO., INC.—for excerpts from Plato, *Parmenides, Thaeitetos, Sophist, Statesman,* tr. by John Warrington, Everyman's Library Edition, 1961. For excerpts from Thomas Aquinas, *Selected Writings,* ed. by M. C. D'Arcy, Everyman's Library Edition, 1950. For excerpts from *Leviathan* by Thomas Hobbes. Introduction by A. D. Lindsay, Everyman's Library Edition. Reprinted by permission of E. P. Dutton & Co., Inc. For excerpts from John Locke, *Second Treatise* in *Two Treatises of Civil Government,* ed. by William S. Carpenter, Everyman's Library Edition, 1924.

HAFNER PUBLISHING COMPANY—for excerpts from Baron de Montesquieu, *The Spirit of the Laws,* tr. by Thomas Nugent; ed. by Franz Neumann, 1949. For excerpts from Jean-Jacques Rousseau, *The Social Contract,* tr. by G. D. H. Cole; rev. and ed. by Charles Frankel, 1947.

HARVARD UNIVERSITY PRESS—for excerpts reprinted by permission of the publishers from R. M. Gummere, translator, Seneca, *Epistulae Morales,* Cambridge, Mass.: Harvard University Press, 1953. For excerpts reprinted by permission of the publishers from W. A. Oldfather, translator, Epictetus, *Discourses,* Cambridge, Mass.: Harvard University Press, 1926. For excerpts from Dante, *The Divine Comedy,* tr. by Geoffrey L. Bickersteth, 1965.

INDIANA UNIVERSITY PRESS—for excerpts from *The Histories of Polybius,* tr. by E. S. Shuckburgh; Introduction by F. W. Walbank, 1962.

ALFRED A. KNOPF, INC.—for excerpts from Albert Camus, *The Rebel,* tr. by Anthony Bower, Random House, Vintage Books, 1956.

LUTTERWORTH PRESS—for excerpts from *Reformation Writings of Martin Luther,* tr. by Bertram Lee Woolf, 1952.

OXFORD UNIVERSITY PRESS—for excerpts from *Il Principe,* by Niccolo Machiavelli, translated by Luigi Ricci, revised by E. R. P. Vincent and published by Oxford University Press, 1906. Reprinted in *The Prince and The Discourses,* Random House, Modern Library, 1940.

RANDOM HOUSE, INC.—for excerpts from *Basic Writings* of *Saint Augustine,* ed. by Whitney J. Oates, 1948.

GEORGE B. SABINE—for excerpts from Cicero, *De republica* in *On the Commonwealth,* tr. by George H. Sabine and Stanley B. Smith, Bobbs-Merrill, n. d.

SCM PRESS LTD.—for excerpts from John Calvin, *Institutes of the Christian Religion,* I & II, tr. by Ford Lewis Battles; ed. by John T. McNeill, Library of Christian Classics, 1960.

THE UNIVERSITY OF CHICAGO PRESS—for excerpts from Karl Jaspers, *The Future of Mankind,* by permission of The University of Chicago Press. Copyright © 1961 by The University of Chicago. All rights reserved.

THE WESTMINSTER PRESS—for excerpts from *Institutes of the Christian Religion,* I and II, Library of Christian Classics, Vols. XX and XXI, edited by John T. McNeill and translated by Ford Lewis Battles. The Westminster Press. Copyright © 1960, W. L. Jenkins. Used by permission.

JOHN WILEY & SONS, INC.—for excerpts from David Easton, *A Systems Analysis of Political Life,* 1965.

To Claire

PREFACE

A book is what it is. Cut its pages properly and, inescapably, its virtues and vices are spread before all who can read and care to read. This makes the writing of prefaces a precarious enterprise, whether they are meant to serve as enticements or diversions. Should you therefore be overcome with curiosity about Plato, by all means proceed at once to page 5, where begins a well-meant chapter on that estimable sage. With or without prefatory preparation, you will find that if the chapter works you will want to read further—not just in McDonald, though that would be nice, but in Plato, which is even nicer.

This book, which examines the contributions of major Western political thinkers from ancient Greece to the present, includes a revision of my *Western Political Theory: The Modern Age,* which analyzed political thinkers from the seventeenth to the twentieth centuries. The present volume is thus a big book of commentary born in an age of small paperbacks and anthologies. In this sense, it is unconventional—influenced perhaps by the political philosophers in its pages who have questioned convention.

Some skeptics will wonder what can justify the attempt to compress more than two thousand years of political thinking into a few hundred pages. Their skepticism should be respected, for such sanity as the world knows is much in tempered skepticism's debt. In my 1962 preface I suggested that my aim was not to save the world or to make money (though, if the truth be known, I was opposed to neither aim), but rather to fulfill a "long-felt need in the author to write a book." That need having so long ago been met, I must find another justification for this second book. A second book, I am happy to report, is easier to write than a first book and provides even more pleasure in the writing. But it takes longer, because a second book is a less reliable excuse for avoiding service on committees. One way or another a decade of my life has spanned the writing of this book. Though I have tried to make the experience appear painful, I have in fact learned much of worth, much that I treasure, in writing this book. If others learn something in reading it, I shall be doubly grateful.

In the 1962 preface I most soberly thanked

a good many friends and scholars for manifold aid and comfort. Most of them should be thanked again for this volume. But instead I will merely mention a few others who have been generous with their expertise for the sake of this volume: Herbert Deane, Josiah Gould, Harry V. Jaffa, Harvey C. Mansfield, Jr., Leonard Munter, Frederick Sontag, and Theodore Waldman. Typists Mrs. Gladys Burton and Mrs. Shirley Martin each deserve special kudos. Thanks are due also to Pomona College and the Danforth Foundation for leave time and an Award, respectively, which made possible two periods of sustained research and writing in Cambridge, Massachusetts, and Claremont, California.

My youngest son—who at four months of age was induced to accept full responsibility for all errors of fact or interpretation in the 1962 book—is still my youngest son, but he is now six years old and a standout in first-grade research techniques. He stoutly refuses to shoulder additional burdens. I have no choice but to take the blame myself for the defects in what follows.

L. C. M.

Claremont, California

A NOTE ON THE PAPERBOUND EDITION

This volume is part of a variant printing, not a new or revised edition, of *Western Political Theory: From the Origins to the Present.* Some users of that book have requested a three-volume version that would enable them to fit the text into the particular patterns of their teaching and scheduling. To meet that request, the publishers have prepared this printing, consisting of three separate volumes that exactly reproduce the text of the one-volume version of *Western Political Theory: From the Origins to the Present.* Part One, now subtitled *Ancient and Medieval,* contains Chapters 1 through 7 of the original text; Part Two, *From Machiavelli to Burke,* contains Chapters 8 through 17; and Part Three, *Nineteenth and Twentieth Centuries,* contains Chapters 18 through 28. Since the variant printing is intended as a convenience to instructors and students, some of whom have had occasion to use the one-volume version, the original pagination, index, and list of selected readings are retained in the new printing. The difference between the one-volume and three-volume versions of the book is a difference only in form.

CONTENTS

WESTERN POLITICAL THEORY

PART 1

ANCIENT AND MEDIEVAL

1

INTRODUCTION

The beginning of politics lies wrapped in largely impenetrable myths. The residue of early political consciousness comes to us in legends, stories, and symbols of uncertain origin. Moses, Solon, and Romulus are the great political founders. The potency of these myths is not to be underestimated. Not merely for some distant, innocent, bygone race did they give shape to the fearful unknown in order to make it bearable or turn joy into an image to make it expressable. Myths, even political myths, are still with us; they express, as someone said, "what never was but always is." We must not be misled by the trivialization of a society in which the queen is a beauty contest winner, the princess is a telephone, and king-size refers to a cigarette. Myths of nature, of the heroic, of the divine are transformed but not destroyed by a scientific age.

We need, for example, a ruler, and we prefer him in the heroic mold. He will surely seek and may possibly find a new land of milk and honey for us, but if the stockmarket drops, "confidence" in the administration is questioned. He will surely fight and may possibly defeat our enemies, whose demonic countenances are recorded in endless cartoons. He will surely invoke the God of our fathers to sanctify our common purposes; and if those purposes are frustrated, he will call in other gods. Because the leader will invariably carry in his person the dignity of a revered past and the hopes for a promising communal future, he cannot lightly be condemned. All sorts of minor vices—including gluttony, bribery, and wife-stealing—may be tolerated in him; but let him seem weak and indecisive, let him reveal cowardice in a crisis, and his people will turn on him with a vengeance. We need a hero to maintain, however thinly, the presumption that affairs are under control. The responsibility for vast, disturbing events tends to fall on one man, as Julius Caesar, Louis XVI, Herbert Hoover, and Nikita Khrushchev discovered.

We need, for example, a law to allay our fears of evil men who, leaping out of shadows, would rob us blind. We need a law to warm our hopes that justice is at hand. The long, involuted paragraphs neatly stapled on blue paper, the fancy curlicues on gilt-edged certificates, the seals, the signatures, and black-robed judges are all part of the necessary mythology of the law. Mutual trust, the essence of the contract, cannot be seen; but all the visible images warn us and reassure us of the communal interest in honesty. The lawyer's Latin reminds us of how old and deeply rooted this interest is.

The sanctified ruler and the sanctified law exist because somewhere in the recesses of common memory occurs a conjunction of the instinct for survival and the instinct for gregariousness. Men do not want to be alone in the world, yet men do want to *be*. So for each man and each group in each time there is an elusive working out of a way to best protect himself and hence survive not merely as a discrete, lonely individual but as a member of a community—a band of fellows united by shared experience. The most important community is the one for which we would die. In different ages it has been a family, a clan, a tribe, a gang, a class, a sect, a church, a city, a state, or a nation; rarely has it been a sex, a generation, or a profession.

The line thus drawn between "us" and "them" is the line that demarcates a public and brings politics into being. When the public wants to know what its leaders are up to and can stimulate the "publicity" about them it needs in order to know, then politics in its ripest sense has come into being. In this sense, only some government is political.

Even consensual-political government does not extirpate myth, however. Myth was and is and shall be not because men are too stupid to state things directly but because what is most important to men can be stated only indirectly. The Greeks gave us many myths, but they gave us much more. They gave us the vocabulary of politics and the first self-conscious reflections on politics. Plato used myths and knew their power; but he also analyzed, speculated on, philosophized about politics. Politics is what the *polis* did and what it might do. The past tense is made present not merely in the lingering classicism of the language of politics (a lingering that is not so mere as it often seems) but in the very forms of our law courts, assemblies, councils, and even the Greek and Roman columns on our public buildings. All these testify to a conception of politics as a form of communal action that is peculiarly Western.

The special identification of politics with the West is matched by the special character of philosophy in the West. The love (*philia*) of wisdom (*sophia*) is confined to no single culture but the Greeks gave it a name and a habitation. We would do well to remember, however, that every abstraction is not wise and every wise writing does not guarantee wisdom in its readers. Aristotle disparaged theory (*theoria*) as mere abstraction cut off from the juices of life. His aim in the *Ethics* and *Politics* was not theory but practical wisdom (*phronesis*). Plato thought genuine philosophy could not be transmitted by writing but must leap as a spark from person to person. Every thought is not theoretical and every theory is not philosophical.

Of what use is political theory? The question is badly put, and our answer may not be definitive simply because political theories can be used in an infinite number of ways: to fill idle hours or to fill crossword puzzles, to rationalize past actions or to rant at the neighbors, to reveal distinctions or to conceal distinctions, to solve the problems of men or to comfort men in their failure to solve problems, to inspire awe at the complexity of history or to explain human choice by subhuman processes. (The easy transformation of theory into "useful" ideology is the subject of a closing peroration in Chapter 28.)

Political theorists are not agreed among themselves about what political theory is or what its uses should be. Some strive to portray the quality and conditions of an ideal state, to present a vision of perfection capable of propelling mankind into the good life. Some seek with equal determination to generalize about man, the political animal, with utter realism—to strip away all façades, all illusions that blind the unsophisticated to the way things really are. Others, of less emotional temper, generalize with great caution and are forever reminding us of the base of hard data that supports the generalization. Some think of political theory as a branch of philosophy. Some say it is a field of political science. "It is identical with the history of ideas," asserts Professor A. "Yes," says Professor B, "but it should not be." The most durable theorists may be the system-builders, those for whom normative perfection and factual validation are secondary to logical structure, esthetic coherence, and self-conscious suggestiveness.

The system-builders necessarily use the metaphors of their time. Despite the bewildering variety of theoretical approaches, the tendency to see the political order as analogous to something else seems inescapable. It may be compared to parts of the soul (Plato), or to the human body (John of Salisbury), or to God's heaven (Aquinas), or to a physical mechanism (Hobbes), or to a computer (David Easton). The very idea of a political order or system, which was held by virtually all the theorists we will consider, may be but a variation on the myths of paradise and eternal harmony that go deep into our culture. Even Machiavelli's power was but an instrument of harmonious order. (To say that political theory participates in the great myths of our culture is not to make them ideological. Myths and ideologies are almost opposites. *Myths* are past-oriented narratives that compress into concrete images an indeterminate number of figurative meanings. *Ideologies*—a nineteenth-century word and phenomenon—are logical patterns extended into the future as bearers of a fixed number of literal meanings.)

To ask theorists dead a thousand years to abide by our restricted, formal definitions of theory is futile. To justify the reading of political theory by asking how we may use it is not only premature but philistine. A theory that does not solve our particular problem—be it Vietnam or urban poverty—is not automatically inferior. There is a common theoretical basis that gives relevance and worth to the major political theorists. We can even give brief preliminary guidance on what to look for in theorists of the body politic, be that body spiritual, corporeal, mechanical, or electronic. In studying their works, look for language, look for thought.

Unlike economics and sociology, politics is peculiarly linguistic. The stuff of politics is a network of reverberating promises, oaths, bargains, threats, and obligations. The political content of basic terms—*law, governor, rights, authority, community*—arises from the fact that they can be used and understood by the man in the street. When scholars give political terms too technical a meaning, they not only lose the man in the street—they lose their grip on the political as well. The layman also recognizes that language always arises and acquires meaning in a particular historical context; it is the bearer of historical experience. Our historical context is the record of Western civilization itself. Look, therefore, to the linkages of language that bind together the theorists of the Western tradition and bind us to them.

And think about their thought. Go as far into their thought processes as the heavy barriers of time, vocabulary, and defective reporting permit. We must not be too quick to twist past thought into the shape of our own problems. Every man seeks philosophic help until his dying day; if he did not, he would read nothing and talk to no one. None of us would read Nicholas of Cusa, or even Plato, were this not so. Yet help comes only if we can be sufficiently patient to listen. And the thirteenth or seventeenth centuries can be no help to the twentieth until we have looked and listened patiently enough to sense their deeper difference and their deeper similarity. Our patience, surprisingly, is often rewarded with a different kind of help: we understand what it means to speak of knowledge as its own end. The delight in seeing as Aristotle saw, in piecing together the conclusion that Rousseau drew, stands by itself, quite apart from any use those perceptions have for our theories and our problems. That is why this book focuses on men first and theories second and why we are not overeager to point out relevance and influence. In scholarship, as in everything else, protracted preparation for life is only half-living; the full life is always now, in the delight of the moment.

Partly because we speak their language, we are privileged to share in some measure with the great political theorists of the past their delight and occasionally their agony in seeing new relationships, in forming new meanings, and in voicing new convictions about an area of life of utmost importance to human beings. Whatever else they have done, political theorists in the Western tradition have been conducting a dialogue with each other. The best way to grasp the nature of political theory is not to acquiesce in an abstract definition of its nature but to participate in the dialogue that is the vehicle of its functioning, for, as we have suggested, the proper definition of political theory is itself one of the issues of political theory. Such a prospect may be motivation enough to lead us beyond introductions and beyond textbooks. The attractiveness of nonuseful knowledge is apparently as basic to our nature as gregariousness and the desire to survive, however much our utilitarian society would deny it. Indeed, our imprudent enjoyment of apparently useless knowledge may be an essential part of our humanity. If politics begins in man's gregariousness and desire to survive, it cannot end there: ants and bees also survive gregariously, but they do not know the sorrow and joy that fill the lives of political animals.

2

PLATO

Who has not heard of Plato? He is both the philosopher's philosopher and the layman's symbol for all philosophy. He is so ancient and so venerable that it is easy for us to assume that everyone has read him and that because they have, we need not. Both assumptions are questionable. As in reading all ancient writers, the trick in reading Plato is to walk the shaky line between excessive veneration and apathetic detachment. Plato *does* speak to us. The continuing profusion of articles and books on the man are not all symptoms of cathartic antiquarianism. Our whole culture—including our language, our politics, our ways of thinking—is indelibly stamped by ancient Greek and Platonic thought.

But if we believe he is worth reading, we must also remember he speaks to us in a language and from a culture not fully our own. Take the language. The Greeks, we are told, had a word for everything, but not many of us study those words these days; and even in times past, when every well-bred young man knew his Greek and Latin, the message often came through garbled. To illustrate the difficulty of vaulting the language barrier, let us compare several English renditions of the same passage in Plato's Greek by scholars of repute. The passage is chosen, not because it is difficult to translate, but because it is well known and important to the argument of the *Republic,* from which it comes.

> remember the original principle. . . . one man should practice one thing only, the thing to which his nature was best adapted;—now justice is this principle, or a part of it.[1]

> we have laid down as a universal principle that everyone ought to perform the one function in the community for which his nature best suited him. Well, I believe that that principle, or some form of it, is justice.[2]

> that which we first established . . . as what ought always to be done. . . . that everyone ought to apply himself to one thing relating to the city to which his genius was naturally most adapted.[3]

> what at the commencement we laid down as a universal rule of action. . . . that every individual ought to have some one occupation in the

[1] Bk. IV, Sec. 433*a* in the Stephanus standard pagination, which will be used throughout. *The Republic,* trans. by Benjamin Jowett (1881), in C. M. Bakewell, ed. (New York: Scribner's, 1928), p. 159.

[2] *The Republic of Plato,* trans. by F. M. Cornford (New York: Oxford Univ. Press, 1945), p. 127.

[3] *Plato's Republic,* trans. by H. Spens (1763) (London: Dent, Everyman's, 1906), p. 125.

state, which should be that to which his natural capacity was best adapted.[4]

what we put forward at the very start as the first principle of our society. . . . everyone was to have some one special sort of work in the society, the work which he was naturally most able to do?[5]

Is the statement a rule of action, a universal principle, a principle of our particular society, or merely a starting place in our narrative? Does it apply to work in the city, the state, the community, the society, or, as in Jowett, everywhere? Are natural capacity, natural ability, natural function, and natural genius all the same? Are suitability (Cornford) and adaptability (everyone else) the same? Is "occupation" comparable to "special sort of work," to "function," or to "one thing only"? The so-called dead languages are not really dead when they can produce as much contention as the pages of any journal of philology reveal. The lesson for those of us ignorant of Greek is clear: whether or not we aspire to become Platonic scholars, we must not take Platonic scholarship for granted in the pages that follow.

LIFE[6]

Plato was born of a distinguished Athenian family in 427 B.C.—in the closing days of the golden age of Pericles and just after the beginning of the fateful Peloponnesian War with Sparta. He was born about the same time that Pericles died, during the fourth year of the Archidamian War. The events are relevant to an understanding of Plato's thought:

The death of Pericles at the beginning of the Peloponnesian War had marked the moment when the men of thought and the men of action began to take different paths, destined to diverge more and more widely until the Stoic sage renounced his local allegiance to become a citizen of the universe. . . . To Plato, this drifting apart of the men of thought and the men of action was a disastrous calamity, indeed the root of the social evils of the time.[7]

Plato's mother, Perictione, was the niece of Critias, one of the oligarchs of Athens during the anarchic period immediately following the defeat of Athens by Sparta (404 B.C.). She was a member of a family whose ancestry allegedly went back to Solon—indeed, even beyond that revered lawgiver to the god Poseidon. Plato's father, Ariston, died when Plato was young, leaving four children: Plato; two other sons, Adeimantus and Glaucon, who were older than Plato and who appear in the *Republic;* and a daughter, Potone. The widow married Pyrilampes, a

[4] *The Republic,* 3rd ed., trans. by John L. Davies and David J. Vaughn (1866) (London: Macmillan, Golden Treasury, 1935), p. 134.

[5] *The Republic,* trans. by I. A. Richards (New York: Norton, 1942), p. 82.

[6] *A note on biography.* There are those who would say that biography is of little use in the study of political theory. Their position is that the validity of any particular theory cannot be confirmed by study of the life of the man who produced it, but only by study of the theory itself and the data it attempts to explain. If, however, one is attempting to understand how theories come to be produced, that is, to make a theory about theories, one would have to study systematically the biographies of a thousand or so theorists in order to say anything significant about the general relation of biography to the production of theory. Both these points are well taken. Why, then, include biographical material on the men whose theories have been selected for special study in this book? The answer is twofold: (1) Most of us can become more emotionally and therefore intellectually involved with a theory when he knows something about the man who produced it. The intellect is not so cold and detached that it can do its work unstimulated by contact with personality. If so, teachers and colleges would be superfluous to education and isolated men would not go mad. Put crudely, an encounter with Hobbes the man may help us stay awake through soporific passages of his theory. (2) Of all theory political theory especially involves speculation about people, what they will do, and why. Even though a few bits of biography cannot provide a general theory about theories, we can, perhaps, understand better what Rousseau meant by "society" when we see what "society" did to him and for him. Whether Hobbes was a Christian may change our understanding of what he said about the Church. We should not be scornful of fragmentary knowledge and ephemeral correlations. In many cases, this is all we can know.

[7] Cornford, in the Introduction to his translation of Plato's *Republic,* p. xxiv.

friend of Pericles, and had another son, Antiphon—who appears in Plato's *Parmenides.* Plato was raised in a household frequented by important political figures.

The details of Plato's life are not known. If Aristotle is correct, he was first a student of the Heraclitean philosopher Cratylus. He was a close friend but not necessarily a regular pupil of Socrates' from the time he (Plato) was twenty—Socrates would have been over sixty—and was present at the trial of Socrates eight years later. After the trial Plato and other friends of Socrates are said to have withdrawn from Athens to the city of Megara. Plato traveled in Italy and Sicily and possibly Egypt and other parts of Africa before his return to Athens to found the Academy. One of the results of these travels was his friendship with Dion, the son-in-law of Dionysius I, ruling tyrant of Syracuse, where Plato was later to indulge his fruitless hopes for the establishment of a philosopher-king.

The Academy was founded some time around 387 B.C., when Plato was forty years old. Its name came from the northwestern suburb of Athens where it was located—near a shrine to Academus, a local hero. A school of remarkable durability it was, for it lasted over nine hundred years, until it was closed by Justinian in 529 A.D. The Sophist Isocrates, unlike the wandering Sophists before him, had already established a permanently based school, but his aim was to give students the practical arts of oratory and rhetoric that would equip them for success in the world of affairs. Plato sought nothing less than to give his charges a thorough mastery of science and philosophy. The rivalry between the two men is well recorded. Plato once called the students of Isocrates smatterers. (If Isocrates' school had been equipped with athletic scholarships, we would be able to draw some parallels with modern schools.)

In 367 B.C., when Plato was sixty, Dionysius I of Syracuse died, leaving the throne to his son Dionysius II. The new king was young and weak, and an influential figure behind the scenes was the new king's brother-in-law, Dion, Plato's long-time friend. The situation seemed to provide a rare opportunity to apply the theories of training enunciated in the *Republic*—training that would turn a king into a philosopher-king. Plato went to Syracuse to help in the education of the young ruler. But Dionysius soon tired of the rigors of geometry drill. Not only did the pedagogical experiment fail miserably, but Dion was banished. Some think the political pessimism of *Theaetetus* and the *Statesman* are reflections of Plato's Syracuse experience. Others regard the *Statesman* and the later *Laws* as less pessimistic than the *Republic* and feel the significance of the Syracuse venture has been exaggerated.[8]

Plato died in 347 B.C. at the age of eighty-one—at a wedding feast, according to legend. Whether he married or left any descendants is unknown. A nephew, Speusippus, took over the Academy, and he was followed by Xenocrates. Plato's greatest disciple, Aristotle, departed to tutor the young Alexander and, when he returned to Athens in 335 B.C., began another school. Perhaps the greatest value of the Academy to us is that it preserved, probably in their entirety, the works of Plato.

Works

Without going into the prodigious store of scholarship expended on the problem of dating Plato's writings, we can mention the four periods into which a number of scholars would organize the whole output.[9]

(1) The early dialogues are called Socratic, not only because Socrates is the central character in each one, but because their sub-

[8] See, for example, Ernest Barker, *Greek Political Theory: Plato and His Predecessors* (New York: Barnes & Noble, 1960), pp. 126–27; Eric Voegelin, *Order and History,* Vol. 3, *Plato and Aristotle* (Baton Rouge: Louisiana State Univ. Press, 1957), pp. 14–16; David Grene, *Greek Political Theory, the Image of Man in Thucydides and Plato* (Chicago: Univ. of Chicago Press, 1965), Ch. 12.

[9] See A. E. Taylor, *Plato, The Man and His Work,* new ed. (New York: Dial Press, 1936), pp. 16–22. See also his *The Mind of Plato* (Ann Arbor: Univ. of Michigan Press, Ann Arbor Paperbacks, No. 41, 1960), pp. 23–30.

jects and their arguments seem to reflect the interests and arguments of the historical Socrates more than do the later dialogues. The *Apology* is virtually a reporter's account of the trial of Socrates. The form of these early dialogues is genuinely dramatic; the style is literary and fresh. They include the three associated with Socrates' death—the *Apology, Crito,* and *Euthyphro*—several minor dialogues, and *Gorgias*. *Gorgias,* which we soon shall discuss, was probably written just after Plato organized the Academy.

(2) The second group of dialogues, written until around 380 B.C., are marked by less concern with what is generally taken to be Socrates' point of view—even though Socrates is still a central character in the discussions—and more concern with Plato's special philosophic interests, especially the theory of forms. This group includes *Meno* (education), *Protagoras* (knowledge as virtue), the *Symposium* (art and love), *Phaedo* (immortality), the *Republic* (justice), and *Phaedrus* (the science of rhetoric). These were written at the height of Plato's literary power and combine literary force and philosophic insight in a unique way.

(3) The third group of dialogues is concerned more with dialectic than with style and personality. These four dialogues have overlapping dramatis personae and refer to each other. The rôle of Socrates diminishes. Three concern problems dealt with by the Eleatic philosopher Parmenides: *Parmenides* (the one and the many), *Theaetetus* (epistemology), and the *Sophist* (logic). The fourth, the *Statesman* (sometimes called *Politicus*), we shall examine in detail shortly.

(4) The last group finds the dramatic form of the dialogue retained only perfunctorily at best. These works—*Philebus* (ethics), *Timaeus* (cosmology), and the *Laws*—tend to be long lectures by one protagonist in which Socrates is given but a bit part. In the *Laws,* as we shall see, Socrates disappears altogether. This rambling work gives evidence that it was written by an old man. It was probably completed a short time before Plato's death in 347 B.C.

It is no doubt a useless pleasure to speculate more than a little about circumstantial influences on Plato. He was old enough to fight for Athens at the end of the Peloponnesian War, but we do not know whether he did. It is probable that he thought little of the oligarchy established in Athens after the defeat by Sparta, despite his family's connection with it. Certainly he thought even less of the revived democratic regime that put Socrates to death.

We must, however, speculate about the relationship of Socrates to Plato. Thanks to the early Socratic dialogues, we can do so with some information at hand.

SOCRATES

Socrates, like Jesus of Nazareth, left no writings of his own by which to be remembered. His influence was face to face. Almost all we know of Socrates we know through Plato, but the very fact that Socrates is a conspicuous character in the Platonic dialogues covering certain subjects and an inconspicuous character in those dealing with others suggests that he was not a mere foil for Plato's ideas. Yet the literary Socrates was more than a historical figure:

" 'Socrates' in Plato is neither, as some of the older and more uncritical expositors used to assume, the historical Socrates, nor as is often taken for granted today, the historical Plato, but the hero of the Platonic drama."[10]

There can be, of course, no question about the historical existence of Socrates. He was ridiculed in the plays of Aristophanes. He was described affectionately, but not very perceptively, by Xenophon. A fragment remains of a dialogue about him written by Aeschines, one of his students. Xenophon and Plato do not contradict each other in the essentials of their descriptions of Socrates, though Plato is more concerned than Xenophon with the content of his philosophy.

The democracy that tried Socrates was a

[10] Taylor, *The Mind of Plato,* p. 32.

very different democracy from that of the Periclean age. After the Spartans under Lysander defeated Athens in 404, an oligarchic Commission of Thirty was sent up (involving both Critias and Charmides, relatives of Plato); but after eight months its repressive rule was overthrown. Though Socrates had distinguished himself for bravery during the Peloponnesian War, his tenuous association with that war's traitor, Alcibiades, and later with the discredited Critias and Charmides was pretext enough for blackening his character with the populace when the new democratic regime undertook its unstable rule.

The charges of worshiping new gods (not of heresy with reference to the old gods) and of corrupting the young were conceived and applied with some ambiguity. This was partly because the amnesty of 403 made earlier events irrelevant and partly because Anytus, the chief instigator of the trial, could not permit the real reason for Socrates' trial to be made known, for the truth was that Socrates' constant questioning was making the already insecure politicians feel more insecure. The death penalty proposed by the prosecutor Meletus—who was Anytus' flack—was clearly meant to do no more than drive Socrates into exile, where he would no longer bother the leaders. After having been found guilty by a 281–220 vote of the jury, Socrates was allowed to propose an alternate penalty to that suggested by the prosecution, as was the custom in such cases. But he irritated the jury of citizens by stating, "If I am to propose the penalty which I really deserve, I propose this—a public maintenance in the prytaneum."[11] And so when Plato, Crito, and his other friends urged Socrates to pay a fine, which they would gladly contribute, it was too late, and Socrates was condemned to death.

It was in the equanimity of his dying as much as in his words that Socrates made a deep impression on endless generations of thoughtful men. His words in the *Apology,* Plato's account of the trial, stand as a monument to the man. At the bidding of the Delphic oracle Socrates had searched for wisdom, only to find that the men reputed to be wise were ignorant and did not know it: "I seem . . . to be a little wiser . . . on this point: I do not think that I know what I do not know."

But he does know that evil cannot overcome a just man; therefore death is not to be feared or allowed to color judgment. He says that, if offered a choice of dying or giving up philosophy,

> I should reply: "Athenians, I hold you in the highest regard and affection, but I will be persuaded by the god rather than you; and as long as I have breath and strength I will not give up philosophy and exhorting you and declaring the truth to every one of you whom I meet. . . ." And I think that no greater good has ever befallen you in the state than my service to the god. For I spend my whole life in going about and persuading you all to give your first and greatest care to the improvement of your souls.[12]

Possibly it was the setting of a court-chamber confrontation with political accusers that prompted such an extreme expression—for Socrates, as he subsequently points out, had once been a senator—but the philosophic mission he exalts is made to be wholly incompatible with holding office:

> There is no man who will preserve his life for long, either in Athens or elsewhere if he firmly opposes the multitude, and tries to prevent the commission of much injustice and illegality in the state. He who would really fight for justice must do so as a private citizen, not as an office holder, if he is to preserve his life, even for a short time.[13]

Socrates could not refrain from involvement in politics because he could not withdraw

[11] *Apology,* in *Euthyphro, Apology and Crito,* trans. by F. J. Church, in Robert D. Cumming, ed. (New York: Liberal Arts Press, 1948), p. 43. Subsequent quotations from the *Apology* and *Euthyphro* are from this edition.

[12] *Ibid.,* pp. 35–36.

[13] *Ibid.,* p. 38. That Plato is looking backward as well as forward may be inferred from his view in the *Republic* of the ideal state as an attempt to recapture a *polis* good enough to be worthy of having Socrates as senator.

from the community of which he was a part. But neither could he accept official responsibility. Here are the lineaments of the problem of the man of thought and the man of action with which Plato was concerned in two of his dialogues, *Gorgias* and the *Republic.*

Philosophy

What stands out in the Socratic words that seem to be most validly historical is a curious mixture of humility and arrogance. Humility clings to his claim to know nothing, yet there seems to be arrogance in his references to the signs whereby God directs him in a special way.

Underlying the first posture is the belief that "the unexamined life is not worth living"; from this it follows that continual, searching, skeptical inquiry must be part of a worthwhile life. Underlying the second is the belief that evil could not overcome a good man in life or death; from this comes an air of virtuous certitude. Part of the irritation Socrates generated in the Athenians was born of the way he seemed to undermine traditional authority with a method of questioning that enabled him to deny the worth of his own knowledge at the same time. People do not like gadflies—the term was Socrates' own—whose purposes are too subtle for general consumption. Though a loyal son of Athens, Socrates was "irresponsible" in his passion for truth—as all uninhibited seekers after truth must seem. But, at the same time, his protestations of ignorance often seemed feigned. After leading a sometimes bewildered but always submissive Euthyphro through a dialectical labyrinth in a quest for the meaning of piety, for example, Socrates says,

> Certainly, Euthyphro, if you had wished, you could have answered my main question in far fewer words. But you are evidently not anxious to teach me. Just now, when you were on the point of telling me what I want to know, you stopped short. If you had gone on then, I should have learned from you clearly enough by this time what is piety. But now I am asking you questions and must follow wherever you lead me; so tell me, what is it that you mean by piety and impiety? Do you not mean a science of prayer and sacrifice?[14]

Socrates so confuses poor Euthyphro that he dashes off at the end of the dialogue rather than begin the tortuous inquiry a second time.

We must remember that Socrates is not merely playing games. Euthyphro, in the first place, is struggling with a real problem, namely whether he should charge his own father with impiety. In leaving Euthyphro confused as to the meaning of piety, Socrates has helped him to an answer of sorts for a practical problem. All of Socrates' ethical inquiries begin and end with practical problems—none more practical than his own dilemma of whether to flee or to accept the sentence of death at the hands of the Athenian *demos* after he had been convicted of impiety, the very subject discussed with Euthyphro. In the second place, in asking Euthyphro what seem to be entrapping questions, Socrates is following what he thinks is the only method that can carry one from falsehood to truth. It is the method of the dialectic, a winnowing-out process through which the logical implications of statements and their opposites are relentlessly pursued until a residue of axiomatically assured propositions remains. Although the method of the dialectic displayed in almost all of Plato's dialogues is partly a literary device, using it is also one of the highest tributes Plato could pay to Socrates. In the light of this method "a science of prayer and sacrifice" is not the contradiction in terms it may sound like to modern ears. Science (*episteme;* in Latin, *scientia*) in its classical usage meant all wisdom and explanation, the body of true knowledge. For reasons we shall examine when we look at Plato's theory of forms, such knowledge was deductive and not inductive.

[14] *Euthyphro,* p. 18.

GORGIAS

The political themes of the *Republic* are anticipated in the dialogue *Gorgias* (pronounced with hard G's) with fewer metaphysical excursions to complicate the picture. But like everything else that Plato wrote, the dialogue carries us beyond its opening question. Gorgias was a well-known Sophist, a teacher of rhetoric. The subject of inquiry is the nature of this profession. But the real protagonist against whom the Socratic view is directed here is Callicles, a strong, self-assured, unsentimental young man who is not known outside of this dialogue. Callicles is the counterpart of the *Republic*'s Thrasymachus (who was a real person) and is a more effective contender for their shared viewpoint.

Gorgias puts up scarcely any defense when Socrates leads him over the dialectical trail to the conclusion that the rhetorician, despite his skill, is merely a creator of beliefs and not a teacher of truth. Soon Gorgias' pupil Polus is engaged with Socrates in the familiar dispute over whether a man ignorant of true justice can be happy and Polus weakly concedes that to do wrong is worse than to be wronged. The unexamined assumption at this point is that wrong for the individual and wrong for the *polis* are identical, so that, for example, just punishment benefits both the individual being punished and the group doing the punishing. Socrates therefore concludes that rhetoric may be useful to the unjust man who wishes to befuddle those who would punish him, but that it is of no use to the man who does not intend to do wrong. For such a man, philosophy, not popular persuasions, is the highest authority.

But just when we think Socrates' forensic victory will be too easy, Callicles steps into the fray and accuses Socrates of using a rhetorical trick—the very practice he has been condemning—in order to trap the hapless Polus. Deliberately, says Callicles, Socrates has confused the distinction between convention and nature. It is conventional morality, not natural morality, that holds the doing of wrong to be uglier than the suffering of wrong. If we look at nature herself, says Callicles, and not the laws made by weak and timid men, we find the stronger always lording it over the weaker. Therefore, the only meaning of truly natural justice is the rule of the strong. And in such an environment philosophy, however charming, can ruin a man. It is mainly a plaything of the young and innocent. When a weak man is slapped in the face by a powerful one, the weak man's philosophy does him little good.

Socrates pays Callicles the compliment of calling him a superior touchstone for the testing of his own theories, then brings the knife to bear on Callicles' assumption that the better and the stronger are one and the same. Callicles, a hard man to ruffle, replies, "I shall be glad to tell you precisely: they are the same."[15] But upon being pressed further, Callicles is required to contend that by strong he means not only physically superior but more intelligent and more courageous. A strong man is one who has the capacity to fulfill his desires, whatever those desires may be.

There follows an examination of whether the good and the pleasurable can properly be regarded as the same. Socrates offers a parable of leaky jars, which, like men without discipline and restraint, cannot hold the goods of this life. Pleasure is not the same as goodness, says Socrates, for pleasure happens *to* a man, whereas goodness is a quality *in* him. Even fools and cowards can know pleasure. Therefore the mere fulfillment of desire is compatible with being a cowardly fool, a type Callicles presumably does not admire. Callicles is forced to back out of the trap by granting that some pleasures are better than other pleasures.

Socrates pushes on to reiterate themes familiar to readers of the *Republic*—the analogy of the ruler with the physician and the standard of harmony in the body politic:

[15] *Plato's Gorgias,* trans. by W. C. Helmbold (New York: Liberal Arts Press, 1952), p. 57. Subsequent quotations are from this edition.

I think that "healthy" is the right word for order in the body; from it health and other physical excellencies arise. . . . And the word for harmony and order in the soul is "lawful" and "law" by which men become law-abiding and orderly. These qualities, then, are justice and self-control. . . . it is these qualities which the moral artist, the true orator, will have in view in applying to men's souls whatever speech he may use; to these he will apply absolutely every one of his actions. Whether he bestows a benefit or takes one away, he will always fix his mind upon this aim: the engendering of justice in the souls of his fellow citizens.[16]

For a moment it seems as if Callicles will drop out of the discussion entirely, and Socrates presses his advantage with hortatory lectures on the dangers of power and on the corruption of the souls of tyrants.

With Callicles in rout, Socrates tends to take over the end of the dialogue in a manner that betrays his (or Plato's) disgust with contemporary Athenian politics, for he portrays even Pericles as having failed in his responsibilities as a leader because he left the citizens "wilder than he found them." All politicians are condemned: "We are unaware of a single good politician in our state." With a reference to the possibility of his death at the hands of his fellow Athenians, Socrates boldly and rather defiantly asserts, "In my opinion I am one of the few Athenians (not to say the only one) who has attempted the true art of politics, and the only one alive to put it into practice." Philosophy becomes the "true" politics, even when its practice is doomed to immediate rejection.

The dialogue ends with a recitation of the myth of Cronus, in which the three sons of Zeus are charged with the responsibility of deciding which among the dead shall go to the islands of the Blessed to live in complete happiness and which shall be sent to the prison house of retribution. It turns out that Hades is overpopulated with politicians. It is "they who, through irresponsible power, commit the most fearful and incurable crimes." The concluding warning is stern. There is only one way to spend one's days: "To live and die in the pursuit of justice and the other virtues. Let us follow it, then, and urge on everyone else to do the same and to abandon that way in which you put your confidence and your exhortations; for your way, Callicles, has no value whatever."

The defect of *Gorgias* is that it assumes but does not examine the contention that justice for the individual is justice for the state, and vice versa. Without the vice versa this assumption is curiously close to certain eighteenth- and nineteenth-century liberal beliefs. Even the derision hurled at politicians fits the mold. The comparison of Plato to the moderns is tantalizing but shallow, for in the *Republic* he does examine the contention in its entirety. We must look at that work's consideration of justice, but first let us briefly summarize the theory of knowledge that underlies the *Republic*'s theory of the state.

[16] *Ibid.*, pp. 78–79.

POLITICS AND PHILOSOPHY

Plato was torn by a basic conflict about his civic role: on the one hand, he was unable to participate in politics and disdainful of public leaders who had been unable to beat Sparta and then had seen fit to execute the noblest man in their midst. Yet, on the other hand, he had been raised in an atmosphere of political authority and had acquired from Socrates himself a deep respect for civic virtues and the responsibility of better men to work for justice in the common life of the *polis*.

The fact that Plato was in a practical sense pulled in two directions may have contributed to the duality of his philosophy. He was and yet was not a utopian. What seemed to be here, now—the life that most men accepted—was corrupt and base; but what was *really* here, now—the dimension of reality veiled by the world of shadowy appearances—was universally true and good and beautiful. This attitude reflects a degree of otherworldly mysticism that seems confirmed by

Plato's view that the highest truths of philosophy cannot be communicated in words. As he put it most strongly in his Seventh Epistle, writers on philosophy

> can, in my opinion, have no real acquaintance with the subject. I certainly have composed no work in regard to it, nor shall I ever do so in the future; for there is no way of putting it in words like other studies. Acquaintance with it must come rather after a long period of attendance on instruction in the subject itself and of close companionship, when, suddenly, like a blaze kindled by a leaping spark, it is generated in the soul and at once becomes self-sustaining.[17]

Because Plato had this esoteric, mystical bias, it is not surprising that he distrusted the democratic crowd-pleaser. But there was a positive as well as a negative side to Plato's distrust of politics, for he believed that the pleasures of the contemplative life have[18] many attractions. Nowhere are they more wistfully described than in *Theaetetus.* To the orator and man of affairs, who is filled with low cunning and overwrought with anxieties from having constantly to please people, the philosopher often appears clumsy and stupid; he is the laughingstock even of servant girls. It never occurs to him to become involved in political rivalries. He is set apart:

> he knows no evil of any man, never having meddled with such things; and so in his perplexity he merely looks an ass. When people cry up their own or other men's virtues, his mirth is so clearly unaffected that he is set down as frivolous. When a tyrant or king is eulogized he imagines that he is listening to the congratulations offered to some shepherd or herdsman for a record yield of milk; only it strikes him that the animal tended and milked by monarchs is more surly and malicious than are sheeps and cows, and that such a herdsman, shut up in his castle and without a moment's leisure, must inevitably grow as rough and uncouth as do shepherds in the mountain folds. When he hears that so-and-so is wonderfully rich, owning ten thousand acres or more of land, he is not impressed, being used to contemplate the whole wide world.[19]

But when the philosopher leads the man of the world away from the narrow concerns of personal wrongs and rewards to questions of the nature of justice and injustice in themselves,

> then, I say, when that small, shrewd, pettifogging mind has to render its own account, then indeed our philosopher comes into his own. This time it is the other who feels dizzy—dizzy from hanging at such an unwonted height and gazing downward from mid-air. Dumbfounded, stammering, he becomes a laughing stock.[20]

At such a height only the philosopher can be serene: he has "acquired the style of conversation which alone can rightly celebrate the life divine and that of truly blissful men." Insofar as words can express the fruits of this blissful life, what did Plato discover at these dizzying heights? At this point we must turn to an exposition of the theory of forms, which lies at the heart of his contribution to Western philosophy and political thought.

THE THEORY OF FORMS

The starting point with Plato is the belief that the metaphysical is superior to the physical—superior morally, cognitatively, and in its eternal reality. The physical, the world of sense, is full of birth and death, growth and decay. The metaphysical, the world of thought, enables us to grasp and order transient sensual impressions and is therefore more enduring than the sensual. The physical appears and disappears; it exists fragmentarily. The metaphysical is the essential reality behind (or above) existential appearances.

[17] Seventh Epistle, sec. 241*c–d*, in *Thirteen Epistles of Plato,* trans. and ed. by L. A. Post (Oxford: Clarendon Press, 1925), pp. 93–94.

[18] See Sebastian DeGrazia, "Politics and the Contemplative Life," *American Political Science Review,* Vol. 54 (1960), pp. 447–56.

[19] *Theaetetus,* secs. 174–75, in *Parmenides, Theaitetos, Sophist, Statesman,* trans. by John Warrington (London: Dent, Everyman's, 1961), pp. 107–08.

[20] *Ibid.,* p. 108.

Plato, like other Greek philosophers, was impressed by mathematics. The superiority of the intellect over the sensual—"passions" and "appetites" would be closer to his terminology—was most easily demonstrated by overt or covert mathematical reasoning. For example, it can never be proven by the senses —we would say "empirically"—that two parallel lines will never meet, but it can be proven axiomatically by Euclidian geometry. Science for Plato was not an experimental method but rather the body of principles derived from deductive reasoning on the model of mathematics.

This will strike many as a curious reversal of assumptions between ancient science and modern science. The modern physical scientist is likely to say that, while metaphysics can provide some interesting speculations, these are never more than mere speculations. What certainty and precision exist come only through rigorous experimental methods. This is what Francis Bacon meant when he said the new method is "continually to dwell among *things*," meaning material things. Plato suggests in *Timaeus* that physical science contributes "likely stories" about causation and the cosmos but lacks the finality of mathematics and metaphysics. Again in *Phaedo* his protagonist accuses physicists of forgetting that "obligation is the ligature which connects all things." He did not mean by this that values in our modern usage somehow predetermine facts, but rather that the good is a principle of order in the universe.

We may illustrate the Platonic distinction between the physical and the metaphysical by the familiar example of the rose. What we see in a rose is a collection of colors, shapes, and textures, that last month did not exist and next month will not exist. We attach the name "rose" to this collection only because we have a mental conception (an *eidos*[21] in Platonic language) of what objective qualifications must be met by any candidate for roseness. It is the Platonic claim that such mental conceptions have more reality than sensual impressions. Mental conceptions, or forms, are the true objects of thought. Moreover, the more general the ideas, the more inclusive, unified, and fixed, and hence the more "real" they become.

Almost anyone can have an accurate collection of the simpler ideas, or forms—shoes, boats, chairs, cows.[22] But only those who have an innate capacity for intellection and who subject themselves to long and rigorous discipline will have accurate conceptions of the more general forms—beauty, justice, friendship. The latter, however, are no less real than the former.

The Line

Book VI of the *Republic* offers the illustration of a line dividing the visible order from the intelligible order. Each of these two realms is, in turn, divided into two. The lowest part of the visible realm (A) is what Plato calls images (*eikon*), or shadows. In the next part (B) are the actual things of which the images are only likenesses. Whereas the images produce in the mind only imaginings, the actual visible objects produce beliefs (*pistis*).

Now consider how we are to divide the part which stands for the intelligible world. There are two sections. In the first (C) the mind uses as images those actual things which themselves had images in the visible world; and it is compelled to pursue its inquiry by starting from assumptions and travelling, not up to a principle, but down to a conclusion. In the second (D) the mind moves in the other direction, from an assumption up towards a principle which is not hypothetical; and it makes no use of the images employed in the other section, but only of

[21] Although the Greek *idea* is the source of the English "idea," it is usually translated "form" with reference to Plato's thought, since the English "idea" suggests mental images—mere mind-stuff—without the necessary participation in substantial, eternal essences required by Plato's usage. The primary meaning of *eidos* is "shape" or "look."

[22] The Platonic forms, Aristotle held, were not appropriate to artifacts, but only to "natural beings" (*Metaphysics*, 1070^a).

Forms, and conducts its inquiry solely by their means.[23]

To repeat, in the sphere of belief or appearance are found, first, images and, secondly, perceptions of visible objects. In the sphere of knowledge the mind first uses visible objects to construct hypotheses that lead to conclusions and secondly uses forms to reach first principles by means of philosophic contemplation. Characteristically, Plato uses mathematics to illustrate the intermediate forms. A student of mathematics, for example, can postulate as a conclusion drawn from prior axioms and observations that the sum of the angles of a triangle equals 180°. He can if he chooses draw a triangle on a blackboard to illustrate the conclusion. This chalky triangle will not, however, be *the* triangle about which he is talking, for a drawing is but a wavering representation of the perfect, formal triangle. At the higher levels, the forms do not have even imperfect visible and tangible counterparts. They are beheld only by the mind's eye. In this case the mind is said to move not "down to a conclusion" but "up to a principle." It is important to note that Plato does not deny the reality of the visible world. The four stages of belief and knowledge discussed here are degrees along a line of *aletheia* (literally, the unveiling), one word that was used to mean both truth and reality.

Although in *Phaedo* Plato suggests there is an infinite plurality of forms, in the *Republic* he establishes a definite hierarchy. The beliefs (*pistis*) based on more or less systematic reference to physical things are superior to, and a restriction upon, the bare perception of physical images (*eikasia*). The beliefs are, in turn, subordinate to the embodiments of the forms and the forms are subordinate to and embodiments of their archetypes in the single source of being (*nous*), the whole realm of essence. Opinion (*doxa*) operates at the second level, deductive thinking (*dianoai*) at the third, and the highest rational insight (*noesis*) at the fourth.[24] Yet this must not be thought of as a mechanical ladder the philosopher climbs until at last he has reached the top rung—a final form called the good. It is probably incorrect to regard the good (*agathon*) as a form at all. Plato deliberately precedes his categorical analysis of the line with the allegory of the sun.

> the Sun is not vision, but it is the cause of vision and also is seen by the vision it causes. . . . [It stands] in the same relation to vision and visible things as that which the Good itself bears in the intelligible world to intelligence and to intelligible objects.

> while you may think of it [the Good] as an object of knowledge, you will do well to regard it as something beyond truth and knowledge and, precious as these both are, of still higher worth. And, just as in our analogy light and vision were to be thought of as like the Sun, but not identical with it, so here both knowledge and truth are to be regarded as like the Good, but to identify either with the Good is wrong.

> the Sun not only makes the things we see visible, but also brings them into existence and gives them growth and nourishment; yet [it] is not the same thing as existence. And so with the objects of knowledge: these derive from the Good not only their power of being known, but their very being and reality; and Goodness is not the same thing as being, but even beyond being, surpassing it in dignity and power.[25]

The Platonic Vision

In one passage Plato speaks of the "Form or essential nature of Goodness." But despite this we should no doubt regard the good as a prerequisite to the forms just as the sun is a prerequisite to colors. It is for this reason that Taylor can compare Plato's good—not his god—to the Christian God. That such a

[23] *Republic,* sec. 510*b*, trans. by Cornford, p. 224. Subsequent quotations are from this edition.

[24] See F. M. Cornford, *Plato's Theory of Knowledge* (New York: Harcourt, Brace & World, 1935). For a realist interpretation, see John Wild, *Plato's Theory of Man* (Cambridge, Mass.: Harvard Univ. Press, 1946), pp. 176–87.

[25] *Republic,* secs. 506–07, Cornford, pp. 219–20. Plato's theory of vision as a kind of fire is developed in *Timaeus,* sec. 45*b*, 67*c*–68*d*.

comparison is possible is enough to raise doubts about the rationalism of Plato, if that term is meant to suggest the capacity of unaided intellect to reason its way to truth. The good is not simply truth in this sense. Nor is it what we would call a value. The final vision of truth for Plato is a type of revelation. There is always an element of the mystical in revelation, a communication of what cannot be communicated with merely verbal symbols. Hence, as Plato implies in the Seventh Epistle, metaphysical discussion must lean upon metaphor and analogy, which point to rather than describe.

It is necessary to add that Plato himself never claims for disembodied reason what the caricature of the rationalist would claim. (For one thing the dialogue form made it easy to leave a good many questions open-ended.) The *love* of wisdom, not the possession of some specified quantity of it, is the mark of the philosopher. It comes neither to those who are complacent in their stupidity nor to those who are complacent in their knowledge, but to those who aspire.[26] Philosophy begins in emotion rather than thought—or perhaps we would be more true to Plato to say that it begins in thought but is consummated in emotion.

THE *REPUBLIC*

Justice

The *Republic* is an inquiry into the nature of justice. But is it concerned primarily with justice in the individual or justice in the state—or is there no distinction between the two? The answer hinges in part on how one interprets Plato's view that "the state is man writ large." And how one deals with this issue is related to one's overall estimate of Plato's orientation. Some find in Plato what amounts to an otherworldly distaste for things political. Others, like Werner Jaeger in his monumental study *Paideia* (the Greek term for education), suggest that the political theorist in Plato is more fundamental than the philosopher. Perhaps Ernst Cassirer represents a middle position: "To [Plato] as well as to St. Augustine the home of the philosopher was the *civitas divina,* not the *civitas terrena.* But Plato did not allow this religious tendency to influence his political judgment. He became a political thinker and a statesman not by inclination but from duty."[27]

Let us examine this issue by summarizing the *Republic* itself. The setting is about the time of the Peace of Nicia, 421 B.C., when Socrates would have been about fifty, Plato a mere child. The dialogue opens with an attempt to define justice. Cephalus, the worldly old businessman at whose home the conversation takes place, offers a conventional and trite definition of *justice* as "honesty in word and deed."[28] This is soon shown to be inadequate, for might it not sometimes be just to withhold the truth from a madman? The old man's son, Polemarchus, tries to help him out by refining the definition to helping friends and harming enemies. Polemarchus is made to seem ridiculous almost too easily when Socrates shows him that his definition implies that justice must be the greater as a man has a greater skill at fighting or building, for then he can harm or help with greater effectiveness. Hence a skillful thief could be the just man. But Socrates carries the discussion beyond the negative by suggesting an idea contrary to conventional Athenian morals and probably to contemporary morals as well: namely that *any* harm

[26] The experience of a disciplined quest followed by revelatory insight is portrayed in several Platonic dialogues. Compare the *Symposium,* sec. 210, with the *Republic,* sec. 508. The other side of the coin is the sense of limitation of analysis by itself. *Theaetetus* provides three negative answers to the question, "What is knowledge?" "At least," says Socrates, "you know what you don't know. That much and no more my art can accomplish" (*Theaetetus,* sec. 210, in *Parmenides, Theaitetos, Sophist, Statesman,* trans. by Warrington, p. 155).

[27] Ernst Cassirer, *Myth of the State* (Garden City, N. Y.: Doubleday, Anchor, 1955), p. 74.

[28] There seems to be deliberate irony in Plato's designation of Cephalus as the defender of conventional Athenian morality: Cephalus was an alien, originally from Syracuse.

to a man, any lasting, permanent harm, could only make him less just. Surely, argues Socrates, the function of justice cannot be to make others less just.

Plato dispenses with conventional justice with perhaps less than its due to clear the stage for the cynical views of Thrasymachus, whose might-makes-right position we have already seen expressed by Callicles in *Gorgias.* Thrasymachus defines *justice* as the interest of the stronger, but is soon forced to explain that he means not simply physically strongest but ablest, most skilled; this, of course, brings in the element of moral valuation he wished to avoid. Socrates introduces the first of many analogies with the physician, whose art as art must be evaluated not by what it does for him but by what it does for others. Thrasymachus takes refuge in the empirical case: the ruthless businessman and the ruthless ruler often get the best of the deal, and if their depredations are on a grand enough scale, they are sanctioned by the community. In answer to this Socrates comments, in effect, that, while a social power may seem to confer authority, properly conceived authority is nothing less than rightful power. The shepherd who abuses his own sheep is not for long regarded as a model of the shepherd's art. Yet, Socrates concedes a good part of Thrasymachus' empirical argument, for he agrees that the powerful frequently rule in their own interest alone, and are, indeed, corrupted by power itself. (This is a judgment for which Lord Acton was to become noted in the nineteenth century.) The creeping utopianism of Plato is evident even at this early stage in the *Republic* when Socrates wistfully comments that "the heaviest penalty for declining to rule is to be ruled by someone inferior to yourself. That is the fear, I believe, that makes decent people accept power. . . . If there could ever be a society of perfect men, there might well be as much competition to evade office as there now is to gain it."

Now that Thrasymachus has fallen by the wayside, we start afresh. A more sophisticated version of his case is stated by Glaucon, Plato's older brother, who presents what has been called a prototype of later social-contract theories—that justice is what the community consents to call it. Glaucon introduces the story of the magic ring of Gyges, which has the power to make a man invisible. No one, he suggests, if given this power and enabled to get away with anything, would treat his neighbors in the manner usually called just. Hence, justice must be a matter of community definition. In practice, he suggests, it is better to seem virtuous than to be so—as Machiavelli was later to suggest.

Adeimantus, the other brother, suggests that the illustration is not complete. It is not enough, he says, to ask whether the supposedly just man would find an appeal in justice if injustice were profitable to him. One must also look at the pressure of society itself to make a man less than just. Even parents presently teach their children to cultivate the appearance of justice for the rewards it will bring rather than to respect justice for its intrinsic worth. Glaucon was looking at the individual who flouts the social convention of justice; Adeimantus is indicting the social convention itself. There is an evident ring of righteous indignation in Adeimantus' words. The two brothers are not, it is clear, genuine allies of Thrasymachus; they are pushing Socrates to make the strongest possible case.

At this point Socrates shifts the discussion from justice in the individual to justice in the community, ostensibly on the grounds that, as a nearsighted man would benefit from having an inscription he was reading set in larger type, so our company of inquirers could see problems of individual justice writ large in the community. And so he proceeds to "build up our imaginary state from the beginning." In implicit refutation of Glaucon's earlier social-contract theory, Socrates shows that the state[29] arises naturally out of the fact that no individual can be self-sufficing.

[29] That is, the *polis.* The two terms are often used interchangeably even though the modern state is quite different from the Greek *polis.* "Community" (*koinonia*) is still another concept but it is used interchangeably with *polis* in this passage.

Specialization of function—some men producing shoes, some growing food, some setting up shops, and so on—is the principle of the new state. Eventually the state may become luxurious and ever more specialized until even a separate class of warriors is set up. Plato calls these warriors the Guardians (later the group will be divided between the mere fighters and the philosophic rulers) and discusses their proper education. Foster has pointed out that Plato neglects to clarify the distinction between the first *polis* he describes —the natural product of human interdependence—and the ideal *polis* he later describes—a city ruled under the guidance of philosophy. The ideal *polis* may not be natural in quite the same sense as the first *polis*. The smooth historical transition from one to the other may conceal a theoretical chasm.[30]

In discussing the education of the Guardians Plato takes up the question of censorship for the sake of instilling proper motives, including respect for the deities. He cites numerous offending passages from Greek literature that must be expurgated if the gods are to be thought of as doers of good and not evil. Plato's defense of censorship in these passages has caused twentieth-century critics to speak of his "totalitarian" methods; but perhaps these critics are overly harsh—even in libertarian America do we permit ridicule of national gods in the textbooks of the young? Extended discussion of the physical, moral, intellectual, and esthetic training to be given the Guardians up to the age of twenty follows the discussion of censorship. At twenty, the Guardians are divided into the subclass of warriors, called Auxiliaries, and the true Guardians, or rulers. To encourage acceptance of the scheme, Plato recalls a myth of men born of the earth and made of gold, silver, or iron and brass. These represent the Guardian, Auxiliary, and artisan classes, respectively. Children are assigned to the station in life fitting their metallic quality. Stations, however, are not inherited. A silver parent may produce a golden, iron, or brass child. Plato speculates that it might take several generations for this "convenient fiction" to be believed (he would depend upon the common feeling that early childhood experience is but a dream) so that persons would eventually "care more for the commonwealth and for one another" than they would the biological family.

The Guardians are subjected to a Spartan regimen. They can possess no private property, they eat meals in common, and in general they live like soldiers on bivouac. To Adeimantus' interjection that they will not be particularly happy Socrates answers,

> though it would not be surprising if even these people were perfectly happy under such conditions, our aim in founding the commonwealth was not to make any one class specially happy, but to secure the greatest possible happiness for the community as a whole. . . . you must not press us to endow our Guardians with a happiness that will make them anything rather than guardians.[31]

A state so endowed, provided at least that it stays small enough, will have far greater unity and, consequently, greater strength than other states torn by division between rich and poor. A strong, small state will be able to defeat softer, larger states if necessary. Plato is sometimes accused of shortsightedness in not seeing the ultimate decline of the city-state form and assuming the perpetuity of what he knew. (The charge falls even more frequently upon Aristotle, who, from his association with Alexander, is supposed to have foreseen the possibilities of military empire.) But Plato was aware of the Persian empire. Since he was constructing a model *polis,* an ideal, he may also have constructed something of a model world in which it could exist, for Plato may well have felt that the *polis* was too precious to lose and that the prospect of a world of gigantic empires, while not quite unthinkable, was hardly worth thinking about. In any case the smallness of the *polis* is justified in part by the rigorous

30 Michael B. Foster, *The Political Philosophies of Plato and Hegel* (Oxford: Clarendon Press, 1935), Ch. 1.

31 *Republic,* sec. 420*b*, p. 110.

demands for civic education (*paideia*) that Plato puts upon it. A *polis* too large has no unity and requires constant legislative regulation; this, in turn, encourages innovation, which is not to be commended. Proper education leads to self-regulation and Plato sees education therefore as an alternative to legislation. The *polis* as "man writ large" means that, just as there are self-indulgent moral invalids among individuals, so there are self-indulgent moral invalids among states—always doctoring themselves with legislation.

Virtue

What is the goal of education? No less than virtue itself. The four components of virtue are wisdom, courage, temperance, and justice. Each is examined in the *polis* and, in consequence, in the individual. The high place given to knowledge by Plato is evident in his description of each of these virtues. *Wisdom* is the highest form of knowledge; *courage* is knowledge of that of which one ought or ought not to be afraid. *Temperance* is mastery of oneself, but such mastery is "a kind of orderliness." Unlike courage, which tends to reside in a part of the *polis,* however, temperance extends throughout the whole.

Finally we return to justice, the theme of the whole work. The meaning of justice is not put forth in the same categorical fashion as are the meanings of the other virtues. It is what is left over after the other virtues have been elucidated. It has something to do with the performance within the community of the function for which nature has best fitted a man. This means that each order in the community—tradesman, Auxiliary, or Guardian—does its own work and minds its own business. But Socrates reminds the group that their concern for justice in the state is but an extension of the original question of the meaning of justice in the individual and brings the conversation back to the individual plane.

He asks, if there are three basic elements of the state, are there three basic elements in the soul? His method of answering this question may strike us as a bit artificial. By adopting the logical tenet that a given element cannot operate in opposite ways at the same time, he attempts to prove that different elements are at work in the human soul. One part of us says, "Take this drink"; another part of us says, "Do not take this drink." Socrates says that the latter part is the rational part, disciplining faculty; the former is the appetitive part, a derivation from physical needs. A third, distinct from both reason and physical appetites, is called the spirited part, the drive revealed in anger, indignation, or moods of revenge. These three elements in the soul match the three basic elements in the *polis;* therefore, just as justice in the state consists of each element's doing what nature has best fitted him to do, so justice in the individual is a balance between the three elements, with, of course, reason performing its proper function of ruling. "The just man does not allow the several elements in his soul to usurp one another's functions. . . . Only when he has linked these parts together in well-tempered harmony and has made himself one man instead of many, will he be ready to go about whatever he may have to do." Injustice, in turn, is a sort of civil strife between the three elements, whether in man or *polis.*

In *Phaedrus,* Plato presents the well-known myth of the chariot, which is a useful supplement to the idea of the three parts of the soul. The soul is said to be like a power composed of two winged horses and a charioteer. The horses are difficult to drive as a team, for one represents the passionate and appetitive—a powerful but unruly beast—and the other represents the spirited nature. The charioteer is Reason, who must assert his authority over the horses if the whole assemblage is to ascend toward heaven, which is its destination. The unruly horse is prone to drag the lot back to earth. Only the driver is capable of comprehending what bliss may be in store in the nether regions. The most pertinent implication to be drawn from this quite complicated myth is that Reason does not have some kind of omnipotent status, but is dependent upon the support of the horses. Without Reason's vision they would never exert themselves to leave the ground, but without their strength Reason would never be able to leave the ground. Another important implication is the significance of aspiration, which we have noted earlier. Reason is more than a mechanical ordering principle. Without its aspiration, the horses could not become winged creatures capable of carrying the whole aloft. Finally, although the whole dialogue is basically apolitical (it is concerned mainly with the nature of *eros*), the three parts of the soul illustrated by the myth can justifiably, on the authority of the *Republic,* be rendered three parts of the state. The part is dependent on the whole, the driver and his horses are a single power, and Reason *or* the reasoning class is moved by aspiration as much as by cold logic.

Little need be said in either attack or defense of the *Republic*'s rather notorious communism of wives. Women are to be eligible for membership in the Guardian class because they have qualities entitling them to it, but they must also then subject themselves to the rigorous discipline required in the training of Guardians. The communism of wives is anything but promiscuous. After declaring that practicality is being set aside in the discussion, Socrates explains a rather elaborate procedure whereby the best would be mated to the best at periodic marriage festivals. The grounds, drawn by direct analogy from the breeding of cattle and horses, were strictly eugenic. Between marriage festivals the Guardians would be required to practice continence. The paraphernalia of a festival were in large part necessary so that those of inferior stock but still within the Guardian class would blame their luck and not the ruler for their less than ideal marriage partners. Offspring of these marginal unions would presumably be thrust out into the lower classes. But even the offspring of the favored unions would be delivered immediately to the nurses, who would raise them for the *polis.* The new mothers would nurse the new babies but would not know which babies were theirs. The children would not call all the Guardians father or mother, as some summaries of Plato have implied, but all children born at a particular time would regard as father or mother those Guardians who had taken part in a particular marriage festival. The object of all this, of course, was the unity of kindred souls, "the greatest good that a state can enjoy." Sons would feel pain and joy for many mothers, and fathers would have the greatest solicitude for many daughters. And for inanimate property as well, "mine" would be replaced with "ours."

In a brief discussion of the usages of war Plato shows himself a relatively humane commentator according to the standards of his time: Greeks should not be made slaves; the dead should not be looted; houses should not be pillaged and burned; the purpose of war is not to destroy but to "bring . . . adversaries to reason by well-meant correction"; foreigners should be treated as Greeks treat each other.

Then we arrive at the heart of the *Republic,* the dilemma of the philosopher-king. Once again Socrates is forced by one of his discussants, this time Glaucon, to disavow the problem of practicality. "We did not set out to show that these ideals could exist in fact. . . . suppose a painter had drawn an ideally beautiful figure complete to the last touch, would you think any the worse of him, if he could not show that a person as beautiful as that could exist?" It is stated as axiomatic that theory can never be fully realized in practice, for what is true and real is in the realm of thought, not the realm of action. This no doubt makes Plato a utopian, but a more self-conscious one than the nineteenth-century reformers who tried to give society a blueprint for action; for Plato was in one way quite a realist: he faced honestly the enormous difficulty of putting his scheme into practice while refusing to dilute it in order to sell it to his audience.

Unless either philosophers become kings in their countries or those who are now called kings and rulers come to be sufficiently inspired with a genuine desire for wisdom; unless, that is to say, political power and philosophy meet together, while many other natures who now go their several ways in the one or the other direction are forcibly debarred from doing so, there can be no rest from troubles, my dear Glaucon, for states, nor yet, as I believe, for all mankind; nor can this commonwealth which we have imagined ever till then see the light of day and grow to its full stature.[32]

Thought and Action: The Philosophic Ruler

How may the nature of the true philosopher be combined with that of the ruler? The philosopher is concerned with thought; the ruler is concerned with action. The philosopher stands apart from the passions of his time; the ruler is immersed in them. The philosopher cares not for the approval of the multitudes; the ruler depends upon it for success in his chosen vocation. The philosopher will suspend judgment rather than render a verdict that may be untrue; the ruler knows that in many cases it is more important to act than to act correctly. The philosopher continually refines distinctions; the ruler must frequently blur distinctions to hold together the divergent factions of his clientele. The combination of philosopher and king is a theoretical question of immense practical significance; it is divorced from practice in Plato only in the sense that how one gets from one to the other is not of primary interest.

To answer the question of whether philosophers are utterly useless to the state, Socrates lapses into the familiar analogy of the ship of state. When the rabble crew has mutinied and taken over the ship, they are not likely to defer to the expert in navigation, who seems to them a mere stargazer and talks a language they do not understand; they do not realize how much they need him. Similarly, the philosopher seems useless to the *polis* only because the citizens do not realize how much they need him. The philosophic nature demands courage, magnanimity, quickness to learn, good memory, and, above all, a consuming love of truth. Hence the majority can never be philosophical and the wall between the majority and the philosophical seems impenetrable. But what is even more serious, the public is capable of dragging would-be philosophers to its side of the wall and keeping them there through psychological compulsion, as Plato tells us in a memorable passage attractive to antidemocrats in all ages:

> Is not the public itself the greatest of all sophists, training up young and old, men and women alike, into the most accomplished specimens of the character it desires to produce?
>
> When does that happen?
>
> Whenever the populace crowds together at any public gathering, in the Assembly, the lawcourts, the theatre, or the camp, and sits there clamouring its approval or disapproval, both alike excessive, of whatever is being said or done; booing and clapping till the rocks ring and the whole place redoubles the noise of their applause and outcries. In such a scene what do you suppose will be a young man's state of mind? What sort of private instruction will have given him the strength to hold out against the force of such a torrent, or will save him from being swept away down the stream, until he accepts all their notions of right and wrong, does as they do, and comes to be just such a man as they are?[33]

Only the occasional superhuman statesman escapes this debilitating pressure.

Obviously, it is difficult to communicate the subtleties of truth to clamoring multitudes, or even apathetic multitudes, and the problems of foreign policy in the mid-twentieth century suggest that we are no more free of this difficulty than was fourth-century Greece. But, while Plato's contrast between philosophic and nonphilosophic natures seems well grounded, his wholesale dismissal of democracy rests on somewhat dubious analogies. While it is quite true that the ship of state would flounder without the services of a skilled navigator and a skilled captain, it is wrong to imply, as Plato does, that they are therefore better qualified than ordinary citizens to decide what the destination of the

[32] *Ibid.*, sec. 473*c–e*, pp. 178–79.

[33] *Ibid.*, sec. 492*b–c*, p. 199.

ship ought to be.[34] One does not have to know how to get to Trinidad to decide that one should go there. Presumably the owners of ships make this kind of decision on the grounds of their own interests and then inform the expert of their decision. If there is an expertise of choosing destinations, it differs from the expertise of navigation. But is there such an expertise? Is there any scientific or philosophic way to determine whether the proper destination for the U. S. S. United States is Port A or Port B? Plato would say yes, on the basis of an epistemological position that, in current language, identifies judgments about facts with judgments about values.

Plato, like elitists in our day, points to the poor judgments of the masses in matters of poetry and art and equates this with weakness in political judgment. Again, the two kinds of judgment may be quite different. Poetry and art are subtle, esthetic, precious, and full of private meanings—uncommon by definition. But politics by definition pertains to what is common. And perhaps common meanings require common rather than special definition. The analogy of the physician and his patient may be somewhat more pertinent than that of the sea captain and his crew. A diseased body politic may have a greater need to put itself in a physician's hands than a wandering ship of state has to put itself under a ruthless master. But even here the esoteric method of diagnosis and prognosis appropriate to bodies corporeal may have no counterpart in the diagnosis and prognosis of bodies politic. How citizens feel may be more relevant than how rulers think.

But this caveat about Plato's assumptions does not undermine the logic of his discussion, based upon those assumptions, of the philosopher-king. The problem remains: how does one get the successful politician, who is almost of necessity full of ambition, to give up his ambition in order to become a philosopher without at the same time making him give up the profession of politician? A gifted youth drawn toward philosophy who also has the attributes of a leader will be zealously used by those who see how much he can do for their party. If he sticks to philosophy, he is cut off from political power. If he goes along with the politicians, his love of philosophy is corrupted and "Philosophy is left forlorn, like a maiden deserted by her nearest kin." (Some think Adlai Stevenson represented a modern case study in this poignant dilemma.)

Plato's answer to this problem poses another dilemma. Since a philosopher cannot get power in a nonphilosophic society, society must be made worthy of the philosophic nature. Thus, before a philosopher can produce a perfect state, a perfect state must produce a philosopher. But Plato is not willing to put it quite so starkly. He must hold out some hope: "Our plan is difficult—we have admitted as much—but not impossible." And after condemning the public himself—but indicting conniving politicians much more—Plato has Socrates say, "My dear Adeimantus, you must not condemn the public so sweepingly; they will change their opinion, if you avoid controversy and try gently to remove their prejudice against the love of learning." But the task of reform is nevertheless so herculean that there is little gentleness in what Socrates proposes: to scrape clean the canvas of society and humanity in order to begin a new picture. In practice this means sending out into the country all above the age of ten and seeing what can be done with the youthful remainder.

The Allegory of the Cave

It must not be thought, however, that Plato is playing into the hands of reforming megalomaniacs who would like nothing better than to scrape clean a canvas or two. Recall what was said about the best taking

[34] Bernard Crick suggests that the analogy of a convoy of state is superior to that of a single ship of state. The modern state is many ships, under different commanders, centrally coordinated. See *In Defense of Politics*, rev. ed. (Baltimore: Penguin Books, 1964), p. 118.

power only to prevent the worst from having it. The same reluctance of the philosophic spirit to order people around may be inferred from the famous allegory of the cave. We have already seen how the sun served as a symbol of the true and the good. The same device of light and shadow is used here to describe the cave that is the dwelling place of humanity. Men are physically restrained from looking at anything but the wall of their cave, where flicker shadows of objects passing in front of a fire-light behind the men. The speech of those carrying the objects—figures of men, animals, etc.—echoes off the walls so that the observer believes the shadows themselves are speaking. It is a continuing puppet show in which the spectator believes the puppets to be real men. To be such spectators is the lot of most men. If one of the cave-dwellers is hauled out of the cave into the sunlight, he is blinded by the dazzle and thinks he must surely be in some kind of bad dream. But as he gets used to the sunlight and as objects become visible to him, he comes to realize that he is actually for the first time seeing reality and not the mere shadows of reality. But plunged into the darkness of the cave again, he is unable even to distinguish the shadows until his eyes adjust to the darkness. The cave-dwellers laugh at him and his wild tales of the outside world. If he tried vigorously to set them free, they would even try to kill him. This is the situation of the philosopher as he tries to bring the light to men sunk in ignorance. Thinking they already see, they see not. "In the world of knowledge, the last thing to be perceived and only with great difficulty is the essential Form of Goodness. . . . Without having had a vision of this Form no one can act with wisdom, either in his own life or in matters of state." So the allegory of the cave has meaning for both the individual and the *polis,* and it suggests the difficulty faced by the would-be philosopher and leader of the people.

With what might tentatively be termed an egalitarian note, Socrates observes that all men have the power of sight; therefore it is not the task of one who would educate men to put the power of sight into their eyes. Even evil men may be very keen-sighted, but their range of vision is exceedingly narrow. They are clever rather than wise. The task is to get men to look in the right direction. This requires a conversion of the soul. This conviction underlies the whole tradition of liberal education. Truth is not implanted in the student; he must look for it himself. So also, by extension, the modern liberal tradition has found political ramifications in this belief. A democratic state does not give the people the answers but enables them to look for themselves. Unlike Enlightenment champions of egalitarianism, however, Plato believed society would always remain a cave.

Plato may be a utopian, but he does not turn his back on political responsibility. Man comes out of the cave almost by accident. The philosopher goes back into the cave, not because he wants to, but because he ought to. If the ignorant should not govern, neither should the wise neglect to govern:

> The ignorant have no single mark before their eyes at which they must aim in all the conduct of their own lives and of affairs of state; and the others [idle devotees of culture] will not engage in action if they can help it, dreaming that, while still alive, they have been translated to the islands of the Blest.[35]

To Glaucon's objection that it may work an injustice upon the sages to force political work upon them, Socrates replies that our concern is not to make one class happy but to ensure the welfare of the whole community. The reverse of this is that, if men seek to find happiness in politics in order to fill otherwise empty lives, not only will their hunger for power be unsatisfied, but the state will be ruined by internecine conflict.

The Decline of the State

In the construction of political models or ideal types, Plato is also concerned with models of progressively undesirable states. In Book VIII of the *Republic* he constructs

[35] *Republic,* sec. 519*c*, p. 233.

four such models. The Greeks had a cyclical view of history: degeneration and renewal were assumed to take place almost on the pattern of the changing seasons. So it was with Plato's view of the cycle of bad states. But more important than the assumed causal link between his models is the assumption that "if there are five forms of government, there must be five kinds of mental constitution among individuals." This is but another way of stating that the state is man writ large.

Plato first outlines a system based on the Spartan model and calls it *timocracy,* or government by the principle of honor (*timé*). When reason loses its control over the community as the result of bad marriages, blunders in educational administration, and other causes of divisiveness, the spirited, or honorific, element in man and the state comes to the fore and the philosophic loses out. Intellectuals will be distrusted and private property will muddy the devotion of the Guardian class. Wealth will not yet be flaunted, but its pleasures will be tasted in secret. Exploits in war will count for more than gifts of speech in winning office, and the man of ambition will become typical of the whole.

The next move down the slide to chaos is the *oligarchic state,* though what Plato described is not merely the rule of the few but more specifically *plutocracy,* or the rule of the rich. The flow of gold into private coffers infects the timocratic man until money means more than virtue. Laws are tampered with in order to avoid taxes, and certain men get their fingers into too many lucrative pies and defeat the principle of specialization. As the rich grow richer, the poor grow poorer, and beggars begin to be seen in the streets. Beggars, thieves, and pickpockets are a sound clue that plutocracy has taken over. Their morality is but a reflection of the morality of their betters, who exude a conventional honesty only because it is prudent in furthering their acquisitive desires. The rich are restrained by fear for their fortune, but the ignoble desire for easy money has eaten away their integrity.

The next to the last station in the recession is *democracy,* or the rule of the people. It comes because "a society cannot hold wealth in honour and at the same time establish a proper self-control in its citizens. One or the other must be sacrificed." The plutocracy's inability to curb riotous spending means that some men of ability sink with debt into the mass, where they display their talents by fomenting revolution. The usurers —Plato did not believe in interest—stretch their luck and the rich become lazy and effeminate until finally it is easy to persuade the poor that they are poor only because they are too cowardly to take the wealth away from the rich. Civil war begins.

The democratic man is less easily described than the timocratic or plutocratic man because the essence of a democratic state is the toleration of all sorts of individual pleasures. With a magnificent indifference to a man's background, democracy will promote to office anyone who can claim loudly enough to be the people's friend.

In each of his descriptions of the alternate states, Plato has pictured a father and a son to make concrete the way political orders become part of individual character. The father represents the old way of life and the son represents the new. The battle between political factions takes place literally within the soul of the young man until he allows himself to go with the tide or forces himself to stand against it. It is the characteristic of democracy to confuse the young with flattering names and imprecise conceptions: anarchy is called freedom; waste is called magnificence; impudence is called a manly spirit; luxuries are called necessities. Participation in politics is sporadic and only half thought out. The democratic man, like the state of which he is a part, bounces from feast to famine and, if lucky, back again. Though it would be foolish to attempt to draw fine parallels between Plato's prototypical constitutions of the past and the societies of our own day, only the obtuse would argue that the motivations and tendencies he describes have no counterpart in twentieth-century political life.

At the end of the line despotism,[36] or government by the lustful man, arises out of democracy. The democratic greed for liberty[37] makes it easy for unprincipled leaders to find their way to the top. When the virus of liberty has spread to impossible lengths, when even the children and the dogs become anarchists, a violent reaction sets in and the people turn to the one in power who best promises to rid them of strife. The despot takes over, punishes, chastens, invents scapegoats, is ruthless with critics. As beggars were the clue to plutocracy, the appearance of bodyguards around the ruler is a sign that despotism has arrived.

In the early days of a despot's rule, "he has a smile and a greeting for everyone he meets; disclaims any absolute power; makes large promises to his friends and to the public; sets about the relief of debtors and the distribution of land to the people. . . ." But after he has disposed of his more troublesome enemies one way or another, his regime becomes less beneficent. And when economic problems begin to chafe the people, the despot finds that provoking foreign wars is a handy policy for keeping critics occupied and in jeopardy.

Those who do not flee the despotic society reflect in their own personalities the character of despotism. No less than members of other regimes, they incorporate the prevailing style of life. In this case the untamed lawlessness of our more depraved dreams becomes waking reality. The qualities of "drunkenness, lust, and lunacy" are combined. One cursed with a despotic character is sometimes a master and sometimes a slave, but he does not know friendship and therefore does not know freedom. He knows not the pure pleasures of the just and the wise but only the illusory pleasures of self-indulgence.

At the end we are brought back to Thrasymachus' contention that injustice is more profitable than justice. For Plato the whole record of the decline of the state stands as persuasive evidence that injustice only enslaves the best part of man's nature to the worst and therefore can never be profitable.

THE *STATESMAN*

It is always risky to specify categorically the content, let alone the message, of a Platonic dialogue. The *Republic* deals with the nature of justice but also with the best state and the best education. The *Statesman* ostensibly seeks only to define what the statesman is, but other themes intrude. We can say that the *Statesman* stands between the *Republic*'s concern with ideal metaphysical essences and the *Law*'s concern with constitutional details. Since it deals sympathetically with the constitutional regime, the *Statesman* may be made to seem a reversal of the *Republic*'s antidemocratic position. But proconstitutional and prodemocratic may not be the same.

The *Statesman* forms a triad with *Theaetetus* and the *Sophist*. It is suggested at the end of *Theaetetus* that the characters reassemble the next day. They do, as portrayed in the *Sophist* and the *Statesman,* but Theodorus brings with him a friend, a stranger from Elea, the early center of Stoicism in Italy. This man is allegedly a disciple of Parmenides and Zeno, but it soon becomes apparent that he is not a typical Stoic. Some

[36] For some reason Cornford translates *tyrannos* as "despot" rather than "tyrant." Jowett, Shorey, Barker, and others use the latter term in these passages. Though frequently used as a synonym for "despot," "tyrant" has two meanings: "a bad ruler" or "an extralegal ruler." Some tyrants in the latter sense, such as Pisistratus of Athens or Periandros of Corinth, could be regarded as good rulers. Though a tyrant would often be a monarch (a single ruler), he would never be a king (*basileus*). A despot (*despotes*) is a bad ruler, though originally the term simply meant "master of the house."

[37] It may be well to remind ourselves that many theorists, most notably Alexis de Tocqueville, have identified democracy not with liberty but with equality and have indeed made the two ideals quite antagonistic. Plato assumed that liberty and equality went together in the democratic state. Many modern theorists, more sympathetic to democracy than Plato, assume likewise.

think he speaks for Plato himself. Unlike earlier dialogues, there is really no dialogue, but rather an almost unbroken exposition by the anonymous stranger.

Socrates, the usual exponent, lapses into silence as the stranger leads Theaetetus on and on to a true definition of the sophist in one dialogue and as he leads Socrates the Younger willingly along to a defensible definition of the statesman in the other.[38] A. E. Taylor notes that, although the subject of the *Statesman* is similar to that of the *Republic* and hence a role for Socrates could easily be expected, the purpose of the *Statesman* was not only to define its title subject but to demonstrate the "method of division" as a logical procedure, a method demonstrated even more pointedly in the *Sophist.* It is a moot question at many points whether Plato is using philosophical issues—for example, the problem of extremes and the mean—to clarify the problem of the statesman or the problem of the statesman to clarify philosophical issues. Since a dogmatic, neatly packaged statement of Plato's tenets is bound to distort the character of his work, it seems best to approach Plato dialogue by dialogue.

The Kingly Science

Statesmanship, or the kingly science, is initially stated to be a theoretical and not a practical science—that is, it is not rooted in action in the same way as is carpentry, for example. Yet, it *is* related to action as pure contemplation is not, for it is a branch of theoretical science considered directive rather than critical. It does not merely judge but also guides others on the basis of that judgment. Some men guide others on the basis of borrowed authority. Because the statesman directs others on the basis of inherent authority, he is further classed with the self-directive.

On and on the division and subdivision go. Statesmanship concerns production, but production of animate and not inanimate beings, of animate beings taken collectively and not individually, and so on through the animal kingdom—the land creatures, the bipeds, the nonfeathered bipeds—until Socrates the Younger, like us, begins to wonder whether his leg is being pulled. But the protagonist, while not above playfulness, is apparently quite serious in saying at the beginning of the dialogue that the method of division requires at each point "an equal division so far as that is possible."[39] Here he objects to jumping directly from the discussion of the rule of animate beings to the rule of human beings. To divide all animate beings into human and nonhuman is possible, he says, but lopsided. In order to glorify itself, a crane could just as well classify all living things into cranes and noncranes. (This degree of humility, it strikes us, is not typical of humans in their dealings with other animals.)

At any rate, what could become endless zoological taxonomy does not materialize, for the Eleatic stranger suggests a new beginning and shifts to the quite different plane of myth.[40] The stranger now speaks of an early age when the gods reversed the order of the rising and setting of the sun. Time itself was reversed, and men, rather than being deposited in the earth after death, were born from the earth to grow younger and younger. At times, it seems, God guides the progress of the world, at other times He leaves it alone. When left alone it travels in the oppo-

[38] Since the stranger explains in the beginning of the *Sophist* that sophist, statesman, and philosopher are three distinct types, scholars have long but inconclusively speculated on whether there is a missing dialogue on the philosopher or whether one of the other existing dialogues is intended to complete the series. See Taylor, *Plato,* p. 375, *n.* 1, and literature cited there. See also Frederick Sontag, "Plato's Unwritten Dialogue, 'The Philosopher,'" *Proceedings of the Twelfth International Philosophical Congress,* pp. 159–67.

[39] *Statesman,* sec. 265, in *Parmenides, Theaitetos, Sophist, Statesman.* Further quotations from the *Statesman* will also be from this admirably fresh translation.

[40] For extended discussion of the myths of the *Statesman* see G. R. Levy and J. A. Stewart, eds., *The Myths of Plato,* new ed. (London: Centaur Press, 1960), pp. 179–207. See also George Grote, *Plato and the Other Companions of Socrates,* new ed. (London: Murray, 1885–88, 4 vols.), Vol. 2, p. 480, *n.* 5.

site direction according to the innate character of the life that animates it. (The divine is noncorporeal and exempt from change.) But the world cannot forever be the author of its own movement else it would be itself divine—that is, "that which carries with it all things that are moved." Men in that early age were watched over and protected by the god Cronos, and life was lush. Following the great upheaval of God's withdrawal, the world, "remembering as best it can the instructions of its author and father," allowed primitive chaos gradually to gain control, until once again God took over. Here the traditional myth ends. But one of Plato's techniques is to use traditional myths for new purposes, and so the stranger here adds that after another reversal of the cosmic order man is left helpless against wild beasts and is forced to learn the arts of collective self-protection, from which all political forms derive. Plato's "state of nature" is prepolitical, as it was to be for the political theorists of the seventeenth and eighteenth centuries, but it is also prehistorical, a mythological construction of an age of divine rule. (Rousseau was, in this respect, closer to Plato than either Hobbes or Locke was.)

By means of the myth Plato shows that the "shepherds of men"—the initial, provisional definition of the statesman—in the age of Cronos were gods and not men. The primary purpose of the myth is simply to show that in the current age kings are men and not gods. Plato is eliminating from consideration supermen—Nietzsche's *Übermensch*—who would make the task of defining the statesman unrealistically easy. The rather high flown cosmology actually serves a naturalistic purpose.

In clearing up the earlier ambiguity between godly and human shepherds of men, the stranger also strikes at another error in the previous employment of the method of division—namely that attention was given to the types of flocks ruled at the expense of attention given to the meaning of "rule" or "care for." The shepherd of the age of Cronos actually fed his flock. The leader of men has a more modest role: he "minds" his flock or "tends" it (*epimelia, therapia*). Though the stranger admits to having "loaded ourselves with so enormous an amount of myth that we could not avoid using too much of it," he has by this method steered the discussion toward defining the true art or science of *earthly* kingship, and we begin again the method of division as we distinguish between guardianship imposed by force and guardianship voluntarily accepted.

The dialogue ends by using the weaving of wool as a paradigm to explain the relationship of auxiliary arts to the Guardian's art. But along the way there are a number of digressions, including a sophisticated discussion of how paradigms work in the education of the young and an examination of two kinds of measurement: measurement according to mutual relationships between different modes of existence, as in a comparison of extremes, and measurement by reference to a mean, or that which is proportionate.[41]

Continuing the analogy with weaving, Plato looks at the types of government within which the problem of rulership must be considered and enunciates a sixfold classification of government. This classification is almost identical with that presented by Aristotle in the *Politics* and is frequently attributed to his authorship. The scheme is, of course, the rule of the one, the few, and the many, in their good and bad forms. The rule of one is more likely than the rule of the few or the many to display skill at ruling, which is even rarer, Socrates the Younger tells us, than skill at chess. But the presence of this skill is, in any case, more important than mere structure.

In one of his few assertions of independence in this dialogue Socrates the Younger objects at this point and seems to induce the stranger to examine the function of law. Law is compared to a doctor's prescription, which

[41] A. E. Taylor calls these two kinds of measurement intrinsic, or absolute, and extrinsic, or relative, and points out that, whereas modern science regards its measuring function as primarily extrinsic, both kinds of measurement were appropriate for Plato and Aristotle, who regarded science as no less a process of measurement. (*Plato,* p. 399) See also Plato's *Philebus* and Aristotle's *Nicomachean Ethics,* Book VI.

can be changed or modified by the doctor at any time as the condition of the patient changes. A prescription, says Plato, is at best an imperfect substitute for an absent doctor. It is a convenience rather than a necessity. So also a sea captain is not tied to a written code that would bind his judgment in doing what is necessary for the safety of his ship and his passengers. The theory of the consent of the governed is explicitly dismissed with the same analogy of the doctor: "Suppose a doctor cannot persuade a child, a man or a woman to undergo a course of beneficial treatment, but, being a master of his art, obliges the patient to accept the treatment in defiance of written rules. What will this constraint be called? Surely not a sin against medical science."

The Second-best State

So far we are hearing the familiar strains of the *Republic*. But there is at this point an almost surprising reversal of position or shift of interest from the ideal of the *Republic* to the need for law in the second-best state typical of the historical world:

> STRANGER. . . . A real monarch such as we have described would be acclaimed as controlling and administering the one and only perfectly right constitution.
>
> SOCRATES THE YOUNGER. Of course.
>
> STRANGER. But since in fact, as we are agreed, kings are not produced in states like queen bees in hives, unique both in body and soul, it seems that we must get together and compile legal codes as near as possible according to the pattern of the truest form of government.[42]

The whole thrust of the dialogue now moves in the direction, not of extolling the philosopher-king, but of defending the necessity of a constitutional regime.

Many pretend to master the art and science of statecraft who master only the art of persuasive speaking, or rhetoric; the latter is a subordinate art, as is the exercise of the military and the judicial functions. Like the master art of weaving, which is more than carding and spinning and the other subordinate arts, the kingly function "interlaces the various strands."[43]

This function is not an easy one, for there is no easy, natural harmony among the strands being integrated. Courage and wisdom are both part of virtue, but they are often "fiercely hostile to one another." With considerable perspicacity Plato notes how men who favor speed tend to give it a favorable name, such as vigor, whereas men who favor slowness use their own euphemisms, such as reserve or moderation. Hence both types of persons conceal from even their own view the extent to which their preferences are antagonistic to those of others in society. If one or another of these types of persons becomes represented by a faction and if the faction becomes dominant, danger to the whole community results. Those "of a most retiring disposition, ever anxious to lead a quiet life . . . unconsciously lose all aptitude for war." On the other hand, "the more vigorous sort" are "forever trying to commit the state to some new war . . . exposing their country to so much powerful hatred. . . ." Americans have called these two types doves and hawks.

It is the job of the statesman, then, to balance these two temperaments—which is not the same as mixing good and bad elements—like the warp and woof of the weaver's art, mixing them eugenically as well as in the distribution of offices:

> Herein lies the whole kingly art of weaving: never to allow a divorce of the moderate from the vigorous character, but to bind them together by means of common opinions, honors and glories, as well as by mutual exchange of undertakings, so as to produce a supple and, as we say, a close knit web.

Measured by the critical attention they have received the *Republic* has tended to

[42] *Statesman,* sec. 301, p. 282. Compare the *Laws,* Book IV. The stranger even expresses some surprise that states ruled by more than one survive as well as they do.

[43] The stranger earlier listed seven classes of auxiliary things required by any art: raw materials, instruments, containers, vehicles, coverings, amusements, and nutriments. (Sec. 287–88)

overshadow the *Statesman;* but the latter has had a significant influence on subsequent thought. From the *Statesman* Aristotle undoubtedly acquired his basic distinction between theoretical and practical wisdom and also his conception of a science of statesmanship.

THE *LAWS*

The dialogue on the laws is often dismissed as the turbid utterance of an old man—one who, in the *Republic,* had been capable of lyric idealities but who is now reduced to garrulous practicality. The work is Plato's longest; it is virtually a monologue by an "Athenian stranger," presumed to be Plato himself, with the Spartan Megillus and the Cretan Clinias putting in bits and snatches. The style has deteriorated, but the content should not be brushed aside. The three old men of the dialogue are playing the role of advisors to a newly founded fictitious city in Greece, and it would be absurd for them not to be practical. The Athenian stranger is concerned with reviewing a great stretch of political history and this, too, keeps the discussion close to earth.

Book I begins with a discussion of the central purpose of Spartan and Cretan institutions: the representatives of those polities argue for the priority of a military prowess capable of defeating all enemies. The Athenian argues that peace and not war should be the aim of all lawgivers. From this the dialogue proceeds to an inquiry into the nature of true manliness, the proper use of wine, and, in Book II, the function of poetry and music in the education of the young. It is agreed that the ability to withstand the seductions of pleasure is a virtue comparable to bravery in battle. There are spirited exchanges on the morals and mores of various cultures.

In Book III the sages look at politics, or, more precisely, at how a city comes into being. The description is reminiscent of the *Republic,* though it is more historical, but it leads to a different conclusion from that of the *Republic*—namely that there are only two basic forms of constitution, the rule of one man and popular rule. The most stable regime is one that combines both aspects in the form of a mixed constitution. Moderation, not perfection, is the pervasive theme of the *Laws:*

> if anyone gives too great a power to anything, too large a sail to a vessel, too much food to the body, too much authority to the mind, and does not observe the mean, everything is overthrown, and in the wantonness of excess runs in the one case to disorders, and in the other to injustice, which is the child of excess.[44]

> CLEINIAS. And now, as regards friendship and wisdom and freedom, tell us what you had in mind when you were about to say that the legislator should aim at them.
>
> ATHENIAN. Hear me, then: there are two mother forms of states from which the rest may be truly said to be derived; and one of them may be called monarchy and the other democracy; the Persians have the highest form of the one, and we of the other; almost all the rest, as I was saying, are variations of these. Now, if you are to have liberty and the combination of friendship with wisdom, you must have both these forms of government in a measure; the argument emphatically declares that no city can be well governed which is not made up of both.
>
> CLEINIAS. Impossible.
>
> ATHENIAN. Neither the one, since it was exclusively and excessively attached to monarchy, nor the other, since it was similarly attached to freedom, observed moderation.[45]

This emphasis on the mixed constitution inaugurated a line of political theorizing that was to run through some of the most famous theorists of the Western tradition—from Aristotle to Montesquieu, to the *Federalist* papers, though it was later to take on a more technical meaning than it had in the *Laws.*

In Book IV the three men turn to the de-

[44] *The Dialogues of Plato,* 4th ed., sec. 691*c*, trans. by Benjamin Jowett (London: Oxford Univ. Press, 1953, 4 vols.), Vol. 4, p. 260. Subsequent quotations are from this volume of this edition.

[45] *Ibid.,* sec. 693*d–e*, p. 262.

tails of constructing their new constitution. They consider geography, isolation from neighbors, immigration, and commerce. The *polis* would be agrarian rather than industrial because the effects of the commercial spirit are both threatening to character and likely to lead to imperialistic aggressions. In what seems like a surprising statement for Plato, the Athenian says that the most plausible way to get the kind of wise legislation they are looking for is to pair a wise statesman with a young, intelligent tyrant. The desired change comes most easily because the tyrant has the most flexible means of control. Monarchy is the next most likely to be won over to wise legislation, then democracy, and last oligarchy.

Yet, despite the shift from perfection to plausibility in the *Laws,* Plato was no less aware here than he was in the *Republic* of the extent of the dilemma involved in trying to unite power with wisdom:

> The difficulty is to find the divine love of temperate and just institutions existing in any powerful forms of government, whether in a monarchy or oligarchy of wealth or of birth. . . . When the supreme power in man coincides with the greatest wisdom and temperance, then the best laws and the best constitution come into being; but in no other way.[46]

Later the Athenian stresses the evil of laws addressed to this or that class rather than to the good of the whole state:

> States which have such laws are not polities but parties, and their notions of justice are simply unmeaning. . . . that state in which the law is subject and has no authority, I perceive to be on the highway to ruin; but I see that the state in which the law is above the rulers, and the rulers are the inferiors of the law, is preserved, and has every blessing which the Gods can confer.[47]

Although Plato is here concerned with law rather than with the more abstract problem of justice, it is not stretching the truth to say that the same moral conviction—namely that the good of the *polis* is superior to the preferences of any individual, even a ruler—operates here as in the *Republic.*

Law and Respect

In the form of a hypothetical speech to the founders of the new Cretan city, the Athenian eulogizes the majesty of law and relates it to the reverence due parents. One is reminded of the Periclean funeral oration. The address continues on into Book V, where the Athenian examines what kinds of respect are due ourselves and others. In the course of this development he enunciates a version of the golden rule—namely that, if good will is to be maintained, one ought to overvalue the services others perform for him and undervalue the services he performs for others. The speech is full of homely wisdom, such as, "The best way of training the young is to train yourself at the same time; not to admonish them, but to be seen always doing that of which you would admonish them."

Plato's versatility is revealed once more in the way he shows that the life of virtue, while it must be justified quite apart from any pleasure it produces, is, at the end, also the most pleasant life:

> He who knows the temperate life will describe it as in all things gentle, having gentle pains and gentle pleasures, and placid desires and loves not insane; whereas the intemperate life is impetuous in all things, and has violent pains and pleasures, and vehement and stinging desires, and loves utterly insane; and in the temperate life the pleasures exceed the pains, but in the intemperate life the pains exceed the pleasures in greatness and number and frequency.[48]

The Character of the City

After these and similar exhortations in the preamble to his laws, the Athenian plunges into the details of the new city: it should be permanent and it should be kept small.[49] It

[46] *Ibid.*, sec. 711*e*, 712*a*, p. 280, p. 281.
[47] *Ibid.*, sec. 715*b*, *d*, pp. 284–85.
[48] *Ibid.*, sec. 733*e*–34*a*, p. 302.
[49] Plato suggests (sec. 737) that a population of 5040

should be balanced so that it is strong enough to defend itself but not afflicted with the kind of expanding population that leads to aggressive actions against neighboring cities. It should practice colonization rather than permit the local population to become too large, but the careful regulation of marriage and the family should make this unnecessary. Plato stresses that the very best state would be without private interests in property, or even in women and children—the ideals of the *Republic* are by no means abandoned. But in this more plausible *polis* neither land nor women would be held in common. Even here, however, in order to prevent the insidious encroachments of commercialism, Plato insists that neither interest nor credit be permitted. To help guarantee efficiency and honesty in dealings, there would be a rigid standardization of currency and weights and measures.

The city would be divided into twelve tribes, so that each tribe could assume certain civic duties for one month each year. Property values would be more or less equalized among the twelve. The magistracy would be composed of a body of thirty-seven "guardians of the law" (*nomophylakes*)[50] between the ages of fifty and seventy. Three would be chosen from each tribe, and one additional man would be elected in order to break ties. The great council, or representative body, would have 360 members, ninety from each of four property groups, selected by an elaborate voting scheme that would take a week to execute. More votes of the poor than of the rich would be needed to elect the representative of the rich and more votes of the rich than of the poor would be needed to elect the representative of the poor, so that the moderate factions in each group would prevail. Though distrustful of the poor, Plato was no admirer of the rich: "I can never assent to the doctrine that the rich man will be happy; he must be good as well as rich. And good in a high degree and rich in a high degree at the same time, he cannot be."

It is not surprising that the highest single executive position in Plato's *polis* of the *Laws* is that of the Minister of Education. In Book VII Plato spells out the most elaborate schemes of education for children from prenatal days on: the types of exercise, the uses of gymnastics, music, and what is perhaps the first permanently organized secondary school ever known,[51]—everything is covered. What impresses us is Plato's fear of private autonomy and innovation, which no doubt boil down to the same thing. Once the best is set up, nothing must be allowed to tamper with it, for change can be only for the worse. Hence, logically enough, even the poets must be censored. This treatment of the state is reminiscent of the *Republic,* where we find a chronicle of the decline of the state but nothing about its ascent.

Plato's legal devices for the regulation of agriculture and the market need not detain us, but it is of interest to note that his examples of the law of property appear again and again in Western history—from Justinian's *Institutes* to Grotius' *De jure belli et pacis*. In Book IX the Athenian stranger reviews the confused state of criminal justice in contemporary societies and shows how it is partly due to departure from the correct philosophical position that "all men do evil involuntarily." The common judicial test that attempts to determine whether an act is voluntary or involuntary and concludes with a verdict of "not guilty" if it is involuntary is

would be convenient, since that figure is evenly divisible by fifty-nine different divisors, including every number between one and ten. This would make it easy for the magistrates to subdivide the population for purposes of revenue or defense. The most masterful study of Plato's *Laws* in light of recent archeological studies is Glenn R. Morrow, *Plato's Cretan City, A Historical Interpretation of the Laws* (Princeton: Princeton Univ. Press, 1960).

[50] The Guardians (*phylakes*) in the *Republic* were not so circumscribed by law (*nomos*) as were their counterparts in the *Laws*.

[51] Since the school was permanent, its teachers would have to be paid; and since free citizens could not demean themselves by accepting pay, the teachers would have to be aliens.

confused from the outset. Plato shifts the judicial test from the accused to the victim: did he merely suffer a hurt, in which case a civil suit for damages is appropriate, or did he suffer an infringement of right, in which case the accused has committed a criminal offense? "There is no such thing as a voluntary crime." Penal measures, it follows, must be aimed at correction rather than mere punishment—though he feels that physical pain is an acceptable method of correction.

The Religion of the City

In his discussion of natural theology in Book X Plato seeks to unite three forms of religious belief that heretofore had been separable and, in practice, probably would remain separable. The beliefs about the gods extolled by the poets, commanded by the legislators, and rationalized by philosophers all rested on somewhat different bases. Plato wanted harmony among them; but, in a way, since the political good was uppermost in his mind, it can be said that for him the legislative motive dominates. The poet clearly loses and the philosopher triumphs, for Plato could never quite cease being the philosopher.

He carefully tries to refute three varieties of heresy. Listed in order of their increasing degree of harm to the *polis* they are (1) atheism, (2) the belief that there are gods but that they are indifferent to men, and (3) the belief that men can escape divine judgment by bribing the gods or through other means. In the process of demonstrating that soul or mind (*psyche*) is the cause of cosmic movement, Plato analyzes ten meanings of *kinesis* (movement, energy). If soul is the cause of bodily movement, it must be prior to and greater than bodily movement and also hidden from the senses, which can perceive only bodily movement. Hence the case against the heretic:

ATHENIAN. And this soul of the sun, which is therefore better than the sun, whether riding in the sun as in a chariot to give light to men, or acting from without, or in whatever way, ought by every man to be deemed a god.

CLEINIAS. Yes, by every man who has the least particle of sense.

ATHENIAN. And of the stars too, and of the moon, and the years and months and seasons, must we not say in like manner, that since a soul or souls having every sort of excellence are the causes of all of them, those souls are gods, whether they are living beings and reside in bodies, and in this way order the whole heaven, or whatever be the place and mode of their existence;—and will anyone who admits all this tolerate the denial that all things are full of gods?

CLEINIAS. No one, stranger, would be such a madman.

ATHENIAN. And now, Megillus and Cleinias, let us offer terms to him who has hitherto denied the existence of the gods, and leave him.

CLEINIAS. What terms?

ATHENIAN. Either he shall teach us that we were wrong in saying that the soul is the original of all things, and arguing accordingly; or, if he be not able to say anything better, then he must yield to us and live for the remainder of his life in the belief that there are Gods.[52]

After the discussion of religion Plato returns to such mundane matters as the regulation of wills, orphans, sorcerers, robbery, and begging. (Begging will not be permitted, but no one—not even slaves—will be allowed to starve.) In all these details of daily life in the *polis* Plato accepted a good part of Attic custom, modifying it where he thought necessary.

The Nocturnal Council

More derided than anything else in the *Laws* is Plato's concluding reference to the Nocturnal Council. With this council, it is generally believed, Plato surrendered the viable constitutional structure he had set up to

[52] *Laws,* sec. 899*a–c,* pp. 69–70. Close attention to this part of the *Laws* will help dispel some of the popular misconceptions about Platonism. Plato argues, for example: (1) Matter itself is not evil; evil stems instead from some inferior soul or souls who represent a principle of disorder in the universe. (2) A soul (*psyche*), or that which moves itself, is not the same as a form (*idea*). (3) God is a soul, not a form, and, though there may be more than one god, there are not many. Plato is not a pantheist.

the veto of a collective substitute for a philosopher-king. The charge is probably a bit extreme, too easily made by those eager to fit Plato into a Procrustean bed of elitism. That the Council was to have philosophic qualities is quite correct. They were to be men trained in astronomy and the mathematical sciences, able to grasp the causal priority of soul in the universe, and possessed of that rare philosophic capacity to see the one in the many. It is not so surprising that the aged Plato should want to keep alive the dream of a philosophic rulership. He as much as acknowledged that it was still but a dream:

> Dear companions, if this our divine assembly can only be established, to them we will hand over the city; none of the present company of legislators, as I may call them, would hesitate about that. And that which a little while ago we described as a dream, when we blended reason and mind in one image, will be accomplished in reality, if only our governors are chosen with care, and rightly educated; and being educated, and dwelling in the citadel of the land, may become perfect guardians, such as we have never seen in all our previous life, by reason of the saving virtue which is in them.[53]

The Nocturnal Council would be composed of the entire Board of *euthynoi,* or high court—which also audited the magistrates—the ten senior *nomophylakes,* the minister and ex-minister of education, and ten coopted men between the ages of thirty and forty. Some of the members should be experienced travelers. The name was derived from the fact that the group would meet before daybreak to plan civic business in advance of the formal operations of government. As the brain of the entire political system, it would brood over all. Sinister prospects are not hard to imagine, but clearly Plato's intention was not that tyranny be sanctioned. The elaborate safeguards Plato discusses for the process we would call reasonable search and seizure are proof of that. But, still, the Nocturnal Council, in addition to stimulating the right kinds of scientific research, could regulate travel and punish heresy. This is enough for some to regard Plato as a champion of the closed society.

[53] *Ibid.,* sec. 969*b–c*, pp. 543–44.

CONCLUSION

This chapter has presented but the briefest of summaries of those dialogues of Plato that bear most directly on political subjects. The aim has been to stay close to the Platonic text and to avoid excessive interpretation. In contemporary political writing the name of Plato has been pasted like a revenue stamp on a variety of theories regarded as absolutist, elitist, and utopian. Since these theories cover an amorphous collection of past and present human experiences, perhaps it is useful to have a five-letter word to epitomize them. But the usage frequently does a disservice to a man of remarkable perspicacity and subtlety; and, what may be worse—since Plato is beyond being offended—it inhibits the understanding of Plato. For absolutism, elitism, and utopianism are, in our day, negative terms, and we read writers with bad labels prejudicially if we read them at all.

To call Plato an elitist is probably fair. The assumption that superiority occurs rarely in the human species was common to his teacher, his class, and his age. His dislike of innovation is a partner to his dislike of the open, action-oriented politics of fifth-century Athenian democracy. It may also be fair to call him a utopian if we mean one who constructs models of nonexistent places, but not if we mean one who has no respect for reality. Why would a nonrealist be concerned with describing so accurately the grim conditions of despotism? But whatever we say about Plato's elitism and utopianism, it seems quite unfair to call him, as so many do, an absolutist. We must remind ourselves once again that the Plato we know was a dramatist who gave us no definitive statement of his philosophy in propositional form. In Plato as in Socrates irony was a prominent element; but there is no good reason to reject his assertion that his philosophy is not written down because it cannot be written down.[54] Even if we think the *polis* of the *Republic* or the *Laws* is, in some sense, absolutist, to call their creator an absolutist is something like calling Faulkner decadent because he wrote about the decadent.

It is quite justifiable to play the agnostic with Plato and claim that it is impossible to know for certain what he thought—but this is not very useful. It is also justifiable—and more useful—to draw some tentative conclusions about Plato's thought from a consideration of the themes and insights that appear again and again in his work. These would surely include his emphasis upon the incompleteness of sensory data, the value of careful definition, respect for skills appropriate to a special function, the demonic character of undisciplined emotion, and—what at this point seems most crucial—the pedagogical value of dialectic and myth. Why does Plato lead us along through various refinements of concepts and then abruptly switch to another track before he reaches a satisfactory definition? Completeness, airtight construction, and impenetrable dogmatism are the marks of the absolutist. But Plato is determinedly incomplete. Why does he continually throw myths into the discourse, a device of such ambiguity that it seems an intentional counterweight to the supposed precision of dialectic? Hans Kelsen suggests that Plato does so because what he is attempting is the formulation of an ideology suitable for an autocracy—indeed, says Kelsen, it is "the ideology of every autocracy."[55] By a "method of substitution," says Kelsen, the meaning of justice in the *Republic* is made to depend upon an understanding of reason, and the meaning of reason is made dependent upon an understanding of the good, and the meaning of the good is put beyond examination. The secret of justice lies hidden in the heart of the ruler, for his knowledge is inexpressible in terms comprehensible to ordinary mortals. The role of myth and censorship is, then, to provide a propagandistic rationale for submission.

Kelsen's case, however, requires too many dubious assumptions to be convincing. His imputation of Plato's will to power is, for example, supported by questionable evidence drawn from the Syracuse experiment. It is a great strain on the imagination—especially given the tragic undertones of the *Republic,* where the rulers of the just state are unhappy and are likely to be killed for their efforts—to regard Plato's tribute to the philosophic life in *Theaetetus* as a decoy to conceal his actual preference for the political life. As for Socrates' caginess in avoiding final definitions, does this not fit his dialectical role, which is to ask rather than to answer questions?

The common view is more plausible than Kelsen's. It holds that Plato's incompleteness and his use of myths and models were simply the devices of an imaginative writer aiming to instruct his readers. But, if so, what is the content of this instruction? If it is knowledge of justice, the political form of the good, it is a strikingly ambiguous content. Kelsen errs, not in calling attention to the ambiguity, but in attributing it to base motives. Perhaps the incompleteness and ambiguity are inseparable from the content of Plato's teaching. In a remarkably penetrating article Philip Merlan has suggested that the body of Plato's work is aimed at the refutation of dogma rather than at its construction, at keeping both himself and his readers free of illusion and hence open to new truth. In the early Socratic dialogues the function of refutation is explicit: Socrates leads a confused young Euthyphro into deeper and deeper confusion on the

[54] Seventh Epistle, in *Thirteen Epistles of Plato.* We might also note *Phaedrus,* in which Socrates says of a man's thoughts: "It won't be with serious intent that he 'writes them in water' or that black fluid we call ink, using his pen to sow words that can't either speak in their own defense or present the truth adequately" (*The Collected Dialogues of Plato,* sec. 276*c*, trans. by R. Hackforth, in Edith Hamilton and Huntington Cairns, eds. [New York: Pantheon, 1961], p. 522).

[55] *What Is Justice?* (Berkeley: Univ. of California Press, 1957), p. 109.

question of how to define piety until Euthyphro (who had condemned his own father for impiety) runs off in chastened dismay. In the later dialogues the young men are often shadowy background figures. They do not need to be refuted because they already know they are not wise, and they have no personal interest at stake. The older men, not uneducated but miseducated, have to be refuted. The present-day reader, too, may be miseducated by what has transpired between Plato's time and our own and may benefit by a refutory challenge. But since the reader cannot literally become a part of the dialogue, refutation must be indirect, and myths are a useful device to this end. They are ambiguous. They interrupt the logical flow of the dialectical inquiry. They force us to struggle for meanings: "Instead of instructing they prepare. Myth, dialectic, refutation; all of them are aimed in some manner at the hearer and relate him to himself rather than offer him direct instruction."[56]

One cannot, of course, say that Plato's writings were without philosophic content. There is, for example, the Platonic theory of forms. But in *Parmenides* Plato himself offers one of the best refutations of this theory. The dialogue form not only stimulates thought in the reader; it helps preserve intellectual freedom in the writer as well.

What of the content of Plato's politics? Some say it is autocratic, but it is a strange kind of autocracy that forces philosophers to become rulers against their own wishes and that denies to the alleged autocrats private property, physical comfort, the right to choose a marriage partner, and the right to bring up one's own children. The Guardians are denied control of the very things most men assume everyone is capable of handling for himself. The aim of these restrictions may well be to preserve the modesty of the elite, to prevent the formation of delusions of grandeur, to dissipate the feeling (especially strong among the gifted) that one knows what is best for oneself. To Plato, sophistry was the art of those who did not bother to ask ultimate questions, those who took the world for granted. The Sophists were his perennial enemies. But Plato respected men who possessed professional knowledge—the physicians and navigators who provided him with recurring analogies for rulership—and whose knowledge was special rather than general, practical rather than ultimate. Indeed, this is what makes the philosopher-king such an anomalous creature. He had to be skilled in the arts of running the world, but wise enough not to take the world or himself for granted. The discipline imposed on the *Republic*'s rulers served this end. The *Republic*'s "ideal state is the actualized method of refuting sham knowledge and sophistry, in short an objectified Socratic refutation."[57]

In the *Laws,* which describes Plato's second-best *polis,* the function of political and philosophic refutation is not abandoned but, quite the contrary, imposed on everyone. In the *Republic* the prideful self-will of the experts is broken; in the *Laws* no one escapes, not even the domestic animals.[58] All self-illusions are destroyed so that the good may be achieved. But Plato never defines the good for us. The lawgivers of the *Laws* are no clearer on this point than the philosopher of the *Republic.* The reader is kept in the same uncertainty in which the ideal *polis* would keep its citizens:

> Thus Plato's political intentions do indeed throw some light on his writings. The state is for Plato a kind of philosophical communication just like his writings, and even more effective than they, because it addresses itself to a greater number of people and makes use of much stronger means of compelling attention. But this new form of communication does not, after all, communicate anything either; its only effect is to destroy the illusion in which Plato finds us

[56] Philip Merlan, "Form and Content in Plato's Philosophy," *Journal of the History of Ideas,* Vol. 8 (1947), p. 411.

[57] *Ibid.,* p. 420.

[58] See sec. 923*a*, 942*a–e*, 944*e*.

caught, by applying pressures and compulsions of various kinds. By destroying that illusion it makes us receptive to a communication. Both the content of Plato's writing and the indirect form in which it is communicated serve the same purpose.[59]

Behind Plato's dialogues, therefore, we find not a hidden view, but a personality. "Plato's philosophy dismisses us cross-examined rather than instructed."[60]

Apollo, watching a blacksmith, asks if the beautiful glow of molten metal cannot be combined with a fixed and permanent shape. The blacksmith replies that it cannot be done. To keep from being consumed by the fire, the metal must be allowed to cool off and harden, to be given structure at the expense of its glow. To preserve Plato we have cooled him off and hardened him into doctrine. But even today, the doctrine is not what compels us to read Plato; it is the converting effect of the life-giving dialogue.

[59] Merlan, pp. 422–23.

[60] *Ibid.*, p. 429. The limited evidence available on Plato's oral teaching seems to support Merlan's view. See Harold Cherniss, *The Riddle of the Early Academy* (Berkeley: Univ. of California Press, 1945). It does not appear that philosophy as such was taught in the Academy. This would seem to vitiate Kelsen's claim (*What Is Justice?* p. 91) that the Academy was a metaphysical sect. Thomas Thorson, ed., *Plato: Totalitarian or Democrat?* (Englewood Cliffs, N.J.: Prentice Hall, 1963), despite its crude title, shows something of the radically divergent views presently taken on the issue of what Plato really meant.

3

ARISTOTLE

Reading Aristotle is not like reading Plato. One is neither caught up in a dramatic dialogue between human protagonists and antagonists nor attracted by felicitous prose. Cicero praised Aristotle's flowing style, but a present-day reader is immediately aware that, whatever else may be said of the English translations of Aristotle's known works, they cannot be made to flow gracefully. The explanation is that what we have are not polished writings but what are probably lecture notes compiled by Aristotle or his students. Virtually the whole body of Plato's writings are preserved for us, but his lectures are lost. With Aristotle, the reverse is true. We know from experience how exciting borrowed lecture notes are; we also know how useful they can be, especially when the lecturer is now silent but once had much to say about almost everything.

LIFE

Aristotle was born about 384 B.C. in Stagirus, on the Chalcidic peninsula in Thrace, a bit east of the modern Salonica. The distinction between the Greek and the barbarian, which was deeply felt there, was to forever color Aristotle's thinking. This area had been ruled by the Athenians during the time of Pericles, but early in the fourth century the Chalcidic cities had tried to form an independent federation. This movement was forcibly put down by Spartan forces. With the blessing of the Spartans, these cities came under the control of Macedon at the time Aristotle was a baby and were later incorporated into the Macedonian kingdom.

Aristotle's father, Nichomachus, was the court physician to Amyntas III, father of Philip of Macedon: "This early connection with medicine and with the rough-living Macedonian court largely explains both the predominantly biological cast of Aristotle's philosophical thought and the intense dislike of 'princes' and courts to which he more than once gives expression."[1] When Aristotle was quite young, his father died. At eighteen he was sent to Athens for exposure to higher education at Plato's Academy. He arrived the year Plato was in Syracuse, but this scarcely

[1] A. E. Taylor, *Aristotle* (New York: Dover Publications, 1955), p. 8.

denied him contact with the master: Aristotle remained at the Academy for twenty years.

After Plato's death in 347 B.C. Aristotle went to Asia Minor to join a friend and fellow student, Hermias, who had just been made monarch of Atarneus in Aeolis. Aristotle married Pythias, the niece of Hermias, and had a happy time studying marine biology along the Aeolic coast. But in 345 B.C., as the result of a Persian plot, Hermias was assassinated. Aristotle sadly departed for Macedon, where he became tutor to the crown prince, a young man who, as Alexander the Great, would lead one of the most spectacular series of conquests of all time. Many stories concerning Aristotle's influence on Alexander have grown up—helped along by Plutarch's *Lives.* The temperaments of the two men were very different, and there is little evidence that much of Aristotle's scientific detachment and philosophic rigor rubbed off on Alexander. There is evidence, however, that Alexander took the trouble to send Aristotle some zoological specimens during the course of one of his later conquests. After Philip of Macedon had been murdered (336 B.C.) and the young Alexander mounted the throne, Aristotle returned to Athens and resumed his scientific work.

At about this time Speusippus, Plato's successor as head of the Academy, died. Perhaps Aristotle expected to be elected the new president, but Xenocrates was chosen instead. Soon after (335 B.C.), Aristotle opened his own school, the Lyceum, in a gymnasium attached to the temple of Apollo Lyceus. Since instruction was given in the portico (*peripatos*), the Lyceum has come to be called the school of the peripatetics. The Platonic Academy at this time tended to stress mathematics; the Lyceum, biology and politics.

Aristotle was soon to suffer from an ironic display of public passion. When Alexander died (323 B.C.), Athens was seized with an anti-Macedonian agitation. Because of his previous association with Alexander, Aristotle was the victim of popular abuse. Only shortly before, when Alexander had hanged a relative of Aristotle's for daring to criticize the conqueror, Aristotle's supposedly pernicious influence on the hapless man had been an issue. Now, in a manner reminiscent of the case of Socrates, Aristotle was charged with impiety. This was largely a pretext to cover underlying political reasons, namely Aristotle's connection with Antipater of Macedonia. Unlike Socrates, however, Aristotle chose to escape with his friends. He went to Chalcis, where he died the following year at the age of sixty-two or sixty-three.

Works

We have two versions of Aristotle's lectures on ethics: the *Nichomachean Ethics,* compiled by Aristotle's son Nichomachus, and the *Eudemian Ethics,* compiled by the mathematician Eudemus. The fifth, sixth, and seventh books of the former are identical with the fourth, fifth, and sixth books of the latter. Aristotle's other major works are the *Metaphysics, Politics, Rhetoric, De Anima* (*On the Soul*), *Physics, Poetics, Prior Analytics,* and *Posterior Analytics* (the logic).

There is one exception to the statement that we have no finished writing of Aristotle: *The Constitution of Athens,* a recent archeological discovery, is the sole survivor among 158 constitutional studies made by Aristotle and his students.

Taken together, Aristotle's works constitute one of the most impressive intellectual achievements of recorded history. They earned for him in the later Middle Ages the supreme accolade of recognition simply as The Philosopher.

THE *ETHICS*

Political Science and the Good

A word of explanation for the amount of attention we shall give to the *Ethics* in relation to the *Politics* may be necessary in advance. Aristotle himself as much as states that the *Ethics* is but a preface to *Politics.*

Politics is at the beginning, at the end, and in the center of the *Ethics*. In the conclusion of the *Ethics* Aristotle says that we must turn now to the subject of legislation and constitutions "in order to complete to the best of our ability our philosophy of human nature." He then outlines what amounts to the contents of the *Politics* and says, "When these have been studied we shall perhaps be more likely to see with a comprehensive view, which constitution is best, and how each must be ordered, and what laws and customs it must use, if it is to be at its best. Let us make a beginning of our discussion."[2]

Political science as master science

Every art and every inquiry aims at some good, Aristotle tells us in Book I of the *Ethics*. But there is a difference between ends that are activities and ends that are products: the former have an intrinsic worth—the activity of playing the clarinet, say—the latter an instrumental worth—the clarinet itself. Of course, there is a hierarchy of ends, often, in which some ends are both intrinsic and instrumental, depending on which side of the relationship one views them from. Aristotle's illustration is that bridle-making is a product-directed end subordinate to the more intrinsically worthful art of riding; but the art of riding may, in turn, appear instrumental if viewed under the more comprehensive art of military strategy.

The master arts, such as military strategy, are those that subsume a variety of other arts; they are clearly preferable to the lower arts. The highest master art is politics, for its end is no less than the good of man. The master statesman must have in the highest degree a perception of the *good,* or that which is desired for its own sake, and which, like the target for the archer, gives direction to his aim.

Precision is not to be sought in all subjects alike; the subject political science investigates admits of "much variety and fluctuation of opinion." It is "the mark of an educated man to look for precision in each class of things just so far as the nature of the subject admits." Because it takes very good judgment to cope with the great diversity of activities incorporated within political activity, political science is not for the young: ". . . a young man is not a proper hearer of lectures on political science; for he is inexperienced in the actions that occur in life . . . and further . . . he tends to follow his passions . . . because the end aimed at is not knowledge but action."

The goods of life

Political science aims at the highest good for man, which ordinary men as well as superior men seem to agree is happiness. But, starting as we must, says Aristotle, with the facts of the world, most men identify the good, or happiness, with pleasure. The aim of pleasure characterizes a common type of life. But there are two other modes of life: some men seek not pleasure but honor; they lead the political life. Others seek not only honor but virtue; they believe that honor is superior to pleasure yet that honor is not an end in itself. Most men seek honor to be assured of their goodness; otherwise they would not value the acclaim of men of practical wisdom who know them at close hand above the acclaim of distant and ignorant persons. So virtue would seem to be higher than honor and the end for which honor is valued.

Is virtue, then, the end of the political life? This would appear to be an incomplete conclusion, says Aristotle, for virtue may be compatible with suffering, misfortune, and dishonor. Aristotle states rather abruptly that the third and last mode of life is the contemplative—which is, we infer, most closely

[2] *Nicomachean Ethics* (henceforth *N. E.*), Bk. X, 1181^{b}, *The Works of Aristotle,* trans. and ed. by W. D. Ross (Oxford: Clarendon Press, 1925), Vol. 9. The same translation, complete, is also in Richard McKeon, ed., *Introduction to Aristotle* (New York: Random House, Modern Library, 1947). Greek references are to *Opera Omnia, Graece et Latine* (Paris: Firmin-Didot et Sociis, 1927), Vol. 2. Page references will be to the Berlin Greek edition edited by I. Bekker (1831 *et seq.*), with "a" and "b" referring to columns. Since these citations have become standard in virtually all subsequent editions and translations, no other page references are needed.

related to virtue. (The life of money-making and wealth does not, he notes, stand by itself, since wealth can never be more than instrumental—it is always sought for the sake of pleasure or honor.) But Aristotle promises to discuss the contemplative life later. His discussion turns out to be very much later, at the end of the *Ethics* (1177^a*ff.*).

Again Aristotle seems to shift rather abruptly—perhaps because we are reading only his lecture notes—to the problem of universal good, the highest end. This inquiry was made "an uphill one" by his friend Plato's theory of forms. Without going into all the subtleties of the argument, we may say that Aristotle challenges Plato's notion that the good is one Idea—a common element in all things. There is not one science, or body of knowledge, but many pertaining to the good in all things.

Being and the good

People disagree on the degree of Aristotle's pluralism. A full treatment of this problem could require an exposition of his *Metaphysics*,[3] but suffice it to say that he clearly believed that the science of ethics and the science of being were separable—for he separated them: ". . . even if there is some one good which is universally predicable of goods or is capable of separate and independent existence, clearly it could not be achieved or attained by man; *but we are now seeking something attainable* [our italics]." Men interested in practical knowledge, observes Aristotle, are likely to derive very little benefit from knowledge of the good itself. A doctor does not set about studying health in the abstract, but the health of man, or perhaps even the health of a particular man. Ethics is such a study.

Immediately after Aristotle explains the separation between ethics and metaphysics, he goes back to the initial question:

> Let us again return to the good we are seeking and ask what it can be. . . . clearly not all ends are final ends; but the chief good is evidently something final. Therefore if there is only one final end, this will be what we are seeking, and if there are more than one, the most final of these will be what we are seeking.[4]

This concern for a final end may seem to contradict what we have just quoted to show Aristotle's disdain for the Platonic good. There is in Aristotle, it is true, what sometimes appears to be an excessive eagerness to disagree with Plato; but quite apart from this, it must be remembered that what Aristotle is talking about here as the final end is (a) final for man only, not for all creation (as a biologist, Aristotle saw more readily than some that man is only one animal among many) and (b) hypothetical, for he writes, "*if* [our italics] there is only one final end." The analogy of the physician studying health is instructive. Aristotle was certainly not averse to speculation if it was appropriate to the facts and within the limits of precision imposed by the subject matter of the inquiry. Happiness is the final good for man because it is never sought for the sake of something else but is always desirable in itself. It "is something final and self-sufficient, and is the end of action." Aristotle points out that the test of self-sufficiency applies not simply to man in isolation but to man in relation to family, friends, and fellow citizens, "since man is born for citizenship."

Happiness

There is a danger that we will misunderstand Aristotle's emphasis on happiness as an end and make of him a hedonist unless we realize that he was not using a term for which some present-day usages of the English word "happiness" are apt counterparts. The Greek word *euphoria,* or subjective good feeling, which we retain in English, is the synonym for what we often mean when we use the word "happiness." But this state can be induced by drugs. *Eudaemonia,* or objective well-being and well-doing, is the Greek term Aristotle was using here.

[3] See Aristotle, *Metaphysics,* 986^a 22–26; 1028^b 21–24; 1072^b 30–1073^a 3; 1091^a 29–1091^b 3; 1091^b 13–1092^a 17.

[4] *N. E.,* 1097^a 15, 26–29.

But even this refinement does not help us very much. Aristotle himself, with that questioning, almost skeptical approach that has endeared him to many, observes that to say happiness is the chief good is to utter what seems a platitude. Further inquiry leads to the conclusion that the function of man is to perform activities of soul that follow or imply a rational principle. As the function of a lyre-player is to play the lyre and that of a good lyre-player is to play it well, so the function of a good man is "the good and noble performance" of those activities—that is, performance with "appropriate excellence." Or, put subjectively, "human good turns out to be activity of soul in accordance with virtue. . . . But we must add 'in a complete life.' For one swallow does not make a summer." A man can suffer many misfortunes; but if he responds well to them, his total life can be judged happy.

The emphasis on performance cannot be overstressed. Aristotle was reflecting the classic Greek practice of measuring excellence by performance in the arts, athletics, military activity, and politics. Virtue could not reside in the spectator; it does not come as a gift of the gods. It depends on nature, to be sure, but also on art and reason, learning and habituation: ". . . political science spends most of its pains on making the citizens to be of a certain character, viz. good and capable of noble acts."

Intellectual and Moral Virtue

Virtue is of two kinds, intellectual and moral. The former results from being taught; the latter, from habituation. States of character arise from activities: *ethike* (moral virtue) is derived from *ethos* (habit). The primary function of legislators is to make citizens morally virtuous rather than intellectually virtuous, for men are not moral by nature—nor are they moral contrary to nature—but they are adapted by nature to receive virtues, which are perfected by habit.

The emphasis on training for virtue has a certain utilitarian cast: Aristotle notes that political science as the practical art of inducing moral virtue by the proper habituation of citizens has as its "whole concern" pleasures and pains, for it is in learning to respond to and use these well that a man becomes virtuous.

But how does the legislator know what is or is not virtuous? The answer is given by Aristotle's famous doctrine of the mean: the good is one but the bad is many, for reasons not exactly like those given by the Pythagoreans. The ethical good is a single point between many points of excess and deficiency. It is worth noting that Aristotle is not so mechanical in stating the doctrine of the mean as some popularizations would suggest. When we think of a mean, we are apt to think of an arithmetical mean or perhaps the fulcrum of a teeter-totter, with excess sitting high on one end and defect low on the other. But Aristotle recognizes, first of all, a problem in the relativity of perception: ". . . the brave man appears rash relatively to the coward and cowardly relatively to the rash man."[5] He writes:

> it is no easy task to be good. For in everything it is no easy task to find the middle, e.g., to find the middle of a circle is not for every one but for him who knows; so, too, anyone can get angry—that is easy—or give or spend money; but to do this to the right person, to the right extent, at the right time, with the right motive, and in the right way, *that* is not for every one, nor is it easy.[6]

Finding the mean, then, is like finding, not the middle of a plank, but the middle of a circle; we must often settle for—"as people say," said Aristotle—the lesser of two evils.

Aristotle acknowledges that the Socratic idea of knowledge as virtue is put in question by the very distinction between intellectual virtue and moral virtue. Having one does not guarantee having the other. Legisla-

[5] Aristotle has some trouble with courage as a mean between rashness and cowardice. He sees that for courage "what is intermediate is in a sense an extreme," since it seems more opposed to cowardice than to rashness, which "is thought liker and nearer to courage."

[6] *N. E.*, 1109^a 24–28.

tors need to study the subtle distinctions between voluntary and involuntary actions. When we say that circumstances forced a man to commit murder, we are often saying too much—we assume that the agent contributes nothing, that the compulsion is, in Aristotle's language, the result of a moving principle outside the agent. This is rarely the case, suggests Aristotle. Much depends on a man's peculiar perception of particular facts. But the variability of perception is no grounds for the dissolution of moral responsibility. We can say, if we wish, that a pleasant object has a compelling power, but "it is absurd to make external circumstances responsible, and not oneself, as being easily caught by such attractions, and to make oneself responsible for noble acts but the pleasant objects responsible for base acts."

That Aristotle is thinking of the practical problems of the legislator is evident from the distinction he draws between wrongs committed involuntarily and those committed voluntarily. Punishment is appropriate, he argues, only when repentance is relevant and repentance is relevant only when a person could have acted voluntarily and therefore responsibly.

Justice

It is not part of our task here to discuss Aristotle's treatment of the various virtues examined in the central part of the *Nicomachean Ethics:* courage, temperance, liberality, munificence, pride, honor, good temper, nonobsequiousness, nonboastfulness, tact, and justice. But justice as a virtue is so central to the life of a *polis* and the speculations of so many scholars have begun with Book V of the *Ethics* that we must review what Aristotle says on this subject.

Justice is, first of all, a state of character, the contrary of injustice; both terms are ambiguous. The just man obeys the law, treats others fairly, and exercises complete virtue, "not absolutely, but in relation to our neighbor." Justice and virtue are in appearance the same, "but their essence is not the same; what as a relation to one's neighbor is justice is, as a certain kind of state without qualification, virtue." Justice is the sum of virtues (each with its intellectual and moral aspect) and at the same time the harmony between them that, for Aristotle as well as Plato, makes goodness in the context of a *polis* possible. Although neither Plato nor Aristotle would put it this way, we might say that justice in the broadest sense is virtue socialized.

But there is also a species of justice that is justice not in this wide sense but in a narrower sense. It pertains to the distribution of honor or money (distributive justice) or to the rectification of injurious transactions between man and man (retributive, or rectificatory, justice).

In the first case, the just is seen as a species of the proportionate, or the equality of ratios, according to some standard of merit,

> . . . for all men agree that what is just in distribution must be according to merit in some sense, though they do not all specify the same sort of merit, but democrats identify it with the status of freeman, supporters of oligarchy with wealth (or with noble birth), and supporters of aristocracy with excellence.[7]

Aristotle uses some simple equations of discrete and continuous proportion to show how one may arrange problems of distributive justice.

Rectificatory justice concerns the righting of wrongs—and is better compared, perhaps, to modern civil suits than to modern criminal suits. Aristotle notes that people go to a judge to correct wrongs because the judge is an intermediary: he stands between extreme claims, between loss and gain, and he restores equality. The Greek word for just (*dikaion*) comes from the word for division into two equal parts (*dicha*); the judge (*dikastes*) is one who bisects (*dichastes*). Rectificatory justice is not, Aristotle notes, simple reciprocity: an eye for an eye is not always just. Proportion is the key, "For it is by propor-

[7] *Ibid.*, 1131ᵃ 25–29.

tionate requital that the city holds together." Money has been introduced into men's relations precisely because it provides a basis for comparing and equating unlike things. The diversity of things bought and sold, however, are not in fact as commensurate as they are made to seem in economic relationships; what is in truth being compared is not the things but the demand for them—a conclusion we may illustrate by comparing the income of a teen-age rock-and-roll favorite with that of the first violinist of the Cleveland Symphony.

Once again we note how close to Aristotle's thinking is the problem of right rule, for he distinguishes political justice—justice between free and equal men who "share their life with a view to self-sufficiency"—and justice by analogy only—the right relationship between master and slave, father and son, husband and wife: ". . . justice can more truly be manifested towards a wife than towards children and chattels, for the former is household justice, but even this is different from political justice." (Different from, and less than, we must stress.)

Natural justice

One of the more controversial passages in the history of Aristotelian interpretation occurs in Aristotle's discussion of political justice. This passage also has great bearing on the long history of natural-law theories. There are two places where Aristotle speaks of natural justice, or the law of nature: the *Nicomachean Ethics,* Book V, Chapter 7, and the *Rhetoric,* Book I, Chapter 13. In the latter Aristotle speaks of "two kinds of law, particular and general" (*idion ton de koinon*) and says that "by general laws I mean those based upon nature" (*koinon de ton kata physin*).[8] This seems to be a slim thread upon which to hang the proposition that Aristotle was the initiator of natural-law theories as they later came to be known, for the *Rhetoric* is a handbook for orators and lawyers—a how-to-do-it book more than a philosophic treatise.

In Chapter 15 of the *Rhetoric* Aristotle notes that a lawyer is well advised to appeal to positive law when his case is strong and to natural law when his case is weak. At the least, one should be skeptical about attempts to read too much into the *Rhetoric,* even though it is clear there as elsewhere that Aristotle believed that the problem of justice and injustice was common to all men.

The reference in the *Ethics* raises more problems:

> Of political justice part is natural, part legal —natural, that which everywhere has the same force and does not exist by people's thinking this or that; legal, that which is originally indifferent, but when it has been laid down is not indifferent, e.g., that a prisoner's ransom shall be a mina or that a goat and not two sheep shall be sacrificed. . . . Now some think that all justice is of this sort, because that which is by nature is unchangeable and has everywhere the same force (as fire burns both here and in Persia), while they see change in the things recognized as just. This, however, is not true in this unqualified way, but is true in a sense; or rather with the gods it is perhaps not true at all, while with us there is something that is just even by nature, yet all of it is changeable; but still some is by nature, some not by nature.[9]

Which is which, Aristotle goes on to say, is evident, even though both are changeable. By nature the right hand is stronger, "yet it is possible that all men should come to be ambidextrous." Convention determines that measures for corn and wine will vary from place to place; "constitutions also are not the same, though there is but one which is everywhere by nature the best."

If there is a justice that is everywhere the same, and hence by nature, there is also injustice that is everywhere the same, and hence by nature. Set apart from each of these are specific acts of justice and injustice, which

[8] *The "Art" of Rhetoric,* trans. by J. H. Freese (Cambridge, Mass.: Harvard Univ. Press, The Loeb Classical Library, 1926), pp. 139–41. *Koinon* is sometimes translated "universal" rather than "general"—which may be part of the trouble. The *Rhetoric* uses *nomos* for "law" in these passages, whereas *dikaion* (law, just, or right) is used elsewhere.

[9] *N. E.,* 1134^b 18–30.

Aristotle says are just and unjust not by nature but by enactment. He concludes the passage by promising to examine later the nature and number of species of each of these. Unfortunately, this examination occurs in a set of lectures, possibly another book for the *Politics,* either never written or written and lost.

Universal law?

The question of theoretical import is whether Aristotle was consciously propounding a universal realm of law discoverable by reason and superior to and determinative of positive law, or whether his statements were more modest and descriptive. The context suggests the latter, for it implies that both conventional justice (*nomikon dikaion*) and natural justice (*physikon dikaion*) are changeable, and that both justice and injustice may be "by nature." Wormuth suggests that this distinction between natural and conventional justice is no more than the traditional legal distinction between two types of offense, those that are regarded as bad in themselves (*mala in se*) and those that are regarded as bad only because they are prohibited by law (*mala prohibitor*). Murder would be an example of the former and parking overtime would be an example of the latter. Such a distinction can be maintained without a metaphysical theory that defines true law—even though Aquinas thought otherwise. "Perhaps his [Aristotle's] division of positive law into natural and legal justice is the strongest evidence that he had no conception of a natural law which annuls positive law. He believed that laws were good or bad, but he never denied the name of law to bad laws."[10]

As Aristotle points out in Book X, law must have compulsive power, "while it is at the same time a rule proceeding from a sort of practical wisdom [*phronesis*] and reason [*nous*]." Without law we cannot be made good because laws habituate us to good behavior and "we are not made good or bad by nature."[11] But this is no guarantee that, as Aquinas would later argue, an unjust law was no law at all or that law must be in conformity to nature. The view that these natural-law theories find their roots in Aristotle is not tenable. For Aristotle, "Justice is essentially something human."

Aristotle upholds this belief in Book V, Chapter 10 by his treatment of equity. The law is universal in form, but sometimes universal statements are incorrect when applied to specific cases. The adaptation of the law to the facts by decisions in equity is like a sculptor's adaptation of his guidelines to the shape of a stone. Equity, then, "is a sort of justice and not a different state of character."

Practical Wisdom as the Art of Politics

We can say little of the discussion of intellectual virtue (*aretés dianoutikes*), scientific knowledge (*episteme*), and practical wisdom (*phronesis*) in Book VI of the *Ethics* except to note that for Aristotle practical wisdom, or prudence, is the special virtue of the political leader. Practical wisdom is neither an art (*techné,* or how to make things), which requires and is limited to a specialized area,[12] nor is it scientific knowledge, which requires demonstration about things that are universal and invariable. No limitation or demonstration is possible when first principles are variable, as they are here. *Practical wisdom* may be summarized most simply as wisdom about means, good judgment about what is to be done, combined with the capacity to act.

This is not to say that deliberation is ex-

[10] Francis D. Wormuth, "Aristotle on Law," in Milton R. Konitz and Arthur E. Murphy, eds. *Essays in Political Theory; Presented to George H. Sabine* (Ithaca: Cornell Univ. Press, 1948), p. 59. For a contrary interpretation see Ernest Barker, *The Political Thought of Plato and Aristotle* (New York: Dover Publications, 1959), pp. 326–28. Leo Strauss argues that Aristotle identifies natural right with political right and that the justice of the best regime is natural justice in *Natural Right and History* (Chicago: Univ. of Chicago Press, 1951), pp. 156–63.

[11] Aristotle also says, "None of the moral virtues arise in us by nature" and "Legislators make the citizens good by forming habits in them."

[12] Although Aristotle later speaks of practical wisdom as "the art of politics."

cluded from practical wisdom. Quite the reverse. It is scientific knowledge that excludes deliberation, for one does not deliberate about invariable things. *Philosophic wisdom* (*sophia*) is scientific knowledge combined with intuitive reason (*nous*) that grasps first principles. We would not say, notes Aristotle, that practical wisdom, or the art of politics, involves the highest or best knowledge, since it involves only knowledge of man and "man is not the best thing in the world."

In a preview of the *Politics,* Aristotle divides practical wisdom into household management, legislation (the controlling part, concerned with universals in a city), and politics more narrowly conceived, which, in turn, has two parts: the deliberative and the judicial, both concerned with particulars. In an observation of striking timelessness, Aristotle points to the way men concerned with only their personal material interests often presume to think that they alone have practical wisdom; they call politicians busybodies for aiming too high and trying to do too much. With delightful understatement he adds, "yet, perhaps one's own good cannot exist without household management, nor without a form of government. Further, how one should order one's own affairs is not clear and needs inquiry."[13]

After probing the reaches of practical wisdom in Book VI, Aristotle concludes that, while for Socrates reason is virtue, for Aristotle virtue increases reasoning. Then, characteristically, as Book VII opens, he says: "Let us now make a fresh beginning." He examines continence and incontinence and their relationship to knowledge, appetite, and choice. He discusses the nature of pleasure and pain, a subject, he says significantly, that belongs "to the province of the political philosopher." But the details of Aristotle's discourse on the nature of pleasure and pain are less significant for us than his discussion of friendship in Book VIII.

[13] Such inquiry, Aristotle repeats, is not for the young: ". . . a boy may become a mathematician, but not a philosopher."

Friendship

Friendship is so central to the good life and the political life as Aristotle conceives it that it is difficult to understand the discussions of the *polis* in the *Politics* without some familiarity with the discussion of friendship in the *Ethics.* Books VIII and IX of the *Nichomachean Ethics* are devoted wholly to the subject of friendship. This indicates the importance Aristotle attached to the subject. Without friends a man can scarcely aspire to full humanity. "With friends men are more able both to think and to act." When men are friends, they have no need for justice; but when they are just, they still need friends. "Friendship seems . . . to hold states together and lawgivers . . . care more for it than for justice."

There are many degrees of friendship. The highest form involves equality, awareness of the other, reciprocity, and wishing the other well. The purpose of the best *polis* is to make such friendship possible. At a lower level is friendship of utility, such as that among old people who need to assist each other, and friendship for pleasure, such as that among young people who enjoy each other's company in a fleeting way. The highest form of friendship is not, of course, without utility and pleasure, but these follow from mutual good will and affection without forming the essence of the relationship. Friendship and justice are united by a common criterion of proportionate duties:

> How man and wife and in general friend and friend ought mutually to behave seems to be the same question as how it is just for them to behave, for a man does not seem to have the same duties to a friend, a stranger, a comrade, and a school fellow. . . . equals must effect the required equalization on a basis of equality in love and in all other respects.[14]

At still a third level Aristotle placed what we might call pseudofriendships, relationships between unequals. These include father-son, elder-younger, husband-wife, and ruler-subject friendships. That one of the basic

[14] *N. E.,* 1162^a 29–31, and 1162^b 3–4.

assumptions of Aristotle's ethics is fundamentally opposed to one of the basic assumptions of Christian ethics is clear at this point: "In all friendships implying inequality the love also should be proportional, i.e., the better should be more loved than he loves . . . for when the love is in proportion to the merit of the parties, then in a sense arises equality, which is certainly held to be a characteristic of friendship." Consequently, friendship between a master and his slave is impossible. Mothers, however, seem to violate the rule of proportion, for they love their offspring, says Aristotle, even when they are not loved in return.

Friendship in all of its forms depends on community (*koinonia*). All forms of community are parts of the political community, for all share in the purposes of life aimed at by legislators: "All the communities, then, seem to be parts of the political community; and the particular kinds of friendship will correspond to the particular kinds of community." At this point Aristotle, rather surprisingly, reviews the three basic forms of political constitution (*politeia*) and their three perverted forms—subjects that form an important part of the *Politics,* as we shall see, and also match the categories of Plato's *Statesman.* In each constitution, says Aristotle, the degree of justice present is closely related to the degree of friendship present. The king, for example, displays the friendship of a father to his subjects.

The unanimity found among men of good will—which is not the same as identity of opinion but is rather a mutuality of spirit—is, says Aristotle, properly called political friendship. It is by contrast a mark of our contemporary conception of the nature and purpose of politics that most people today would look on a political friendship as something a bit unsavory.

Politics, Happiness, and Contemplation

Book X, the last book of the *Ethics,* is divided between two subjects referred to earlier in the work, pleasure and happiness. Our concern here is with the political, but the political as conceived by Aristotle, not by us—hence we must reemphasize the degree to which, for Aristotle, the political is bound up with the quest for virtue. Book X, Chapter 6, reviews the relationship between pleasure, virtue, and happiness—which by now should be fairly familiar to us.

Except for happiness, which is an end in itself, we choose everything for the sake of something else. But good men seek happiness through *virtue,* or the doing of "noble and good deeds," and bad men, including those who put "despotic position" ahead of virtue and reason, "have never tasted pure and generous pleasure" and hence "take refuge in bodily pleasures." Happiness is an activity; a virtuous life requires exertion. Amusement is valuable as relaxation, for no one can work continuously; but happiness does not, as so many think, lie in amusement.

So much is granted. But a problem arises for our understanding of political virtue when we consider the ultimate appeal of contemplation:

> If happiness is activity in accordance with virtue, it is reasonable that it should be in accordance with the highest virtue: and this will be that of the best thing in us. Whether it be reason or something else that is this element which is thought to be our natural ruler and guide and to take thought of things noble and divine, whether it be itself divine or only the most divine element in us, the activity of this in accordance with its proper virtue will be perfect happiness. That this activity is contemplative we have already said.[15]

Reason is "the best thing in us" and the objects of reason are "the best of knowable objects." Moreover, the self-sufficiency that has been a cardinal value for Aristotle throughout "must belong most to the contemplative activity." "Happiness extends, then, just so far as contemplation does. . . . Happiness, therefore, must be some form of contemplation."

The introduction of the subject of contem-

[15] *Ibid.,* 1177^{a} 12–19.

plation at the very climax of the *Ethics* raises five basic and interrelated questions. In light of all we have said so far we must try to resolve them before we can proceed to *Politics*. It must be said at the outset that, though we may read Aristotle with care and though some questions offer more difficulty than others, the answers to all of them are to some extent ambiguous. The questions are:

(1) Is contemplation itself a form of activity?

(2) Does the self-sufficiency of contemplation preclude friendship?

(3) Does the self-sufficiency of contemplation preclude the doing of noble deeds?

(4) Is contemplation human or divine?

(5) Is contemplation consistent with political life?

(1) *Contemplation as activity*. The first is a more or less technical question we will not attempt to plumb. Suffice it to say that Aristotle uses "activity" in several ways in the *Ethics*. Speech and the doing of deeds are, on the one hand, set apart from internal mental operations associated with contemplation. But, on the other hand, a mental operation (*energeia*) is also a kind of activity, for in its generic sense *energeia* could apply to both. Activity as what is practical would be *praktikos;* as doing deeds, *praxis;* as principle of work, *ergon*.[16] To call contemplation an activity, therefore, could mean that it is an inner rather than an external activity.

(2) *Contemplation and friendship*. Aristotle comments explicitly on the relation of contemplation to friendship. We cannot contemplate nothing. In finding something worthy of our contemplation we should look for the highest and most inclusive thing—and this turns out to be the worthy actions of a good man who is our friend. Another's action is easier to contemplate than our own —Freud would have understood why—yet, if our friendship is genuine, our friends' actions are in part our own as well. So we resolve a dilemma: though contemplation is self-sufficient, a man can contemplate truth "better if he has fellow workers."[17]

(3) *Contemplation and noble deeds*. Whether or not mental activity is properly called activity, complete self-sufficiency would seem to imply that man need not perform external actions. But this implication would be inconsistent with Aristotle's claim that "to do noble and good deeds is a thing desirable for its own sake." It would also be inconsistent with his repeated criticism of the Socratic dictum that knowledge is virtue. (Arguments do not, Aristotle says, make men good.) Finally, it would be inconsistent with Aristotle's unquenchable practical bent: "Surely . . . where there are things to be done, the end is not to survey and recognize the various things, but rather to do them; with regard to virtue, then, it is not enough to know, but we must try to have and *use* it, or try any other way there may be of becoming good."

The resolution of this difficulty is so bound up with the resolution, if it may be called that, of the next that we must suspend the former until we can examine the latter.

(4) *Contemplation and divinity*. Is the life of contemplation human or divine? After describing the contemplative life, which aims at no end beyond itself, and suggesting that it is superior even to the life of the statesman —for his great art is aimed at making the contemplative life possible—Aristotle abruptly interjects, "But such a life would be too high for man; for it is not in so far as he is man that he will live so, but in so far as something divine is present in him. . . . If reason is divine, then, in comparison with man, the life according to it is divine in comparison with human life."

From this we might well conclude that

[16] "A theoretical science ends in truth, as a practical science ends in action (*ergon*)" (*Metaphysics* 993^b 21). For a contrast between the *vita activa* and the *vita contemplativa* as different ways of life in Greek experience, see Hannah Arendt, *The Human Condition* (Chicago: Univ. of Chicago Press, 1958), pp. 12–21.

[17] It must be noted, however, that in discussing the contemplation of worthy friends in Book IX, Aristotle appears to be using the concept of contemplation in a less technical sense than in Book X, where the contemplation is of philosophic wisdom (*sophia*).

the gods can contemplate but we mortals have other fish to fry and must therefore be about our business. But, curiously, Aristotle seems to advise us to be divine and human at the same time: ". . . we must . . . so far as we can, make ourselves immortal, and strain every nerve to live in accordance with the best thing in us." We must, it seems, transcend our humanity; yet we do not transcend humanity in contemplation either, because "reason more than anything else *is* man."

This description of the tension between the mortal and immortal in man is what made possible the "Christianizing" of Aristotle—his assumption that man was imbued with a spark of divinity. But the attempt to turn Aristotle into a Christian was erroneous, because the spark of divinity in the Scriptures was not reason and the God of the Scriptures acted in the world rather than contemplated. What sort of actions can we assign to the gods, asks Aristotle. Not justice, for why would they make contracts and return deposits? Not liberality, for to whom would they give? Not bravery, for what risks could they run? All our actions must appear "trivial and unworthy" to gods. Still the gods live: "Now if you take away from a living being action, and still more production, what is left but contemplation? Therefore the activity of God, which surpasses all others in blessedness, must be contemplative; and of human activities, therefore, that which is most akin to this must be most of the nature of happiness." And he who exercises reason must be "most dear to the gods."

Yet Aristotle does not say even to the man possessed of unusual reason, "Go off by yourself and sit trancelike, gazing at your navel." The life of action in the world is secondary to contemplation—again, this is unlike the Hebrew or Christian concept of action as primary—but is not therefore to be abandoned: ". . . in a secondary degree the life in accordance with the other kind of virtue is happy; for the activities in accordance with this befit our human estate. Just and brave acts, and other virtuous acts . . . seem to be typically human. . . . the moral virtues must belong to our composite nature." And the doing of these virtuous actions requires "external prosperity." To act we must be healthy and to be healthy our bodies "must have food and other attention." (We do not, however, need many things to be virtuous: "We can do noble acts without ruling earth and sea.") Nor must we —as modern political theorists tend to do—identify the exercise of contemplative reason with "mere theory." Reason brings to the test the facts of living, which requires experience of what these facts are. Hence the philosopher, who in the last analysis is superior to the statesman, is never a "mere theorist."

(5) *Contemplation and political life.* We have already answered the question of the relationship between contemplation and political life by looking at the gods. With regard to virtue, "it is not enough to know, but we must try to have and use it." Yet this use of knowledge produces a higher knowledge, which is the object of contemplation and which is truly divine. Philosophers cannot live without the protection of the good *polis,* the *polis* cannot live well without the knowledge of the philosophers, and men cannot become philosophers without the experience of the *polis.* Hence the *polis* is an educational venture in which law is the chief instrument by which men become good: ". . . surely he who wants to make men, whether many or few, better by his care, must try to become capable of legislating."[18]

The Sophists presume to teach politics, but they do so without the actual experience of legislating. They are like medical men who read books only but do not study patients. After receiving this warning against impracticality we read on and find Aristotle summarizing the contents of a forthcoming study on the structure and practices of constitutions and legislation: "When these have been studied we shall perhaps be more likely to see with a comprehensive view, which constitution is best, and how each must be ordered, and what laws and customs it must use, if it is to be at its best. Let us make a

[18] "You can't legislate morality" has become a commonplace of our individualist American politics. Aristotle's position is that morality must be legislated.

beginning of our discussion." The end of ethics is but the beginning of politics.

THE *POLITICS*

The *Polis* as End

In the first book of the *Politics* Aristotle distinguishes between political associations and other associations. The household (*oeconomia,* from which we get our "economics") is concerned with "mere life," that is, biological procreation, sustenance, and nurture. These are the familial functions, made necessary when male and female by natural instinct unite. In this association men are similar to other animals. Out of such relationships arise, for the sake of self-protection, villages and small monarchies, with the king usually occupying the position of a surrogate father. "The fact that men generally were governed by kings in ancient times, and that some still continue to be governed in that way, is the reason that leads us all to assert that the gods are also governed by a king. We make the lives of the gods in the likeness of our own—as we also make their shapes." But when a number of villages join together and hence achieve the "height of self-sufficiency," we reach the *polis,* "the final and perfect association." But it is necessary to qualify this statement immediately in order to avoid misunderstanding resulting from the use of the word "perfect": ". . . or rather we may say that while it *grows* [comes into being] for the sake of mere life, it *exists* for the sake of a good life."

> Because it is the completion of associations existing by nature, every polis exists by nature, having itself the same quality as the earlier associations from which it grew. It is the end (*telos*) or consummation to which those associations move, and the nature of things consists in their end or consummation; for what each thing is when its growth is completed we call the nature of that thing, whether it be a man, or a horse, or a family. Again, the end, or final cause, is the best.
>
> From these considerations it is evident that the polis belongs to the class of things that exist by nature, and that man is by nature an animal intended to live in a polis.[19]

Behind these famous words lies a philosophical system that must be understood at least in part if the words themselves are to be understood. Students reading the *Politics* without reference to the *Metaphysics*—not to mention the *Ethics*—often take as pointless what has in fact an almost technical precision. For example, what does it mean to say that the nature of a thing is its end? "Nature" is a translation of *physis,* from which we get "physical" and "physics." The root of the word pertains to birth, to origination; but in the Latin *natura,* this is connected with the idea of the primitive, as it may also be in our minds when we think of natural man. But the Greek *physis* was primarily connected with the idea of growing. With this meaning, therefore, we think of natural man not as a primitive but as a growing man or a grown man. To this Aristotle added a special understanding of the process of growth in nature or by nature.

The four causes

In the *Metaphysics* Aristotle develops the theory of the four causes (*aitia*).[20] Ridding our minds of the usual connotations of the word "cause" helps us to understand this

[19] *Politics,* 1252^b 32–1253^a 4, trans. by Ernest Barker (New York: Oxford Univ. Press, 1958), p. 5. Subsequent page references are to this edition. Benjamin Jowett's translation (*The Works of Aristotle,* W. D. Ross, ed. [Oxford: Clarendon Press, 1921], Vol. 10) is more literal and less cluttered, but Barker is better on political terminology. Greek references are from *Politics,* in Greek and English, trans. and ed. by H. Rackham (Cambridge, Mass.: Harvard Univ. Press, Loeb Classical Library, 1932). Barker divides each Book into chapters and sections, but, as Rackham points out, a given chapter and section number can mean twelve different places in as many editions. Because Barker collates his pages with the standard Bekker references page by page but not line by line, it will be necessary to give both Bekker page and line and Barker page references in footnotes to follow.

[20] *Metaphysics,* Bk. I, 983^{a-b} and Bk. V, 1013^{a-b}. See also Book II, Chs. 3 and 7, of the *Physics.*

theory. *Explanatory factor, approach to reality, frame of reference, orientation*—any one of these might be a more apt term. The four causes are material, formal, efficient, and final. The *material cause,* or factor, is simply matter, the physical substance of whatever is under consideration. The *formal factor* consists of the abstract essence, the definition, the mental conception drawn from or imposed upon matter. This may be closely identified with the Platonic theory of forms. The *efficient factor* is what we today usually mean by "cause," the immediate source of change in anything, that which produces effects. The *final factor* is what a person, thing, or event will become. The material factor of a chair is wood; the formal factor, an idea in a carpenter's head; the efficient factor, the movement of the carpenter's arms and hands and tools in a certain way; the final factor, the use to which a chair is put—a seat for a person who might declare with satisfaction, "Now, *this* is a chair!"

This same explanatory framework can be imposed on anything that exists. This is what Aristotle does with the *polis* in the *Politics.* He looks at the human and associational materials of the *polis,* the ideas of it in the heads of Plato, Phaleas, and others, the ways lawgivers have put together particular *poleis,* and —here and in the *Ethics*—the uses served by the *polis.* The *polis* is obviously more complex than a chair and not so obviously less artificial. It lies somewhere between mere nature—the acorn becoming the oak—and artifice—the carpenter making a chair.

When Aristotle says, "the *polis* exists by nature and . . . it is prior to the individual," we need to know that it is prior both temporally—you were not born a stateless creature—and ontologically—a whole is prior to its parts, for without it the part cannot complete itself.

Thus it is the intention of nature that man live in a *polis:* "There is an immanent impulse in all men towards an association of this order."[21] Bees, too, are naturally gregarious and live in society, but man alone has been given language and he alone has a perception of good and evil, the just and the unjust. He alone *constructs* the *polis* with rational intention as well as instinct. His art cooperates with nature—or frustrates it. Hence, "Man, when perfected, is the best of animals; but if he be isolated from law and justice he is the worst of all." Outside of a *polis* man is either a beast or a god.

The Household

In Chapters 3–13 Aristotle outlines the elements of the household—the relations of master and slave, husband and wife, and parent and child—as well as the art of acquisition, which gives them all the necessities of life.

Aristotle cannot foresee the impact of automation, which would take place over two thousand years hence, but with his usual precocity he can imagine its precondition: men will always need subordinates until such unlikely day as inanimate instruments learn to do their own work "as if a shuttle should weave of itself, and a plectrum should do its own harp-playing." But even here a distinction must be made between instruments of production (*poiesis*) and instruments of action (*praxis*), for the former make things that exist and persist beyond the immediate act of use, whereas the latter are complete in themselves. Production is of course necessary, but "Life is action not production" and the slave, while he may make things, "is a servant in the sphere of action." Thus in the realm of the household Aristotle sees a perpetual need for slaves.

The natural slave

Some argue that slavery is unnatural and exists only because of the exercise of force. But Aristotle replies that, while some men are slaves by convention only, others are natural slaves: "Anybody who by his nature is not his own man, but another's, is by his nature a

[21] Aristotle also says man is by nature meant even more for marriage than for living in the *polis,* but the more here seems to mean in the order of time rather than in the order of final development.

slave." Aristotle invokes the analogies of the soul ruling the body, men ruling animals, males ruling females ("the relation of male to female is naturally that of the superior to the inferior"), to justify the rule of masters over natural slaves: "It is better for them . . . to be ruled by a master." The natural slave can, unlike animals, apprehend the workings of reason in others and hence obey commands, but he is "destitute of it himself." He differs from animals, who do not even apprehend reason, "but the use which is made of the slave diverges but little from the use made of tame animals."[22]

Surely here is a confusion of observation with justification. That men *are used* like animals says nothing on the point of whether they *should be used* like animals. Aristotle only compounds the error by adding physical differences to the hypothetical mental differences between natural master and natural slave: the latter (by "nature's intention") have great physical strength for the menial duties of life, whereas the former ("upright in carriage") are "useless for physical labor" but "useful for the various purposes of civic life. . . ." This distinction is complicated, if not invalidated, by the fact that military service is for the freeman and is part of civic life.

We are apt to be impatient with Aristotle for his defense of natural slavery, but we must note his honesty in pointing out how often conventional slaves are not natural slaves. There are slaves by law who have not only freemen's bodies but freemen's souls. He reviews the arguments of those who say that to make slaves of vanquished enemies is always just (because military superiority has been demonstrated) and those who say that it is never just. Both arguments are ambiguous, and Aristotle suggests a third position: superiority in goodness alone justifies the possession of slaves. This is why, he says, that Greeks do not like to call prisoners of war slaves unless they happen to be barbarians. In any case, there is only suspicion and enmity when master and slave do not merit their position, and "a community of interest and a relation of friendship" when they do.[23]

Suffice it to say that, in the context of his day, Aristotle could not be regarded as an arch-conservative on the issue of slavery—his contemporaries may have regarded his analysis as an attack. Some today would argue that in describing the natural slave Aristotle was only describing what modern man has become—the servant of production and householding rather than the master of them. Likewise, we are aware of how far we have departed from Aristotelian assumptions when we read further in Book I about property, household management, and the art of acquisition.

Property: use and exchange

What we call economics is close to the art of acquisition, whereas Aristotle's *oeconomia* was household management, which is sharply separated from the art of acquisition: "That the art of household management is not identical with the art of acquiring property is obvious." The aim of the household is the good life, and property is but a means to this end. Moreover, too much property is a barrier to the moral purposes of the household.

Aristotle now puts great emphasis on the distinctions between nature (*physis*) and convention (*nomos*) and between art (*techné*) and nature, which he used in discussing statesmanship. It is clear that he thinks some ways of acquiring property are natural and hence desirable and other ways are conventional and, unless held within severe limits, hence undesirable, if not immoral. Aristotle's bias against monetary speculators and for agrarian producers is marked. All articles of property, he says, have use value and exchange value. A shoe is produced for the purpose of being worn. That it may be ex-

[22] As Aristotle's argument on slavery becomes increasingly difficult to sustain, he seems to shift from saying the natural slave has some reason to saying the natural slave has no reason.

[23] Slaves in Attica, we should remember, were not set apart by dress, were protected by law against exploitation, were often treated as members of the family, served in the civil service, and could purchase their freedom.

changed for money is incidental to its proper use, for "the shoe has not been made for the purpose of being exchanged." A *barter system,* or exchange of goods for other needed goods, is preferable to a money system: "When used this way, the art of exchange is not contrary to nature," though Aristotle concedes that, as dependence on foreign imports grows, a money currency becomes inevitable. The trouble is that some men strive to develop an art of profit-making derived solely from the experience of exchanging goods for money. They lose sight of the real—the natural—purpose of the goods. Because money can be stored up, they see the possibility of unlimited wealth; and this possibility destroys their balance: ". . . the fundamental cause of this state of mind is men's anxiety about livelihood, rather than about well-being." Of course, Aristotle regarded *usury,* or making a profit from currency itself, as the most unnatural of all the unnatural modes of acquisition. This, he says, "is hated most and with most reason."

Excessive concern for livelihood—the material aspect of life—destroys concern for well-being—which is not necessarily to be identified with the spiritual or nonmaterial aspect of life but with objective excellence (*arête*), which the *Ethics* spelled out for us. Our idea of economic man is a perversion of Aristotle's householding man (*oeconomicos*), for the latter is "concerned more with the good conditions of human beings than with a good condition of property." Aristotle's conception of the man of practical wisdom is the "serious man" (*spoudaios*), one able to manage a household or a *polis.* The *epistemic* man, the man of philosophic wisdom, is even more to be honored.

Ideal States and Actual States

In Book II of the *Politics* Aristotle looks not at the household but at the *polis,* and not at the Athenian *polis* as it is but at a number of *poleis* as they ought to be. The Book has three parts: Aristotle first offers a critique of the ideal-state theories of Plato, Phaleas, and Hippodamus; then he offers a critique of three existing states—Sparta, Crete, and Carthage; finally he reviews the works of famous lawgivers who, in a sense, combined the practical and the theoretical.

At the outset Aristotle notes that he will not offer here his own suggestion for the ideal state—he offers it in Books VII and VIII—but will consider instead what others regard as ideal, what they would wish for as a form of political association if the material conditions that are the subject of Book I were satisfied.

Critique of Plato

Aristotle criticizes Plato on two grounds: first he questions whether, in Socrates' words, "The greatest possible unity of the whole *polis* is the supreme good," for if the *polis* becomes more and more unified, it "will eventually cease to be a *polis* at all." In fact, it will turn into a household, for it is the intermeshing of diverse elements that distinguishes a *polis* from a household, a tribe, or an alliance. Self-sufficiency, argues Aristotle, is more desirable than unity, and the *polis* can be more self-sufficient than the household only at the expense of unity. (Such self-sufficiency requires, however, the kind of proportionate distribution of goods discussed in Book V of the *Ethics.*)

Second, even if unity were of the highest worth, would Plato's proposals for common property and community of wives and children be the right means to that end? Aristotle thinks not. There will be an ambiguity in the use of "mine" and "not mine" where all share ownership of property, wives, and children collectively. That men should say "mine" of thousands of sons in a magnanimous way is highly impractical, but that they should say it in a nonmagnanimous sense would be highly dangerous: ". . . the result will be that every son will be equally neglected by every father." This would lead to "a watery sort of fraternity" with family feeling "diluted and tasteless," as if a little wine had been "mixed with a great deal of water."

In addition to the practical difficulties of

transferring offspring from one rank to another and of limiting "unnatural affection" when paternity is common, Aristotle argues against Plato's communism on the grounds that it destroys the occasion for two important virtues, respect for the family and generosity (liberality) with one's property. Aristotle suggests that pleasure and pride in one's own property is a "feeling implanted by nature" and is not to be censured.

In all this Aristotle does not, perhaps, take sufficient account of the imaginative character of Plato's *Republic* but treats it as one might treat a blueprint for social reform. The *Republic,* as we have seen, is demeaned when taken this way. Whether Aristotle consciously or unconsciously misinterpreted the *Republic* is uncertain.

Also, Aristotle does not make it clear that Plato's communism applies not to the whole *polis* but to the Guardian class only. Indeed, we must recall that the *Republic* deals with what a philosophic ruler must be and with what justice is rather than with how to organize an entire *polis.* The *Republic* goes into little detail on any but the Guardian class. Plato does make quite clear, however, that the farmers will own private property. Yet Aristotle says, "We are not told whether these farmers, as well as the guardians, are to have property in common." In fact, it is not fair to talk about common ownership in the *Republic* at all, since the Guardians, with their Spartan discipline and rigorous duties, scarcely participate in the ownership arrangements of the other classes. Aristotle is quite correct, however, in noting that Plato's Guardians do not achieve personal happiness in exchange for their sacrifices.

It is perhaps ironic that Aristotle's realism does not challenge Plato's utopianism and its assumptions about what we would call *human nature,* or what men are capable of. Instead Aristotle accepts the Platonic vision of goodness and then questions Plato's particular institutional arrangements for bringing these human powers into realization.[24]

[24] See Eric Voegelin, *Order and History* (Baton Rouge: Louisiana State Univ. Press, 1957), Vol. 3, pp. 322–23.

W. L. Newman suggests that Aristotle is finding enough wrong with Plato, pushing a bit too hard, in order to justify another attempt at a best constitution. To this observation Barker adds, "the same may be said to be true of the somewhat grumbling criticism of the *Laws* which follows."[25] Aristotle complains of Plato's digressions, says the *Laws* really is essentially the same as the *Republic* as far as institutions are concerned, and quarrels with the 5,000 limit on the number of citizens.[26] Plato, we are told, neglects foreign affairs and is not sufficiently definite on allocations of property; he is content to distinguish the rulers from the ruled with a simile; he dismisses the distribution of farm-houses as "another subject which needs further consideration . . ." and so on. Aristotle eventually relaxes his grip on Plato, but not until Plato's political garments are tattered.

Critique of Phaleas

Phaleas of Chalcedon (5th Cent.), Aristotle's next subject of analysis, seems less personal a target than Plato. Phaleas' views on the need for equal distribution of property are mainly the occasion for Aristotle to display his quite remarkable knowledge of Hellenic laws and to set forth his own position: ". . . it is not enough merely to establish the general principle of equality of property. . . . It is more necessary to equalize men's desires than their properties; and that is a result which cannot be achieved unless men are adequately trained by the influence of laws."

For all his practical concern with property, Aristotle never ignores the moral significance of the *polis.* A modicum of property will mitigate crimes committed out of physi-

[25] From Newman's notes on the *Politics.* Quoted in Barker, p. 55*n.*

[26] Aristotle actually is in error in using the figure 5,000. It is, as we saw, 5,040, a number selected for numerical rather than practical reasons. 5,040 is divisible by 12 as well as by all the integers from 1 to 10. Aristotle missed the element of playfulness in Plato's use of this term and the importance of playfulness for philosophic insight. See Voegelin, *Order and History,* Vol. 3, p. 293, and Johan Huizinga, *Homo Ludens* (Boston: Beacon Press, 1955), Ch. 9.

cal want; but only a temperate disposition will cure men of committing crimes to obtain release from some unsatisfied desire that gnaws at them. Finally, only philosophy will cure them of committing crimes out of pure lust for pleasure: "Men do not become tyrants in order to avoid exposure to cold." Despite the fashion of economic interpretations of events, a study of twentieth-century riots, revolutions, and tyrannies would seem to bear out Aristotle on this point.

Critique of Hippodamus

Hippodamus of Miletus (5th Cent.) was a town planner and, according to Aristotle, the first non-statesman to write on the form of constitutions. He was "without practical experience" and perhaps for this reason, Aristotle says later, advocated laying out streets in straight lines. He seemed to consult mathematics more than experience and he advocated three classes, three divisions of land, and three sets of laws for each *polis*. He advocated a supreme court in which the judges (i.e., jurors) would be allowed to render qualified verdicts, and he proposed a law for public maintenance of orphans. This proposition leads the worldly-wise Aristotle to comment that such a law already exists in Athens and elsewhere.

Aristotle the practical man is willing to rebut Hippodamus and his ivory tower with regard to the voting procedure of courts by giving a rather formal, logical defense of the *status quo*. To give civic honor to innovators, as Hippodamus suggests, might lead to political disturbances, says Aristotle; but he does not show how. He does reveal "sad confusion" in many of Hippodamus' proposals; but his basic concern is to show that everything cannot be written down in politics, that, while laws must sometimes be changed, they should be changed with "great caution" and that changing practices in the arts is not the same as changing the operation of a law: "It is from habit (*ethos*), and only from habit, that law (*nomos*) derives the validity which secures obedience."[27] And changing habits takes time.

Actual states

Aristotle now turns to actual states that have in some measure approached the ideal. He analyzes Sparta not only in terms of its formal constitution but in terms of how it works in practice. Because of Sparta's heavy emphasis on the military, the men are often away and the women have acquired inordinate power through their husbands rather than directly. The laws on property and inheritance are not well-ordered, either, for they have encouraged great disproportions in land ownership: a few people, often women, own a large part of the land. The Ephorate, a council of five Ephors (overseers) drawn from the people, has acquired such power that even the Spartan kings[28] court its favor, and Sparta is in danger of becoming a democracy without the guidance of adequate written rules. Aristotle says that the Council of Elders, chosen by acclamation as judges for life, has been subject to bribery and undue influence because men must declare themselves openly as candidates for election. This has encouraged the wrong kind of man to seek the office: "The man who deserves the office should have it whether he wants it or no. . . . No one would seek election as councillor unless he had . . . ambition. Yet ambition and avarice are exactly the motives which lead men to commit nearly all intentional crimes."

There are many other defects of the Spartan system, but the chief one—as Plato has already noted in the *Laws*—is that the Spartan ethos is so directed toward military values, "goodness in war," that the Spartans "did not know how to use the leisure which peace brought."

The Cretan constitution, says Aristotle,

[27] Some translate *ethos* in this context not as "habit" but "custom."

[28] Recall that Sparta had a system of two kings, each with less power than we usually associate with kings.

has many features in common with that of Sparta and is alleged to be modeled after it. But the Cretan constitution is inferior to the Spartan one in several respects. The *Cosmoi,* though somewhat like the *Ephoralty,* is distressingly casual in its methods of appointment yet it still manages to deny the people at large an opportunity to participate. The Cretan constitution is, in fact, scarcely a constitution at all, but a *dynasteia,* an oligarchic tyranny. The Cretan nobles are able to split the people into factions headed by kings who quarrel interminably with each other. This is, says Aristotle, "the dissolution of political society." The only thing that saves Crete is its island isolation.

Aristotle admires the Carthaginian constitution on practical grounds: "It is proof of a well-ordered constitution that Carthage . . . has had no civil dissensions worth mentioning, nor any attempt at a tyranny." Nevertheless, there have been deviations from the pure principle of aristocracy in the direction of democracy and oligarchy. The assembly can consider a matter even if the two kings (Suffetes) and the Council of Elders have agreed not to submit it to the people. The trend has been toward the election of magistrates on the basis of wealth as well as merit, which imbues the whole *polis* with "a spirit of avarice" and has made even kingships and generalships open to purchase.

In his discussion of these and many other details of the Spartan, Cretan, and Carthaginian constitutions, chosen because they "are justly held in high regard," Aristotle shows his sensitive concern for a balance of classes, institutions, and influences. But this balance is not simply a reduction to the lowest common denominator, for Aristotle is also concerned with the principle or virtue that animates the whole state: he is able to see the political and moral weakness in Sparta's emphasis on military strength as well as the political and moral strength in Carthage's principles, despite the deviations from them, of election according to merit and leisure for the meritorious.

The *Polis* and Its Citizens

Book III is perhaps the most important book of the *Politics.* It begins by asking, "What is the nature of the *polis?*"[29] The *polis,* Aristotle tells us, is a compound (*syntheton*) made up of individual citizens; this "compels us to consider . . . what a citizen really is." A citizen (*polites*) does not become such because he happens to reside in a certain place or because he has certain legal rights, such as the right to sue in the courts; nor can young children and old and infirm men be citizens "in the strict and unqualified sense. . . . The citizen in this strict sense is best defined by one criterion, 'a man who shares in the administration of justice and the holding of office.'" The citizen is one who is eligible both for discontinuous offices—those for which no person may serve more than one term—and for what Aristotle calls indeterminate offices—those without a time limit, such as a judgeship or a position as an assembly member. Defining "citizen" is difficult because there is no broad common denominator: there are a variety of offices that citizens may fill and a variety of constitutions under which they may live.

Aristotle grants that it is easier to apply his definition to a citizen of a democracy than to a citizen of a polity, in which all legal powers may be exercised by specialized agencies. Hence Aristotle amends his initial definition, one who shares, to one "who enjoys the *right* [our italics] of sharing in de-

[29] Barker, p. 92. Compare Jowett, "What is a state?" in *The Works of Aristotle,* Vol. 10; Rackham, "What exactly is the essential nature of a state?" in *Politics,* p. 127; and Voegelin, "What really is the *polis?*" in *Order and History,* Vol. 3, p. 325. Taking *ti pot* as an idiom, perhaps the most literal translation of *ti pot estin e polis* would be "What in the world is the *polis?*" Once again we see how elusive meanings in translation are. The opening lines of Book III, which are rendered in English in fourteen lines by Jowett, require twenty-nine lines of Barker's English. Voegelin argues that "nature" and "essence" improperly suggest the viewpoint of the philosopher, whereas the viewpoint of Book III as a whole is really that of the statesman seeking standards for political rule. We might add that the viewpoint of the descriptive political scientist is also present.

liberative or judicial office" within a *polis,* when the latter is "a body of such persons adequate in number for achieving a self-sufficient existence."

In practice, of course, most *poleis* base citizenship on parentage rather than on Aristotle's definition. There are further difficulties: What of the original founders of a *polis?* Aristotle asks; they are certainly citizens. Or what of those who have acquired constitutional rights as a result of a revolution? This is a more complicated question, for the revolution may be based on unjust principles and "Can a man who is not justly a citizen be really a citizen . . . ?" Aristotle recalls his own definition and concludes that, to be practical, one must call such persons citizens. But whether they are *justly* called citizens is not yet answered, for this question requires examination of the *polis* of which they are a part. What constitutes the identity of a *polis?* It is certainly not walls, or a place on the map, or even the permanence of its members: "Old members are always dying and new members are always being born . . . shall we thus apply to the state the analogy of rivers and fountains, to which we ascribe a constant identity in spite of the fact that part of their water is always flowing in and part always flowing out?"

This analogy, says Aristotle, is not conclusive, because a *polis* may change its identity even while none of its inhabitants change. A chorus, first tragic then comic, changes its identity even without changing its members. If the musical mode is changed from Dorian to Phrygian the same notes combine to form a different sounding chord. In the same way, a constitution (*politeia*)[30] determines the identity of a *polis:* citizens are notes; the constitution is the musical mode.

The good man and the good citizen

But if the constitution is to have a character separable from its individual members, a further question arises: "whether the excellence of a good man and that of a good citizen are identical or different." Using the familiar ship analogy, Aristotle points out that each sailor performs different functions aboard ship, yet each is judged by the contribution his work makes to the purpose of the whole ship. Likewise, a citizen's role must be seen in relation to the common purpose of his *polis.* Nor should it be thought that Aristotle the aristocrat put good name or proper family connections ahead of civic excellence. Those who contribute the most to the well-being of the *polis* should justly receive the most in recognition from it, even though others surpass them in wealth and descent. But there are many different kinds of *poleis,* so "there cannot be a single absolute excellence of the good citizen. But the good man is a man so called in virtue of a single absolute excellence. It is thus clear that it is possible to be a good citizen without possessing the excellence which is the quality of the good man."

We cannot imagine even a good state being composed of only good men, for any *polis* is composed of unlike elements; yet in their different ways, the members of a good state must all display something of the excellence of the good citizen. Aristotle is the eminent pragmatic realist here in accepting both the diversity of *poleis* and the diversity of traits among citizens. Yet there lingers the inference that citizen and man are ultimately one and hence their virtue is ultimately one. In one case the two are identical: "We may thus assume that, in the case of the ruler (*politikos*) the excellence of the good citizen is identical with that of the good man."

In a rather labored logical pirouette of the sort Aquinas was later to make, Aristotle notes that, while a ruler must know only how to rule, a citizen must know how to both rule and be ruled. Hence must not the citizen know more and be more virtuous than the ruler? Aristotle argues that, on the one hand, neither ruler nor citizen, insofar as they are participants in governance, need master the lesser arts of menial service, for manual laborers can be directed intelligently

[30] *Politeia* is sometimes translated as "regime." The term is closer to the idea of biological structure than to legal restrictions.

without the director acquiring their skills.

On the other hand, the ruler is not exempt from the knowledge of how to obey, which is appropriate to the citizen, for, as the old army maxim—old even then—expressed it, "You cannot be a ruler unless you have first been ruled." In fact, citizens and rulers need to share all forms of goodness (temperance, justice, courage) save one: prudence (*phronesis*). Prudence completes the virtue of the good man and also separates the good ruler from the good citizen.

Aristotle seems to have shifted ground. Having started with the suggestion that the goodness of citizens is relative to their *polis,* he now tells us that good citizens—presumably everywhere—have temperance, justice, and courage. And from the claim that the good ruler has a single absolute excellence, he has moved to the claims that knowledge of ruling and being ruled are different and that the good ruler must have both. The latter is not a fundamental difficulty, for presumably singular virtue can have different aspects. The former difficulty does seem to be fundamental, and we will need to observe whether and how it is resolved.

Can a mechanic be a citizen? In some *poleis* he is; but in the best states he is not, for he does not have the leisure. Only in a good *polis* can the good man and the good citizen be identical and then only in the person of the citizen who has the ability to be a statesman. Does this create an obligation for *poleis* to enable good men to become statesmen?

Forms of Rule

We are brought back to the starting place —the problem of the good man and the good citizen—but we are also led forward. What kinds of constitutions are there? A constitution (*politeia*) "may be defined as 'the organization of a *polis,* in respect of its offices generally, but especially in respect of that particular office which is sovereign in all issues.' The civic body [*politeuma*] is everywhere the sovereign of the state." For example, in a democratic *polis* the people (*demos*) constitute the *politeuma;* in an oligarchic *polis* the few (*oligoi*) constitute the supreme authority. It is evident, therefore, that there are a number of different types of constitutions. All serve in some measure the natural gregarious impulse of men and a perceived common interest: "It is an evident fact that most men cling hard enough to life to be willing to endure a good deal of suffering, which implies that life has in it a sort of healthy happiness and a natural quality of pleasure."

Aristotle repeats that it is natural that masters should rule slaves and householders their household (wife, children, and servants), but that under a constitution stressing equality it is proper that men should hold office by turns. Aristotle sounds a bit like the old-generation deplorer of the young generation in stating that "Today the case is altered." Men seek profit from public office as if they were sick and wanted health from their office. "Those constitutions which consider only the personal interest of the rulers are all *wrong* constitutions, or *perversions* of the right forms. Such perverted forms are despotic, whereas the *polis* is an association of freemen [*koinonia eleutheron estin*]."

Although Aristotle's tone is still descriptive, there is no equivocation in his sharp distinction between right and wrong forms of government. This distinction is based on the criterion of the end (*telos*) of the *polis* and the nature of political rule. The end of the *polis* is self-sufficiency and the "common interest [*koine sympheron*] . . . judged by the standard of absolute justice [*haplos dikaion*]."[31] It is the nature of political rule to be directed to the good of the *polis* and not merely to private interest.

Classification by number

Superimposed on these two categories of proper rule and corrupted rule are three cate-

[31] By thinking of *koine sympheron* as "common interest"—which no doubt came through the Latin *communem utilitatem*—we can be easily misled into images of nineteenth-century liberal, individualistic, and contractual society. Rackham's "common advantage" may be a little better.

gories based on the criterion of number: rule by one, by few, and by many. Rule by one is kingship and its perverted form is tyranny; rule by the few is aristocracy and its perverted form is oligarchy; and rule by the many is polity (*politeia*—now used in a special sense) and its perverted form is democracy. In each of the perverted forms, the interests of the ruling group (*politeuma*) rather than the interest of the whole is uppermost.[32]

Mere number, however, turns out to be an inadequate basis of classification. For in practice what may be most significant about the many (*demos*) is that the poorer classes predominate; and what may be significant about the few (*oligoi*) is not that they are always the best (*aristos*) but that they are most often the rich (*plousios*). Hence the conflict between oligarchy and democracy is most often a conflict between plutocracy and rule by the lower economic classes.

Both democracy and oligarchy—and Aristotle continues to use these designations, even though he is now talking about poor and rich—have their own warped sense of justice. True justice is equality for those deserving equal treatment; but the democrat seeks equality for all, whether they deserve it or not, and the oligarch favors unequal treatment for all—that is, a rule of privilege whereby those who have keep what they have and those who have not are out of luck. Advocates of oligarchy and democracy agree on the meaning of equality in *things* but not on the meaning of equality in *persons*. These standards are of course faulty, but "most men, as a rule, are bad judges where their own interests are involved."[33] Defenders of oligarchy and democracy are in error not only about their own claims but about the end of the *polis* itself. They think that the right distribution of property is somehow the highest end of the *polis* and the reason why people associate together in a *polis:* "But the end of the state is not mere life; it is, rather, a good quality of life." Were it otherwise, slaves and animals could form their *poleis,* but this is of course impossible:

> any polis which is truly so called, and is not merely one in name, must devote itself to the end of encouraging goodness. Otherwise, a political association sinks into a mere alliance, which only differs in space from other forms of alliance where the members live at a distance from one another. Otherwise, too, law becomes a mere covenant—or (in the phrase of the Sophist Lycophron) 'a guarantor of men's rights against one another'—instead of being, as it should be, a rule of life such as will make the members of a polis good and just.[34]

No statement could more sharply illustrate the contrast between the classical conception of the *polis* and the modern conception of the liberal state. Even in the age of the welfare state one hears repeatedly that it is both futile and wrong for government to try to mold an individual's sense of right and wrong. Yet for Aristotle this was the very purpose of government and the standard of good legislation. And when he says, "otherwise . . . law becomes a mere covenant . . . a guarantor of rights," he is doing nothing less than condemning the social-contract state as an example of obvious defectiveness. Modern advocates of social democracy or the welfare state may have abandoned the social contract and may accept an activist role for the state, but even they see as the primary purpose of politics the provision of fair shares of property to all—or, as Aristotle would somewhat scornfully put it, the encouragement of "mere life" rather than a "good quality of life."

Sovereignty

Does this mean that the better sort of men should be sovereign[35] in the *polis?* Aris-

[32] Cp. *N. E.,* 1160^b, where "timocracy" replaces "polity"; *Rhetoric,* Bk. I, Ch. 8, 1365^b–66^a, where Aristotle speaks of democracy, oligarchy, aristocracy, and two kinds of monarchy; and Plato's *Statesman,* 301–03, where the original sixfold classification was expounded, though Plato, unlike Aristotle, did not give a name to the good form of democracy.

[33] The equal or unequal treatment in question here refers to the distribution of offices.

[34] *Politics,* 1280^b 6–13, p. 119.

[35] *To kyrion,* which is translated "sovereignty," means *lordship,* or the capacity of giving validity to acts. This

totle sees difficulty in having any one group with final sovereign power and thus barring other groups from civic honor. Even rule by the one best man is defective in this respect. The answer would seem to be that no man or group of men but rather the laws themselves should be sovereign—a "government of laws, not men," as our founding fathers would put it.

But Aristotle is realistic enough to see that even this does not solve all difficulties, for the law itself is biased toward the groups that established it. Because this is the case, Aristotle entertains the thought that there may be something to be said for government by the many after all. Even though they may be inferior individually, "it is possible" that collectively the many may surpass the few best in the quality of deliberation. By combining many qualities—as in the judging of music or poetry, for example—they may achieve a greater sense of unity and a higher quality. Aristotle is quick to qualify this conclusion, however, and notes that some popular bodies behave like herds of beasts. "All the same . . . there is nothing to prevent the view we have stated from being true of *some* [Barker's italics] popular bodies."

A further question is, what are the matters over which any such sovereign body should exercise its sovereignty? Solon, with some wisdom, did not let the mass of citizens serve as magistrates but gave them the functions of electing the magistrates and calling them to account when their terms were over. However, can people not fitted to serve in a particular calling best judge that calling? The conduct of doctors, notes Aristotle, is passed on by a board of doctors rather than by a board of patients. However, the best judge of a house may not be a committee of house-builders but of house-users, "and the diner—not the cook—will be the best judge of a feast."[36] But Aristotle finally returns to the point that "rightly constituted laws" should be the final sovereign, except in contingent matters where personal decisions must be made.

Quality and quantity

Good laws and a just constitution are not easily acquired, for in practice it is exceedingly difficult to balance the claims of quality and quantity. This problem fascinates Aristotle. Even if there is some sort of constitutional balance between the good, the wealthy, the well-born, and the many; are there not difficulties if the good or the wealthy are very few in number? "The claims of both may be justly challenged by the masses; for there is nothing whatever to prevent the many—collectively if not individually—from being better, or richer, than the few." In such a case should the lawgiver direct legislation to the benefit of the many? Aristotle's answer is not altogether satisfactory; he says the lawgiver should strive to satisfy neither the good few nor the not-so-good many but to do what is for the benefit of the whole *polis* and "the common good of its citizens." This is what a politician probably thinks he does when he succeeds at maximal redistribution of discontent; but Aristotle had a more reflective, more precise image of the common good than many present-day practitioners seem to have.

What happens, however, if the sum of many lesser goodnesses does not add up to the goodness of a few? What if there are a few, or even one person, "so pre-eminently superior in goodness that there can be no comparison between the goodness and political capacity which he shows (or several show, when there is more than one) and what is shown by the rest . . ."? Such a one would surely be "like a god among men"; he and his counterparts "are a law in themselves." Visions of Plato's philosopher-king,

is a slightly different sense from the modern (post-Bodin) conception of *sovereignty* as the final power of commanding in the state.

[36] One is reminded of A. D. Lindsay's discussion of the democratic argument that "only the wearer knows where the shoe pinches" in *The Modern Democratic State* (New York: Oxford Univ. Press, 1943), Ch. 11. Athenian citizens had the right to arraign a magistrate who was breaking the law. The popular assembly (*ecclesia*), however, did not enact basic legislation but only proposed legislation to a judicial commission.

Machiavelli's prince, and Rousseau's legislator leap to our mind. They are the lions against whom the rabbits in Antisthenes' fable were claiming equal rights. It is because such persons exist, says Aristotle, that democratic states practice ostracism and that oligarchies pull down outstanding men. Indeed there may be a kind of justice in this "policy of levelling." Proportion is important: a painter would not permit an oversize foot to mar his canvas, however beautiful it was. The trouble is that most acts of ostracism do not have even this expedient form of justice to recommend them but are done "in a spirit of mere faction [*stasiastikos*]." However, when a man who is truly "of outstanding eminence in goodness" comes along, the "natural course" is simply to make him permanent king.

The rule of law

This remark provides the transition to a concluding discussion of five forms of kingship. We will discuss only the last form, absolute monarchy, because it raises the theoretical question of personal rule versus the rule of law. There is some thrashing about and considerable repetition of points previously made. Aristotle appears to be putting arguments in opposition to one another and summarizing the views of others, but in the end he turns out to be speaking his own views. As Plato suggested, the free intelligence of a gifted man is better than the deadness of fixed law. A physician bound to a rule book is hampered in the arts of healing. But law is free of passion—indeed, reason free of passion becomes Aristotle's definition of law—and even the most intelligent man can be aroused to passion. Almost any single man is more liable to corruption than a whole people. The analogy to a physician is not apt, says Aristotle, because the physician's aim is inevitably to cure while the politician's aim may be deflected toward favoring friends or gaining self-serving power. An able king who had complete power to deliberate on details within a framework of general laws would obviously be best. But problems of succession often bring conflicts of sovereignty to a head, since kings with real power wish to secure their offspring's claim to authority. Moreover, a king's bodyguard is always a threat to the rule of law.

> What has just been said is sufficient to show that in a group whose members are equal and peers it is neither expedient nor just that one man should be sovereign over all others. This is equally true whether laws are absent, with the one man ruling as a law in himself, or are present; it is true whether the one man is a good man ruling over the good, or a bad man ruling over the bad; it is even true when the one man is superior in goodness . . . unless his superiority be of a special character.[37]

This "special character" is another reference to the appearance of a most unusual semidivine figure. The fact is, Aristotle is unable and unwilling to offer a ringing defense of absolute monarchy. He closes Book III on an equivocal note, but one that is also respectful of law and distrustful of monolithic power.[38]

The Varieties of Constitutions

Book IV is ostensibly a taxonomic inquiry into the varieties of constitutions. At the outset Aristotle outlines in a systematic way the topics to be covered, including what types of constitution there are, which ones are preferable for which civic bodies, how they may be established, and how they may be preserved. Subsequently, he departs rather freely from this projection. Moreover, the classificatory schemes do not always coincide with each other and there is some repetition. This suggests to some scholars that two different drafts are included in Book IV. The main distinction among constitutions is not the familiar sixfold one but the distinction be-

37 *Politics,* 1287^b 41–1288^a 5, p. 150.

38 Book III is incomplete. It breaks off in mid-sentence and the same words reappear in a completed sentence at the start of Book VII. This and other evidence has led some scholars to rearrange the order of books so that Book VII follows Book III, but we feel there are insufficient grounds for departing from the traditional arrangement.

tween democracy and oligarchy, each of which has its own subspecies.

Democracy

Democracy, which is nominally the rule of the many in a strictly numerical sense, is in fact the rule of a class: the nonwealthy freeborn, provided they are a majority. There are several parts of this class—farmers, mechanics, merchants, serfs, maritime workers, soldiers, and others—working together like the parts of an animal. Aristotle sketches five varieties of democratic constitutions with varying degrees and forms of participation in rule. In the fifth, however, the people rather than the law are the final sovereign. In this situation demagogues may rise to power because, as it may be truly said, "A democracy of this type is not a true constitution. Where the laws are not sovereign, there is no constitution." The people do not rise up en masse and crush out the law. It is the demagogues (playing the role played by the flatterer in tyrannies) who criticize whatever the magistrates do and cry, "Let the people decide," an invitation the people readily accept. Residents of American states with provisions for direct democracy written into their state constitutions are no strangers to this phenomenon.

Oligarchy

The varieties of oligarchy include: (1) those states in which property qualifications are high enough to exclude the poor; (2) those in which property qualifications are high enough to include only the very wealthy; (3) those in which office is hereditary under the rule of law; (4) those in which personal rule has succeeded the rule of law. This last variety is the counterpart of the lawless democracy. This type of oligarchy is called a dynasty (*dynasteia*), which for the Greeks had overtones of illegality the English word "dynasty" does not have.

There are many variations and complications within these four types of oligarchy. On one hand, the laws may allow for equality of participation in politics, but the economic means to do so—especially the availability of leisure—may be lacking. On the other hand, a system of state payments to the poor to attend the assembly and the courts may give this group inordinate power because the rich may be too busy taking care of their private concerns to attend.

Mixed constitutions

Polity and all but the purest form of aristocracy—that in which rule is not simply by the best (*aristoi*), but by the best according to a standard of absolute moral good—may be viewed in the context of the chapter as forms of mixed constitutions. Some men have downgraded polity by refusing to believe that the rule of law could exist where the poorer classes legislate or that it could fail to exist where the better classes legislate. With that passion for making distinctions that has always marked the philosopher, Aristotle points out that these men confuse two senses of the rule of law: having people who obey the law whatever the law happens to be and having good laws to obey. Good laws may in turn be judged as best either relatively or absolutely. Among other confusions, Aristotle notes, most *poleis* he would call polities are by their spokesmen "embellished . . . by a higher title" of aristocracy, just as their rich men are embellished with the higher title of gentlemen. The public relations syndrome was not unknown even in ancient Greece. Of the elements of free birth, wealth, and merit, Aristotle suggests that among mixed constitutions the name polity be used for a mixture of two elements and the name aristocracy for a mixture of all three. In any case, "aristocracies and 'polities' are not far removed from one another."

Democratic and oligarchic elements can be blended in many ways—some elections may be held by lot (democratic) and some by vote (oligarchic); the state might pay the poor for sitting in court (democratic) and fine the rich if they do not sit in court (oligarchic)—"it is a good criterion of a proper mixture of democracy and oligarchy that a mixed constitution should be able to be described indifferently as either."

Middle-class government

After a brief and wholly descriptive chapter on tyranny, Aristotle takes up—in Chapter 11, perhaps the most important chapter of Book IV—the best practicable constitution: that in which the middle classes dominate. Specifically referring to the doctrine of the mean as found in the *Ethics,* Aristotle is more concerned here with ethical and sociological categories than he was in the prior discussion of mixed government, which was somewhat more concerned with mechanisms.

The very rich and the very poor are less able to be guided by reason than members of the middle class: the latter suffer least from ambition. They are less afflicted by envy, like slaves, or by contempt, like wealthy masters. They regard their fellow citizens as equals and peers and hence are capable of friendship (*philia*). This is important, for "Community depends on friendship."

Hence a large middle class is a prerequisite for the best, or most practicable, political society. If possible, the middle class should be larger than the other two classes combined; if not, it should be larger than either singly. There is the least likelihood of faction with a large middle class, and, as proof of its value, Aristotle says that the best legislators—Solon, Lycurgus, and Charondas—all came from the middle class. But this is not to say that middle, or mixed, constitutions are common. Indeed, they are exceedingly rare. The masses and the rich, once they have power, are too suspicious of each other to permit the growth of neutral power in the center:[39] "One man, and one only, of all who have hitherto been in a position of ascendancy, has allowed himself to be persuaded to agree to the setting up of such a type."[40]

The rarity of this practical ideal does not, however, fill Aristotle with despair. One can arrange constitutions on a vast spectrum from those of lesser merit to those of greater merit on grounds of intrinsic worth. Even at the theoretical level the less than perfect can be appreciated. One can appreciate, too, the variations in particular circumstances that supersede formal requirements: "One sort of constitution may be intrinsically preferable, but there is nothing to prevent another sort from being more suitable in the given case; and indeed this may often happen."

Aristotle has thus distinguished among (1) the ideal state in the Platonic sense; (2) the practical ideal, the middle-class state he talks about in this chapter; and (3) certain actual states that may have their own special virtues. These careful distinctions and Aristotle's calm acceptance of different levels of reality give him the estimable stamp of both the scientist and the philosopher, which in his terms, of course, are identical.

Quality and quantity revisited

In response to the query, "What and what sort of constitution is suited to what and what sort of persons?"—a question that would seem to be wholly qualitative in character—Aristotle returns to his favorite problem of the balance of quantity and quality. He repeats in somewhat greater detail the various devices for encouraging and discouraging participation in government by different classes and, in an interesting digression, notes that an increase in the number able to participate in politics paralleled a shift in

[39] We speak of power, but the Greek word *dynamis* does not have the connotations of personal influence that our English "power" has; it is rarely if ever used by Aristotle in the *Politics* in this sense. Barker's translation sometimes uses "power" when *dynamis* does not appear in the text. For example, Jowett's "the best political community is formed by citizens of the middle class" seems superior to Barker's "the best form of political society is one where power is vested in the middle class" (1295^b 35–36). Jowett, on the other hand, regularly translates *politeia* as "government" rather than as "constitution."

[40] Such a flat assertion has naturally piqued the curiosity of classical scholars. Who was this one man? Scholars have suggested sixteen different names. Paul Andrews reviews them all and claims that Aristotle's friend Hermias of Atarneus (see above, p. 38) must be the man ("Aristotle, *Politics,* IV, 11, 1296^a 38–40," *Classical Review,* n.s., 2 [1952], pp. 141–44).

military strategy from reliance on cavalry to reliance on infantry.

Separation of powers

The final parts of Book IV deal with what has come to be called in modern times the separation of powers—in this case, the separation among deliberative, executive, and judicial functions. Although these sound like our legislative, executive, and judicial branches, the similarity is deceptive. The deliberative element would have much broader powers than today's legislatures; it would decide issues of war and peace; make and break treaties; enact laws; levy penalties of death, exile, and confiscation; appoint magistrates and call them to account. There would be various ways for the whole body of citizens to participate or be checked in participation in these functions. The citizens might, for example, meet in relays rather than as a single body, or they might have authority over only some of these areas, or they might merely respond to the reports of magistrates. Yet all these methods can be called democratic. They become oligarchic when property qualifications, or the principle of co-optation, or some other principle of exclusion is applied.

If a deliberative body is to be democratic and have quality, too, "a democracy will do well to apply [a] plan of compulsory attendance to the deliberative assembly." The deliberation is better when "all deliberate together"; Aristotle is not wholly unfamiliar with the idea of representation and suggests that it is in the interests of a democracy to have all parts of the *polis* represented. Oligarchies, however, benefit by screening devices and preliminary councils and by allowing the people a right of veto but not of initiation.

The executive element, by contrast to the deliberative element, would be more restricted than our concept of this term suggests. It would consist basically of the magistrates, who would enforce the law, make inspections, measure the corn for distribution, give instructions, and maintain order.

The law courts (*dikasteria*) would form the third branch of government. There were many kinds of courts in Aristotle's lexicon and in his experience: courts for the review of magistrates, for the interpretation of the constitution, for the drafting of contracts, for the trial of homicide cases, for the trial of aliens, and so forth. The composition of these courts and the mixture of popular and oligarchic elements in them allow for a wide variety of modes of selection, which Aristotle enumerates with rather little discussion.

Book IV, a mine of procedural lore, ends abruptly, with no summary statement.

Revolution

Book V is on revolution viewed within the general problem of what makes states decline. The inspiration of Book VIII of Plato's *Republic* is evident. *Stasis,* the word usually translated as "revolution," or sometimes as "sedition," has a narrower connotation than that which we usually give to revolution. The Greek term refers to any situation in which two groups use violence or illegal behavior to overcome each other and might better be translated "political struggle."[41] More exhaustively, Newman suggests it is the act of forming a combination "for the attainment of some political end by legal and illegal means."[42]

Inequality is the basic reason for *stasis,* or to be more exact, for feelings about unequal treatment. Both democracy and oligarchy embody "a sort of justice," but each falls short of absolute justice, so that, when either side is denied what its special conception of justice seems to require, it is tempted to turn

[41] The Greek *stasis* should not be confused with the English "stasis," which is derived from the Greek *histanai,* "to stand." See Marcus Wheeler, "Aristotle's Analysis of the Nature of Political Struggle," *American Journal of Philology,* Vol. 72 (1951), pp. 145–61.

[42] Newman's notes on the *Politics.* Quoted in Barker, p. 204*n.* A complete change, a revision of basic institutions, which we often think of when we hear the word "revolution," might better be suggested by the Greek *metabole.* Aristotle distinguishes the two at 1301^b 5–13 and 1304^b 6–8.

to sedition. Aristotle notes that the truly superior persons, those most justified in rebelling when their rights are denied, are usually the last to make the attempt. Most are not much interested in that equality which is proportionate to desert: "Some take the line that if men are equal in one respect, they may consider themselves equal in all; others take the line that if they are superior in one respect, they may claim superiority all round." How much contemporary political *stasis,* national and international, is explainable in just such terms? If profit and honor are the principal aims of *stasis,* they may also be keys to some of the emotional states that lead citizens to rebel. Insolence and profit-making by those in authority may lead to popular resentment, as may the leader so far superior to the general body of citizens that he is beyond their understanding. Fear of and contempt for rulers are other stimuli to rebellion. (But Aristotle does not include greed in his catalog of stimuli.) There are social causes of revolution, too: the disproportionate increase in one part of the state—the poor, or the nobles, for example—destroys the harmony and symmetry to which people have become accustomed. Finally, there are more incidental occasions of *stasis* —election intrigues, bad appointments, the atrophy of important laws, and the introduction of dissimilar racial stocks without time for assimilation—which are largely attributable to the negligence of rulers. What is striking is that, though Aristotle sees the centrality of the division between rich and poor, he never explains the causes of *stasis* in terms of simple economics but rather in terms of what we might call moral issues—honor that is affronted, resentment that is aroused, conceptions of justice that clash. Such an emphasis contrasts sharply with the Marxian interpretation of revolution, but Aristotle's concept may still have explanatory value when applied to Marxian revolutions.

Aristotle warns us that sweeping changes can result from petty disputes if the conditions are ripe, because of either general discontent or one magistrate's power becoming too great.

Changes from democracy to oligarchy are usually the work of demagogues—their "wanton license," their "false accusations," and their flattery of the people, who are made to believe that popular sovereignty is above even the law. In the old days demagogues became tyrants, says Aristotle, but nowadays they lack the military skill and settle for becoming oligarchs.

Practical political preservation

A host of historical illustrations, many of them obscure, illustrate how oligarchies may be disrupted by internal cliques, corruption, and external resistance. The same fate may be in store for aristocracies and polities. The purpose of learning what destroys constitutions, says Aristotle, is to know how to preserve them. (Political science is a practical science.) So Aristotle gives us a lengthy list of rules for preserving constitutions. They range from the very general (equals should be treated equally) to the very specific (audit the financial books annually: ". . . to prevent the embezzling of public funds, the outgoing officers should hand over such funds in the presence of the whole civic body; and inventories of them should be deposited with each clan, ward, and tribe"). The gist of the whole section is that care should be taken in small matters as well as in large ones, for the pressures for political change can build up rapidly and the rudiments of justice ought to be maintained: democracies should not be too harsh on the rich, and oligarchies should pay attention to the poor. This is not moral exhortation so much as practical advice.

Aristotle is always trying to come to terms with reality. In outlining the qualifications for good rulers—loyalty, ability, and goodness—he notes that military skill is rare whereas financial skill is rather common. In getting a man for military office, therefore, more attention has to be paid to his expertise than to his goodness, though it is of course reassuring to know that the latter is also of high quality. A treasurer or property custodian, however, should be picked more for his character than for his skill or the coffers will be looted.

"The greatest, however, of all the means we have mentioned for ensuring this stability of constitutions—but one which is nowadays generally neglected—is the education of citizens in the spirit of their constitution." In a democracy citizens will need to display the democratic spirit, and in an oligarchy, the oligarchic spirit. This does not mean that they should do things that delight the extreme partisans of either form of government; it means that they must carry out those actions by which one form or the other will survive. This statement, as well as many others about democracy, may well confuse the modern reader if he is thinking of democracy as, in Lincoln's words, government of, by, and for the people. We tend to subsume good ends as well as good means in our concept of democracy. Democracy was more simply rule *by* the lower classes for Aristotle. Rule by the better classes was presumably better, thought Aristotle, but in either case the worth of the rule and the durability of the rule had to be judged not simply by which class ruled but by how and toward what purpose it ruled. The self-enrichment of a particular class was an unworthy and ultimately untenable aim, whatever the class. Conversely, loyal, disciplined magistrates and rulers and educated citizens, capable of supporting moderate positions toward other classes, were necessary to the preservation of the *polis,* whichever class ruled.

Extreme democracy

Aristotle concludes Chapter 9 by noting that a false conception of liberty is apt to develop in extreme democracies, where the will of the majority is put above the law. The extreme democrat begins by conceiving of liberty as a function of equality and of the sovereignty of the majority—a conception Aristotle may not personally endorse but credits with validity in its own terms. The democrat then moves toward the indefensible conception of liberty as doing whatever he likes and living, as Euripides says, "for any end he chances to desire." Such a person would argue that to live under the discipline of a constitution is slavery; but, says Aristotle, it ought to be regarded rather as salvation (*soteria*).[43]

Tyranny

Although Aristotle had relatively little to say about monarchy in Book IV, in Book V he says rather more than is necessary about how kingships and tyrannies, two forms of monarchy, are brought down by revolt and rebellion. Aristotle offers a Machiavellian touch in Chapter 11 as he summarizes how tyrannies may be preserved: by "lopping off" outstanding men; by forbidding the gathering of cultural societies; by using secret police; by forcibly drafting men for public works, such as the Egyptian pyramids; by systematically impoverishing subjects through taxation; by carefully sowing discord and stimulating wars. The list is not at all unfamiliar to observers of twentieth-century dictatorships. The utilization of mass media and mass parties are no doubt unique to modern totalitarianism, but Aristotle has captured the central tactical mission of every such system: "in a word, the adoption of every means for making every subject as much of a stranger as is possible to every other." Later he says, "Tyranny is never overthrown until men can begin to trust one another." It is clear that Aristotle has no admiration for tyrants, however dispassionate he is when summarizing their devices:

> Tyranny is thus a system which chooses bad men for its friends. Tyrants love to be flattered, and nobody with the soul of a freeman can ever stoop to *that;* a good man may be a friend, but at any rate he will not be a flatterer. . . . It is a habit of tyrants never to like a man with a spirit of dignity and independence.[44]

To preserve a tyranny it may be necessary to put on the trappings of kingship, the

[43] Aristotle does not state a valid definition of liberty to counter this invalid one, but we may infer that it would prefigure Montesquieu's concept of doing what the laws permit.

[44] *Politics,* 1314^a 2–6, pp. 245–46.

visage of moderation, sobriety, and military discipline: a grave but not harsh manner, a disdain for opulence, and an adherence to the forms of religious piety. The hint of hypocrisy that flows through these remarks once again reminds us of Machiavelli, but this time with a difference: Machiavelli's prince was, for the sake of power, a skilled showman; Aristotle's tyrant masquerading as proper king receives no moral justification, but his literary creator does offer a hope for partial redemption: if the tyrant tries hard enough to appear noble, his subjects will be better, his rule will be longer, "and he will himself attain a habit of character, if not wholly disposed to goodness, at any rate half-good—half-good and yet half-bad, but at any rate not *wholly* bad."

Democracy and Liberty

In Book VI Aristotle undertakes a new program of studies that sounds a bit like the old program of studies in Books IV and V. Having analyzed the operations and decline of democratic and oligarchic constitutions, he now sets out to state in detail their principles of construction. But he falls into considerable repetition and never completes the task. Book VI, like its predecessor, breaks off in mid-sentence.

The underlying idea of the democratic constitution is liberty, which is really a certain conception of justice—namely, the enjoyment of an arithmetical equality between citizens. A by-product of this concept, as we have seen, is the idea of each free man living as he likes, though this is not necessarily consistent with the idea of the sovereignty of the majority. Somewhat prematurely, Aristotle suggests one of his formulas for reconciling numbers with property but notes wistfully

> To find theoretically where truth resides in these matters of equality and justice, is a very difficult task. Difficult as it may be, it is an easier task than that of persuading men to act justly, if they have power enough to secure their own selfish interests. The weaker are always anxious for equality and justice. The strong pay no heed to either.[45]

Aristotle outlines, in order of his own preference, the construction of democracies based on societies of farmers, shepherds, artisans and large societies where no single class can dominate. Then—paying attention to military functions and the duties of magistrates—he examines the construction of various styles of oligarchies.

Man, *Polis,* and Empire

Book VII is different from the other books of the *Politics* in that it seems to be taken from the exoteric discourses (*logoi*) Aristotle delivered to the general public rather than from the esoteric discourses he gave to the students of the Lyceum. The opening passages on what makes the happy man and hence the happy *polis* are familiar to those who know the *Ethics.* Chapter 1 is, says Aristotle, a "philosophic preface." There are two central questions in Chapter 2. The first is whether the felicity (*eudaemonia*) of the *polis* is the same as that of the individual (*anthropos*). This question is handled summarily: "*All* are agreed that they are the same." Men who value wealth want the *polis* to be wealthy; men who are tyrants want the *polis* to be tyrannical; men who judge individuals by their goodness also judge *poleis* by their goodness. At first glance this statement may seem to contradict the assertion of Book III that the good man and the good citizen are not necessarily the same, but it does not. Even while granting the separation of the individual and the *polis,* one can invoke the same standard of goodness to judge both: the standard of goodness for the *polis* is in turn the criterion for the good citizen.

Mastery and empire

The second question of the chapter is whether a self-contained *polis* is better than an expansive *polis,* such as Sparta. This question

[45] *Ibid.,* 1318^{b} 1–6, p. 262.

implies a choice between two ways of life, the political and the philosophic. This is "a matter of no small moment" for individuals or *poleis,* though the *polis* is Aristotle's concern here. How a *polis* can be anything but political is apt to bewilder us at this point; what Aristotle is really contrasting is internal versus external politics. One *polis* aims at the highest cultural goods, while of course being political as a means; another *polis* is animated by a drive to overcome and control neighboring *poleis:* "In Sparta, for instance, and in Crete the system of education and most of the laws are framed with a general view to war."

Aristotle seems to express genuine wonderment at the fact that only in politics is coercion accepted as a professional tool. Doctors are not expected to use coercion on their patients, "But when it comes to politics most people appear to believe that mastery is the true statesmanship; and men are not ashamed of behaving to others in ways which they would refuse to acknowledge as just, or even expedient, among themselves."[46] Nature intends animals to be subject to control and so we go out to hunt them for a banquet, says Aristotle. But nature intends men to be free, and we do not hunt them as we hunt animals—yet an aggressive *polis* that pursues a policy of offensive war seems to do exactly this.

The significance of this passage can hardly be overestimated. Here in a few brief lines are bound up all the great Aristotelian themes: a nature that intends, man who is free by virtue of his reason, a statesmanship that is directed toward guiding men to the good rather than mastering them, and a *polis* that is free by virtue of its self-sufficiency and communally friendly by virtue of its small size and that disdains to impose on the outsider what it would not impose on itself.

Though they probably lack Aristotle's understanding of nature, present-day critics of foreign policy who argue for the inviolability of self-determination express something of his implied condemnation of treating men as animals, as things to be controlled. Aristotle's point is more subtle than a mere condemnation of aggressive warfare. Men should be led but not controlled. One can argue that in coping with seven million or 200 million persons it is impossible not to treat them as integers. It is foolish to ask leaders not to manipulate. Exactly. Why else did Aristotle treat the *polis* as necessarily small in size? It would be going too far to make a modern liberal democrat out of Aristotle by overemphasizing his references to free men. But the point needs to be made that Aristotle was hardly a blind reactionary who clung to the ideal of the self-sufficient *polis* only because he lacked the imagination to see how politics might develop. Indeed, he says, "Most men are believers in the cause of empire, on the ground that empire leads to a large accession of material prosperity."[47]

Thought and Action

Though he indicated earlier (Book VII, Chapter 2) that his concern was the *polis* and not the individual, Aristotle now (Chapter 3) returns to the problem of the individual: is the solitary way of thought and contemplation better than political activity for the individual? Characteristically, Aristotle seeks a mean between those who opt for contemplation (*theoria*) and those who opt for action (*praxis,* or *the doing of deeds*). The former are right in holding that having the free life (*eleutherou bios*) is better than being master of any number of slaves. But they are wrong to think that all rule must be like that of a master (*despotikos*) over slaves. Moreover, it is wrong to praise inaction over action. Felicity (*eudaemonia*) is itself a state

[46] Cp. Book I, 1252^a 8, where Aristotle repudiates the idea that being a statesman is like being a master over slaves.

[47] On this point, see Charles N. R. McCoy, "The Turning Point in Political Philosophy," *American Political Science Review,* Vol. 44 (1950), pp. 678–88. See also his *The Structure of Political Thought* (New York: McGraw-Hill, 1963), Chapter 2. McCoy argues that modern man—intimidated by empires, big bombs, and production—has become Aristotle's "natural slave."

of activity. But it does not follow from this that the ruler with the most power is thereby capable of doing the most noble deeds. Whatever success is gained by violating the law is more than canceled out by what is lost in virtue. Sharing is just for those equal in virtue. It is contrary to nature, and hence not good, for the inferior in virtue to rule the superior in virtue. A purely passive goodness is not enough; a "capacity for being active in doing good" is also important:

> If we are right in our view, and felicity is held to consist in "well-*doing*," it follows that the life of action is best, alike for every state as a whole and for each individual in his own conduct. But the life of action need not be as is sometimes thought, a life which involves relations with others. Nor should our thoughts be held to be active only when they are directed to objects which have to be achieved by action. Thoughts with no object beyond themselves, and speculations and trains of reflections followed purely for their own sake, are far more deserving of the name of active. "Well-doing" is the end we seek: action of some sort or other is therefore our end and aim; but even in the sphere of outward acts, action can also be predicated—and that in the fullest measure and the true sense of the word—of those who, by their thoughts, are the prime authors of such acts.[48]

So, for the individual and the *polis,* isolation does not mean inactivity so long as there is thought: "If it were not so, there would be something wrong with God himself and the whole of the universe, who have no activities [*praxeis*] other than those of their own internal life."

By this resolution, Aristotle makes the whole struggle between defenders of the life of action and defenders of the life of thought seem spurious. Thought is action, and the most worthy action depends on thought. When Aristotle discusses education later in Book VII (1333^a), he repeats the familiar distinctions between speculative reason, practical reason, and the ability to obey rational principle. All are activities; those who can attain all will naturally seek the highest, which is speculative reason: ". . . in the sphere of action we may further distinguish acts which are merely necessary, or merely and simply useful, from acts which are good in themselves." War is a means to peace. And practical, external actions are means to *leisure,* or the space in which one may perform acts good in themselves. "The legislation of the true statesman must be framed with a view to all of these factors."

[48] *Politics,* 1325^b 14–22, p. 289.

The Best *Polis*

These philosophic considerations are but prefatory to Aristotle's grand theme of the ideal *polis* begun in Book II, illumined by the discussion of the best practicable *polis* in Book IV, and now resumed in Book VII. We must treat his remarks in summary fashion: the size of the population should be large enough to make self-sufficiency possible but small enough to enable citizens and leaders to know each other's characters and to let one voice be heard by all. It is difficult, if not impossible, for a very populous state to maintain the habit of obedience to law. Likewise, the territory of a *polis* should be moderately sized, easily surveyed, accessible from both land and sea, and easily defended against enemies. (The distance of the Peiraeus, the port city, from Athens was ideal—close enough to be economic but far enough to keep alien influences at a distance.)

Aristotle's assessment of the quality of the ideal population betrays a certain parochialism: the people of Europe have spirit (*thymos*) but little intelligence (*noesis*); the people of Asia have intelligence but little spirit; the Greeks, located halfway between the two, have both intelligence and spirit. The quality of spirit is important, for "this faculty of our souls not only issues in love and friendship: it is also the source for us all of any power of commanding and any feeling for freedom. Spirit is a commanding and an unconquerable thing." But the power of commanding (*archon*) does not justify harshness toward the stranger—as Aristotle implies that Plato argues—for magnanimity is the mark of durable rule.

In outlining the ideal social structure,

Aristotle states a now familiar position on the value of the median—in age and property as well as in other things—and on the need for a leisure class: he believes that property should be owned privately but used in common; he supports common dining at public expense and suggests that worship be paid for by the state. Each property owner should own one plot near the center of the city and another plot near the frontier of the *polis* to ensure his support in case of border wars. Those who do the farming should be slaves. Water pipes, street layouts, and city walls receive Aristotle's attention. There should be a free square of the city where citizens gather and old men play games and from which all merchandise must be excluded. The market square should be some distance away.

Education in the *Polis*

Education and leisure

Referring to the *Ethics* in Chapter 13 of Book VII, Aristotle distinguishes between *arête,* the good that is a product of necessity —of conditions that are given—and *kalos,* the good that is intrinsically good and hence unconditional. As an example, Aristotle notes that a just penalty for a crime is an act of goodness, but one forced on the judge and the *polis* by necessity. The *polis* must be equipped to act and act well in all such areas "where fortune is sovereign." But intrinsic goodness comes from man without the goad of necessity. Here we are in "the realm of human knowledge and purpose," where the real art of the legislator can come into play.

A *polis* can be good without every citizen being good, but ideally each citizen should be good in the unconditional sense. This goal will be approached only through education and the right use of the three means to human goodness: natural endowment, habit, and rational principle. The last element tunes the other two into a harmonious whole, and the statesman in the ideal state is an expert in such tuning.

Even though Aristotle is now presumably describing the ideal state and not the best possible state he described in Book IV, he cannot bring himself to construct a Platonic philosopher-king. He talks of the possibility of a surpassing class of heroic men almost like gods and notes that the writer Scylax says such a class exists in India. "But that is a difficult assumption to make, and we have nothing in actual life" like such a gulf between subjects and rulers. Thus influenced by sober reality, Aristotle concludes that in his ideal system "all should share alike in a system of government under which they rule and are ruled by turns." Aristotle does not deny that there must be a reasonable gulf between ruler and ruled. But if, for example, the ruled are young people who know that one day they will be called upon to rule, they will not resent being governed. Indeed, some kinds of work usually considered menial and often done by slaves "may none the less be the sort of work which young freemen can honorably do. It is not the inherent nature of actions but the end or object for which they are done, which make one action differ from another in the way of honor or dishonor."

We have already referred to that part of Book VII in which peace is seen as the aim of war and leisure as the aim of action. Properly educated citizens will see these goals in the right perspective. They will understand that truly good acts of both the individual and the *polis* are unaffected by necessity and utility. They are acts appropriate to leisure, not reactions to necessity. Good citizens of the good *polis*—here Aristotle refers to the discussion of citizenship in Book III—will not be victims of the present "vulgar decline into the cultivation of qualities supposed to be useful and of a more profitable character." Many warlike states are militant because all they know how to do is fight; they are insecure when peace comes. Their leaders have given their citizens no training in the proper use of leisure. Such a generalization is not irrelevant to the modern world.

One of the unique attributes of the brief presidency of John F. Kennedy was his embodiment of an authentic political concern for cultural excellence. The popular response to good art, music, and architecture —not necessarily the governmental dictation of standards in those areas—was for him a matter of public as well as private attention. He consciously adopted the classical stance: culture must be cultivated.

This, of course, is not to say that the military virtues are not virtues: courage and endurance are required before leisure can be obtained; temperance and justice are required both before and after acquiring leisure. Nor are the joys of peace and leisure automatic and uncorruptible: the enjoyment of leisure can give way to indulgent luxury, to which, says Aristotle, "a special measure of shame" should be attached because the promise of the leisured is so much greater than for workers.

It is important to note that Aristotle, unlike most moderns, does not link leisure (*schole*) to recreation (*anapausis*) and amusement (*paidia,* or *what children* [*pais*] *do*). The latter are more closely tied to the very opposite of leisure (*ascholia*), which is business, or occupation, done not for its own sake but as a means to something else. Recreation and amusement provide rest and diversion from occupation or sometimes preparation for it. Leisure is not a release from activity but a more intensive form of activity, performed for its own sake and consisting primarily of the cultivation of the mind (*diagoge*). That the original product of *schole,* namely schools, should have become so devoted to *ascholia,* to occupational preparation, is one of the great ironies of modern times. The age of automation, however, is allowing us to look anew at both the old and the new meanings of leisure.

Education and music

The last part of Book VII is devoted to the proper age of marriage; the regulation of marriage, birth control, and adultery; and the censorship of plays for children. Book VIII sets out to cover the specifics of education (*paideia,* not to be confused with amusement, *paidia*), but, like a number of other Aristotelian writings, it is incomplete.

Aristotle notes the lack of agreement about whether the moral training of children or the development of their understanding is to take precedence, and, indeed, about which subjects are most appropriate for which job. At this point one can only infer that Aristotle believes the subjects are inseparable. He is explicit in stating that education should be a state affair and not a private one. Repeating what he said earlier about education for leisure, he makes it evident that there should be two classes of training: one for mechanical (*banausos*) and therefore useful subjects, the other for the cultivation of the mind and spirit. The four subjects Aristotle outlines are reading, writing, physical training, and music. The first two, he grants, are useful in a sense but, above this, have intrinsic worth and are certainly necessary as means to the end of right activity in leisure. Physical training, too, is worthwhile for all classes, but Aristotle criticizes Sparta for overemphasizing the kind of athletic rigor and professionalization that is valuable to only the competitive few and actually debilitating to those who should be devoting their time to mental activity.

Music is ideal for education of the higher sort, although it can also provide simpler pleasures of relaxation, because it can reproduce in the individual "images of states of character"—anger, sorrow, and calm—which can lead to a significant "change of soul," both through the development of special sensitivity and the purging (*katharsis*) of unwanted passion. Aristotle is deep in a discussion making several comparisons—the worth of musical performance versus that of listening; performing by flute versus performing by harp or song; and the relative purposes to be served by Dorian, Phrygian, and Mixolydian modes (names presentday musicians will recognize)—when the Book abruptly ends. We are pleased to note, however, that the Dorian mode is best for the young because it is in the position of the mean.

CONCLUSION

A summary of Aristotle's political thought and a sweeping evaluation of its significance for the history of political thinking seems called for at this juncture, but the call will go unheeded for two reasons: both the *Ethics* and the *Politics* are flat and expository summaries themselves, and summaries of summaries are especially tedious. If the reader has not found the meaning of Aristotle in the interstices of his steady systematic examination of problem after problem, he will not find it in a quick, overripe formula distinguishing realism from idealism. The significance of Aristotle for subsequent ages, however, will find ample testimony in the pages that follow. We do not leave "The Philosopher" behind with this chapter.

A word might be said, however, about the irony of this eminent man of reason ending the *Politics* with a defense of the moral and purgative uses of music. The irony is more apparent than real. Neither Plato nor Aristotle was the captive of disembodied reason to the extent that frequent caricatures make them out to be. They were neither without passion nor against it, but rather for a life in which reason could harness, use, and channel passion. In emphasizing the simultaneously personal and political benefits of music, Aristotle was following the know-thyself tradition begun by Socrates; in the fine balance he struck between the inner person and the outer institution he symbolized the transition from a primitive shame culture to a less primitive guilt culture.[49]

If one point must cap the many made in this chapter, let it be this: music was not for Aristotle, as it is for us, private enterprise; and politics was not for him, as it is for us, a public compartment of private experience. Like so many other things, music was for him part of the inclusive scheme of public training for personal virtue that finds its justification, not in private, fragmentary satisfactions, but in the *telos* of a good *polis* full of good citizens who are also good men—men who know how to rule and how to be ruled in turn.

[49] See E. R. Dodds, *The Greeks and the Irrational* (Berkeley: Univ. of California Press, 1964), Ch. 2. Incidentally, Dodds's description of the twisting, gyrating, jerking, orgiastic dances in ancient Greece and elsewhere as reflecting rebellious attitudes and serving a cathartic function has a striking similarity to the dances of American adolescents of the 1960s.

4

THE STOICS AND ROME

Stoicism as a school of thought was durable, cosmopolitan, and diverse. It lasted from Zeno, who was born in the fourth century B.C., to at least Marcus Aurelius, who died in the second century A.D. It numbered among its adherents men from several cultures: Zeno was a Phoenician, born in Cyprus, who studied in Athens; Panaetius was born in Rhodes but migrated to Rome; Poseidonius was a Syrian Greek who lived in Rhodes; Seneca was a Spaniard in the Roman court of Nero; Epictetus was a Greek slave; and Marcus Aurelius was a Roman emperor. The tenets of Stoicism were not monotonously similar: Zeno was a materialist who studied with Crates the Cynic; Panaetius abandoned the materialism of Zeno and introduced an element of Platonism; Poseidonius was an eclectic excelling in mathematics, astronomy, and history.

THE EARLY STOICS

Though we shall be concerned in this chapter chiefly with later Stoic thought and its influence on Roman political thinking, we need to summarize briefly the soil out of which it grew.

Zeno

As a young man Zeno (c. 336–264 B.C.)[1] traveled from his native Cyprus to Athens, arriving there shortly after Aristotle's death. After studying under several Athenian philosophers, he founded his own school in about 301 B.C. The name Stoic came from the painted porch (*stoa poikile*), which, like the stoas frequented by other philosophers of other persuasions, became Zeno's academic base. Zeno, like many others who sought Socratic wisdom, had come to the home of Socrates. And because the Cynics (*cynos,* dog), too, invoked the name of Socrates, Zeno for a time associated with them. The Cynics—not to be confused with modern cynics—neglected the subtler and more fundamental aspects of Socrates' thought in order to glory in his spirit of rugged independence, his capacity to rise above painful external circumstance, and his criticism—

[1] This Zeno should not be confused with the fifth-century Zeno, student of Parmenides and author of the worrisome paradoxes with which philosophy professors begin their courses in the history of philosophy.

but not, as the Cynics imagined, denial—of the conventional. In their defiance of the conventional, they became virtual anarchists and Zeno, his intellectual ambitions unsatisfied, left their company.

Zeno was a radical materialist. From Heraclitus he took the idea that the basic stuff of the universe was fire—though not really fire as we know it but rather a diffuse physical matter of some kind. The soul was for him a special kind of fire in the body. God was simply the basic fire—everywhere and in everything. The world, Zeno thought, is completely ordered and completely deterministic. At birth man's mind is a blank tablet on which objective material events write their record. Universal ideas have no objective existence whatsoever. But in trying to fashion some kind of ethics compatible with this view, Zeno foundered.

Cleanthes, Zeno's successor in Athens, sought a way out of Zeno's flat determinism. Man, he said, is a microcosm of the universe; man is rational; therefore the universe is rational—a valid syllogism, but not necessarily therefore true. But since man is not perfectly rational, the universe cannot be completely determined. Man's purpose is to conform to the universe, that is, to become fully rational. The wise man is the perfectly reasonable man. One of the difficulties of this position became clear when the Stoic Chrysippus noted that there had been only three wise men in the history of the world: Hercules, Ulysses, and Socrates. Chrysippus made no provision for degrees of rationality and wisdom: one either joined this select company or struggled in blindness. It is not hard to understand why Stoicism in the third century B.C. was not the most popular of philosophies. A century later Carneades was among the Skeptics who poked holes in the logic of Cleanthes and Chrysippus and made fun of their ethical standard, a standard which, almost by definition, was unattainable.

Panaetius

The man who saved Stoicism from death by ridicule was Panaetius (c. 180–109 B.C.), who carried Stoicism to Rome, where it found a friendly home. Basically, he introduced degrees of rationality. Each man, he said, carries with him a touch of fire, that is, god, which can be developed toward the norm of complete rationality. In his book *On Duties,* Panaetius set forth the ideas that gave substance to the later Stoicism. Its most significant tenets came directly from this collection of ideas, which can be summarized under four headings:

(1) The universe is rational and rationality is man's nature.

(2) The reason common to all men is the ground of their universal brotherhood.

(3) Virtue is a discipline of the will that can make a man impervious to pain and suffering and give him self-sufficiency (*autarkeia*).

(4) Self-denying duty is the highest virtue.

In the remainder of this chapter we shall illustrate these four tenets by drawing from the works of three later Stoic philosophers: Seneca, Epictetus, and Marcus Aurelius. Then we shall examine in somewhat greater detail the political thought of the lawyer and orator Cicero. Finally we shall see how Stoic ideas affected the development of Roman law.

RATIONAL NATURE

The Stoic belief that nature is rational must be distinguished from the belief that everything is rational. The concept of nature, unknown to early civilizations, arose as a philosophic concept with Greek speculation. It refers, according to one of its present-day defenders, not to "the totality of phenomena" but to the essence of things discoverable without reference to the prescriptions of ancestral authority or to the authority of one's social group.[2] It thus refers to what a man may learn outside of local custom, social and religious mores, and historically conditioned

[2] Leo Strauss, *Natural Right and History* (Chicago: Univ. of Chicago Press, 1951), pp. 81–89.

beliefs—for presumably nature is unaffected by any of these. How much and what is left to study under the heading of nature, given these qualifications, is one of the perennial issues of political theory.

The Greek philosophers generally distinguished between nature (*physis*) and convention (*nomos*) and the Stoics were the inheritors of the fruitful problems pointed to by the distinction. Parmenides, the Eleatic philosopher of the sixth and early fifth centuries B.C., stimulated generations of philosophic speculation when he argued that because the world is one, as Thales had contended, change is an illusion. If, however, nature were identified with this monistic world, nature would become an all-inclusive category and no category outside of itself, such as reason, could be brought to bear to explain it. If everything just *is* and nothing changes, there is nothing much to be said about anything. This could and did lead to disenchantment with questing after the essence of things, to philosophical skepticism, and led to the Sophists' contention that knowledge of the arts of social survival is as much knowledge as anyone can gain, for "man is the measure of all things." It is, curiously enough, a very short jump from saying everything is natural to saying everything is conventional. The Sophists made that jump. There is a certain similarity between the Sophists' emphasis on how to succeed as a marketable technique and modern skeptical naturalism, which knows the how of a great many things but has given up the search for the why.

As we have seen, Socrates enunciated most clearly an ethical alternative to *nomos,* though it was described as conscience or the voice of the god, rather than as *physis.* The internalized *arête* of later Greek drama paralleled this view of Socrates'. Plato, too, found an alternative to *nomos* in the universal forms, the true ideas that mind alone could grasp. These were beyond nature—not *physis* but *meta-physis.* Plato believed that physical phenomena tended to be confined to appearance rather than to reality, to belief rather than to knowledge. Physical explanations, he said, were only "likely stories." Aristotle found an orderliness in the physical world clearly independent of human judgment. He seemed to postulate an objective good discoverable in nature—although perhaps we should say objective good*s*, since each subject appropriate to human inquiry had its own end. As we have noted, Aristotle refers to natural justice (*physikon dikaion*) in the *Ethics* and the *Rhetoric,* but he does not flatly state that it is eternally unchangeable or that is exists independent of human initiative. To assert the latter remained for the Stoics.

The Stoics found reason (*ratio*) in nature; indeed, this was their name for the element of orderliness in all creation. But no part of nature more significantly revealed this orderliness, they thought, than the human mind. We must not, however, think of the Stoic concept of reason as that of a limited cognitive function, nor a skill at logical manipulation, nor even the power of "reasoning" as we are apt to use that term, but as the Greek *logos*—the word of life, the structure of reality, a divine essence (*daimon*) found in the center of things. The term is perhaps more religious than philosophical, though philosophy itself was more of a religion than we can easily recognize. The works of the three Stoics we have selected as representative—Seneca, Epictetus, and Marcus Aurelius—indicate how much they are concerned with living the right kind of life, viewed more internally than externally. They were familiar with Plato and Aristotle and the more technical problem of ontology[3] but their conclusions on these questions tended to be but backdrop assumptions for their advice to men who would nourish worthy souls.

Seneca

Seneca (3 B.C.–65 A.D.) was born in Spain and was brought to Rome when very young. He studied philosophy and law but he gave

[3] See Seneca, *Epistulae Morales,* No. 58, "On Being." On the breadth of the conception of reason, see Marcus Aurelius. *Meditations,* Bk. IV, sec. 4; Bk. VI, sec. 23; Bk. IX, sec. 1.

up the practice of law when he inherited his father's sizeable fortune. For offending Caligula and later Claudius, he was exiled for eight years (41–49 A.D.) to Corsica, where he suffered with his asthma and composed tragedies. He was restored to favor by the ambitious Agrippina, mother of eleven-year-old Nero, to whom Seneca became tutor and mentor and to whom he addressed a series of treatises expounding Stoic philosophy. When Nero became emperor, Seneca added to his own riches with shrewd investments and, some say, high-interest loans; yet he lived an ascetic life, though he never claimed to have achieved for himself the model Stoic life his writings set forth. After the great fire of 64, Seneca contributed most of his fortune to rebuilding Rome. Despite his important role as advisor in Nero's regime, he longed to withdraw and eventually succeeded in withdrawing to his Campanian villa, where he wrote (63–65) his scientific essays, *Questiones Naturales* (*Inquiries Concerning Nature*), and the most mature of his works, *Epistulae Morales* (*Moral Essays*), addressed to his friend, Lucilius, governor of Sicily and Epicurean poet. When Seneca spurned a messenger from Nero, Nero commanded him to die, and, at last true to his professed Stoic detachment from worldly concerns, he calmly opened his veins and did die, taking at the end a cup of hemlock as if to imitate Soccrates.

"Comely slaves and beautiful houses," said Seneca, are of no real worth to a man, for they are "on the outside." What is important is what is "in the man himself," that which

> cannot be given or snatched away, that which is the peculiar property of the man. Do you ask what this is? It is soul [*animus*] and reason brought to perfection in the soul. For man is a reasoning animal [*animal*]. Therefore, man's highest good is attained if he has fulfilled the good for which nature designed him at birth. And what is it which this reason demands of him? The easiest thing in the world—to live in accordance with his own nature.[4]

But what is this nature to which we are to conform? It is not always easy to tell:

> Nature sends forth all these things towards the same goal. Whatever is will cease to be, and yet it will not perish, but will be resolved into its elements. To our minds, this process means perishing, for we behold only that which is nearest; our sluggish mind, under allegiance to the body, does not penetrate to the bournes beyond [*ulteriora*]. Were it not so, the mind could endure with greater courage its own ending and that of its possessions, if only it could hope that life and death, like the whole universe about us, go by turns, that whatever has been put together is broken up again, and that the eternal craftsmanship of God, who controls all things, is working at this task.[5]

As microcosm is to macrocosm, the soul of the wise man, for Seneca, is to God—or more specifically, to God as divine logos, existing above God as fate. There is a double usage of the term "God" in Seneca, just as there is a double usage for the term "nature." On the one hand, nature is revealed in sense experience; on the other hand, nature is triumph over sense experience: ". . . nature is insistent and cannot be overcome," says Seneca, and he shows this by noting that a man will die if he does not eat. But "Nature does not care whether the bread is the coarse kind or the finest wheat; she does not desire the stomach to be entertained but to be filled." Man, who is meant to imitate nature, should be concerned with eating but unconcerned about the quality of what he eats. This may be regarded as a criticism of the Epicureans (see p. 81, *n.* 19) and their principle of pleasure as a primary value. Seneca also criticizes the Epicureans for paying too much attention to the senses: "We Stoics maintain" that the Good is not a matter of the senses,

[4] *Epistulae Morales,* No. 71, "On the God Within Us," trans. by R. M. Gummere (Cambridge, Mass.: Harvard Univ. Press, Loeb Classical Library, 1953), Vol. 1, pp. 277–79. Subsequent page references will be to this edition. Though it is supposedly easy to live in accordance with nature, Seneca also says, "this is turned into a hard task by the general madness of mankind; we push one another into vice."

[5] *Ibid.,* No. 71, "On the Supreme Good," Vol. 2, p. 81.

but "a matter of the understanding, and we assign it to the mind."

Seneca compares the distinction between the sense of touch and the sense of sight to the distinction between all the senses and reason: the sense of touch is gross and cannot distinguish very small objects; the sense of sight is fine and can distinguish the smallest particles. So it is between the senses and reason: only the foolish man puts reason in the service of the senses; the senses must be the servant of reason. But confusion enters with this point, which seems to make the naturalness of reason open to question or at least to limit reason to a small part of nature. The Good, says Seneca, is nonexistent in a tree, or a dumb beast, or a child (at least under seven years old), "Because there is no reason in these." Yet elsewhere in the same epistle he refers to reason as the "governing element" in all things. Does he mean that trees, beasts, and children contain no governing element?

Epictetus

Epictetus (c. 60 A.D.–?), a deformed son of a slave woman and hence himself a slave, was born in Hieropolis, Phrygia. We have very few facts about his life. Even the name Epictetus is arbitrary: it means, "bought" and was but a servile designation. After passing with different owners from one city to another, he was sold to the cruel Epaphroditus, a prominent member of Nero's court, who uncharacteristically permitted Epictetus to hear lectures on philosophy and who eventually freed him. Epictetus taught in Rome until Domitian banned all philosophers. He then settled in Nicopolis, in Epirus, where his lectures were widely popular. One student, Arrian of Nicomedia, later governor of Cappadocia, recorded his lectures with what scholars seem to agree was remarkable fidelity and later published them in Greek as the *Discourses*. Still later Arrian compiled the shorter *Encheiridion* (or handbook) of Epictetus, which some Christian ascetics used as a guide to monastic life. The emperor Hadrian knew and honored Epictetus, who is said to have lived to a ripe old age.

Epictetus faced more directly than Seneca this problem of natural reason and rational nature. Yet he did so in terms that reinforced only the spiritual rather than the natural flavor of reason.[6] In one of his *Discourses* Epictetus defends the familiar Stoic ideas that all things are united in one, that the earth is influenced by heaven, and that order is found in all nature: "For how else comes it that so regularly, as if from God's command, when He bids the plants flower, they flower, when He bids them put forth shoots, they put them forth, when He bids them bear their fruit, they bear it, when to ripen, they ripen."[7] The human body, says Epictetus, shares in the same divine process of growth; but unlike plants, man has the capacity to acquire memories and to think about the whole:

> on being moved by these impressions, your will falls upon notions corresponding to the impressions first made, and so from myriads of matters you derive and retain arts, one after the other, and memories. All this you do, and God is not able to oversee all things and to be present with all and to have a certain communication from them all?[8]

As did Seneca, Epictetus sees man as a lesser representation of God. God is one who resides inside man as well as outside him. No man is the equal of Zeus, "Yet none the less He has stationed by each man's side his particular genius [*daimon*]—and has committed the man to his care—and that to a guardian who never sleeps and is not to be beguiled. . . . God is within, and your own genius is within."[9] This genius within is

[6] The affinity of Epictetus' philosophy with many elements in Christian thought has often been noted. For example, see F. W. Farrar, *Seekers After God* (London: Macmillan, 1906), Part II.

[7] *Discourses*, Bk. I, Ch. 14, "That the Deity Oversees All Men," trans. by W. A. Oldfather (Cambridge, Mass.: Harvard Univ. Press, Loeb Classical Library, 1926), Vol. 1, p. 101. Subsequent page references will be to this edition.

[8] *Ibid.*, p. 103.

[9] Very similar expressions are found in Seneca, *Epistle* 41, and Marcus Aurelius, *Meditations*, Bk. V, sec. 27.

equated with reason but not with arid intellect. It is the divine spark, hence *daimon,* by which true insights are received and right judgments are made. Much of the layman's notion of the philosopher as a venerable sage, impervious to petty afflictions, derives from the picture of the Stoics, which is not altogether inaccurate when judged by their lives. Philosophy was not for them an academic discipline but a way of life. But if reason is the key to such a life, "reason" obviously means more than simply rigorous intellectual calculation. Otherwise it would not make much sense to say, as, for example, Marcus Aurelius does, "To the rational creature the same act is at once according to nature and according to reason."[10]

Marcus Aurelius

Marcus Aurelius (Marcus Annius Aurelius Antoninus) (121–80 A.D.) was born in Rome to a distinguished family of Spanish descent. When his father died, the infant Marcus was taken into the home of his rich grandfather, then a consul. Emperor Hadrian knew and liked the boy and emperor Antoninus Pius adopted him as a son. Overpoweringly educated—he had seventeen tutors—he knew Stoic philosophy well, especially that of Epictetus, and when he was but twelve years old he followed a rigorously ascetic Stoic regimen. When he became emperor in 161, he was the beneficiary of the conscientious rule of Antoninus and the brilliant rule of Hadrian and he continued the legal reforms Hadrian had begun. He was a Stoic philosopher-king as much as possible, but his own writings reveal his awareness that he could not be a Platonic philosopher-king: Marcus was too regally trained and too conservative to "scrape the canvas clean." He was also sometimes too goodhearted for the interests of firm authority. But when challenged by Germanic tribes in the North, this man who hated war gave himself wholly to defending the Empire, personally leading his soldiers in battle for seven years. Two years after he won a provisional victory, he died, leaving the sceptre to his undisiciplined and voracious son Commodus. Marcus is remembered chiefly for his book of *Meditations,* composed rather incongruously in a spirit of impressive tranquility amid the tumult of the Northern battles.

In his *Meditations* Marcus Aurelius reveals fewer contradictions than Seneca and less dogmatism than Epictetus, if only because he is less confident and more humble. Perhaps this lack of dogmatism is due to the fact that the treatise by which we know him was an attempt not to teach the world but to commune with himself. Though he confesses his own dissatisfaction with the study of physics and his own work within it, he does, however, acknowledge that one must study external reality in what we would call a nonjudgmental way if one is to obtain "assured conceptions [*theorematon*] on the one hand of the Universal Nature [*olou physeos*] and on the other of the special constitution of man." "The sound eye should see all there is to be seen, but should not say: I want what is green only. For that is characteristic of a disordered eye."

There is a kind of scientific detachment as well as merely world-weariness here. Its aim, we must remember, was more to achieve perfection of soul than to acquire objectively verifiable knowledge for its own sake: "Make thy own scientific system of enquiry [*theoretikon methodon*] into the mutual charge of all things, and pay diligent heed to this branch of study and exercise thyself in it. For nothing is so conducive to greatness of mind." One who would be a scientist in Marcus' sense "gives up all engrossing cares and ambitions, and has no other wish than to achieve the straight course through the Law, and by achieving it, to be a follower of God." By contrast with the easy assimilation of impressions in Epictetus' theory of reason, Marcus fights the tug of imagination, or opinion, within himself: "Well-being is a

[10] *Communings With Himself,* Bk. VII, sec. 11, trans. by C. R. Haines (Cambridge, Mass.: Harvard Univ. Press, Loeb Classical Library, 1916), p. 169. Subsequent page references will be to this edition. *Meditations* is the more frequently used title, though *Communings With Himself* is closer to the Greek original.

good Being, or a ruling Reason that is good. What then doest thou here, O Imagination? Avaunt, in God's name, as thou camest, for I desire thee not!"[11] Again, "Overboard with opinion and thou art safe ashore. And who is there prevents thee from throwing it overboard?"

When opinion is thrown overboard, what is left? Reason and nature are, to be sure, but also God, Zeus, Cause, Force, Soul, Mind, Universe, Law, Truth, Destiny, Necessity, Providence, Fiery Fluid, Ether, and Pneuma. For all these terms were used by the Stoics to help explain the workings of the—what shall we say?—Universe, Providence, Nature, and around once more. Because all these worked, presumably, toward one end, the Stoics were hard put to reconcile such workings with the idea of free will implied in choosing to throw opinion overboard or even in choosing to follow nature. No wonder that Marcus said, with characteristic honesty, "Things are in a sense so wrapped up in mystery that . . . even the Stoics themselves find them hard to comprehend."[12]

UNIVERSAL BROTHERHOOD

The cosmological shortcomings of the Stoics did not, as we shall see, detract from their influence nor do these defects nullify the political and moral significance of some of their conclusions, especially their belief in universal brotherhood.

Because in greater or lesser degree reason resides in all men and because nature is everywhere the same, all men, according to the Stoics, are citizens of the *cosmopolis,* or universal society. The conception of citizenship in such a vaguely defined body politic was itself necessarily vague but it did break the conceptual confines of the Greek *polis.* And in its practical effect the idea of universal brotherhood no doubt mitigated to an indeterminate degree some of the harshness of slavery: "Kindly remember that he whom you call your slave sprang from the same stock, is smiled upon by the same skies, and on equal terms with yourself breathes, lives, and dies. It is just as possible for you to see in him a free-born man as for him to see in you a slave." And so saying, Seneca ridiculed those men who felt degraded for having had to dine with slaves. Few men are not slaves to something—to lust or greed or ambition—Seneca argued, and "No servitude is more disgraceful than that which is self-imposed."

It is part of the universal design of nature, said Marcus, that men should be brought together in brotherly affection. Even birds come together to form colonies, "as it were, love-associations":

> So then all that shares in the Universal Intelligent Nature has as strong an affinity toward what is akin, aye even a stronger. For the measure of its superiority to all other things is the measure of its readiness to blend and coalesce with that which is akin to it. . . . At the present time it is only the intelligent creatures that have forgotten their mutual affinity and attraction, and here alone there is no sign of like flowing to like. Yet flee as they will, they are nevertheless caught in the toils, for Nature will have her way.[13]

This belief in brotherhood was not, however, a belief in cheery good feeling toward all fellow men. The social reserve of the Stoic could not easily be broken down: "We

[11] The capitalization and Shakespearean rhetoric should be attributed to translator Haines and not to Marcus. "Well-being" here is the Greek *eudaemonia,* which reminds us of Aristotle's use of this concept in the *Ethics.* But a definition of the term that would be closer to Marcus' meaning is that of the Stoic Chrysippus: "harmony of our *daimon* with God's will."

[12] Part of the Stoics' difficulty was their attempt to make everything—even God, virtue, the Good—corporeal. See Seneca, *Epistle* 106, "On the Corporeality of Virtue," and Marcus Aurelius, *Communings,* Bk. IV, sec. 40; Bk. X, sec. 1.

[13] *Communings,* Bk. IX, sec. 11, pp. 239–41. The operation of a universal interdependence and sympathy (*sympatheia*) was very compelling to the Stoics. See Epictetus, *op. cit.,* Bk. I, Ch. 14; Cicero, *De divinatione,* Bk. II, Ch. 34.

ought to enter cautiously into . . . social intercourse with . . . laymen, remembering that it is impossible for the man who brushes up against the person who is covered with soot to keep from getting some soot on himself." Given his life in Nero's court, it is not surprising that Seneca should advise, "You are wrong to trust the countenances of those you meet. They have the aspect of men, but the souls of brutes; the difference is that only beasts damage you at the first encounter; those whom they have passed by they do not pursue. . . . But man delights to ruin man."

Despite the value of Seneca's strictures against those who would artificially degrade the hapless slave, there is an element of condescension in his position and a smug tone in *Epistle* 109 as he takes up the topic, "On the Fellowship of Wise Men": "Good men are mutually helpful; for each gives practice to the other's virtues and thus maintains wisdom at its proper level."[14] Seneca suggests that we seek out the wise man and shun the fool. This may be good advice to college admissions officers, but it renders no brotherly service to the fool.

SELF-SUFFICIENCY

The fact is that the Stoic belief in universal brotherhood and the equality of all men was in constant tension with some of their other beliefs, namely the worth of self-sufficiency (*autarkeia*), resignation to the world, a disciplined will that could ignore suffering, freedom as internal control, and the nobility of suicide.

When we speak of the Stoic virtues today, we mean primarily the ability to endure suffering without complaint. This capacity was achieved by the Stoic philosopher by internal and external withdrawal: Seneca wrote, "Let us . . . in so far as we can, avoid discomforts as well as dangers, and withdraw to safe ground, by thinking continually how we may repel all objects of fear." Seneca regarded the three main objects of fear as physical want, fear itself—anticipating Franklin D. Roosevelt—and the violence of the mob, which delights in putting men on "the cross, the rack, the hook, and the stake which they drive straight through a man until it protrudes from his throat." "Do you ask me what you should regard as especially to be avoided? I say, crowds."

Calm detachment no doubt requires a degree of physical distance. But true freedom for the Stoic is internal. A man is free if he voluntarily limits himself to what is within his power: "He is free who lives as he wills, who is subject neither to compulsion, nor hindrance, nor force, whose choices are unhampered, whose desires attain their end, whose aversions do not fall into what they could avoid." A slave, hence, can be free and an emperor without self-discipline can be a slave. Freedom, therefore, is utterly divorced from any logical connection with politics.

Yet circumstances seem to be the master of us all. The body may be compelled by many things. Man's assent, however, may not be compelled. What if a man is threatened with the loss of all he regards as necessary to life? Will not his assent be coerced then? "Do not set your heart upon them, and they will not be necessary to you. Do not say to yourself that they are necessary, and they will not be." Epictetus pushed this argument to its logical limit. Because the body may be compelled, one must give up thinking of the body as one's own. This, in turn, means being willing to accept death rather than assent to what one does not willingly choose. Epictetus quotes Diogenes as saying, "The one sure way to secure freedom is to die cheerfully."[15] (The example of Soc-

[14] An important topic for Epictetus was "how . . . you may avoid ever being so intimately associated with some one of your acquaintances or friends as to descend to the same level with him" (*Discourses*, Bk. IV, Ch. 2).

[15] No such saying of Diogenes appears elsewhere in surviving documents. A story often repeated but possibly apocryphal tells of Epaphroditus twisting his slave Epictetus' leg in some instrument of torture. Epictetus uttered

rates' dying is frequently cited to illustrate Diogenes' point.) With such a frame of mind, says Epictetus, a man can no more be enslaved than can a fish, for a fish lives in his own element—water—or lives not at all. The nobility of Epictetus' position seems reduced by his equating human freedom with the freedom of fish to swim.

Acceptance of the paradox that the willingness to die can give meaning to life did not begin nor end with the Stoics but much of its moral force was derived from them, especially insofar as the belief was mirrored in heroic acts of resignation. The connection with Christianity at this point is obvious—so obvious that many have overlooked the radical differences between the two ways of life. And it would come as something of a shock to these people to find an eminent Christian theologian of the twentieth century speaking of Stoicism as "the only real alternative to Christianity in the Western World"[16] both because he assumes Stoicism to have continuing potency and because he sees it as opposed to Christianity. The appeal of Stoicism is precisely in this genuine courage in confronting death. But this courage is gained as a result of cosmic resignation and of faith in reason as an indwelling divinity that cannot be touched by suffering. Christian courage, by contrast, comes from faith in cosmic salvation and in a divinity that suffers from man and with man. The latter in particular would be inconceivable to the Stoic.

The theological consequences of Stoic *autarkeia* are beyond our scope here, but the political and moral consequences are worth emphasis. Improvement of one's soul by means of withdrawal from the world is apt to leave the world in worse shape than it was before. The ethics of Stoicism is an ethics of being; the ethics of Christianity, at least as interpreted from the Synoptic Gospels, is an ethics of doing. Christian ethics are not necessarily political, but Stoic ethics are avowedly apolitical. Christians are declared slaves of Christ; the whole aim of Stoicism was to avoid enslavement to anything. If one accepts responsibility for only what one can rationally control, one can move toward moral perfection by drastically reducing the scope of one's human associations. And one can simultaneously avoid personal responsibility for the larger social problems of the world. Perhaps it is symbolic of this avoidance that there is no pervasive sense of guilt in Stoicism and there is still much appeal in it. Some of this appeal is felt, on the one hand, in present-day Freudianism, insofar as Freudianism emphasizes personal self-understanding and rational adjustment to nature and, on the other hand, in certain varieties of existentialism, with their emphasis on the personal need to confront death as the central fact of existence.

DUTY

If withdrawal and self-adjustment were the final words on Stoicism, however, there would be no grounds for treating the subject in a history of political thought. Curious, is it not, that all three Stoic spokesmen we are considering were close to Roman emperors and that one became an emperor himself? However apolitical their theology and ethics may have been in the abstract, they were very political in practice. This leads to some interesting and sometimes distressing consequences.

Duty is often thought of as a primary Stoic virtue and the central link between Stoic philosophy and politics. But in the Stoic texts we find that, while duty is often praised, it is usually only in passing. One must accept without complaint the duties appropriate to what one is—a man, a son, a brother, or, perchance, a councillor of a city—for fate has decreed what one shall be.[17]

no cry of pain but only said quietly, "If you go on, you will break it," and when the leg was indeed broken, said, "I told you that you would break it."

16 Paul Tillich, *The Courage To Be* (New Haven: Yale Univ. Press, 1952), p. 9.

17 See Epictetus, *Discourses,* Bk. II, Ch. 10; Marcus Aurelius, *Communings,* Bk. VI, sec. 44.

One accepts the duties of political leadership in much the same spirit as one accepts the duties of being hard of hearing. The duties of citizenship are not treated very specifically because citizenship in the world community is what is important and this has little to do with local rules, regulations, and opportunities:

you are a citizen of the world, and a part of it, not one of the parts destined for service, but one of primary importance; for you possess the faculty of understanding the divine administration of the world, and of reasoning upon the consequences thereof. What, then, is the profession of a citizen? To treat nothing as a matter of private profit, not to plan about anything as though he were a detached unit, but to act like the foot or the hand, which, if they had the faculty of reason and understood the constitution of nature, would never exercise choice or desire in any other way but by reference to the whole.[18]

A ruler will gain little more concrete advice on how to rule well from reading the Stoics, though he will gain much advice on how to live well. Political strategy would seem to be inseparable from planning ahead, but Seneca, in *Epistle* 101, writes "On the Futility of Planning Ahead": every day should be lived as if it were the last, for no man owns tomorrow; one should worry about nothing, for worry is a sign of false values; one should live nobly, which often means that one cannot live long. Seneca seems to contradict himself in *Epistle* 107, "On Obedience to the Universal Will," where he counsels practice in meeting dangers so that panic will become an uncharacteristic response: "We must see to it that nothing shall come upon us unforeseen." But that does not invalidate his more general advice: "Whatever happens, assume that it was bound to happen, and do not be willing to rail at Nature."

Epictetus discharges us from the need to honor tyrants and Marcus admonishes us not to become Caesarified. Marcus sets before us as a model emperor his foster father Antoninus, who was great because he was good, that is, patient, modest, long-suffering—traits that offer us no criteria for right political decisions.

The contrast between the apolitical Epicureans[19] and the political Stoics is often exaggerated. True, the Stoics believed in a universal reason that could unite all men in brotherhood, while the Epicureans took the individual as ultimate. True, the Stoics accepted the rational duty of participation in the world of affairs, while the Epicureans found the highest good in the pleasures of solitary contemplation. But the primary task of both was to penetrate through convention to nature itself by the employment of right reason; and the Stoics, while personally more political, were often not far behind the Epicureans in their indifference to the intellectual task of formulating viable political standards: the Epicureans rejected society; the Stoics accepted society but not the responsibility for its philosophic sustenance.

Self-interest Higher than Duty?

Philosophic withdrawal mixed with personal involvement led to a practical shift from Greek virtue to interest as the basis of politics.[20] Though friendship was important

[18] Epictetus, "How We May Discover the Duties of Life from Names," *Discourses,* Bk. II, Ch. 10, Vol. 1, p. 275.

[19] Epicurus (342–279 B.C.), the founder of Epicureanism, was born in Samos, studied in Athens (where he was attracted by the materialism of Democritus), lectured in Asia Minor, and, in 306 B.C., settled in Athens to teach. The aim of philosophy, Epicurus argued, is to free man from fear, especially fear of the gods. Metaphysical speculation is futile. Pleasure is the highest good and virtue is but a means to this end. But it *was* a means; Epicurus was no advocate of undisciplined revelry. He saw understanding as the highest virtue and also the highest pleasure. Lucretius (c. 94–55 B.C.), author of *De rerum natura* (*On the Nature of Things*), was the chief Roman Epicurean. By the time of the later Stoics, Epicureanism was widely misunderstood as counseling license and in Greek Asia "Epicurean" became an epithet almost as bad as "atheist" or "Christian." But Seneca quoted widely from Epicurus and defended the practice of Epicureanism. See *Epistulae Morales,* No. 8.

[20] This point is ably argued by Sheldon Wolin in *Politics and Vision* (Boston: Little, Brown, 1960), Ch. 3.

to the Stoics, it was a more anemic conception of friendship than that of the Greeks, both because the Stoic was not supposed to let anyone's misfortune upset his own emotional tranquillity and because friendship could no longer be confined to the protective warmth of the close-knit *polis*. Friendship was therefore more easily debased into political expediency, or using one's "friends" to advance oneself in the power game.

The Stoic seeks good things of the mind; but when he is confronted with a social or political situation where different men and different values compete, his response is almost a shrugging "Every man for himself." There is even a certain cynicism, in the modern sense, in Epictetus' counsel: if commanded to hold a chamber pot for another man, would it be degrading to do so? "That is an additional consideration which you, and not I, must introduce into the question. For you are the one that knows yourself, how much you are worth in your own eyes, and at what price you sell yourself. For different men sell themselves at different prices." We must take for granted that men will look out for themselves first and foremost: ". . . It can no longer be regarded as unsocial for a man to do everything for his own sake. For what do you expect? That a man should neglect himself and his own interest? And in that case how can there be room for one and the same principle of action for all, namely that of appropriation to their own needs?" Given a situation where politics means the accommodation of interest conflicts, the chief political agent tends to be the lawyer. This was true of Rome and it has been true of the United States.

CICERO

The best-remembered Roman lawyer is Marcus Tullius Cicero (106–43 B.C.). He does not quite qualify as a Stoic philosopher, for he was too skeptical about the gods, but as an avowed eclectic he was a reflector of Stoic ideas. Yet his fame as a writer and orator and his representative Roman confidence in law as an object of allegiance make him worthy of attention. In appraising his Stoicism, we must remember that he was born a century before Seneca and two centuries before Marcus Aurelius. Cicero emphasized the settlement of disputes by legal process during a period of unusual political turbulence, when the balance of the Roman Republic was breaking down. Such an emphasis is not surprising when one considers that skill in the law was Cicero's chief source of personal strength at a time when the avenue to political success had become military heroics. That political ambition was part of Cicero's make-up does, indeed, cast a shadow on any claim to philosophic purity—or at least, religious piety—that may be made in his behalf. In his private letters, not written for publication, there is no sign of the piety that appears in most of his orations and in many of his essays.[21]

Life

Cicero was born near Arpinum, halfway between Rome and Naples. He was tutored in literature and Greek and studied law with Scaevola, the greatest jurist of his day. An apt pupil, he mastered the art of oratory with unusual adeptness. As a young lawyer he attracted attention by prosecuting a favorite of the dictator Sulla; but to avoid Sulla's revenge he went to Athens, where he studied oratory and philosophy for three years, and then to Rhodes, where he studied rhetoric with the famous Molo and Stoic philosophy with Poseidonius. Cicero returned

[21] This is not to say that he always concealed his skeptical frame of mind: "In most things my philosophy is that of doubt," he wrote in *De divinatione,* Bk. II, Ch. 12, trans. by William A. Falconer (Cambridge, Mass.: Harvard Univ. Press, Loeb Classical Library, 1953), p. 401. Subsequent page references will be to this edition. And he made fun of the idea of eating Ceres, the god of corn, and drinking Bacchus, the god of wine, in *De natura deorum,* Bk. III, Ch. 16. *De divinatione* was an attempt to criticize dependence on local and special gods.

to Rome in 76 B.C., at the age of thirty, and married a wife wealthy enough to enable him to go into politics. In 75 B.C. he became quaestor in Sicily and gave that island a remarkably just administration. In 70 B.C. he brought suit in Rome against the Sicilian propraetor, or governor, Senator Caius Verres, for extortion and corruption and prosecuted him successfully. With the resulting reputation, Cicero was able to become praetor in 66 B.C. and consul in 63 B.C.

Born of the middle, or equestrian, rank, Cicero resented the privileged misrule of the aristocracy but feared even more the mob rule threatened by radical leaders, such as Catiline—about whom, unfortunately, we know only from his enemies. Cicero's policy was what he called *concordia ordinum* (concord of the orders), which meant in practice cooperation between the aristocracy and the business class against the plebeians. Catiline ran for the consulate while a secret army waited in Etruria to support him. But after Catiline lost the vote, Cicero turned his dazzling oratorical abilities against him in the Senate: "How long, pray, will you abuse our patience, Catiline?" The result was that Cicero aroused resistance to Catiline and prevented an insurrection, the possibility of which had at first been only half-believed. Cicero was hailed by some as a savior of Rome; but he alienated others by accepting the laurels too readily, by neglecting the poverty that gave Catiline his cause, and by circumventing Roman law in executing Catiline's followers before the right of appeal could be exercised.

After the formation of the First Triumvirate (Crassus, Pompey, and Caesar) in 60 B.C., Cicero's political fortunes declined. In 58 B.C. he had to flee to Greece to escape the threat of permanent banishment launched by the popular tribune Clodius. Thanks to Pompey and Cicero's brother Quintus, Cicero was recalled next year to become the advocate of the Triumvirate in the Senate. But the triumvirs left the city on military ventures and Rome deteriorated into a series of sordid struggles between bands of ruffians led by Clodius and Milo. When Clodius was murdered, Milo was accused and Cicero defended him. He lost the case and left, in 51 B.C., to govern Cilicia for a year. Without having given up his legal career, Cicero had spent the previous four years in disappointed semiseclusion writing books, including *De oratore, De republica,* and *De legibus.*

"The die is cast," said Caesar as he crossed the Rubicon to make civil war on Pompey; but Cicero, flitting uncertainly from one to another of his several villas, still sought a reconciliation between the two. After Pompey was defeated, the civil war became a social revolution and Cicero's son-in-law joined the radicals. With desperate hope for the constitution of Rome, Cicero contritely welcomed Caesar when he returned from Egypt with Cleopatra; and, after the mighty general's final victories, Cicero used his oratorical powers to praise Caesar for his generosity to former enemies. "If anyone is gracious," wrote Caesar, "it is Cicero: but I doubt not that he hates me bitterly."

Depressed by the dictatorship of Caesar and crushed by the death of his own daughter, Cicero again withdrew into literature and philosophy. From 45 to 44 B.C. he wrote five works on oratory and twelve works on philosophy, including *De officiis* (*On Duty*). The Ciceronian corpus also includes fifty-seven orations and 774 letters, many to his friend Atticus. After the murder of Caesar in 44 B.C., Cicero became a leader of the faction opposing Mark Antony and made a series of speeches that came to be called the *Philippics,* after Demosthenes' speeches against Philip of Macedon. After the Second Triumvirate (Antony, Octavian, and Lepidus) was established in 43 B.C., Cicero was one of many marked for death, although Octavian's acquiescence to his execution was grudging. In the days before his death, Cicero revealed his "usual vacillations before danger and his courage at the decisive moment."[22]

[22] G. C. Richards, *Cicero, A Study* (Boston: Houghton Mifflin, 1935), p. 209. See also Lily Ross Taylor, *Party Politics in the Age of Caesar* (Berkeley: Univ. of California Press, 1961); H. Strasburger, *Concordia Ordinum* (Frankfurt: Noske, 1931); and Henry J. Haskell, *This Was Cicero* (New York: Knopf, 1942).

By the order of Antony, he was murdered and his head and right hand put on public view in the Forum.

The Dialogues

Though we have only fragments of *De republica* and *De legibus* was not finished, there is enough material extant to provide us with a fair sample of Cicero's political thought. *De republica* is modeled on Plato's *Republic* and *De legibus* on Plato's *Laws;* the dialogue form is followed throughout. *De republica* is in six books: the first three deal with the best form of government, the history of the Roman state, and justice, respectively. The last three books, dealing with education and the statesman, exist only in fragments. The three extant books (of a probable five) of *De legibus* discuss the nature of law and list the religious and secular laws necessary to effect the mixed state described in *De republica.* Justice is the central theme of *De republica* and Scipio is the chief protagonist of Cicero's views. Scipio[23] was the distinguished patron of the Scipionic circle, which included the poet Terence, the satirist Lucilius, and the Stoic philosopher Panaetius. The Scipionic circle was united by its love of Greek literature and philosophy but it also aimed to refine the Latin language and employ it with precision as a bearer of wit and wisdom. Apart from Scipio himself, the only figure prominent in the actual circle and in Cicero's dialogue was Laelius, an able soldier and eloquent orator.

Although the Scipionic circle, being composed of admirers of Greece, saw Cato as an opponent because of his anti-Greek bias, Cicero nevertheless pays tribute to Cato in the early pages of the *De republica* "because he chose to ride the storms and tempests of public life until advanced age rather than to live a life of ease amid the calm and restfulness of Tusculum." Cicero's praise of Cato implies his disapproval of the Epicurean philosophers, who felt that a wise man was obliged to stay out of politics. Hence, at the outset, Cicero asserts the importance of politics and applauds the "love for noble actions, which nature has given to men that they may defend the common weal."

The difference between Cicero and his supposed model Plato—and perhaps the difference between Greeks and Romans generally—is immediately apparent. Cicero declares that statesmen, who are able to oblige all men to follow a certain course by authority and the use of punishment, are more worthy of esteem than teachers, who can influence but few. No philosophy is as valuable as "a state firmly established under public law and custom." Moreover, "Cities 'mighty and imperial,' to quote Ennius, ought to be considered superior to hamlets and outposts." (Quintus Ennius was an important Latin poet and dramatist and a friend of Cato.) The world of the *polis* has become the world of the *imperium.*

Cosmology and politics

The character of Scipio in Book I continues the effusive paean to public duty begun by Cicero in the preface, but then, because two suns have been seen in the sky, turns the discussion to cosmology. Laelius, having just joined the discussion, asks sarcastically whether all the public problems have been settled, since the topic is now what goes on in the sky. In good Stoic fashion, Philus, an orator who was elected consul in 136 B.C., responds: ". . . our home is not a structure of four walls, but it is this entire universe, which the gods have given us as a habitation and as a country, to be shared in common with them. Surely if we remain in ignorance of these cosmic problems, we must remain

[23] Publius Cornelius Scipio Africanus Minor (185–129 B.C.), also called Aemilianus, was the son of Aemilius Paulus and the adopted son of Publius Cornelius Scipio, who was, in turn, the son of Publius Cornelius Scipio Africanus Major, the general who defeated Hannibal in 202 B.C. The Scipio who is our subject was also a brother-in-law of the famous brother tribunes, the Gracchi. His troops destroyed Carthage in 146 B.C. Though there were eight prominent Scipios in ancient Rome, there was, fortunately for our sense of chronology, only one Scipionic circle.

ignorant of many important matters." Philus continues by referring to Archimedes' genius in constructing his astronomical globe and in explaining the movement of planets in unequal and different orbits.

The astronomy is but prefatory to humanistic concerns, however, for it sets up Scipio's query: "What, I ask, can a man think glorious in human life, who has contemplated these realms of the gods? What can he regard as enduring, who has learned the nature of eternity? What meaning can fame have for him who has seen how small is the earth . . . how insignificant is that part of the habitable globe to which we are limited?" Scipio is asking questions similar to those asked by twentieth-century men disturbed by the relativism inherent in modern physical science.

He answers his own question by stating that the man who seeks security in physical things will surely fail. Only the man who refuses to call material objects good will avoid being unsettled by his smallness in the cosmos:

Only such a man may truly claim all things as his own, not by a title derived from the law of the Quirites, but by virtue of the right which inheres in wisdom; not because of a formal contract under the civil law, but by virtue of that general law of nature which forbids that anything should belong to anyone, except to a man who knows how to use and employ it wisely. . . . What military command, what magistracy, what kingly prerogative excels the power of him who looks down upon the world, who thinks that everything in it is human and inferior to wisdom, and who therefore reflects only upon eternal and divine truths.[24]

An element of Platonism is obvious here, but a break with Plato is also apparent: Plato's man was never a citizen of the universe looking down on the world; he was always in the world and a citizen of his *polis,* for citizenship meant being a member of the city. Nor does Cicero want to be known only as a spokesman of Greek thought. Through the mouth of Scipio, Cicero separates himself from the Greeks but, interestingly, seems to make politics rather than philosophy the chief point of separation: ". . . bear this in mind: that I am neither wholly ignorant of Greek researches nor minded to accord them preference over our own authors, especially in the field of politics." "I deem the Romans to be no more barbarians than the Greeks."

The commonwealth

Yet, ironically, it is precisely on the subject of politics, and especially on the defense of the "mixed constitution," that Cicero seems most in debt to the Greeks. Scipio begins the discussion of politics with a definition of *res publica:*

The commonwealth, then, is the people's affair; and the people is not every group of men, associated in any manner, but is the coming together of a considerable number of men who are united by a common agreement about law and rights and by the desire to participate in mutual advantages. The original cause of this coming together is not so much weakness as a kind of social instinct natural to man.[25]

The people is not a mere multitude, but citizens bound together in a certain way—an idea Edmund Burke would labor hard to demonstrate in the face of the liberal individualism of the eighteenth century. But, given a restricted conception of "people," the

[24] *De republica,* Bk. I, Ch. 17, in *On the Commonwealth,* trans. by George H. Sabine and Stanley B. Smith (Indianapolis: Bobbs-Merrill, Library of Liberal Arts, n.d.), pp. 122–23. Subsequent page references will be to this edition unless otherwise indicated. The passage seems to be a close paraphrase of the philosophy of the Stoic Chrysippus.

[25] *Ibid.,* Ch. 25, p. 129. The English of Sabine and Smith is not a literal rendering of the Latin *Est igitur, inquit Africanus, res publica res populi,* which, literally, would be, "The public thing is the people's thing." But C. W. Keyes in the Loeb edition prefers "property" for *res* (Cambridge, Mass.: Harvard Univ. Press, 1928. Latin, p. 64, English, p. 65); and Sabine and Smith, following the Carlyle brothers, prefer "affair" (See R. W. and A. J. Carlyle, *A History of Mediaeval Political Theory in the West* [New York: Barnes and Noble, 1953], Vol. I, Part 1). We might say that the wealth that is common to all men is composed of those things that have become public affairs.

distinction between *res publica* and *res populi* is not always clear: ". . . every people, which is a number of men united in the way I have explained, every state, which is an organization of the people, every commonwealth, which, as I have said, is the people's affair, needs to be ruled by some sort of deliberating authority in order that it may endure." The ambiguity lies in the uncertain implication that the people organized (*res populi*) may require an external standard of right to qualify as a commonwealth (*res publica*).

Cicero's consideration of "deliberating authority" does not resolve the uncertainty, for under this head he merely looks at traditional forms of government and the problem of tyranny. The statements of what constitute monarchy, aristocracy, and democracy add little to Plato or Aristotle. At the request of Laelius, Scipio gives the arguments in favor of each form of government: democracy is "a habitation for liberty" and, according to its defenders, the only form that can be truly called a commonwealth. Yet democracies have difficulty in maintaining equal rights and in recognizing degrees of merit and therefore often "degenerate into the irresponsible madness of a mob." Aristocracies uphold the ideal of merit, but often rich men acquire power and cling to the label aristocrat after the substance has gone. Scipio concedes the benefits of wise rule by one man but devotes more words to the perverted form, tyranny.

Asks Laelius, "But of the three simple forms of state, Scipio, which do you especially approve?" And Scipio answers, "I do not approve any one of them considered separately and by itself. I prefer rather the mixed form, which is a combination of all three, to any one taken by itself." If forced to choose, he would take monarchy, where the ruler is an affectionate father, but "I prefer monarchy for the love which a king bears to his subjects; aristocracy for its wisdom in counsel; and democracy for its freedom. When I compare them, I find it hard to decide which feature we desire the most." The surprising preference for monarchy, spoken by a Roman aristocrat, is explained perhaps by the Platonic psychology, which is adopted without much question. Reason is the ruling part of the soul and commands the emotions in much the same way that ruling authority in the state must command lesser persons; "an authority which is not a unit cannot exist." Aquinas picked up this argument in Cicero and made it the basis for his defense of monarchy in *De regimine principum*. He also uses the familiar Platonic analogies with physicians and ship captains and even quotes Plato—though in fact the quotation appears to be a paraphrase—on the slide from democracy to "boundless license."

Though no clear, logical line is established, this discussion of the general problem of authority is the occasion for a turn in Book II to those authorities especially important to Romans, their ancestors. Hence Scipio turns to the Roman commonwealth as a model of good rule.

Ancestral authority

Cicero's minute attention to the historical origins of Rome—or to what he imagines to be the historical origins of Rome—in a work supposed to be modeled on Plato is a clue to the significant difference between Roman and Greek conceptions of authority: for Rome, the historic founding is everything; for Greece, the founding is more metaphysical. In what is a fine piece of combined self-praise and Roman chauvinism, Cicero has Laelius say to Scipio:

> In truth . . . you have begun the discussion in accordance with a new principle which is not to be found anywhere in the works of the Greeks. For Plato, the prince of philosophers, who has no superior as a writer, chose his own ground that he might construct a commonwealth according to his fancy. His was a noble state, no doubt, but incongruous with human life and customs. The other Greek philosophers discussed the kinds of states and their principles but failed to treat any concrete example and type of the commonwealth. You, it seems to me, are likely to combine the concrete with the general. You have so begun the discussion that you prefer attributing your own discoveries to others

instead of setting them forth in your own person, as Socrates does in Plato's "Republic." Moreover, with respect to the location of the city, you show the principles behind the measures which Romulus adopted either by accident or necessity. Your discussion, in fine, does not wander but deals with one commonwealth alone. Go on, therefore, as you have begun. Already, indeed, I seem to see what may be called a perfect state unfolding as you discuss the rest of the kings.[26]

What Scipio has told his auditors is the familiar story of Romulus founding Rome: how he had chosen an "unbelievably favorable" location for a city, free of the military hazards and corrupting influences of seaports (Scipio inaccurately disparages Carthage and Corinth on these grounds); how the Sabine women "of good family" had been seized and given in marriage to the men "of the best Roman families"; how Romulus had made peace with the Sabines and divided their mutual followers into three tribes, a division which became the basis of all Roman government; how he had learned what Lycurgus at Sparta had learned, that good rule requires the support of a council of leading citizens; and, finally, how "Romulus placed chief dependence upon the auspices—a procedure which continues even at the present day to contribute greatly to the safety of the state."[27]

How much of this Cicero believed to be actual history is not clear. He states that it is important for citizens to hold to the tradition that Romulus was the son of Mars, even though it is clear that he does not believe this. He probably believed much of the rest of the story, however, and it was believed for centuries after him. Yet the chronology is undoubtedly confused at many points. In describing the assembly of Centuries supposedly set up by King Servius, for example, Cicero is actually describing the *comitia centuriata* as it existed much later.[28]

In Book II Cicero reviews the traditional history of the kings of Rome and intersperses the survey with discussions of how such *poleis* as Sparta work. The corruption of the kingship into a tyranny under Tarquinius is presented not only as an example of tyranny—with references to Plato—but as a decisive historical event in the history of Rome, for, according to Cicero, it was after Tarquinius that the title of king became anathema to the Roman people and the dual consulship was begun. The first consul, Valerius, decreed that henceforth no Roman citizen could be executed or flogged before he was permitted appeal to the Centuries. According to Cicero's history, Larcius was chosen first dictator ten years after the consulate had been established. Later the power of the Senate was limited by the creation of two tribunes of the *plebs* (the populus minus the patricians).[29]

[26] *Ibid.*, Bk. II, Ch. 11, pp. 164–65. See also Ch. 30.

[27] *Imperium* and *auspicia* represented two aspects of the power of ancient Roman kings: the human and the divine. *Imperium* included plenary and comprehensive powers "over all persons and in all causes supreme." *Auspicia* provided the means of testing the will of the gods, whose favor had approved the choice of the king and guaranteed his power. Thus the Roman king was half priest, even though he was not regarded as divine. When he died, *auspicia* returned to the *patres* in the Senate, who provided for the transition to the new magistrate. See Sir Frank E. Adcock, *Roman Political Ideas and Practice* (Ann Arbor: Univ. of Michigan Press, 1959), pp. 5–6 and 22.

[28] See Sabine and Smith, p. 174, n. 59. The Roman political institutions before the Republic are conjectural only, but it seems clear that the monarchy that preceded the Republic was in alien Etruscan hands. Scholars dispute whether the revolution that threw the Etruscans out occurred in the late sixth or middle fifth century B.C. The Roman suspicion of monarchy as a form of government and also the system of electing two somewhat countervailing magistrates probably date from this period. See also Adcock, Chs. 1–2; and Leon Homo, *Roman Political Institutions, From City to State,* trans. by M. R. Dobie (London: Routledge and Kegan Paul, 1929), Ch. 1.

[29] The tribunes of the *plebs* (not to be confused with the military tribunes) were originally created to protect the *libertas* of the small man. They had religious sanctity and immunity from arrest. By intervention (*intercessio*) they could restrain the initiative of magistrates. Initially this function was exercised on behalf of individuals but later intervention was justified by the interests of the *plebs* as a class and at times became simply obstructive. Eventually, the tribunes were assimilated into the leadership structure and they presided over the Senate and *comitia*. By the time of Augustus, the em-

Quite apart from the question of historical accuracy—which is a goal difficult enough even in our own day—Cicero's historical review is disappointing even when measured by his own stated aim: "The highest achievement of political wisdom, with which all our discussion deals, is to perceive the tortuous path followed by public affairs, in order that we may know the tendency of each change and thus be able to retard the movement or forestall it." At the end of Book II the character Tubero expresses disappointment in the dialogue, which prompts a shift to the subject of the nature of justice, which occupies the last five chapters of Book II and most of Book III. Unfortunately, much of this is missing; but additional parts of the argument can be pieced together from the letters and *De Civitate Dei* of Augustine; the ***Institutes*** of Lactantius; and other writings of Cicero, especially *De officiis, De finibus* (*On Limitation*), and his letters.

Justice

Cicero follows Plato's idea of justice as a kind of harmony similar in the individual and in the state: "The state achieves harmony by the agreement of unlike individuals, when there is a wise blending of the highest, the lowest, and the intervening middle classes in the manner of tones. And what musicians call harmony in song is concord in a state." The wise statesman is one who can bring this about; but the statesman must never disregard Stoic precepts, for he is one who "has in fact scarcely more than this single duty—for it includes nearly everything else—that he should never abandon the study and contemplation of himself; that he should challenge others to imitate him; and that by the nobility of his mind and conduct he should hold himself up to his fellow citizens as a model."

For the sake of argument Philus takes upon himself the task of defending the view that justice is merely conventional. His argument recalls somewhat those of Callicles in Plato's *Gorgias* and Thrasymachus in Plato's *Republic*. If justice were natural, says Philus, everyone would have the same laws; but it is manifest that varying groups have widely varying laws. And the law is not equal for persons within the same community: "Why may a Vestal bequeath property and her mother not?" Moreover, "Laws . . . are obeyed because of the penalties they may inflict and not because of our sense of justice. Consequently, the law has no sanction in nature. It follows, then, that men are not just by nature." Philus paints the picture, as does Glaucon in Plato's *Republic,* of the good man tortured, beaten, persecuted, and universally condemned as unjust and the evil man heaped with wealth, power, and favor and universally honored as just. He then asks which we would like to be. "What is true of individuals is also true of states. There is no country so stupid as not to prefer unjust dominion to just subjection." If a man is selling his house and points out its faults, is he praised for his justice? No, he is called a fool.

In reply Laelius says that the argument is "monstrous" and that Carneades, if he meant it seriously, is a "scoundrel." Laelius then utters one of the most frequently quoted of the many definitions of natural law:

> There is in fact a true law—namely, right reason—which is in accordance with nature, applies to all men, and is unchangeable and eternal. By its commands this law summons men to the performance of their duties; by its prohibitions it restrains them from doing wrong. Its commands and prohibitions always influence good men, but are without effect upon the bad. To invalidate this law by human legislation is never morally right, nor is it permissible ever to restrict its operation, and to annul it wholly is impossible. Neither the senate nor the people can absolve us from our obligation to obey this law, and it requires no Sextus Aelius[30] to expound and interpret it. It will not lay down one rule at Rome and another at Athens, nor will it

peror could simply take upon himself tribunal powers, even though he was born a patrician. See Adcock, pp. 30–32. 66–67; Homo, pp. 221–22, and *passim*.

[30] Sextus Aelius was consul in 198 B.C., censor in 194 B.C., and author of a work on the Twelve Tables.

be one rule today and another tomorrow. But there will be one law, eternal and unchangeable, binding at all times upon all peoples; and there will be, as it were, one common master and ruler of men, namely God, who is the author of this law, its interpreter, and its sponsor. The man who will not obey it will abandon his better self, will thereby suffer the severest of penalties, though he has escaped all the other consequences which men call punishment.[31]

The same sentiments underlie many Stoic writings and appear again in other writings of Cicero. *De officiis* takes up in Book I the four elements of moral goodness: wisdom, justice, fortitude (which includes courage), and temperance. Nature operating through the power of reason is the essence of each:

it is no mean manifestation of Nature and Reason that man is the only animal that has a feeling for order, for propriety, for moderation in word and deed. And so no other animal has a sense of beauty, loveliness, harmony in the visible world; and Nature and Reason, extending the analogy of this from the world of sense to the world of spirit, find that beauty, consistency, order are far more to be maintained in thought and deed, and the same Nature and Reason are careful to do nothing in an improper or unmanly fashion, and in every thought and deed to do or think nothing capriciously.

It is from these elements that is forged and fashioned that moral goodness which is the subject of this inquiry—something that . . . merits praise, even though it be praised by none.[32]

Interestingly, Cicero makes justice a virtue superior to the other three on the grounds that the other three could not exist without the protection of an orderly society: courage without justice would degenerate into "brutality and savagery"; knowledge divorced from justice "would seem isolated and barren of results." Cicero sees a more complicated question in connection with possible conflicts between justice and temperance: justice, which he identifies here with that "social instinct, which is the deepest feeling in our nature," should not take precedence over temperance, for some acts are so repulsive that a man should not commit them even to save his country. But this conflict exists only from the individual's standpoint. Viewed in larger perspective, thinks Cicero, there is no problem at all:

the problem is the more easily disposed of because the occasion cannot arise when it could be to the state's interest [*intersit rei publicae*] to have the wise man do any of those things.

This, then, may be regarded as settled: in choosing between conflicting duties, that class takes precedence which is demanded by the interests of human society.[33]

But if the interests of human society are obscure, who is entitled to define them? Cicero does not say. It is characteristic of his writings that he takes up questions of considerable significance and disposes of them in a superficial way.

The just war

Cicero applies the concept of justice to warfare in both *De republica* and *De officiis*. The concept of the just war was important to Aristotle and to the subsequent natural law tradition. Cicero writes:

Wars are unlawful which are undertaken without a reason. For no war can be justly waged except for the purpose of redressing an injury

[31] *Ibid.*, Ch. 22, pp. 215–16. The definition is similar to those of Chrysippus and other Stoic philosophers. See also Cicero's *De legibus*, Bk. I, Ch. 6.

[32] *De officiis*, Bk. I, Ch. 4, trans. by Walter Miller (Cambridge, Mass.: Harvard Univ. Press, Loeb Classical Library, 1913), pp. 15–17. Subsequent page references are to this edition. The first two books of *De officiis*, on moral goodness and expediency, respectively, follow the work of Panaetius quite closely. The third book, on the conflict between the right and the expedient, does not and is inferior. The Monastery at Subiaco, in the Sabine Hills, printed *De officiis* in 1465, making it, in all probability, the first classical work to be issued from a printing press.

[33] Cicero views the quality of law from three different angles: *justitia* represents the rational structure, the non-self-interestedness of law; *aequitas* represents the fair and impartial application of law; *fides* indicates the respect, loyalty, and confidence of people for the law. Despite the quotation above, all three seem to be psychological rather than sociological or metaphysical categories. See *De republica*, Bk. I, Ch. 2; *De officiis*, Bk. I, Ch. 19; *De finibus*, Bk. I, Ch. 16, Bk. II, Ch. 18; *De amicitia*, Ch. 22.

or of driving out an invader. No war is to be held lawful unless it is officially announced, unless it is declared and unless a formal claim for satisfaction has been made.[34]

The only excuse . . . for going to war is that we may live in peace unharmed; and when the victory is won, we should spare those who have not been blood-thirsty and barbarous in their warfare.[35]

We immediately think about the Roman military adventures that carved out one of the mightiest empires in history and wonder about Cicero's impartiality on this point. "Our people," he says, "were by this time masters of the whole world because they defended their allies." But he goes even further and argues that a superior people may be engaged in a just war when they take over an inferior people. This is permissible "when the power of doing wrong is taken from wicked men, and when those who have been conquered will be better off, inasmuch as they were worse off when unconquered."

Cicero draws a curious triple analogy between such an imposition of force, God's rule over man, and reason's rule over the lesser elements of the soul. One wonders how this justification can be reconciled with the strict egalitarianism that Cicero maintains elsewhere. In *De legibus,* for example, he says,

there is no difference in kind between man and man; for if there were, one definition could not be applicable to all men; and indeed reason, which alone raises us above the level of the beasts . . . is certainly common to us all, and, though varying in what it learns, at least in the capacity to learn is invariable. . . . In fact, there is no human being of any race who, if he finds a guide, cannot attain to virtue.[36]

[34] *De republica,* Bk. III, Ch. 23, p. 217. Reconstructed from Isidore of Seville. In *De legibus* Cicero places the declaration of war in the hands of a fetial college whose officers, the fetiales, can give or withhold a religious sanction to wars, peace treaties, and the like. See Bk. II, Chs. 9, 14.

[35] *De officiis,* Bk. I, Ch. 11, p. 37.

[36] *De legibus,* Bk. I, Ch. 10, trans. by Clinton W. Keyes (Cambridge, Mass.: Harvard Univ. Press, Loeb Classical Library, 1928), pp. 329–30. Subsequent page references are to this edition.

Cicero does not claim to be a great philosopher; indeed, he admits that the Romans as a whole are not outstanding in philosophy but he does claim that Rome has "produced more men" who are "worthy of the greatest honor for having put into practice the teachings and discoveries of the philosophers." We may well be skeptical of the degree to which Roman conquest was an implementation of philosophy, but nonetheless, political sagacity, shaped and tempered by classical learning, marked a significant tradition of Western statesmanship that included our own founding fathers.

Was Cicero a Philosopher?

Although Cicero was a master of Latin rhetoric, there is considerable ambiguity in his own philosophic position. This is partly a result of the dialogue form he employed and of the many missing parts in what has been recovered from his writings. But the difficulty is more fundamental than this: Cicero is sometimes called an academic Skeptic; sometimes he is classified with the Stoics. It is fair to conclude that he was skeptical about certain Stoic ideas but that he was also impressed by them. We know that in his short periods of withdrawal from political life he was intensely anxious to write *about* philosophy, but perhaps more as a statesman than a philosopher. In *De legibus* he says (as Marcus), "Our whole discourse is intended to promote the firm foundation of states, the strengthening of cities, and the curing of the ills of the peoples. For that reason I want to be especially careful not to lay down first principles that have not been wisely considered and thoroughly investigated."

But what are these first principles and how rigorously does Cicero investigate them? In the passage following the one just quoted, Cicero goes on to say that the first principles he is talking about ought to be compatible with the thought of Plato, Aristotle, Zeno, or any number of other philosophers. Cicero's eclecticism is not covert. The only group he specifically excludes here are the Epicureans.

The exclusion is significant, for a man—and especially a nonphilosopher—will often be more precisely identified by what he is against than by what he is for.

The Epicureans are anathema to Cicero because they recognize no interests higher than individual and material interests and they therefore reject involvement in politics. Cicero seems willing to accept as weapons in his opposition to the Epicureans any of a number of theories that find ultimate reality to be higher than individual and material interests. In *De legibus,* where he seems to speak more clearly for himself as Marcus than he does as any of the characters of *De republica,* he summarizes Stoic thought on natural justice—speaking of what "they" believe: the origin of justice is in law and law "is a natural force; it is the mind and reason of the intelligent man [*mens ratio que prudentis*]." But he is not so concerned about vindicating a particular philosophic position as about vindicating popular respect for philosophy, especially philosophy allied with political authority. He goes on to say, "But since our whole discussion has to do with the reasoning of the populace, it will sometimes be necessary to speak in the popular manner and give the name of law to that which in written form decrees whatever it wishes." And in *De officiis* he once again lowers his sights for the sake of the popular target. He cites the Stoic distinction between absolute duties and ordinary, or mean (*media*), duties and notes:

> the common crowd [*volgus*] does not, as a rule, comprehend how far it falls short of real perfection; but as far as their comprehension does go, they think there is no deficiency. . . . The performance of the duties, then, which I am discussing in these books, is called by the Stoics a sort of second-grade moral goodness, not the peculiar property of their wise men, but shared by them with all mankind.[37]

Furthermore, it was the later Roman jurists and not Cicero who tried to bring the precepts of *jus naturale* into the courtroom. As a practicing lawyer Cicero did not entertain such lofty notions. Moreover, in his theoretical writings as well as in his law practice he can be found to stress the importance of private-property interests at the expense of the noble communal ideals he elsewhere eulogizes:

> The man in an administrative office . . . must make it his first care that every one shall have what belongs to him and that private citizens suffer no invasion of their property rights by act of state. . . . For the chief purpose in the establishment of constitutional states and municipal governments was that individual property rights might be secured. For although it was by Nature's guidance that men were drawn together into communities, it was in the hope of safeguarding their possessions that they sought the protection of cities.[38]

These considerations may help to explain why Cicero offers the traditional history of Rome in *De republica* and supports the need to revere it without appearing too much to believe it himself. They may help to explain why the concept of the just war is carefully expounded and Rome is halfheartedly defended as conforming to it. They may also help to explain Cicero's ambiguity on the subject of freedom: on the one hand, "Nothing, they say, is sweeter than freedom, even to wild beasts; and no citizen possesses freedom when he is subject either to a king or to an aristocracy." But on the other hand, "if the people have the supreme power and if all public business is carried on at their pleasure, we have what is called liberty, but what in fact is license."[39]

In frustration Cicero sometimes seems to accept as a conclusion that "the essential nature of the commonwealth often defeats reason."[40] But it would be surprising if he did

[37] *De officiis,* Bk. III, Chs. 3–4, p. 283.

[38] *Ibid.,* Bk. I, Ch. 21, p. 249. Passages such as this led Charles Norris Cochrane to call Cicero "the first Whig" (*Christianity and Classical Culture* [New York: Oxford Univ. Press, 1957], p. 45).

[39] This statement is part of Philus' argument for the conventionality of justice but it does not eliminate the theoretical problem. See *De officiis,* Bk. I, Ch. 20, where the Stoic idea of freedom as wholly internal is stated noncommittally.

[40] This is the Keyes translation, p. 169. It is a more literal rendition than Sabine and Smith's "there is a

not think that politics was often bound to defeat reason. We would do well to remember the turbulence of his own times: any list of leading statesmen of his day would have to include Crassus, Pompey, Caesar, Cato the Younger, Clodius, Milo, Cassius, Brutus, Antony, and Cicero himself—every one of whom died a violent death! Yet the defeat of reason is no ground for giving up the attempt to rule by reason. And Cicero's attempt to prove "the falsity of the view which records injustice as a necessary part of government" was not made unworthy simply by the difficulty of proof. Given the kind of violence characteristic of his age, it is no wonder Cicero would seek Roman stability by revering the Roman past, by creating an ideal state close to a historical state, and by invoking a religion about which he was personally skeptical.[41]

De republica ends with Scipio's dream, in which his grandfather takes him into the starry heavens, prophesies of his future career, and encourages him in the quest for justice and right rule. The cosmological metaphors are inspired by Plato's *Phaedrus* and *Republic*. What is striking to us is the wistful tone of the younger Scipio's yearning to be free of the burdens of the earth and "the body's prison." Like Plato's philosopher-king, he does not want to go back to the earth-cave where duty lies. Cicero's insistent stress on the importance of politics is never wholly without overtones of the longing to escape politics.

The Influence of Polybius on Cicero

It is necessary at this point to backtrack chronologically in order to acknowledge the influence of Polybius (204?–122? B.C.), the Greek historian transplanted to Rome whose idea of the mixed constitution was reflected in Cicero and in later political writers. Polybius and Cicero are really the only classical Roman political theorists whose work has survived to the present. The discussion of Polybius is both a postscript to our commentary on Cicero and a preface to our commentary on later Roman jurists.

Life of Polybius

Born at Megalopolis in Arcadia, Polybius was the son of a rich and eminent statesman. As a youth he apparently acquired a practical knowledge of military matters and read the leading historians but he probably had only a secondhand acquaintance with the Greek literary and philosophic tradition. In 170 B.C. he was ordered to Rome as a consequence of a Roman purge of Greek leaders suspected of disloyalty. Had he not become a friend of Scipio, Polybius would have been put into custody in some outlying town. But instead he stayed on in Rome, technically a foreign internee but actually a mentor and friend of Scipio, a member of the Scipionic circle, and an acquaintance of the great. The three hundred internees who survived the original arrest were released in 150 B.C., largely due to the influence of Scipio. It is probably true that Polybius had illegally traveled to Spain and Africa with Scipio before his release. Afterwards, he traveled extensively, was present at the fall of Carthage, and later, after the Roman sack of Corinth, worked to secure a favorable settlement between Greece and Rome. It is generally believed that he died from a fall off a horse at the age of eighty-two.

Polybius has been compared to Gibbon: one chronicled the rise of Rome, the other the fall.[42] The history Polybius offers is not,

principle of growth inherent in public affairs that often overrides design" (*op. cit.*, p. 185).

[41] Cicero lists his religious laws in *De legibus*, Bk. II, Chs. 8–9. This list, as his brother Quintus quickly points out, "does not differ a great deal from the laws of Numa and our own customs." Marcus replies that, since the ideal state expounded by Scipio in *De republica* was virtually the same as the early Roman state, it is important that the religious laws be "in harmony with its character" (Ch. 10, p. 399).

[42] F. W. Walbank, in the Introduction to E. S. Shuckburgh's translation of *The Histories* (Bloomington: Indiana Univ. Press, 1962), Vol. 1, p. VIII. Subsequent page references are to this edition. See also Walbank's *A Historical Commentary on Polybius* (Oxford: Clarendon Press, 1957), Vol. 1, Introduction.

he says, directed toward speculations on the founding of cities, toward genealogies, or toward art and science. It is basic political history, done in the manner he calls *pragmatikos:* not a dramatic narration but the elemental facts. This is not to suggest that Polybius was unambitious. Quite the contrary, for he aimed at nothing less than universal history and he reminds his readers with bothersome persistence that he is the first to write scientific history. This did not mean passive historiography. The historian, thought Polybius, should have some personal experience of what he writes about; he liked to go out into the field, inspect the site of battles, interrogate witnesses, and search out living memories. Yet his devotion to fact is not quite what we moderns might expect it to be. The mission of the historian was to teach moral lessons, thought Polybius, and he followed the example of Thucydides and most ancient historians in putting speeches into the mouths of leading personages. He did not, however, make up the speeches out of whole cloth, but attempted to get as close to the actual event as the sometimes dubious sources permitted.

Tyché

Tyché (fortune) was an important concept for Polybius, as *fortuna* was for Machiavelli. Part of its importance was simply Polybius' acceptance of a common Stoic inheritance, even though Polybius himself was not a Stoic; it was a term he could assume was familiar to his readers. Polybius used *tyché* to refer to something more than mere chance but less than a deity, although many Greeks did regard her as a deity and built local shrines to her. *Tyché* was a never very well defined agent or power of change. It has been suggested that Polybius used *tyché* very much the way modern writers use "evolution," as in "the evolution of the party system," without meaning anything too precise by it.[43] In Book XXXVII, Chapter 9, Polybius says his aim is to discover causes without reference to divine agency. Yet Book XXIII, Chapter 10, on Philip of Macedon, finds *tyché* personified as a goddess or as a punishing Nemesis. "She" visits Philip with furies who haunt him day and night.

[43] W. Ward Fowler, "Polybius' Conception of *Tyché*," *The Classical Review*, Vol. 17 (1903), pp. 445–59.

The mixed constitution

There were forty books in Polybius' histories, the last of which was an index. A number have been lost entirely; others have endured in fragmentary form. Only three books depart from a straightforward narrative and of these only Book VI, where Polybius expounds his ideas on the theory of the mixed constitution, will concern us.

Despite his personal mistreatment at the hands of the Romans, Polybius admired the vigor of Roman *imperium* and the supposedly harmonious interrelationships that characterized Roman political institutions, though the decay of republicanism had already begun when Polybius wrote. In Book VI he set out to tell his readers "in what manner, and under what kind of constitution it came about that nearly the whole world fell under the power of Rome in somewhat less than fifty-three years—an event certainly without precedent." He finds it unnecessary to invoke divinity at this point to explain the course of history, for to understand the practical undertakings of a state "we must regard as the most powerful agent for success or failure the form of the constitution."

Polybius adopts Aristotle's sixfold classification of government almost without change (instead of polity and its degenerate form, democracy, Polybius speaks of democracy and its degenerate form, mob rule, or *ochlokratia*), but without giving Aristotle specific credit. The Sparta of Lycurgus is cited as the primary example of the right combination of kingship, aristocracy, and democracy —a combination superior to any single form of government. As we know, the idea of a combination of forms was not unexamined by Aristotle. Perhaps the only novelty in Polybius' treatment is the attempt to apply the theory to the Roman Republic. Like Plato, Polybius finds a natural cycle in the growth and degeneration in these forms.

His discussion of the origin of the state is lucid, direct, and reasonable. The state originates, he argues, in the need for protection. It is natural within human groups, as among lower animals, that the physically strong should be the first leaders. Such a primitive form of rule would have to be called despotism; but in time—with the development of family ties and a sense of gratitude for the protection afforded by parents, elders, and rulers—morality is born: "Then is born also the idea of kingship and then for the first time mankind conceives the notion of goodness and justice and their reverse." If, as is likely to happen, someone shows ingratitude rather than gratitude, not only parents and rulers but others as well are displeased and offended, for they can imagine themselves in the protector's place, and they feel their own gratitude affronted: "Hence arises in every breast . . . the meaning and the theory of duty, which is in fact the beginning and the end of justice." The man who publicly displays this sense of duty in courageous acts for the whole group, and, conversely, the man who fails when others count on him, help give rise to the idea of the honorable and the dishonorable. The ruler receiving honor "becomes a *king* instead of a *despot* by imperceptible degrees, reason having ousted brute courage and bodily strength from their supremacy." This is a "natural process."[44] Natural here obviously means more than biological.

But the process of degeneration is also natural. A cycle occurs in which tyranny replaces kingship and the tyrant is overthrown by an aristocracy, which becomes an oligarchy only to be replaced by a democracy, which is corrupted into mob rule, which is finally terminated by a new despotism. Such a cycle is familiar to readers of Plato. But Polybius is more explicit than Plato in attributing this process to "an undeviating law of nature," because a government that rests on one principle alone is inherently unstable.[45] Lycurgus, says Polybius, recognized this process and for that reason set up the Spartan constitution in which each of the three parts checked the other. But the Spartans had a relatively long period of time free from adversity during which to build their state:

> though the Romans have arrived at the same result in framing their commonwealth, they have not done so by means of abstract reasoning, but through many struggles and difficulties, and by continually adopting reforms from knowledge gained in disaster. The result has been a constitution like that of Lycurgus, and the best of any existing in my time.[46]

Polybius follows a formal pattern in explaining the Roman constitution: the powers of the consuls, the Senate, and the people, are taken up in Chapters 12, 13, and 14, respectively; then the legal checks on each of these are summarized in Chapters 15, 16, and 17. Chapter 18 is a closing summary. The description is generally accurate at the level of formal legality, although, of course, the functions and powers of consuls, praetors, tribunes, and censors changed somewhat from generation to generation. The tribunes, for example, eventually came to act as prosecutors of faulty officials and, at least at certain times, gained a power over the whole magistracy beyond that acknowledged by Polybius. Polybius does not entertain the notion that the tribunes constituted a fourth branch of government and regards the consuls as "supreme masters of the administration." Yet, he notes, with the consuls out of town one could well imagine the government to be an aristocracy, so powerful is the Senate,

44 Physical strength and physical courage are not unrelated to political authority, however, even in the sophisticated America of the 1960s. The simple physical weakness induced by surgery on Presidents Eisenhower and Johnson at least temporarily reduced their political authority by reminding all of their mortality. Had they publicly displayed physical cowardice in confronting their surgery, their political authority would surely have been reduced still more.

45 The Stoic idea of the law of nature probably came to Polybius through his friend Panaetius.

46 *Histories,* Vol. 1, Bk. VI, Ch. 10, p. 467.

especially in its control of the treasury (*aerarium*) and of foreign affairs.

There would seem to be nothing left for the people but in fact they have an important role to play: "For the people is the sole fountain of honor (*timés*) and of punishment; and it is by these two things and these alone that dynasties and constitutions and, in a word, human society are held together."[47] (The conferring of honor is meant to include election to office.) Moreover, the people have "the absolute power of passing or repealing laws." Polybius is referring, though not by name, to the *comitia centuriata,* which, in the latter part of the third century B.C., began sitting as a judicial body.[48] The consuls were dependent on the Senate for money and supplies and on the people for the ratification of treaties; the people could also hold them to account when their term of office ended. The tribunes, in turn, as the special representatives of the people, could veto actions of the Senate; the people assembled could change the law. The people were checked by the Senate because the Senate had absolute control over all public works, upon which many people depended for employment. Moreover, in trials for major offenses, the judges were drawn from the senators. The consuls had power over the people because "one and all" could become subject to the absolute authority of a consul when engaged on a military campaign.

While these relationships did exist, their harmonious functioning was never quite so ideal as Polybius suggests:

> when any one of the three classes becomes puffed up, and manifests an inclination to be contentious and unduly encroaching, the mutual interdependency of all the three, and the possibility of the pretensions of any one being checked and thwarted by the others, must plainly check this tendency: and so the proper equilibrium is maintained by the impulsiveness of the one part being checked by its fear of the other.[49]

What Polybius neglects is the powerful social dominance of the noble families. If not a tribune, then a consul, or a praetor, or a dictator would preside over the *comitia centuriata* at election time. There was much behind-the-scenes manipulation during the elections and, as a consequence, the noble families produced virtually all the office-holders.[50] Later, a new man like Cicero, a member of the equine class, could become a consul; but both Polybius and Cicero underestimated the degree to which an oligarchy could use old forms for its purposes. All men were theoretically eligible for election; but on the grounds that it was an honor, no pay was attached to a magisterial office. This by itself drastically limited the availability of candidates, especially since men did not move directly into the higher offices but went through the ranks, so to speak, by being elected quaestor as early as age twenty-eight. Non-nobles who gained financial independence late in life were too old to start at the bottom in politics. Hence, down through Cicero, only six consuls had come from outside the nobility. Moreover, though every male citizen could theoretically vote, voting was by groups—the curiae, Centuries, or tribes—and the lower in the social scale, the more crowded were the voting units.

After reading the glowing tribute Polybius has paid to the superiority of the Roman commonwealth and the part the mixed constitution has played in making it superior, one is surprised, at the end of Book VI, to find him placing religion in a position of dominant influence: ". . . the most important difference for the better which the Roman commonwealth appears to me to display

[47] See Plato, *Laws,* Bk. III, 697*a–b.*

[48] See Cicero, *De republica,* Bk. II, Ch. 39. Polybius refers to the vote of the people being taken by tribes. It is believed that there was an integration of, or at least coordination between, the tribes and the Centuries at this time, though the exact method of integration is not known. See Walbank, *A Historical Commentary on Polybius,* Vol. 1, pp. 683–88.

[49] *Histories,* Bk. VI, Ch. 18, p. 474.

[50] See Kurt von Fritz, *The Theory of the Mixed Constitution in Antiquity: A Critical Analysis of Polybius' Political Ideas* (New York: Columbia Univ. Press, 1954); T. R. Glover, in *Cambridge Ancient History,* J. B. Bury, ed. (Cambridge, Eng.: Cambridge Univ. Press, 1930), Vol. 8, pp. 1–24.

is in their religious beliefs. . . . a scrupulous fear of the gods is the very thing which keeps the Roman commonwealth together." Polybius credits religion with the fact that the typical Greek statesman—even if watched by "ten checking clerks" and twice as many witnesses —still manages some graft, while in Rome such behavior is rare. Polybius spoke too soon.

Cicero's treatment of Polybius

As we have seen, Cicero follows a well-established tradition in adopting a sixfold classification of states: he follows Plato and Polybius in discussing the cycle of degeneration of states and he virtually adopts Polybius on the virtue of the mixed constitution. Cicero gives Plato credit for the first two ideas but Polybius gets no credit at all.[51] One explanation may be that, ironically, Polybius the historian is excessively abstract as he shows how one pure form breaks down into another pure form and then introduces the mixed constitution as a remedy for instability. Polybius would have us believe that the mixed constitution, once adopted, is almost unchangeable. Cicero the nonhistorian writing at a time of great turbulence had to account for some of the complications introduced by the process of change. He could scarcely have argued that the mixed constitution is unchangeable; indeed, the mixture itself shifted.[52] This does not necessarily make Cicero a notable realist, for, despite his praise of the Roman system as it was, he introduced briefly in the fragmentary Book V of *De republica* the figure of a rector, a kind of Platonic philosopher-king. Ancient writers who paraphrased Book VI suggest that he is wise, just, and semidivine. As Plato omitted the philosopher-king from the *Laws,* Cicero omitted the rector from *De legibus;* but we cannot help but find in this implication of the need for a Roman savior foreshadowings of subsequent Roman emperors toward whom Cicero could scarcely have felt any affection.

The influence of the idea of the mixed constitution

Both Polybius and Cicero were conservative and both neglected certain sociological facts that made the Roman Republic different in practice than in theory. But structure per se meant less to Cicero than to Polybius, for Cicero saw that his concord of orders would require a popular consensus and that without this no structure could preserve the common good. Perhaps for that very reason Cicero, despite his lack of originality, was tremendously influential: ". . . his historical importance . . . is out of all proportion to the intrinsic significance of his thought."[53] His emphasis is basically moralistic but couched in an attractive literary style. Augustine credited Cicero with winning him to philosophy. John of Salisbury, who apparently had a longer version of *De republica* available to him than is presently extant, relied heavily on Cicero. Cicero was one of Aquinas' staple authorities.[54] Yet Cicero's idea of constitutional division and countervailing checks was not appealing to these writers, who emphasized the analogy between the unity of a single ruling God and

[51] *De republica,* Bk. I, Chs. 28–35, 42–44; *De divinatione,* Bk. II, Ch. 2. Compare Plato, *Republic,* 545^{a}–588^{a}; Aristotle, *Politics,* 1304^{b} 17–1316^{b} 27; Polybius, *Histories,* Bk. VI, Chs. 55–56, Vol. 1, pp. 502–04. See the Introduction to the Sabine and Smith edition of *De republica,* pp. 56–64. There are only two references to Polybius in the text of *De republica:* at Bk. I, Ch. 21, Laelius calls Panaetius and Polybius the two Greeks "most thoroughly versed in political science." He must mean, though he does not say, living Greeks. The second reference is at Bk. IV, Ch. 3, where Scipio notes that "our guest" Polybius has only one criticism of ancient Roman custom, namely that education is treated as a private rather than a public matter. The statement is not found in any of the extant works of Polybius.

[52] Though Cicero certainly muddied the waters a bit —and it is well to remember how much of the original *Republic* is missing—Sabine and Smith seem to exaggerate when they state that Cicero's treatment of Polybius' materials was "confusing" and "a contradiction." With only slight manipulation Cicero's cycle of degeneration can be made to fit Polybius'. Compare Sabine and Smith's chart at p. 58 with Polybius, Bk. VI, Ch. 7.

[53] Cochrane, p. 38.

[54] See Edward K. Rand, *Cicero in the Courtroom of St. Thomas Aquinas* (Milwaukee: Marquette Univ. Press, 1946).

the unity of a single ruling monarch. The dominant medieval political literature consisted of moral advice to kings and princes rather than the proposal of devices to restrain them. In fact, good advice outweighed institutional checks by a heavy margin even in Cicero.

Nevertheless, the idea of the mixed constitution did not die out. The end of the Middle Ages brought a change in Church-state relations, which had served as a vital substitute for explicitly political restraints on monarchical power. This change would undoubtedly have led to new constitutional forms even without the ancient examples, but these examples helped right on down to the American Constitutional Convention. Polybius is referred to only once in *The Federalist,* and then as a source of information rather than as a source of political wisdom, and Cicero is not mentioned at all. But references to Greece and Rome are many, taking their place beside references to the New York and New Jersey state constitutions. And, of course, Montesquieu is given credit for his special contribution to the idea of the mixed constitution. Madison speaks of "the celebrated Montesquieu" as the leading authority on the separation of powers: "If he be not the author of this invaluable precept in the science of politics, he has the merit of at least displaying and remembering it most effectually to the attention of mankind."[55] Montesquieu, in turn, was a great admirer of Cicero. Cicero, he wrote as a youth,

> does not issue precepts to us, but makes us feel them. He does not incite to virtue, but attracts us to it. Reading his works one will become repelled by Seneca and his like forever, men who are more ill than those they seek to cure, more desperate than those they console, more tyrannized by passions than those they wish to liberate from them.[56]

[55] James Madison, *The Federalist,* No. 47 (New York: Random House, Modern Library, n.d.), p. 313.

[56] "Discourse on Cicero," in *Mélanges Inédits,* trans. by William Ebenstein in *Political Thought in Perspective* (New York: McGraw-Hill, 1957), p. 90.

ROMAN LAW, NATURAL LAW, AND THE *JUS GENTIUM*

Roman Law

Like the common law in England, the earliest Roman law was based on custom; the early *leges regiae* (laws of the kings) were largely legendary. The Law of the Twelve Tablets (451–50 B.C.) referred to by Polybius and Cicero was the beginning of written law but there is considerable romance attached even to the Twelve Tablets and the primitive spirit of *lex talionis* was not altogether alien to them. The priestly domination of the law ended shortly after the Twelve Tablets but there was rather little law by legislation for some time. The power of custom was so strong that the *comitia curiae* and the *comitia centuriata* as well as the Senate would seek to accommodate it as much as possible.

Roman law developed mainly through the magistrates called praetors, who were first appointed in 367 B.C. The praetor was a bureaucrat as well as a judge. He promulgated edicts annually, setting forth the rules and principles that would guide his actions in office. The system was flexible but also dangerous—as when Emperor Hadrian in 125 A.D. ordered the jurist Julian to write an edict of rules and procedures that would bind everyone and called it the *Edictum Perpetuum*. The praetors administered the *jus civile,* which consisted of the Twelve Tablets, the rather sparse *leges* of the *comitia centuriata,* an interlarding of custom, and, under the emperors, the *lex de imperio*.[57]

The *jus civile* was administered only to Roman citizens as their exclusive privilege. Foreigners under Roman law therefore created a special problem. The concept of the personality of the law—the idea that people take their own law with them wherever they go—has caused problems in all ages, especially in the late Middle Ages. (Even in the

[57] W. W. Buckland, *A Text-Book of Roman Law from Augustus to Justinian,* 2nd ed. rev. (Cambridge, Eng.: Cambridge Univ. Press, 1950), Ch. 1.

twentieth century the United States has tried to have American soldiers who misbehave abroad tried in American military or civil courts rather than in the domestic courts of the countries in question, but we have not always been successful.) With Rome's expanding trade and commerce, her contacts with foreigners became more extensive and more complicated. On some occasions special courts, with nations of both sides participating, were set up to handle disputes.

Finally, in 247 B.C., Rome created the *praetor peregrinus* especially for foreigners. This praetor began to build up a special body of law called the *jus gentium* (law of the peoples), essentially Roman law minus its formalisms and plus some elements from Babylonian, Phoenician, and Greek law. The *jus civile* continued to be administered by the *praetor urbanis* (praetor for the city). Thus there was in effect a dual system of making wills, holding property, and enforcing laws of delict. The *jus gentium,* it should be stressed, was not international law but Roman law *over* citizens of other lands. Roman citizens could not be tried in the provinces and had to return home for trial—a rule Paul found to his advantage.

The dual system was inefficient and the *jus gentium* sometimes gave foreigners advantages that Roman citizens did not enjoy; so the arrangement eventually fell of its own weight. Separate proceedings were abandoned and the *jus civile* was gradually absorbed into the *jus gentium.* Finally, the Edict of Caracalla (212 A.D.) extended citizenship to all subjects of the Empire and the distinction between the two bodies of law lost significance.

The Natural Law and the *Jus Gentium*

What is of significance to us here is the relationship between the *jus gentium* and the *jus naturale* (law of nature), especially as conceived in Stoic philosophy. The *praetor peregrinus* came from a legal background of rigid codes and little legislation. Now he was confronted with cases involving conflict among widely divergent legal systems and tenets. Judgments based on essential fairness (*aequitas*) seemed an almost inevitable way out. Moreover, without actually setting aside the *jus civile,* the praetor could, in his annual edict, set forth new principles of equity. The wide range of discretion of the praetor led to deeper questions: What is equity? What is justice? Is there a law above the law of man? It is not surprising therefore that many jurists should find inspiration in the words of Cicero:

> reason, when it is full grown and perfected, is rightly called wisdom. Therefore, since there is nothing better than reason, and since it exists both in man and God, the first common possession of man and God is reason. But those who have reason in common must also have right reason in common. And since right reason is Law, we must believe that men have Law also in common with the gods. Further, those who share Law must also share Justice; and those who share these are to be regarded as members of the same commonwealth.[58]

Gaius

During the reign of Marcus Aurelius lived a jurist named Gaius (110?–80?), whose *Institutes*—not discovered until 1816—apparently had a strong influence on that great landmark in law, the *Institutes* of Justinian (533 A.D.), the backbone of the *corpus juris civilis.* Gaius saw an almost perfect identity between the *jus naturale* and the *jus gentium:*

> Every human community that is regulated by laws and customs observes a rule of conduct which in part is peculiar to itself, and in part is common to mankind in general. The rule of conduct which a people has settled for its own observance and which is peculiar to that people is termed *jus civile.* Those principles which natural reason has taught to all mankind are

[58] *De legibus,* Bk. I, Ch. 7, pp. 321–23. See also J. L. Adams, "The Law of Nature in Greco-Roman Thought," *Journal of Religion,* Vol. 25 (1945), pp. 97–118; Ernst Levy, "Natural Law in The Roman Period," *Proceedings,* Natural Law Institute, College of Law, University of Notre Dame, Vol. 2 (1949), pp. 43–72.

equally observed by all, and collectively are termed the *jus gentium.* The Roman Law is consequently in part peculiar to the Romans, and in part common to all mankind.[59]

What natural reason, common to all mankind, tells us may surprise some modern readers: "Slaves are *in potestate* [in the power] of their masters by virtue of the *jus gentium,* for we find that in all nations the life or death of the slave is in the hand of the master, nor can a slave acquire other wise than as agent of his master." Such sentiments do not indicate that Gaius was a simple apologist for slavery, however, for he emphasized that "it is unlawful for a Roman citizen or any one else who is subject to the Romans to inflict severe and unmerited chastisement on his slave." There may be some inconsistency in establishing the right to hold slaves by natural reason and then using natural reason to establish the legitimacy of laws preventing the evil exercise of that right. Nonetheless, we can see how it was possible in a few generations to suggest that slavery itself, even though legal under the *jus gentium,* was contrary to natural reason.

The idea of sovereign authority arising from the people, also found in latent form in Gaius, was quite alien to Greek thinkers. The *leges* passed by the popular assemblies, or the plebiscites of the *plebs,* introduced a sense of law that is made. But if law can be made in that fashion by unlettered *plebs,* is law truly identical with right reason or is it merely will? The problem of reason and will in law, which we will examine in discussing Aquinas in chapter 6, has its roots here.

[59] *Institutes,* Bk. I, Ch. 1, trans. by David Nasmith in *Outlines of Roman History from Romulus to Justinian (Including Translation of the Twelve Tables, The Institutes of Gaius, and the Institutes of Justinian) with Special Reference to the Growth, Development, and Decay of Roman Jurisprudence* (London: Butterworths, 1890), p. 200. Subsequent page references are to this edition. See also *The Institutes of Gaius,* ed. and trans. by Francis deZulcuta (Oxford: Clarendon Press, Vol. 1 [text], 1946; Vol. 2 [commentary], 1953). Some of the legal principles that seemed common to the reason of all mankind in the *jus gentium* were (1) self-defense is legitimate, (2) a contract impossible of fulfillment is not binding, (3) a father cannot sue his son, and (4) a child born out of wedlock is related to the mother only (Levy, *op. cit.*).

Justinian

Information on the development of Roman law between the time of Gaius and Emperor Justinian (483–565) is fragmentary and unreliable. But we know from Justinian's *Digest* (533)—extracts from the most important extant legal writing, with title and author listed—of the work of three great jurists of the third century: Papinian, Paulus, and Ulpian. Justinian also ordered his scholars to put together the *Institutes,* following the outline of Gaius' work of the same name, in 553. It was basically a student's manual of the law. The next year came the *Justinian Code,* an attempt to formulate the law as it stood. Justinian hoped it would be definitive and beyond the need for amendment but in fact it was amended quite often during the next thirty years of his reign. The law came from many sources: the *leges* and *plebiscita* we have already mentioned; the *senatusconsulta,* which technically were only recommendations to the magistrates but which took on the force of law in the late Republic; the edicts of praetors, especially Hadrian's *Edictum Perpetuum;* the statutes of the emperors themselves, which in the second century took such forms as magisterial *edicta,* judicial *decreta,* formal answers to inquiries (*rescripta*), and directives to officials (*mandata*); and finally, under certain circumstances the opinion of learned jurists, their *responsa prudentium,* which came to have the force of law even when offered outside of court.

Ulpian

The largest contributor to the *Digest* was Ulpian (170?–228), whose point of view on the *jus gentium* differed sharply from that of Gaius. According to Ulpian, the *jus gentium* and the *jus naturale* were clearly differentiated. The *jus gentium* was not the direct product of natural reason. It had a definite historical origin and, in Ulpian's view, existed in part because of irrational human conflict, strife, and war. The small crack in the union of the *jus gentium* and the *jus naturale* that appeared when Gaius talked of slavery now seemed to have split wide open. Rather ironically, the indiscriminate eclecticism of Justinian's *Institutes* put Gaius and Ulpian almost side by side under the heading *jus gentium:* one said that the *jus gentium* is "that law which natural reason appoints for all mankind" and the other said that, though slavery exists according to the *jus gentium,* it is "contrary to the law of nature." When the student had memorized both passages he had presumably learned the law![60] The view suggests Seneca's claim that natural reason in its pure form exists only in a state of innocence from which all earthly systems of law are a departure. Ulpian's considerable contribution was neglected for a number of years because of the curt dismissal he received at the hands of the eminent Sir Henry Maine.[61]

The *Institutes* of Justinian opens with two definitions taken directly from the *Rules* of Ulpian: "Justice is the constant and perpetual desire of giving to every man that which is due to him" and "Jurisprudence is the knowledge of things divine and human, and the exact discernment of what is just and unjust."[62] The simple idea of justice as giving every man his due received a definitive critique in Plato's *Republic.* This conception of justice nevertheless appears again and again in the history of law down to the present time. It will probably always be strongly held in individualistically oriented societies, such as Rome and the United States.[63]

CONCLUSION

Rome's gift to the Western world, say an endless parade of scholars, was the orderly majesty of Roman law. Yet the Romans themselves were a most disorderly, lusty, brawling lot. There seems to be a paradox here: Rome took pride in what we now quaintly call civilian rule; Roman legions were by tradition forbidden to enter the city in battle dress. Yet almost all her most prominent leaders were men who had been or still were military commanders. Legal protections were of little avail when Caracalla murdered his brother and then murdered twenty thousand alleged friends of his brother. Emperor Commodus used to demonstrate his prowess at archery by using crippled humans for targets. The assassination of rulers and the slaughter of political enemies were chronic in the century after Marcus Aurelius.[64]

A Britisher once said of Americans that they are "a law-respecting, if not a law-abiding, people." Perhaps the same must be said of the Romans. Perhaps the replacement of the relatively unified *polis* by the manifestly heterogeneous cosmopolis led inexorably to conflict, contention, and disorder,

[60] It must be said that for Ulpian the *jus gentium* was not simply evil because it provided for slavery; for him it was good as well because it also provided for the manumission of slaves.

[61] *Ancient Law,* fifth ed. (London: Murray, 1873), p. 50. Ulpian also received a curt dismissal at the hands of the Guard of Emperor Alexander Severus: he was murdered in 228. The law may have been orderly but the law-makers were not. Ulpian's predecessor Papinian was beheaded by Caracalla because he refused to provide a legal justification for the killing of Caracalla's brother Geta. Caracalla's father—who lied, killed, and bribed his way to the throne—was to be the last emperor for eighty years to die in bed.

[62] An excellent brief discussion of later Roman jurisprudence is found in Charles H. MacIlwain, *The Growth of Political Thought in the West* (New York: Macmillan, 1932), Ch. 4.

[63] See *The Federalist,* No. 51. See also Edward S. Corwin, *The 'Higher Law' Background of American Constitutional Law* (Ithaca: Cornell Univ. Press, 1955), pp. 16–18. Judith Shklar wrote, "It is not true that 'giving each man his due' is a totally meaningless formula; it implies a precise end, it aims at a certain type of character. It is only meaningless as a prescription for specific actions" (*Legalism* [Cambridge, Mass.: Harvard Univ. Press, 1964], p. 115). For an interesting comparison of Stoic and nineteenth-century liberal ideals see William D. Grampp, "The Moral Hero and The Economic Man," *Ethics,* Vol. 61 (1951), pp. 136–50.

[64] See Edward Gibbon, *Decline and Fall of the Roman Empire,* J. B. Bury, ed. (New York: Heritage Press, 1946), Vol. 1, Chs. 4–6.

which could be controlled only by force or litigation. A litigious society tends to be one in which values are heterogeneous and privatized. Legal process becomes a substitute for absent ties of communal feeling and custom. Thus the veneration of law was a product of the *polis* and law, itself a product of politics, became a buffer against politics as raw power. This paradox, too, is familiar to twentieth-century Americans.

The Stoic philosophers heightened the paradox by making law the emanation of a beneficent and divine nature. Their glorification of law paralleled their disillusionment with the harsh realities of Roman politics and suggests that they may have looked upon the apolitical Epicureans with envy as well as hostility. The universal community of the Stoics was in fact a political conception, for it was not based upon race, or religion, or economics, or anything other than common personality and common citizenship. But, insofar as law meant morality and politics meant power to the Stoics, it was described in legal rather than political language. This wistful separation of law and politics has characterized the thinking of natural lawyers down to the present day.[65]

[65] Though legal positivists, in opposition to natural lawyers, find legal rules within the power structure rather than outside it, the two camps share the passion for rule-following that Mrs. Shklar calls the ideology of legalism: "Either rules for their own protection must be magically lifted out of politics, or society itself must be made safe for justice by imposing a unity upon it which will make possible a consistent policy of justice according to universally accepted rules. The first is the positivist program, the second that of natural law. Both are equally legalistic."

5

AUGUSTINE

A man notable for the intensity of his religious convictions, Augustine cannot be said to have cared much about politics for its own sake—or even politics for the sake of the good life. Politics for the sake of God? Yes, but Augustine would have thought the emphasis strange. He is not a primary political theorist, but rather a theologian so powerful that his view of man touched almost every subsequent Western political theorist and a spokesman for the Church in the moment when it irreversibly came to terms with the political.

LIFE

Aurelius Augustinus was born November 13, 354, in the North African town of Tagaste in Numidia. Tagaste is today called Souk-Ahras and Numidia was what today is the northeast part of Algeria. Augustine was thus a Berber (from the Roman *barbari,* almost barbarian). In marked contrast to its barren state today, the area of Augustine's birthplace was then rather richly endowed with agricultural wealth. The Numidians spoke their own language, one similar to ancient Egyptian, but in the better class homes, such as Augustine's, Latin was spoken.

Augustine's mother Monica—in the ancient manuscripts "Monnica"—was a Christian but his father, Patricius, who was a member of the town council, was not. Patricius was rather indifferent to religion and Monica was no ordinary Christian. Her piety and persistence were such that before her life ended she had converted not only her son but her husband. In time she gained such a reputation that the Church elevated her to sainthood.

In North Africa generally Christianity seemed to be gaining and paganism declining. The area was noted for its Christian martyrs. At the end of the second century Christians in Scilli and Madauros had been beheaded for refusing to renounce Christ and shrines to these and other martyrs dotted the landscape. The African Christian Church was organizationally strong. The Conference at Carthage in 411 produced six hundred bishops. The Church was, however, plagued with factional and doctrinal difficulties: there were Pelagians, and Donatists, and the non-Christian Manicheans, all of whom we will discuss later, since much of Augustine's polemical energy had to be directed toward meeting their arguments.

Augustine studied under a *litterator* in Tagaste, then went south to study grammar in Madaura. But he was forced to spend one year in idleness in Tagaste when his parents could not afford to continue his education; this suggests that, though his parents were civic leaders, they were not members of the wealthy elite. But after his father died, a wealthy friend and benefactor, Romanianus, sent Augustine to Carthage for the third phase of his education, *rhetoric,* or the arts of eloquence and persuasion in the Latin of Cicero, which even by the fourth century had become a classical language.

In 374 Augustine returned from Carthage to Tagaste to teach grammar. He brought with him his "common-law wife" and a two-year-old son. Because he had become a catechumen (*auditor*) of the Manichean sect, his mother would not let him enter her house.

Before returning to Tagaste, Augustine had read and had been greatly impressed by the celebration of philosophy and the philosophic way of life in Cicero's *Hortensius.* In the game of chronicling philosophic influences from age to age authorities have probably exaggerated the impact of this work on Augustine; for one thing, the work is not intrinsically weighty enough to make a dramatic impact. But Augustine does speak of it in the *Confessions* and it is no doubt symbolic of his changing interests. Now, after returning to Tagaste, he read Aristotle's *Categories.* He was beginning to be troubled by discrepancies in the Manichean doctrine and confronted a supposedly learned Manichean bishop with them. He was amazed at the bishop's ignorance, although he admired the honesty with which the bishop admitted it. Dismayed also by the low quality of his rowdy students, he left for Rome, leaving his protesting mother behind.

In Rome Augustine struggled with ill health, gnawing doubts about the Manichean view of life, and poor success as a teacher. He broke with Manicheism and sympathetically studied the Skeptics. In 384 he heard of a position as teacher of rhetoric in Milan, applied to the Roman authorities, and won the post. Milan was a center of Neo-Platonic philosophy and also the see of the famous bishop, Ambrose. Augustine met Ambrose and heard some of his sermons but he was not yet ready to embrace the Christian faith. The success, financial and otherwise, he enjoyed in Milan brought a parade of his friends, relatives, and former students from North Africa: his mother, his brother, his mistress—who is never named in the *Confessions*—his son Adeodatus, his most devoted disciple Alypius, Romanianus, and several others. His mother wanted him to marry but apparently marrying the mother of his son was out of the question: "The woman with whom I was in the habit of sleeping was torn from my side on the grounds of being an impediment to my marriage, and my heart, which clung to her, was broken and wounded and dropping blood."[1] Leaving the brilliant Adeodatus behind with his father, the unfortunate woman returned to Africa after vowing never to cohabit with another man. But the more proper girl to whom Augustine had pledged his troth was not yet of marriageable age, so, "since I was not so much a lover of marriage as a slave to lust," he took another mistress. That sexual desire plays such an important role in Augustine's theology is, we can see, not irrelevant to his own experience.

The dramatic high point of the *Confessions* comes at its center—at the end of Book VIII, where Augustine tells of his inner anguish as he is wrestling with the decision to turn his back on his lustful life. Overcome with weeping, he leaves his friend Alypius and goes into a garden. "Suddenly a voice reaches my ears from a nearby house. It is the voice of a boy or a girl (I don't know which) and in a kind of singsong the words are constantly repeated: 'Take it and read it. Take it and read it (*Tolle lege*).'" Going

[1] *Confessions,* Bk. VI, Ch. 15, trans. by Rex Warner (New York: New American Library, Mentor, 1963), pp. 132–33. There are countless translations of the *Confessions* but this new one is especially felicitous. Subsequent quotations are from this edition.

into the house, he took the Bible and read the first passage to strike his eye—in the writings of Paul, which Augustine had been reading earlier: "Not in rioting and drunkenness, not in chambering and wantonness, not in strife and envying, but put ye on the Lord Jesus Christ, and make not provision for the flesh in concupiscence."[2] Augustine does not claim, as some of his overzealous interpreters have, that the voice of the child was the voice of God. But he took the whole incident as a divine command and from this point on was a changed person. In April, 387, he, Adeodatus, and Alypius were baptized by Ambrose.

Augustine's conversion was not an isolated, melodramatic event. It was very much a consequence of the mental activity involved in coming to a rejection of skepticism and materialism. In preparing for baptism, he had retired to a country villa, where he discussed religion and philosophy with his friends. Because of this experience and, no doubt, because of the Platonic influence generally, the early Augustinian writings were in dialogue form. Perhaps the best example is *De magistro* (*On the Teacher*), written in 389, which purports to be a discussion with his son and is apparently fairly close to an actual discussion. The strictly biographical narrative in the *Confessions*—which is followed by the theological reflections of Books IX–XIII—ends with the death of Monica at Ostia, near Rome, as the clan heads back to North Africa for a new life. It was not until 1946 that archeologists confirmed that Monica had indeed been buried in Ostia.

Augustine went back to Tagaste, liquidated his father's estate, founded a convent, and suffered through the death of his only son. In 391, as Augustine traveled to Hippo Regius to attempt to convert a rich man, Bishop Valerius ordained him a priest. The same year Augustine founded a second monastery, which Alypius entered and from which Alypius was appointed Bishop of Tagaste in 394. Two years after this, Valerius, the overworked and ailing Bishop of Hippo, appointed Augustine to share his bishopric. At his death in 395 or 396, Augustine succeeded him.

Though one would not imagine it when examining the huge outpouring of writings in the Augustinian corpus, Augustine's life was a life of intense activity. "Like so many gifted men, Augustine was a complex character, a strange compendium of tenderness and inflexibility."[3] Part of his saintliness came in the sacrifices made for his multileveled flock. As bishop he had heavy administrative duties, though he disliked them intensely and eventually turned them over to an assistant. He performed as pastor to the large urban church of Hippo; he was rector of a seminary out of which ten bishops were eventually to come; he traveled much and preached much. The extent of the battles with Manicheism and Donatism were such that Augustine became well known to ecclesiastics throughout the Mediterranean world. In 411 he played a leading role in the Conference at Carthage that condemned the Donatists and in 426, at a rather advanced age, traveled to Milevis to arbitrate a bitter dispute over the issue of a new bishop for that place. On his return to Hippo he finished *De Civitate Dei* (*The City of God*) and gave the bishopric to his coadjutor, Heraclius. In 430 the Roman army, retreating from the invading Vandals, took refuge in Hippo. Augustine died on August 28, 430, as the Vandals laid siege to the city.

THE POLITICAL–THEOLOGICAL SITUATION

The Empire

In the year 313 the Emperor Constantine issued the Edict of Milan, ending years of persecution of Christians, most notably in the recent past under Diocletian. The sig-

[2] Rom. 13:13–14.

[3] F. van der Meer, *Augustine the Bishop,* trans. by B. Battershaw and G. R. Lamb (New York: Sheed & Ward, 1961), p. XVIII.

nificance of the Edict was perhaps more political than religious, for it culminated an era in which a policy of persecution seemed increasingly inexpedient and in which there had been an increasing, if ambivalent, tendency for Roman authority to seek Christian support. The Edict was, by common judgment, a great landmark of toleration: it guaranteed the right of all men to profess their faith, free of state interference or disabilities; it further asserted that others should not prevent a person from discharging the obligations of his religion, thus, in effect, promising freedom of worship and assembly; it restored lands and buildings confiscated during the earlier persecutions; finally, it recognized the Church as a legal corporation. In a way, this implied more than merely a tacit blessing given to Christianity, for it meant the abandonment of the long and deep-seated policy of state control of the spiritual life. Despite the differing interests and aims of Emperors Julian ("The Apostate") and Valentinian, the new hands-off policy remained until the accession of Theodosius in 378.

The shock of Christian legitimacy was as great to the Church as it was to the Empire —not that Constantine himself saw or much cared about the long-range consequences of this method of dealing with a difficult practical problem. Christianity was Constantine's own religion and, while in theory this did not make Christianity an official state religion, the distinction was often hard to draw. He carried the anomalous pagan title *Pontifex Maximus* and was not averse to using it to invalidate the tolerant implications of the Edict of Milan. As Cochrane points out, pagan sects were ruthlessly suppressed and their temples reconsecrated as Christian churches. When, on Constantine's twentieth anniversary, the Church of the Holy Sepulcher was dedicated in Jerusalem, Jews who had tried to rebuild the Temple had their ears cut off or were flogged to death by public authorities.[4] Eusebius of Caesarea was a kind of official theologican to Constantine. With his rhetorical skills he could make the building of the Jerusalem church sound like the fulfillment of all prophecy and make the future Day of Judgment appear a minor matter. Such trends posed a serious threat that Christianity would become merely a success philosophy.

But the Church found itself stronger than it might have imagined in the great Council at Nicaea in 325, when 318 bishops assembled to settle credal and disciplinary matters. The result was the theological squashing of the followers of Arius and the formulation of the Nicene Creed, the great charter of Christian doctrine. But, unfortunately, Constantine, in characteristic fashion, set out with a vengeance to fulfill the implications of the condemnation of the Arians as he understood them, decreeing that all of Arius' books be burned and that those possessing them and refusing to add their bit of fuel to the flames be put to death.

Arianism

Arius, a deacon and presbyter of Alexandria, was condemned and deposed in 320 by his bishop for defective christological views. This ignited a major doctrinal crisis in the Church. Within a short time writers began to choose sides. God, Arius argued, is the begetter of all things and hence must Himself be unbegotten, an uncreated Creator. His essence is eternal and unchangeable. All that is created, or begotten—Son, Logos, Wisdom —must be less than this. The Son has divine qualities and stands in a special relation of grace with the Father, a status unlike any other creature's. But still He is a creature, a human body into which God's spirit has come. Most prominent among the critics of Arius and his predecessors was Athanasius, whose doctrine, to put the matter most simply, was that God Himself had entered into humanity and that Christ is "very God," as is the Holy Spirit. (Arius had put the Holy Spirit in a position subordinate to the Son.)[5]

[4] Charles N. Cochrane, *Christianity and Classical Culture* (New York: Oxford Univ. Press, 1944), p. 208.

[5] For a nineteenth-century liberal exposition of these doctrinal disputes, see Adolf Harnack, *Outlines of the*

At the Council of Nicaea (325), with Athanasius in attendance, the Arian formulas were specifically condemned and Arius and a few others were excommunicated. But this by no means ended the substance of the debate. Lest it seem to the twentieth-century mind that many issues of this time were of needless and irrelevant subtlety, it must be remembered that the threat of relapse into pagan polytheism was omnipresent and that in trying to adapt the faith without destroying it the Church was faced with a formidable task. The Arians believed that monotheism itself was in danger of being lost.[6] Even after the Council of Nicaea, Arians were able to depose some of the orthodox bishops, including Athanasius, and in the East, thanks in part to Emperor Constantius, Arianism came close to being a state religion. But after the death of Valens (378) the Creed became acceptable to the East, for Emperor Theodosius became the protector—indeed, the too zealous protector—of orthodoxy.

The leaders of the younger adherents of Nicaea were the three great Cappadocians: Basil the Great of Caesarea, Gregory of Nazianzus, and Gregory of Nyssa. They collectively put on the mantle of Athanasius. Yet it remained for Augustine, almost a century after the Council of Nicaea, to provide what the Church has regarded as the definitive answer to the Arians in his *De Trinitate,* a course delicately steered "between the scylla of Sabellianism and the charybdis of Arianism."[7]

Manicheism

Mani, a Babylonian prophet of the third century,[8] rejected the Christian idea of sin and saw the world as a struggle between two kingdoms and two gods: the kingdom of light ruled by the Father of Greatness, an underived being, and the kingdom of darkness ruled by a devil. Both light and darkness were conceived of as matter. Human individuals tended to become but the inert playground of these two contending forces. Jesus was hailed by the Manicheans as the guide of souls and, perhaps inconsistently, as a man in appearance only and Mani was regarded as the Paraclete promised by Jesus. The elect of the sect took three vows: (1) no meat, wine, or impure words; (2) no menial labor; (3) no marriage. The *auditores,* such as Augustine, were obliged only to keep the Ten Commandments.[9]

Augustine was attracted to Manicheism initially because the sect rejected what later would become the central Augustinian theme,

---

History of Dogma, trans. by E. K. Mitchell (Boston: Beacon Press, 1957), pp. 242–53. This is the one-volume version of Harnack's massive *History of Dogma* in seven volumes. For Catholic interpretations, see Karl Bihlmeyer, *Church History,* 13th ed., trans. by V. E. Mills (Westminster, Md.: Newman Press, 1958), Vol. 1, pp. 46–48, and Etienne Gilson, *The Christian Philosophy of St. Augustine,* trans. by L. E. M. Lynch (New York: Random House, 1960). For a Protestant view, see Cochrane, pp. 231–60.

[6] Their targets were Origenists, a label drawn from the reputation of Origen (185–250) as one who surreptitiously transformed Christian religion into Greek philosophy. Origenists were accused of Sabellianism (after Sabellius of Lybia and Rome), or Modal Monarchism, whereby the Trinity was seen as merely three different modes, or masks (*personae*), or roles played by the one God. Sabellianism would seem to the distant observer to be quite compatible with the Arians' view but the Arians did not see it that way; they claimed that the language of three was still there and still wrong. Hence Arianism has been called the heresy of common sense, the simple belief that one thing cannot be three things. See H. M. Gwatkin, *Cambridge Medieval History,* H. M. Gwatkin and J. P. Whitney, eds. (New York: Macmillan, 1911), Vol. 1, p. 119.

[7] Van der Meer, p. 425.

[8] Mani died a cruel and colorful death. In 275 the Persian king flayed him alive, then beheaded him, then stuffed his skin with straw and hung the remains from a gibbet. Some sources, however, say he was crucified. In any case it was clear that the priests of the Mazdhan religion had their reservations about him.

[9] The sect had one head, twelve teachers, seventy-two bishops, and many priests and deacons. They believed in prayer and fasting, observed a kind of baptism and Lord's Supper, and had one big yearly feast to celebrate Mani's execution and ascension into heaven. They expected a cataclysmic conflagration to consume the earth—the fire would last 1,468 years—after which light and darkness would be forever separated. Sometimes called the Persian Gnosis, the sect shared with Western Gnosticism a belief in esoteric modes of illumination and in a radical dualism. Unlike Western Gnosticism, however, its dualism was materialistic at both poles.

namely the view that belief must precede understanding. Manicheans claimed to have objective truth that could be demonstrated to all who would listen. But after nine years as an *auditor,* Augustine concluded that the Manicheans started with an assertion of belief just as much as the Christians did. The Christians admitted their prerational belief and were, he felt, more honest.[10]

Donatism

In technical language, the Donatists were schismatics rather than heretics. But they caused the fourth-century Church as much trouble as any group of heretics. The origin of the Donatist schism was mixed up with a complicated set of personal quarrels that need not detain us here. The practical consequence was the establishment of an independent North African Church with its own set of bishops, led, after 313, by Donatus "The Great," who for more than forty years was the schismatic Bishop of Carthage. The more fanatic Donatists joined marauding bands called Circumcellions, who, shouting their battle-cry, *"Deo laudes,"* wantonly attacked persons, homes, and churches. Emperor Constans tried repression; Emperor Julian, having restored paganism, tried toleration. At the end of the century, Emperor Theodosius and his sons issued edict after edict against the Donatists to little avail. In the third quarter of the century it had seemed that the schism would be dissipated by the proliferation of little factions within the bigger faction but this did not happen, partly because there were strong African nationalistic and anti-Roman sentiments as well as religious feelings behind the movement for an independent North African Church. This, of course, explains why the Emperors were as concerned as the Church itself to stamp out Donatism. When Augustine became a priest and later a bishop in the 390s, the sect was as strong as ever.

The theoretical issue that makes this movement interesting concerned the purity of the Church. Under the persecutions of the Christians by Diocletian at the beginning of the fourth century there had been priests who had failed to live up to the call of martyrdom and had surrendered scriptural writings to the state authorities. The Donatists claimed that such traitors to the cause of Christ were unfit to serve as priests and that sacraments served by them would be inefficacious. Into the fifth century the Donatists practiced the rebaptism of those who had been baptized by priests regarded as unworthy. This, to Augustine, was a great sacrilege, for to him, and to orthodoxy generally, the Church had authority not because of the moral superiority of individual members—indeed his understanding of sin precluded anyone from being as pure as the Donatists claimed to be—but because the unity, holiness, catholicity, and apostolicity of the Church as an institution were sufficient to make valid agents of less than perfect mortals. The blasphemy implied in the Donatist position, he thought, was the categorical assurance with which they separated the good from the wicked. Such a consequential division, turning on an evaluation of the innermost secrets of the heart, must be left to God on the Day of Judgment and not usurped by fallible, sinful man.

Theologically, the Donatists were crushed by Augustine's numerous and forceful writings directed against them. These writings were friendly and deferential in tone but full of the arts of rhetoric that Augustine had learned as a youth. Organizationally the Donatist Church was crushed at the bishops' Conference at Carthage in 411. We shall examine the consequences of the Donatist stimulus to Augustine's political thought in due course.

Pelagianism

Arianism in the East; Donatism in Africa; and out of the West came Pelagianism. Pe-

[10] See *Confessions,* Bk. VI, Ch. 5; Prosper Alfaric, *L'evolution intellectuelle de Saint Augustin,* Vol. 1, *Du manichéisme au néoplatonisme* (Paris: Nourry, 1918); Bihlmeyer, Vol. 1, sec. 31; and John J. O'Meara, *The Young Augustine* (New York: Alba House, 1965), Ch. 4.

lagius was a British monk, though not a priest, who came to Rome at the end of the fourth century and wrote a commentary on the Epistles of Paul. He argued that humans, being untainted by Adam's fall, are not compelled to sin. The fall, in his view, had greater consequences for Adam than for the rest of us. His was a moralistic humanism of sorts, with some overtones of legalism, declaring that obedience to God's Commandments as expressed in the Scriptures was not only within the capacity of unaided humans but also sufficient for salvation.

When the Visigoths attacked Rome, Pelagius went to Carthage. But before the bishops' Conference at Carthage met in 411, he had departed for Palestine. Nevertheless, he and a cohort, Coelestius, were condemned by this synod for seven errors of doctrine, the essence of which is summarized above. This defeat of Pelagianism, though seemingly irreversible, was not sufficient to obviate a protracted and energetic debate in which Augustine (for orthodoxy) and Julian of Eklanum (for Pelagianism) became the leading protagonists. Pelagianism stressed reason, moderation, and the individual's responsibility for his own defects. Its thesis that the grace of God is bestowed only according to merit and with the regularity of law rendered the doctrine of grace largely superfluous; Pelagians tended to regard this doctrine as a crutch for Christians. "Pelagianism is Christian rationalism, consistently developed under the influence of Hellenic monasticism; it is stoic and Aristotelian popularized Occidental philosophy, which made the attempt to subordinate to itself the traditional doctrine of redemption."[11]

The last years of Augustine's life were consumed by the Pelagian controversy. He tried to show that the sin of Adam affected his descendants by propagation as well as by imitation.[12] He argued that grace is found not in the external fulfillment of the law but in the inner sanctification of the will.[13] In attacking Pelagius' now lost *De natura,* Augustine said that grace did not come to men because of their merits but as a free gift of God.[14] In his last writings on the Pelagian question, Augustine became so insistent on these themes that he made man seem hopelessly lost and God wholly arbitrary; his exegesis of scriptural passages declaring God's will that all men be saved seemed strained.[15] After Augustine's death, his friend Hilary and Prosper of Aquitaine kept up the anti-Pelagian assault but in somewhat softened tones. And without much comprehension of the issue, the Churchmen of the East did the pope a favor and condemned Pelagianism at a Council in Ephesus in 431.

WORKS

The Augustinian corpus is huge: it includes some three hundred and fifty treatises of one kind or another, five hundred sermons, and another two hundred extant letters. Even now there is not a complete translation into English of all Augustine's writings. Virtually all of them were written as a means of dealing with pressing or emergent political-theological-ecclesiastical crises and this urgency of mood clearly colored Augustine's style, probably for the better. The only significant exception to his polemical orientation was *De Trinitate* (*On the Trinity*), composed from

[11] Harnack, p. 364.

[12] *De peccatorum meritis et remissione* (*Of Sin Rewarded and Remitted,* 412). Augustine, however, still sees sin primarily as disobedience. See Ch. 2, sec. 35.

[13] *De spiritu et littera* (*On the Spirit and the Letter,* 412).

[14] *De natura et gratia* (*On Nature and Grace,* 415).

[15] For example, I Timothy 2:4, dealt with in *De correptione et gratia* (*On Reproof and Grace,* 426–27), Ch. 14, sec. 44. Other works of this period are *De gratia et libero arbitrio* (*On Grace and Freedom of Choice,* 426–27), *De praedestinatione sanctorum* (*On Holy Predestination,* 428–29), and *De dono perseverantiae* (*On the Gift of Perseverance,* 428–29). See Philip Schaff, ed., *A Select Library of the Nicene and Post-Nicene Fathers of the Christian Church,* Vol. 5, *Saint Augustin: Anti-Pelagian Writings* (Buffalo: Christian Literature, 1886–88). The eight volumes in this series that are devoted to Augustine constitute one of the best sources for English translations of Augustine's major works.

400 to 416 between rather than during controversies.

The lack of time for reflection makes all the more remarkable the degree of consistency maintained throughout the works. To be sure, Augustine's views on the punishment of heretics by the state changed, as we shall see; the Pelagian controversy made his doctrine of grace more rigid, as we have seen; and, as he grew older, he shared less of the Platonists' metaphysical bias. But most of the other threads of thought remain untangled.

Augustine's writings can be called a synthesis of classical and Biblical modes of understanding but "synthesis" suggests an architectonic structure quite alien to Augustine's temper. Aquinas was a system-builder but Augustine was not. He was rarely dogmatic —in the modern meaning of the term. His approach to knowledge is more psychological than ontological. His writing style is intensely personal and full of modest disclaimers: in the *Confessions* he writes, "Personally, I would rather say 'I don't know' when I don't know than make that kind of reply which brings ridicule on someone who has asked a deep question and wins praise for an inaccurate answer." His writings were personal in two senses: he talked about himself and spoke directly to the reader and he was interested in the theoretical problem of the person. Of the second we shall have more to say later.

The works of Augustine may conveniently be put into seven categories. The first would be his particularly devotional or biographical works—an imprecise though useful category. The two *Soliloquies* (387), the first things written after his conversion, deal with the problem of the relation of faith to reason in the form of a long opening prayer and a dialogue between Reason and Augustine, which reveal the doubts and confusions of Augustine's mind at this time along with his utter honesty.

The world-famous *Confessions* (397–400), half biography and half theology, is also devotional in spirit. No doubt to the disappointment of some paperback-book buyers, it is primarily a prayer of confession, though it is also a prayer of thanksgiving and a prayer of petition: "I pray that it may be pleasing in the sight of your mercy that I may find grace before you so that the inner secrets of your words may be laid open to me when I knock." At one point in Augustinian scholarship, in the early days of this century, some claimed that the actual conversion of 386, being far more a conversion to Platonism than to Christianity, was not as it was described in the *Confessions*. (Philosophic conversions had more in common with religious conversions in those days than they would today.) But the bulk of more recent scholars have defended the traditional view that, though Augustine certainly saw a sharper conflict between Platonism and Christianity later in his life than he did in 386, the conversion is accurately represented in the *Confessions*.[16]

At the other end of Augustine's life is the so-called *Enchiridion,* or handbook for the faithful, written in response to the request of a friend and actually titled *To Laurentianus on Faith, Hope, and Charity* (421). It is striking that the Platonic idea of evil as negation, the assumption that being itself is good, remains firm from the *Soliloquies* in 387 to the *Enchiridion* in 421. A final member of this category, though of a somewhat different order, might be the *Retractations* (426), a retrospective listing and commentary on all Augustine's writings—at least all that Augustine could remember. This has proved invaluable to scholars interested in the problems of dating manuscripts.

In the second category may be put those early writings reflective of Augustine's youth-

[16] See the discussion of this recent scholarly controversy in John O'Meara's Introduction to his translation of *Contra academicos,* Vol. 12, in *Ancient Christian Writers* (Westminster, Md.: Newman Press, 1951), pp. 18–22. The contention that religious experiences might be deliberately distorted for subsidiary purposes is not wholly unreasonable: "Lying was never an ecclesiastical offense, and rigid veracity cannot be claimed as a constant characteristic of any Christian writer of the period except Athanasius, Augustine, and (outside his panegyrics) Eusebius of Caesarea" (H. F. Stewart, *Cambridge Medieval History,* Vol. 1, p. 571).

ful attempt to assimilate Platonism: *De beata vita, Contra academicos, De ordine*—the three Cassiciacum dialogues. The *Soliloquies* might well fit here, too. The dialogues deal with wisdom and its relation to the happy life, attempts to refute academic Skepticism, and the problem of evil; two lesser works of the time deal with immortality. In 386 Augustine read Plotinus' *On Beauty* and Porphyry's *Return of the Soul.* Both works seem to have influenced him deeply but this, too, has been subject to scholarly controversy.[17]

Of the same genre but superior in quality and influence are *De magistro,* 389, *De libero arbitrio* (*On Freedom of Choice,* 388–95), and *De doctrina Christiana* (*On Christian Instruction,* 397 and, Bk. IV, 426). The first, in the form of a dialogue between Augustine and his son Adeodatus, examines the theory of knowledge, especially with reference to the function of language. The second, one of Augustine's greatest works, takes up in brief compass a whole range of the most difficult theological problems: the nature of evil, the relation of reason to faith, how God's foreknowledge can be reconciled with man's free will, how sin operates in relation to human will, and so on. *De doctrina Christiana* deals, in the first three books, with the meaning of historical records, especially the scriptural record, and how instruction in knowledge about must be distinguished from genuine learning, or knowledge of.

The third category consists of Augustine's anti-Manichean writings, including *De moribus Ecclesiae Catholicae* (*On the Morals of the Catholic Church,* 388); *De utilitate credendi* (*On the Utility of Belief,* 391), and *De natura boni* (*On the Nature of the Good,* 404). The fourth category consists of Augustine's anti-Donatist writings, ranging from *Contra epistulam Parmeniani* (*Against the Letters of Parmeniani,* 398) to *Contra Guadentium* (*Against Guadentium,* 420).

The fifth category consists of one work, *De Trinitate,* 400–16, the exception that can be called anti-Arian but which contains some of the most original of Augustine's thought. It will be examined later, as will the other work that deserves its own category, namely *De Civitate Dei,* which was written, as he makes clear in Book I, as a response to the sacking of Rome in 410 by Alaric and his Goths, in particular as a response to the many disheartened, demoralized persons who felt that civilization was now going under and that the Roman adoption of the soft religion of Christ had been responsible. In the seventh category are the anti-Pelagian writings already discussed.[18]

POLITICS AS THEOLOGY

The foregoing classification of Augustine's writings and the sketch of heretical movements that occasioned their creation help us see more forcefully the truth of the assertion that began our chapter: Augustine's political thought is but an aspect of his theology. We can see this in another way—and see it we must if we are to understand Augustine—by summarizing quite simply his political conclusions and then trying to explain his justification for them:

(1) Coercive government is a necessary consequence of man's inherently sinful condition.

(2) Coercive government is ordained by God and is to be obeyed except when the true worship of God is jeopardized.

(3) Peace and order rather than justice

[17] In 1933 Theiler claimed Augustine got almost everything from Porphyry; in 1934 Henry claimed Porphyry had no influence at all on Augustine. Most scholars are, as usual, inclined to think the truth lies somewhere in between. See O'Meara's summary of this controversy in the Introduction to his translation of *Contra academicos,* pp. 22–23 and also his *Young Augustine,* Ch. 9. Augustine himself may be consulted on the matter in the *Confessions,* Bk. VII, Chs. 20–21 and *De civitate Dei,* Bk. X, Chs. 23–32.

[18] For a listing of all major works see Hugh Pope, *St. Augustine of Hippo* (London: Longmans, Green, 1954), Ch. 9. For discussion of specific works in groupings similar to the above, see Roy Battenhouse, ed., *A Companion to St. Augustine* (New York: Oxford, 1955)

are the chief criteria of efficacious government.

(4) The necessity of government is not diminished by its impurity.

(5) The dictate of peace does not preclude a just, or "righteous," war, for the pacifism of Matthew 5:39 applies to individual martyrs, not to states.

(6) Even though the marks of salvation are internal and not external, government may rightftully restrain heretics. This tenet emerged in the later writings of Augustine.

We can see that the necessity of coercive government (1) implies as a corollary the obligation to obey coercive government (2). We can also see that the priority of peace and order over justice (3) implies as a corollary the acceptance of impurity in government (4). Tenets 5 and 6 relate to special cases of the exercise of governmental power, international conflict, and religious orthodoxy.

Underlying these propositions is a delicate balance of political realism and otherworldiness. Augustine accepted, as the early Church did not, the fact that the end of the earth was probably not imminent and hence political skills and organization were relevant to the Christian life. Gone were the interim ethics of the primitive Christian community. Constantine, whatever his motives, had made Christianity an approved religion and, though Augustine undoubtedly had some reservations about certain usages of Roman power, by and large he accepted this development and even welcomed it, especially when the barbarians began pounding on the door of Christendom. On one hand, he deliberately drew a clear distinction between the desirable martyrdom of individuals and the undesirable martyrdom of worthy institutions. On the other hand, he could never sanctify the powers, passions, and material interests associated with politics as being of ultimate worth. Complete human fulfillment could come not with success and glory in this life but only with the beatitude of the next life.

Yet how can the value of historical existence, now threatened by the barbarian hordes, be measured against the value of eternal felicity? How can one live in the world without giving oneself up to the corrupted values of the world? The tension between these two poles tugged at Augustine's own psyche and stamped his theology. The two cities, the City of God (*Civitas Dei*) and the City of the Earth (*Civitas terrena*) became the symbols of this duality. The metaphors were not new but Augustine gave them a new richness. Both cities are invisible, for their bond of membership resides in the recesses of the human heart. In one case the chief loyalty is to God and things eternal; in the other the chief loyalty is to self and things temporal. Though the credentials of membership are secret, the fruits of membership are evident. In one case they are peace, order, forgiveness, and love (*caritas*); in the other they are violence, vengeance, degradation, and lust (*cupiditas*). Augustine's anguished eye beheld a world where the latter seemed to overwhelm the former and he sadly concluded that membership in the City of God was highly restricted and membership in the City of the Earth was very extensive indeed.

Augustine's unvarnished—some would say jaundiced—look at the human condition left him little basis for optimism. That the human race had been condemned in its origin seemed to him proved by man's

> love of so many vain and hurtful things, which produces gnawing cares, disquiet, griefs, fears, wild joys, quarrels, lawsuits, wars, treasons, angers, hatreds, deceit, flattery, fraud, theft, robbery, perfidy, pride, ambition, envy, murders, parricides, cruelty, ferocity, wickedness, luxury, insolence, impudence, shamelessness, fornications, adulteries, incests, and the numberless uncleannesses and unnatural acts of both sexes, which it is shameful so much as to mention; sacrileges, heresies, blasphemies, perjuries, oppression of the innocent, calumnies, plots, falsehoods, false witnessings, unrighteous judgments, violent deeds, plunderings, and whatever similar wickedness has found its way into the lives of men.[19]

[19] *De Civitate Dei*, Bk. XXII, Ch. 22, trans. by Marcus Dods (New York: Random House, Modern Library,

Not a pretty picture. But to Augustine it is the way life is and, because this is the way life is, "the human race is restrained by law and instruction, which keep guard against the ignorance that besets us, and oppose the assaults of vice, but are themselves full of labour and sorrow."

Above all this, however, stands God in His glory, perfect and exalted. Sometimes He appears as a Neo-Platonic God:

> The Supreme Good beyond all others is God. It is thereby unchangeable good, truly eternal, truly immortal. All other good things derive their origin from him but are not part of him. That which is part of him is as he is, but the things he has created are not as he is. Hence if he alone is unchangeable, all things that he created are changeable because he made them of nothing. . . . all good things throughout all the ranks of being, whether great or small, can derive their being only from God. Every natural being, so far as it is such, is good.[20]

Sometimes this Neo-Platonic God is described in imagery befitting the God of Abraham, Isaac, and Jacob:

> O God, Framer of the universe . . . through whom all things, which of themselves were not, tend to be. God, who withholdest from perishing even that which seems to be mutually destructive. God, who out of nothing has created the world, which the eyes of all perceive to be most beautiful. God, who dost not cause evil, but causest that it be not most evil. . . . God, the Father of truth, the Father of wisdom, the Father of the true and crowning life, the Father of blessedness, the Father of that which is good and fair, the Father of intelligible light, the Father of our awakening and illumination, the Father of the pledge by which we are admonished to return to Thee.[21]

Augustine, it would seem, has unlimited confidence in God the Creator and almost no confidence in man the creature. How is this juxtaposition of hope and hopelessness, of optimism and pessimism, possible? What linkage between God and man remains to prevent the poles from breaking asunder, to prevent Augustine from abandoning God or abandoning man? The answer seems to be that, however depraved the behavior of man, he is naturally good because the image of God is planted within him:

> it is the work of the spirit of grace to renew in us the image of God, in which "by nature" we were made. The fault in man is contrary to his nature, and is just that which grace heals. . . . Accordingly, it is always "by nature" that men do the things contained in the law: those who fail so to do, fail by their own fault. By that fault the law of God was effaced from men's hearts; and so when it is written there through the healing of the fault, the things contained in the law are done "by nature"—not that nature is the denial of grace but that grace is the mending of nature.[22]

We find ourselves, willingly or not, carried to the heart of Augustine's theology, to the problems of sin and grace that so agitated the Pelagian controversy.

SIN

Sin and Adam

After his long list of human follies and vices, which we quoted from the pages of *De Civitate Dei* a moment ago, Augustine states, "These are indeed the crimes of wicked men, yet they spring from that root of error and misplaced love which is born with every son of Adam." The trouble is not love lost but love misplaced—which means misdirected, warped, corrupted. What modern men find difficult to accept in Augustine and perhaps in the Christian tradition generally —besides the difficult problem of so-called

---

1950), p. 846. Subsequent quotations are from this edition.

[20] *De natura boni contra Manichees,* Ch. 1, in *The Library of Christian Classics,* Vol. 6, *Augustine: Earlier Writings,* trans. by John Burleigh (Philadelphia: Westminster Press, 1953), p. 326.

[21] *Soliloquies,* Part I, sec. 2, in *Basic Writings of St. Augustine,* Whitney J. Oates, ed. (New York: Random House, 1948), Vol. 1, pp. 259–60.

[22] *De spiritu et littera,* sec. 47, in *The Library of Christian Classics,* Vol. 8, *Augustine: Later Works,* trans. by John Burnaby, p. 230. In "the mending of nature" the Greeks' art (*techné*) is something of a counterpart to Augustine's idea of grace.

natural evil, or the death or suffering of an innocent—is not so much the proposition that evil is warped love or that man makes his own mistakes and can therefore rightly be condemned—though many, of course, would challenge this, too—but the proposition that these sins of Adam infect all men, everywhere and inescapably, by taint of blood. The modern, liberal mentality shrinks at the fatalism, the inevitability, the arbitrariness he finds in the Adam myth.

It is wrong, however, to think that by the inheritance of Adam Augustine meant a literal physiological transmission of defects, a taint built into the gene structure. He was unconcerned with this and so was Paul. In Romans 5 it appears that Paul thought mankind was "in Adam" in a mystical way analogous to the way Christians are "in Christ." Pelagius said that in sinning each man voluntarily chooses to follow the example of Adam. But Paul, Ambrose, and Augustine felt that sinning involved less deliberate imitation and more self-deception.[23]

The historicity of Adam and his role in the corruption of man—in whatever sense this may be understood—was taken by Augustine as an article of belief given by the Scriptures and hence to be accepted not as a speculative conclusion but as a starting place. It is incorporated into Augustine's thought under his pervasive tenet of "faith seeking understanding." *How* he sought to make sense of this in terms of his own experience—and Augustine constantly referred issues to his own experience; in this sense at least he was always the empiricist—is what interested him and therefore is what should interest us. Whatever one says about the historicity of Adam, the problem of men repeatedly doing the very thing they desire not to do remains as much a problem for us as it was for Augustine. The literature of psychoanalysis is but one demonstration of this.[24]

Sin and History

Finding a solution to the problem of sin through the escape route of Neo-Platonic mysticism was a strong temptation to Augustine. But one stumbling block that stood in his way as a Christian was the reality of the historical process. Perhaps grace, like Platonic illumination, could come from above, but could history be disregarded? For the Platonist good was found in fixity and mentality, whereas evil, or nonbeing, was found in flux and corporeality. Hence contemplation was the path of wisdom, or, in Christian terms, blessedness. But the entry of Christ, the God-Man, into history, His physical death and Resurrection, symbolized for the Christian the importance of corporeality and the importance of history. Augustine could not be simply a Platonist. Sin, if it was to be overcome, was to be overcome in history. Hence the City of God and the City of the Earth are not physically separated but coexisting in time and space.

By such acceptance of historical existence with all its vices, faults, and confusions, Augustine is able to argue that sin may be a means of eliminating sin—a fire that fights fire—through the working out of a divine plan in history, a plan but dimly perceived by man but there nevertheless. God is not conceived of, as He was by certain Stoics, as a puppet master playing with His foredoomed creatures, but rather as a physician using harsh methods to cure a patient for his own good. Augustine compares sin to pain—by the experience of sin we know what sin is and we know of our need to be cured—and writes against Pelagius, "As if a sore were

[23] It is interesting that the Eastern Church, sharing the same terminology, regarded Adam's unfortunate bequest to mankind as being mortality, or physical death, whereas the Western Church has tended to emphasize the inheritance of moral defect.

[24] Augustine did not avoid some painful difficulties in maintaining the anti-Pelagian position. For example, he claims that because of Adam an infant who dies before it is possible to baptize him is nevertheless denied the kingdom of heaven. See *De natura et gratia,* sec. 9, in Oates, Vol. 1, p. 526. But Augustine does try in the *Confessions* to make an empirical case for the innate sinfulness even of infants: "It is clear, indeed, that infants are harmless because of physical weakness, not because of any innocence of mind. I myself have seen and known a baby who was envious; it could not yet speak, but it turned pale and looked bitterly at another baby sharing its milk. All this is well known."

not attended by pain, and an operation did not produce pain, that pain might be taken away by pain." The most stubborn of all ailments to cure is the root sin of pride, for it is the most disguised and subtle. He continues: "For all other sins only prevail in evil deeds; pride only has to be guarded against in things that are rightly done." The paradox that the deepest sin arises in the consciousness of good irritates by its illogic but the experience recurs and will not be dismissed. We know perhaps better than Augustine that such pride is collective as well as individual. He knew that not only the individual but mankind was to be healed by Christ the Physician—indeed this is the only sense in which Augustine becomes political at all. But Augustine scarcely drew the full implications of this. There was a gap between the role of man as ruler and man as child of God that he could not close, despite the famous mirror-of-princes passage (see p. 122 below), and perhaps this gap has not yet been closed. The Augustinian illustrations of sin are almost always individual: "Therefore it is not said to a man: 'It is necessary for you to sin that you may not sin'; but it is said to a man: 'God in some degree forsakes you, in consequence of which you grow proud, that you may know that you are 'not your own' but are His, and learn not to be proud."[25]

In such a view, then, government—even when it punishes us unjustly—may be the means whereby our pride is revealed to us and we are chastened. But what about the pride in government, or, better, in the political organism, the enlarged collective self? Who shall chasten it? Augustine's answer in *De Civitate Dei* seems to be that God will chasten it in His own inscrutable way, but most often by defeat in war: ". . . the durations of wars are determined by Him as He may see meet, according to His righteous will, and pleasure, and mercy, to afflict or to console the human race . . ." Moreover, if sin has become a property of the whole human race, then perhaps redemption of the whole human race will be required to defeat it more than provisionally. But Augustine's other-worldliness, his residue of Neo-Platonism, blocked his development of the political potentialities of such a position.[26]

Here the influence of place and time is clearly evident in the structure of Augustine's thought. Had he been writing in the midst of later struggles between pope and emperor, in the Reformation, or in the age of totalitarianism, who can tell how much more political his thought might have been?

THEOLOGICAL TENETS: A SUMMARY

In trying to give some basis for Augustine's political conclusions we seem to have been driven inescapably to his theological beliefs. Before returning to attack the problem of his political generalizations, let us summarize some of his critical theological tenets:

(1) Men are fallen creatures, recalcitrant children of a righteous and omnipotent God. The pride of men is the mark of their unwillingness to acknowledge God as their Creator and pride is the root of sin. Sin is corrupted love—love of things temporal rather than things eternal, the things of earth rather than the things of heaven. That men love is good; that they love unworthy objects is bad. God alone is purely good. Love of Him is the only purely good form of love.

(2) Men sin voluntarily, though they sin inevitably and though God has foreknowl-

[25] The three quotations are from *De natura et gratia,* secs. 30–32 in Oates, Vol. 1, pp. 540–41. See I Corinthians 6:19. Augustine frankly confesses, however, that he does not know why God does not simply cure pride outright.

[26] See John Burnaby, *Amor Dei, A Study of the Religion of St. Augustine* (London: Hodder & Stoughton, 1938), pp. 29–42; Etienne Gilson, *Introduction à l'étude de Saint Augustin,* 2nd ed. (Paris: Vrin, 1943), pp. 230–31; and J. N. Figgis, *The Political Aspects of St. Augustine's City of God* (London: Longmans, Green, 1921), Ch. 2.

edge of their sinning.[27] Man seems always to choose a course that forecloses further choice and leads him into the trap of sin, where he becomes a helpless prisoner. Augustine writes in the *Confessions:* "I was held back not by fetters put on me by someone else but by the iron bondage of my own will. The enemy held my will and made a chain out of it and bound me with it. From a perverse will came lust, and slavery to lust became habit, and the habit, being constantly yielded to, became a necessity." The lust of which Augustine speaks must not be taken as only or simply sexual passion, although that figured strongly in his early writings. He speaks in *De vera religione* of lust of the flesh, the passion of ambition that drives power-hungry men, and —intellectuals take note—the "lust of the eyes": the drive of curiosity, the desire to know simply for the sake of knowing, which, being separated from religious ends, Augustine regards as evil.

A distinguished Augustinian scholar states the same issue in a somewhat different way. The will, he says, desires the good but cannot carry it out:

> there is something damaged within it. Let us call the cause of that damage "sin," and let us prescribe its remedy, namely man's redemption by God, along with the grace of Jesus Christ which flows from it. Once this is done the economy of the moral life, impenetrable to the philosophers, becomes transparently clear because this is the only doctrine which takes into account all the facts, and especially the following: as long as a will relies on itself to do good, it remains powerless.[28]

Even granting the tenability of the concept of "will"—a concession some contemporary philosophers will not make—the assertion that men sin voluntarily yet of necessity raises certain obvious logical difficulties. These difficulties are enhanced by the ambiguity surrounding the Latin adverb *libere,* one word that must fit several meanings. The most reputable scholars invariably point out that there are at least three different meanings of freedom, or liberty, in Augustine. First, there is the unlimited freedom to choose good or evil in the context of all possible alternatives (*libertas indifferentiae*), a condition that existed only in the brief period before Adam's fall. In Adam's choice, *mankind* made the wrong decision and thereby forever precluded individual men from reversing history and going back to their own private Edens. Lost innocence is unrecoverable.

In their present condition men are bound to choose with a kind of half-free will, a compromised will, a drugged will. At one point in the *Confessions* Augustine compares the situation to our experience of trying to wake up in the morning: when Christ bid him to wake up, to arise from the death of routine experience, Augustine answered with "lazy words spoken half asleep: 'a minute,' 'just a minute,' 'just a little time longer.' . . . For the law of sin is the strong force of habit which drags the mind along and controls it even against its will, though deservedly, since the habit was voluntarily adopted."

On the surface this seems to be a freedom to do wrong only—a curious kind of freedom indeed. But it might help to point out that this "freedom to do wrong" describes only the general condition of sin that infects our every action, including actions of praiseworthy consequence. This condition creates a fundamental orientation of the will. Everyday choices of better and worse, however, are not meaningless, nor is the element of choice in them illusory. Everyday freedom of choice (*liberum arbitrium*) presupposes a spontaneity, a self-determining activity that turns out to be the very definition of will. Augustine never denied that, if the will is coerced, it ceases to be will.

Augustine attacked the Pelagians because they assumed that the first kind of freedom, unlimited freedom, was a realistic possibility

[27] God's foreknowledge is not quite the same thing as predestination. Augustine did not say, as Luther and Calvin did, that the fall of Adam was predetermined. Nor is Augustine's idea of foreknowledge the same as the Stoic idea of *fate,* or the sense of being rigidly bound by an order of causes.

[28] Gilson, *The Christian Philosophy of Saint Augustine,* p. 159.

for man acting in historical situations. They ignored the determination of impressions, motives, and environment, including the part God played in them, for though God does not compel the will, He may prepare it.

> The Pelagians think that they know something great when they assert that "God would not command what He knew could not be done by man." Who can be ignorant of this? But God commands some things which we cannot do, in order that we may know what we ought to ask of Him. For this is faith itself, which obtains by prayer what the law commands. . . . It is certain that it is we that *will* when we will, but it is He who makes us will what is good of whom it is said . . . "The will is prepared by the Lord."[29]

A third kind of freedom[30] is true freedom (*vere libero*), the freedom to do God's will: ". . . the first liberty of the will was to be able not to sin, the last will be much greater, not to be able to sin."[31] This freedom is to be known in its fullness only in heaven or after the Day of Judgment. Through grace men participate to some extent in this kind of freedom while still on earth; men feel intimations of it. But scholars are not agreed on how much Augustine was willing to concede the possibility of achieving *vere libero* on earth; Catholics have perhaps tended to be more optimistic than Protestants on this question.[32]

(3) Man is redeemed by unmerited grace. It seems that man's inevitable turning away from God is his own act, whereas man's not-so-inevitable turning toward God is God's act. Why Augustine thinks this should be so is partly explained by the foregoing discussion of free will. We are free to defy God and do so because we serve ourselves. But we are not free to serve God until he makes us his servants: "Our hope is . . . to be made free by the free One; and that, in setting us free, He may make us His servants of love."[33]

Such grace comes in various ways but above all through the redemptive power of God incarnate in Jesus of Nazareth. Stoic, Epicurean, and Platonic ways of life failed, thought Augustine, because "they all lacked the pattern of divine humility." The road to truth is "first, humility, second, humility, third, humility," for without this "all the good of our joy in any right action is wrested from us by pride."[34] Augustine uses the familiar analogy of Christ as Physician for sick humanity in a striking metaphor: the cure of sin comes only from drinking "the bitter cup, the cup of temptations, wherein this life abounds, the cup of tribulation, anguish, and sufferings. . . . And that the sick man may not make answer, 'I cannot, I cannot bear it, I will not drink'; the Physician, all whole though he be, drinketh first, that the sick man may not hesitate to drink."[35]

Despite I Timothy 2:4, which declares it to be God's will that all men be saved, Augustine does not feel that all men—or even many men—will be saved. Though apparently no one will be saved without baptism, not all those baptized can be assured of salvation. This is evidence enough that the City of God cannot be equated with the Church, for many members of the Church will clearly

[29] *De gratia et libero arbitrio,* Ch. 32, in Oates, Vol. 1, p. 759. The Scripture is Proverbs 8:35. See also *Contra duas epistolas Pelagianorum,* Ch. 1, sec. 37. Augustine was not unmindful of the difficult dilemmas of his position: "If there is no grace of God, how does He save the world? And if there is no free will, how does He judge the world?" (*Epistle* 214, sec. 2, in *Select Letters,* trans. by J. H. Baxter [Cambridge, Mass.: Harvard Univ. Press, Loeb Classical Library, 1930], p. 407.)

[30] By distinguishing between the freedom of fallen man generally and the freedom to do this or that specific act, Herbert Deane finds four kinds of freedom in Augustine. See his *Political and Social Ideas of Saint Augustine,* pp. 25–26.

[31] *De correptione et gratia,* Ch. 12, sec. 33, in Schaff, Vol. 5, p. 485.

[32] Maurice Blondel, "The Latent Resources in St. Augustine's Thought," in M. C. D'Arcy *et al., St. Augustine* (Cleveland: World, Meridian, 1957), pp. 319 and 344–49; Burnaby, *Amor Dei,* pp. 229–31; Mary T. Clark, *Augustine, Philosopher of Freedom* (New York: Desclee, 1958), p. 45; Gilson, *Christian Philosophy of St. Augustine,* pp. 323–24; and W. Montgomery, *St. Augustine* (London: Hodder & Stoughton, 1914), p. 177.

[33] *In Joannis Evangelium tractatus,* No. 41, sec. 8, in Schaff, Vol. 7, p. 232.

[34] *Epistle* 118, secs. 17, 22. Quoted in Burnaby, *Amor Dei,* p. 71.

[35] *Sermons,* No. 38, sec. 7, in Schaff, Vol. 6, p. 381.

not make the grade. It is surprising that there has often been confusion as to the lines of membership Augustine meant to draw between the City of God and the City of the Earth. No one can be a member of both cities at the same time because no one can love the eternal and the temporal at the same time: "Consider a man's love; think of it as, so to say, the hand of the soul. If it is holding anything, it cannot hold anything else. But that it may be able to hold what is given to it, it must leave go what it holds already."[36] The external signs of membership are often misleading: earthly minded men may hold office, even high office, in the Church. The sometimes dirty business of earthly power and authority may be managed by men "belonging to Jerusalem."[37] Augustine believed the church was of absolutely crucial significance—indeed it was Christ's "present kingdom"—but he did not hold it to be the City of God, a fact often abused by subsequent writers.[38]

If we remember that Augustine's charge against the Donatists was precisely that they improperly arrogated to themselves the responsibility of deciding who was and who was not pure in the sight of God, we see that Augustine is left with no basis for judging which of his fellow men were or were not members of the City of God. But if membership is so well hidden from men, how can Augustine know that men cannot love two things, even contradictory things, at once? If the two cities are poles apart (the poles of temporality and eternality), why is it not possible for some individuals to be bouncing back and forth or to be stretched in opposed directions somewhere in the middle of the spectrum? Moreover, if membership is so hidden, how can Augustine know that only a few will be chosen for the City of God? And how can he know that those who are chosen will be unable to resist? Unmerited grace is one thing but irresistible grace is another. In the later years of his struggle with the Pelagians, Augustine was led almost to contradict his doctrine of free will by insisting that the elect were themselves without the power to say no to God. Logically, this would seem to be the last power to be denied to man as man. Without the power to say no to God, man is indeed an automaton. But, as Burnaby said, "nearly all that Augustine wrote after his seventieth year is the work of a man whose energy has burnt itself out, whose love has grown cold. The system which generally goes by the name of Augustinianism is in great part a cruel travesty of Augustine's deepest and most vital thought."[39]

(4) Evil is nonbeing; nonbeing is the absence of good. Augustine never abandoned the Platonic doctrine that being itself is good and that evil never has more than the deceptive appearance of true being, although Augustine acknowledged the reality of the corporeal in a way that Plato did not. "Every existing thing however lowly is justly praised when it is compared with nothingness. Nothing is good if it can be better."[40] "What is called an evil nature is a corrupt nature. If it were not corrupt it would be good. But even when it is corrupted, so far as it remains a natural thing, it is good. It is bad only so far as it is corrupted."[41] In moving once more against the Manicheans in *De natura boni* Augustine says that darkness as well as light may praise God, the one true Good, the Author of all nature.[42] This view makes the character of the Devil difficult to assimilate. For if the Devil is presumably purely evil, this would have to mean that he is nothing. In fact, Augustine does not suc-

[36] *Ibid.*, No. 75, sec. 7, p. 479.

[37] *Enarrationes in psalmos,* No. 61, sec. 8, in Schaff, Vol. 8, p. 253.

[38] "God's Church . . . is the incarnation of the City of God" (B. Roland-Gosselin, "St. Augustine's System of Morals," in D'Arcy, p. 243). F. J. C. Hearnshaw wrote, ". . . *Civitas Dei* which has its latest and most perfect terrestrial manifestation in the Christian Church" (*The Social and Political Ideas of Some Great Medieval Thinkers* [London: Harrap, 1923], p. 41). Cf. Augustine, *Enarrationes in psalmos,* No. 50, sec. 9.

[39] *Amor Dei*, p. 231.

[40] *De vera religione,* Ch. 41, sec. 78, in Burleigh, Vol. 6, p. 265. See also *De natura boni,* sec. 34, and I Timothy 4:4.

[41] *De natura boni,* sec. 4, in Burleigh, Vol. 6, p. 327.

[42] *Ibid.*, sec. 16.

ceed in satisfactorily connecting his scriptural references to the Devil with his Neo-Platonic theory of evil.[43]

TRINITY AND PERSONALITY

Augustine's most impressive attempt to give an ontological structure to these assertions about God, the Good, and being itself—not that Augustine was ever very structural—was *De Trinitate.* Augustine here extracts from various aspects of human experience some fourteen analogies to the Holy Trinity. A similar use of Trinitarian analogies appears in other works as well.[44] Some would argue that by means of this venture Augustine was responsible for the most profound transformation of ancient thought: he replaced the Greek *kosmos* with the human *psyche* as the basic analogy for understanding the inner life of God, resting the operation upon a distinction between the personal and the impersonal scarcely understood by the ancients.

De Trinitate was an answer to the Arian heresy. The Arians held that God and Christ cannot be the same substance because—in good Aristotelian language—God is substance only, without accidents or qualities; He is unbegotten. The Son must be different because He is begotten. This is fallacious reasoning, says Augustine. A man is both begotten and begetting, yet this does not destroy his unity as a person. It is all a matter of relationships. Jesus may be a creature; but He is also a Creator, depending upon what relationship is being considered:

> because the Father is not called the Father except that He has a Son, and the Son is not called Son except in that He has a Father, these things are not said according to substance; because each of them is not so called in relation to Himself, but the terms are used reciprocally and in relation to each other; nor yet according to accident, because both the being called the Father and the being called the Son, is eternal and unchangeable to them. Wherefore also to be the Father and to be the Son is different, yet their substance is not different: because they are so called, not according to substance, but according to relation, which relation, however, is not accident, because it is not changeable.[45]

The Arians neglected the fourth Aristotelian category of relation, which is neither substance nor accident. Father, Son, and Holy Spirit can all be related in one divine substance. Personality as the capacity to be related in several different ways thus becomes an essential attribute of divinity itself. Augustine had earlier spoken of this divine essence as a "mode of order" (*ordinis modus*) or a "principle of unity" (*unum principale*) of which "images" (*imago*) may be seen on earth:

> The mode of order lives in perpetual truth. It has no bulk or temporal process. By its potency it is greater than all space, and by its eternity it remains changeless above the flux of time. And yet without it vast bulk can have no unity, and length of time cannot be kept in the straight path. There could be neither matter nor motion. It is the principle of unity, having neither size nor change whether finite or infinite. . . . it is called his [the Father's] similitude and image because it comes from him. It is rightly called also the Son, and from him other things proceed. But before him is the universal form perfectly identical with the unity from which it springs.[46]

[43] *Ibid.,* secs. 32–34. All power possessed by the Devil, says Augustine, is given to him by God in order that "the good should be proved and the iniquity of the bad should be punished" (sec. 32, in Burleigh, Vol. 6, p. 336). But the Devil also wills his own action and shall in the end be punished for it.

[44] See, for example, *De vera religione,* secs. 7, 38 and 43; *De natura boni,* sec. 3; *De diversis quaestionibus octoginta tribus,* sec. 18; *De Civitate Dei,* Bk. XI, Ch. 25. For a discussion of some of these analogies see Paul J. Henry, S.J., *St. Augustine on Personality* (New York: Macmillan, 1960), pp. 3–12; and Cyril C. Richardson, "The Enigma of the Trinity," in Battenhouse, pp. 235–56.

[45] *De Trinitate,* Bk. V, Ch. 5, in Schaff, Vol. 3, p. 89.

[46] *De vera religione,* Ch. 43, sec. 81, in Burleigh, Vol. 6, pp. 267–68. Augustine often speaks of the relativity of time and space and, indeed, all things save the divine essence. See *De musica,* Ch. 6, sec. 7; *De Civitate Dei,* Bk. XII, Ch. 16; *De genera ad littera,* Ch. 5, sec. 5; *Confessions,* Bk. XI, Ch. 20.

In *De Trinitate* Augustine shows how this principle of order or unity parallels in human psychology the relations among the members of the Holy Trinity; he uses such examples as lover, loved, and love; mind, consciousness, and love; memory, intellect, and will; measure, number, and weight. By such surprising and original means, says Father Henry, Augustine demonstrated how "Divine existence is the ideal of all personal existence—to be fully oneself, but only in dependence upon, and in adherence to, another in the community of unity."[47]

The social and political implications of Augustine's insight into the relational character of personality and the personal character of divinity are tremendous. But unfortunately Augustine did not draw these implications. If man is seen as one who becomes a person (and thereby takes on attributes of divinity) only insofar as he participates in certain kinds of human relationships that are but counterparts of divine relationships, is it not likely that the establishment of certain kinds of familial, social, and even political relationships are central to the creation (begetting) of the kind of people Augustine imagines belong to the City of God? Yet, sensitive as Augustine was to human relations at what we would call the private level, he did not concern himself with the establishment of personalizing social institutions. For Augustine redemption took place in spite of and against earthly loves rather than through them. Grace broke through *within* a personality rather than *between* personalities. Even though he accepted political authority as natural, he felt that the function of political authority was only to maintain external order. The problem of community in the sociopsychological sense remained otherworldly for Augustine. The possibility that grace could flow through human communities other than the Church escaped him.[48]

THE NATURE OF THE STATE

And so, circling around again, we come back to Augustine's political tenets. Their core could perhaps best be summed up by the familiar statement that the state for Augustine is not an instrument for the promotion of the good life but a hospital for the care of the sick, with the possibility for cures largely out of the hands of the hospital staff. The state is necessary, even natural—for sickness is a natural condition of man—but it is hardly necessary and natural in the Greek sense and it is certainly not an instrument for the promotion of private interest in the liberal sense. Since the sickness of man may require some harsh medicine, the patient usually resists what is for his own good. No matter; he must learn to take the bitter with the bittersweet. (And we must not forget that Augustine believed in cures by the grace of God. His pessimism was provisional, not ultimate.) In this life, everyone gets what is coming to him—except the select few who get better than is coming to them. This may be a form of justice but it is not political justice; it is not Aristotle's distributive or retributive justice.

Perhaps no single issue in the interpretation of Augustine's political thought has been so often agitated in recent years as that of whether he regarded justice as an essential attribute of the state. McIlwain's incisive scholarly imagination has made much of the distinction between kingdom (*regnum*) and

[47] *Op. cit.*, p. 10. But Richardson notes that virtually all Augustine's Trinitarian analogies are taken from *within* the psyche of one person and he questions whether Augustine has done justice to the idea of three persons rather than one person: "If the Cappadocians were sometimes in danger of tritheism, Augustine's danger lies in the opposite direction" ("The Enigma of the Trinity," in Battenhouse, p. 247).

[48] A few of the many twentieth-century works that suggest these possibilities are Martin Buber, *I and Thou*, trans. by R. Gregor Smith (Edinburgh: Clark, 1937); John Macmurray, *The Self as Agent* (London: Faber and Faber, 1957); H. Richard Niebuhr, *The Responsible Self* (New York: Harper & Row, 1963); and Max Scheler, *The Nature of Sympathy* (New Haven: Yale Univ. Press, 1954).

city (*civitas*) on the one hand and commonwealth (*res publica*) on the other; he has suggested that, while Augustine conceived of the former as capable of existing without justice, he did not so exempt the Ciceronian *res publica*. Indeed, McIlwain has claimed, Augustine accepted Cicero's definition of the state but wanted to go further and Christianize the concept of political justice that was central to it: ". . . justice and justice alone is the only possible bond which can unite men as a true *populas* in a real *res publica*."[49]

Augustine does indeed cite Cicero's definition—and seems to do so with some sympathy—but only because he is showing that even by Cicero's testimony the Republic did not live up to its ideals. And McIlwain finds shaky support in quoting Augustine's "Justice being taken away, then, what are kingdoms but great robberies?" Though this could mean that justice transforms robberies into kingdoms, the context of the whole chapter makes it quite clear that Augustine is emphasizing the quite nominal character of the distinction that separates robberies from kingdoms. The point is not how great is the difference between the two but how small. The chapter ends with Augustine saying how "apt and true" was the fabled pirate's reply to Alexander the Great: a man is called a pirate for seizing a part of the sea but for seizing the whole earth Alexander is called emperor.

Augustine never dignifies the state much more than this and after citing Cicero's definition he says categorically:

> Rome was never a republic, because true justice has never had a place in it. But accepting the more feasible definitions of a republic, I grant there was a republic of a certain kind, and certainly much better administered by the more ancient Romans than by their modern representatives. But the fact is, true justice has no existence save in that republic whose founder and ruler is Christ. . . . the city of which Holy Scripture says "Glorious things are said of thee, O city of God."[50]

Since Augustine denies even the Church the rightful title to the City of God, suggesting that he meant to identify the latter with any political entity stretches credulity to the breaking point. Hence we can safely say that "true justice" in Cicero's sense does not belong to this world.

NATURAL LAW AND REASON

It would seem to follow that the positive law of actual states partakes of little more than the order-inducing rules of any well-run robber band. Is there room in such a conception of law for anything approaching natural law? There is, of course, the law of the Scriptures. But in Augustine's treatment even this is a remarkably inward-turning law. (As Figgis notes, Augustine is as antithetical to the Jewish tradition as he is to the classical ideal of the *polis*.)

> because men desiring those things which are without, even from themselves have become exiles, there hath been given also a written law: not because in hearts it had not been written, but because thou was a deserter from thy heart. . . . Therefore, the written law, what crieth it, to those that have deserted the law written in their hearts? *Return ye transgressors to the heart.*[51] (Isa. 46:8)

Or, again, Augustine speaks of natural law not as the law of the Scriptures per se—though the whole context of the passage is scriptural exegesis—but in terms that seem somewhat closer to the classical tradition: "For when will they be able to understand that there is no soul, however wicked, which can yet reason in any way, in whose con-

[49] C. H. McIlwain, *Growth of Political Thought in the West* (New York: Macmillan, 1932), p. 158. In this controversy, George H. Sabine, in *History of Political Theory* (New York: Holt, Rinehart and Winston, 1937), p. 192, *n*. 14, sides with McIlwain against A. J. Carlyle in Hearnshaw, p. 50, and Figgis, Ch. 2.

[50] *De Civitate Dei*, Bk. II, Ch. 21, p. 63. Prior quotation is from Bk. IV, Ch. 4, p. 112.

[51] *Enarrationes in psalmos*, No. 57, sec. 1, in *Library of the Fathers of the Holy Catholic Church* (Oxford: Parker, 1848), Vol. 3, p. 97. In the Revised Standard Version this is Psalm 58.

science God does not speak? For who but God has written the law of nature in the hearts of men?"[52] We consult reason, to be sure, but not as it is inscribed in the lucid mind so much as it is written in the conscientious heart.

Whether or not we call Augustine a rationalist, he was certainly not an irrationalist. That he took self-consciousness as the starting point of thought serves only to link him with Descartes. Faith does come first: "We begin in faith and are made perfect by sight. This also is the sum of the whole body of doctrine." Reason is never autonomous: Christ, he says, is to be defended by reason, "which must have its starting point either in the bodily senses or in the intuitions of the mind."[53] But this does not undermine the conviction that thought is indispensable. Indeed, though in one sense belief precedes thought, in another sense thought precedes belief: ". . . it is necessarily the case that everything that is believed is believed after thought has preceded. Though indeed belief is nothing else than thinking with assent. Not everyone who thinks, believes; but everyone who believes thinks. He both believes in thinking and thinks in believing."[54]

The important point is that the seat of the rational and the standard of rationality are, in modern language, more psychological than logical. Rationality is concrete rather than abstract; it is an aspect of the emotional rather than a denial of it. Hence the formulation of abstract universal norms of justice based on a natural law accessible to the reason of all men by means of logical demonstration did not interest Augustine and indeed would have seemed futile to him. Augustine's lack of interest in law as mere abstract right led Figgis to suggest that his replacement of *justitia* with *concordia* parallels the modern distinction between legal right and moral right.[55] A legal obligation separated from spiritual authority would have had no meaning for Augustine. He wrote in *De Civitate Dei:* "For though the soul may seem to rule the body admirably and the reason the vices, if the soul and reason do not themselves obey God, as God has commanded them to serve Him, they have no proper authority over the body and the vices."[56]

SOME POLITICAL QUESTIONS

For anyone interested in systematic political theory a host of bothersome questions spring up at this point: (1) What criteria does Augustine give us for determining the political responsibility of rulers or the political obligation of subjects? (2) Is Augustine's view of historical purpose and governmental responsibility such that civic education is either inconceivable or futile? (3) If the purpose of all institutions is to glorify God, does this mean that all institutions must be subordinate to the Church? Does it mean that state power may be used to coerce nonbelievers into Christian patterns of worship? (4) If the purpose of government is simply to maintain peace so that individuals can find God and if justice is irrelevant to the state, how can Augustine defend the just war?

Christian Rulers and Subjects

The command to rulers and subjects alike—the command for all human action—is "love God." In his famous mirror-of-princes passage[57] Augustine denies that true

[52] *Sermone Domine in Monte,* Part II, sec. 32, in Schaff, Vol. 6, p. 44. See Gustave Combes, *La doctrine politique de Saint Augustin* (Paris: Librairie Plon, 1927), p. 130, and Romans 2:14–16. The original Latin text is in J. P. Migne, ed., *Patrologia Latina* (London: Gregg, 1844–64), Vol. 34, p. 1283.

[53] *Enchiridion,* Chs. 5 and 4, in Oates, Vol. 1, p. 659 and p. 658, respectively.

[54] *De praedestinatione sanctorum,* sec. 5. Quoted by Montgomery, p. 157. *Fides* is usually translated either "faith" or "belief," *credo* being the verb "to believe."

[55] *Op. cit.,* p. 64.

[56] "AUGUSTINE: 'God and the soul, that is what I desire to know.' REASON: 'Nothing more?' AUGUSTINE: 'Nothing whatever' " (*Soliloquies,* No. 2, Ch. 7, in Oates, Vol. 1, p. 262).

[57] The mirror-of-princes device—a genre stretching

happiness comes to Christian emperors from power, wealth, or adulation:

> But we say they are happy if they rule justly; if they are not lifted up amid the praises of those who pay them sublime honors, and the obsequiousness of those who salute them with an excessive humility, but remember that they are men; if they make their power the handmaid of His majesty by using it for the greatest possible extension of His worship; if they fear, love, worship God; if more than their own they love that kingdom in which they are not afraid to have partners; if they are slow to punish, ready to pardon; if they apply that punishment as necessary to government and defense of the republic, and not in order to gratify their own enmity . . . if their luxury is as much restrained as it might have been unrestrained; if they prefer to govern depraved desires rather than any nation whatever; and if they do all these things not through ardent desire of empty glory, but through love of eternal felicity, not neglecting to offer to the true God, who is their God, for their sins, the sacrifices of humility, contrition, and prayer. Such Christian emperors, we say, are happy in the present time by hope and are destined to be so in the enjoyment of the reality itself, when that which we wait for shall have arrived.[58]

The proper motives of proper monarchs are thus other worldly. There is not much guidance here on how to operate a secular political system, although some might see a vigorous theocratic regime hidden in the phrase suggesting the use of power "for the greatest possible extension" of God's worship. We must remember that here Augustine is not telling all rulers what they must do as rulers; he is telling the Christian ruler what he must do as a Christian. In a letter written in 411 to Marcellinus Augustine says that Christian judges should never yield to the spirit of revenge but should use coercive measures in a humane way for the correction of the offender. They should be as "a devoted father" to the defendant and therefore, rather than apply the rack or fire or tear their flesh with hooks, as was the custom to obtain a confession of guilt, they should do as loving parents do with wayward children —beat them with rods![59] A ruler may be led by either ignorance or the necessity of office to torture the innocent. In neither case, says Augustine, is he either happy or guiltless. Yet Augustine does not tell such a ruler to stop the practice; he does not presume to judge the necessity of office. In *De Civitate Dei* he admonishes the ruler, "had he any piety about him," to "cry to God, 'From my *necessities* [our italics] deliver thou me.'"

Most regimes, Augustine knows, will not be humane, even by the crude standards of his day, for the grace to act sacrificially is seldom accepted. And even those rulers who try cannot as officials act in the self-sacrificial manner of those martyrs who would try to live in every way consistent with the Sermon on the Mount. Those who do not resist evil and who turn the other cheek in fact become martyrs, and their blessing shall be in heaven. But a ruler who tried this would soon cease to be a ruler. Here is Augustine's political realism at its most bitterly honest.

If the obligation of rulers is to be humane, the obligation of subjects is to obey. Two favorite passages of Augustine are Romans 13:1, "the powers that be are ordained of God," and Matthew 22:21, "Render unto Caesar the things that are Caesar's." He often speaks of how Christians make good citizens and—though he is not generous in assessing the motives of rulers—when he discusses penal law, he takes for granted, as Aquinas would later do, that rulers apply it for legitimate penal purposes. Men are good, he says, insofar as they love righteousness. No one is good simply through fear of punishment, but "even so, it is not without advantage that human recklessness should be confined by fear of the law so that innocence may be safe among evil-doers, and the evil-doers them-

from the late Stoic to the Renaissance eras—was a means of trying to influence rulers by giving them a favorably distorted picture of themselves on the assumption that rulers, like other men, try to live as they see themselves reflected in the eyes of their beholders. In this case Augustine is delicately if not altogether plausibly identifying his description with the examples of Constantine and Theodosius.

[58] *De Civitate Dei,* Bk. V, Ch. 24, p. 178.

[59] *Epistle* 133, in Baxter, pp. 253–55.

selves may be cured by calling on God when their freedom of action is held in check by fear of punishment."[60]

That the powers that be are ordained by God seems also to be supported by Augustine in his assumption that victory in war is not accidental:

in almost all nations the very voice of nature somehow proclaims, that those who happen to be conquered should choose rather to be subject to their conquerors than to be killed by all kinds of warlike destruction. This does not take place without the providence of God in whose power it lies that any one either subdues or is subdued in war; that some are endowed with kingdoms, others made subject to kings.[61]

What is difficult to assess properly is the margin for discrimination Augustine intended to establish within two sets of apparent contradictions: (1) All things, including all political regimes, work together for the glory of God yet some things, including some political regimes, are better than others. (2) Success on the historical stage is wholly unimportant when seen in the light of eternity, yet the success of some political regimes is to be preferred to the success of other political regimes. Perhaps we can get a handle on the problem by asking how Augustine, granting as much as he does to what a later generation would call "reason of state" and to a rather inscrutable historical process, would distinguish between the worth of, say, Rome and Babylon:

in order to discover the character of any people we have only to observe what they love. Yet whatever it loves, if only it is an assemblage of reasonable beings and not of beasts, and is bound together by an agreement as to the objects of love, it is reasonably called a people; and it will be a superior people in proportion as it is bound together by higher interests, inferior as it is bound together by lower.[62]

There are lower and higher objects of love but the only truly worthy object of love is God Himself. His exalted presence does not annul the fine moral distinctions between men and nations but sets them all, so to speak, over against Himself—puts them all in a common shadow out of the divine light. To speak negatively, ordinary social, political, and economic frailties are regarded by Augustine not as morally neutral but as simply swallowed up by the transcending importance of impiety: ". . . is he who keeps back a piece of ground from the purchaser, and gives it to a man who has no right to it, unjust, while he who keeps back himself from the God who made him, and serves wicked spirits, is just?"

Peace, Order, and History

To speak of reform or improvement in the Augustinian context seems almost bizarre. Society can be reformed only if individuals are reformed. Yet sin is social; it is built into the very fabric of common experience. Nevertheless, it is Augustine's unshakeable faith that this seemingly intractable situation is all part of God's plan for man to work out his salvation. This will happen within the framework of historical sequence but according to a dynamic not bound simply to historical sequence. The following quotation from *De Civitate Dei* shows the way the themes of order and peace are put at the core of Augustine's vision of this divine plan:

The peace of the body then consists in the duly proportioned arrangement of its parts. The peace of the irrational soul is the harmonious repose of the appetites, and that of the rational soul the harmony of knowledge and action. The peace of body and soul is the well ordered and harmonious life and health of the living creature. Peace between man and God is the well-ordered obedience of faith to eternal law. Peace between man and man is well-ordered concord. Domestic peace is the well-ordered concord between those of the family and those who obey. Civil peace is a similar concord among the citizens. The peace of the celestial city is the perfectly ordered and harmonious enjoyment of God, and of one another in God. The peace of all things is the tranquillity of order. Order is

[60] *Epistle* 153, in Henry Paolucci, ed., *Political Writings of St. Augustine* (Chicago: Regnery, 1962), p. 255.
[61] *De Civitate Dei,* Bk. XVIII, Ch. 2, p. 610.
[62] *Ibid.,* Bk. XIX, Ch. 24, p. 706.

the distribution which allots things equal and unequal, each to its own place. And hence, though the miserable, insofar as they are such, do certainly not enjoy peace, but are severed from that tranquillity of order in which there is no disturbance, nevertheless, inasmuch as they are deservedly and justly miserable, they are by their very misery connected with order. They are not, indeed, conjoined with the blessed, but they are disjoined from them by the law of order. And though they are disquieted, their circumstances are notwithstanding adjusted to them, and consequently they have some tranquillity of order, and therefore some peace. But they are wretched because, although not wholly miserable, they are not in that place where any mixture of misery is impossible. They would, however, be more wretched if they had not that peace which arises from being in harmony with the natural order of things.[63]

Many have compared Augustine's sense of a hidden plan working itself out in history with what Hegel would later call the cunning of reason. Is Augustine's plan progressive? Yes and no. On the one hand, Augustine's conception of a universal order was heavily flavored with Platonic idealism and hence drew its significance in part from the idea of an unchanging transhistorical order. This order was quite at odds with the earlier Christian millennialism, which identified the City of God with a coming heaven on earth.

On the other hand, Augustine's discovery of the subjective meaning of time produced a new sense of history, a new sense that each man can and does incorporate the past in himself:

It is now however perfectly clear that neither the future nor the past are in existence, and that it is incorrect to say that there are three times—past, present, and future. Though one might perhaps say: "There are three times—a present of things past, a present of things present, and a present of things future." For these three do exist in the mind, and I do not see them anywhere else: the present of things past is memory; the present of things present is sight; the present of things future is expectation.[64]

[63] *Ibid.*, Ch. 13, p. 690.

[64] *Confessions*, Bk. XI, Ch. 20, p. 273.

Thus Augustine's view of the whole of history as a drama under God's direction ran counter to the cyclical assumptions of the Greeks.

This recognition of the uniqueness and irreversibility of the temporal process—this "explosion of the perpetual cycles"—is one of the most remarkable achievements of St. Augustine's thought. It is true that the change of attitude was implicit in Christianity itself, since the whole Christian revelation rests on temporal events which nevertheless possess an absolute significance and an eternal value. As St. Augustine says, Christ is the straight way by which the mind escapes from the circular maze of pagan thought. But although this change had been realized by faith and religious experience, it still awaited philosophic analysis and definition. This it received from St. Augustine, who was not only the founder of the Christian philosophy of history, but was actually the first man in the world to discover the meaning of time.[65]

Augustine saw secular history as unprogressive but he also saw in history a progress of the Holy Spirit and the continuing possibility of permanent change in individual human will. Thus, says Dawson, while the East continued to mantle its political institutions with an aura of uncritical divinity, the West, largely due to Augustine's influence, at least "made possible the ideal of a social order resting upon the free personality and a common effort towards moral ends." That Augustine was indifferent to secular progress does not nullify a long-run stimulus to secular progressivism arising from his thought. Nor does Augustine's recognition of evil in history nullify his belief that evil is wholly negative:

Both the *Civitas Dei* and the *Civitas terrena* grow in history, as Augustine observed. But they do not have their separate histories. The evil which appears at the end of history is either a corruption of the final good or it is an explicit denial and defiance of that good which would be impossible without the juxtaposition of the good. This is to say that evil is negative and parasitic in origin even though its effect is positive and its power something more than

[65] Dawson in D'Arcy, p. 69.

inertial resistance. Modern tyrannies are not the end product of a long history of tyranny in which ancient evils have been consciously refined to their present consistency of evil. They are rather characteristic corruptions of a mature civilization in which technical instruments have become more effective tools of tyrannical purpose.[66]

Church and State

How did Augustine see the relation of Church and state? The fact that both the Roman state and the Catholic Church opposed the Donatists—though for different reasons—gave Augustine a most practical basis for assuming cooperative Church-state relations to be a norm. The Church teaches civic duties and induces civic tranquillity for the sake of the peace necessary to hear God's word. This includes "love and charity to our neighbor."[67] The state, on its part, has an obligation to take those steps necessary to maintain the peace and not to interfere with the liturgy of the Church.[68]

Deane observes that Augustine's view of Church-state compatibility and mutual helpfulness foreshadows the two-swords doctrine of Pope Gelasius.[69] Perhaps this is so but the foreshadowing is cast in a most ethereal, flickering light. Augustine may have permitted the Church to depend upon secular power but he did not demand it. He was too other worldly for that. The Church could be as true to itself under persecution as under Constantine.

Yet at the same time, Augustine did view the Church in a particularly political way, as Figgis puts it,[70] which can best be understood, perhaps, by seeing how the genuinely apolitical Church developed in the East. And while Augustine preferred small states to large, he preferred a large Church to a small. Moreover, he never doubted that, if anyone can speak for God, it is the Church. Certainly it is not the state: "Consider these several grades of human powers. . . . if the Proconsul himself enjoin any thing and the Emperor another thing, is there any doubt that disregarding the former, we ought to obey the latter? So then if the Emperor enjoin one thing and God another, what judge ye?"[71] But Augustine recognized that the practical problem of distinguishing God's command from the other commands of life could be formidable:

> there are some actions which look vicious and criminal and yet are not sins because they are not offenses either against you, our Lord God, or against human society. For example. . . . Many actions, therefore, which seem disreputable to men are, according to your testimony, to be approved, and many actions that are praised by men are, in your sight, to be condemned. The appearance of the act, the mind of the person who does the act, and the secret promptings of the occasion are all capable of great variations.[72]

Augustine is unable to give any objective standard for determining from the outside, so to speak, which acts are truly disobedient to God. He is too scrupulous for that and the internality of his position remains firm. It is indeed hard to know when God speaks, "But happy are those who recognize your commands."[73] It would seem that we can but hope and pray to follow those commands we do understand. A corollary of such uncertainty as we consider God's commands to another person would seem to be a degree of tolerance for deviant behavior. Given these assumptions at the private level, it might seem fitting that Church-state harmony-through-separation could reign. The Church is concerned with a private and intangible personal peace; the state is concerned with a difficult but nonetheless limited physical peace.

[66] Reinhold Niebuhr, *The Nature and Destiny of Man* (New York: Scribner's, 1949), Vol. 2, p. 318.

[67] *De moribus Ecclesiae Catholicae,* Ch. 30, in Oates, Vol. 1, p. 348.

[68] *Expositio quarumdam propositionum ex epistola ad Romanos,* sec. 72, in Migne, Vol. 35, p. 2083.

[69] *Op. cit.,* p. 172.

[70] *Op. cit.,* p. 72.

[71] *Sermons,* No. 12, sec. 13, in Schaff, Vol. 6, p. 302.

[72] *Confessions,* Bk. III, Ch. 9, p. 65.

[73] *Ibid.* See the similar statement in *De Civitate Dei,* Bk. I, Ch. 26, p. 31.

Under the pressure of events, however, Augustine moved from a position of toleration to one that justified the coercion of heretics and thereby brought the norm of Church-state relations closer to theocratic adhesion. With characteristic honesty, Augustine openly admitted his change: "For originally my opinion was that no one should be coerced into the unity of Christ, that we must act only by words, fight only by argument, and prevail by force of reason."[74] But about 400 Augustine began to change, suggesting that if the state has the power to punish poisoning of the body, it might also have the power to punish the poisoning of the mind.[75] Yet in *Contra litteras Petiliani* of the same period he assures Donatists that the antiheresy laws do not compel right belief but only prevent wrong-doing: "The fear of punishment . . . keeps the evil desire from escaping beyond the bounds of thought."[76]

About 406 Augustine seems to approve for the first time the imposition of penalties on heretics who have committed no criminal acts.[77] This position came into full flower in 408. Then, in a letter to Vincentius, he pointed to the success of the imperial edicts in bringing Donatists back into the fold:

> Could I therefore maintain opposition to my colleagues, and by resisting them stand in the way of such conquests of the Lord, and prevent the sheep of Christ which are wandering on your mountains and hills—that is, on the swellings of your pride—from being gathered into the fold of peace, in which there is one flock and one Shepherd?[78]

But why should such "conquests of the Lord" be made by secular power? Augustine rather ingenuously makes the action by the king a function of the king's Christian conscience. Are we entitled, Augustine asks rhetorically, to say to the kings, "Let not any thought trouble you within your kingdom as to who restrains or attacks the Church of your Lord; deem it not a matter in which you should be concerned"?[79] Rather, says Augustine, "let the kings of the earth serve Christ by making laws for Him and for His cause."[80] He evades the question that seems most pertinent at this point, namely who advises the king on which laws best serve the cause of Christ if it is not the Church.

Augustine's next step away from tolerance is to seek scriptural justification. He does this by a rather strained interpretation of Luke 14:21–24, where the master, finding that the invited guests do not come to his banquet, sends his servant out on the highway to confront passers-by and "compel them to come in."[81] Augustine still agrees that the will cannot be coerced but now says that one can be "exposed to good teaching and example" by force.[82] From 418 on there was a further slide down the slippery path the suppression of heresy seems to follow. In a letter to the priest Sixtus (later Pope Sixtus III) Augustine says that silence on the part of former heretics is not enough, for they are secretly spreading their doctrine—as indeed they were and were almost bound to do. They will need to be forced into defending the true doctrine openly.[83]

It must be noted on Augustine's behalf that he expressed joy that penalties of capital punishment were not being levied against the Donatists; he even intervened with the civil authorities to prevent the execution of a Donatist charged with murder. He consistently maintained that the way to redemption should always be left open and that capital punishment, for whatever purpose, was inconsistent with this. Nevertheless, Augustine, supported by scriptural references, had by now sanctified with his own ecclesiastical blessing a policy based on hard political ne-

[74] *Epistle* 93, sec. 7, in Schaff, Vol. 1, pp. 288–89. Deane, Ch. 6, documents Augustine's change on this issue with admirable thoroughness; this section follows his account. See also Montgomery, pp. 238–42.

[75] *Contra epistulam Parmeniani,* Bk. I, Ch. 10, sec. 16. See Deane, p. 319.

[76] Bk. II, Ch. 84, sec. 184, in Schaff, Vol. 4, p. 572.

[77] *Epistle* 89, sec. 1, *ibid.,* Vol. 1, p. 374.

[78] *Epistle* 93, sec. 19, *ibid.,* p. 389.

[79] *Epistle* 185, sec. 20, *ibid.,* Vol. 4, p. 640.

[80] *Epistle* 93, sec. 19, *ibid.,* Vol. 1, p. 389.

[81] *Sermons,* No. 12, sec. 8, in Schaff, Vol. 6, p. 449.

[82] *Epistle* 135, sec. 13, *ibid.,* Vol. 4, p. 638.

[83] *Epistle* 191, sec. 2, *ibid.,* Vol. 1, p. 555.

cessity—or expediency, depending upon one's viewpoint—a policy that seems inconsistent with his own view of the interiority of true faith. That the state, in which Augustine had little enough confidence in all other respects, should be the agency of such forced obeisance to "true doctrine" seems rather grimly ironic.

War and Morality

Augustine was no war-lover. Wars, he said in *De Civitate Dei,* were always cruel, destructive to the innocent, a product of sinful lusts, the occasion of the "most insane pomp of human glory."[84] Yet, unlike such early Church Fathers as Tertullian and Origen, he was not a pacifist. He accepted the world as it was too fully for that:

> A great deal depends on the causes for which men undertake wars, and on the authority they have for doing so; for the natural order, which seeks the peace of mankind, ordains that a monarch should have the power of undertaking war if he thinks it advisable, and that the soldiers should perform their military duties in behalf of the peace and safety of the community.[85]

Augustine offers two basic criteria of the just war:[86] (1) All defensive wars are just: ". . . the law which demands that a hostile force be repelled for the purpose of protecting the citizens can be obeyed without lust."[87] (2) An offensive war is just if the state "warred upon has failed either to make reparation for an injurious action committed by its citizens or to return what has been wrongfully appropriated."[88] But even just wars are a function of the earthly city: the property restored serves earthly appetites; the peace achieved is for the sake of enjoying earthly goods. The justice of a just war is the natural justice that directs man toward earthly harmony and peace, not the eternal justice of harmony with God's will.

One defect of Augustine is his failure to distinguish between the moral weight to be assigned "the causes for which men undertake wars" and that assigned to "the authority they have for doing so." In practice, the authority seems to be all that matters, for a king making war for the worst possible reason, says Augustine, must still be obeyed by his subjects. Augustine, as Hobbes was to do later, assumed that unquestioning obedience was the prerequisite of peace and that peace was the highest civic good. Augustine granted a single exception to the requirement for obedience: no king could rightfully require a subject to disobey God. If a soldier is asked to worship idols or to throw incense on pagan altars, he may rightfully refuse. For Augustine's soldier military duty is merely an aspect of what one should "render unto Caesar" according to the scriptural injunction. Jesus praises the young centurion of Matthew 8:5–13 for his faith but does not, observes Augustine, tell him to leave the armed service.[89]

And what of the Sermon on the Mount —turn the other cheek, walk the second mile, return no evil for evil? These, Augustine argues, were injunctions meant not for states but for individuals[90] and indeed only for individuals willing to follow a martyr's course. Augustine thought it admirable but unusual for the individual to follow such a course. He considered the Sermon's injunctions irrelevant for states, since a state must survive in order to fulfil its obligation to protect its citizens. Though he does not agree with Cicero that states are intended to be eternal, he does acknowledge that states can be constructed so that they will not die in the way individuals die. At least it can be said that

[84] As does his treatment of the writings on heresy, Deane's treatment of Augustine on war seems definitive. See *Political and Social Ideas,* Ch. 5.

[85] *Contra Faustum,* Bk. XXII, sec. 75, in Schaff, Vol. 4, p. 301. See also the letter to Boniface in 418: "Do not think that it is impossible for anyone to please God while engaged in active military service. Among such persons was the holy David" (*Epistle* 189, sec. 4, in Schaff, Vol. 1, p. 553).

[86] See the discussion in Deane, pp. 160–62; Combes, pp. 284–88; and Paolucci, pp. 162–83.

[87] *De libero arbitrio,* Bk. I, Ch. 5, sec. 12, in Burleigh, p. 119. Cf. *De Civitate Dei,* Bk. I, Ch. 21.

[88] *Quaestionum in Heptateuchum,* Ch. 6, sec. 10, trans. by Deane in *Political and Social Ideas,* p. 312.

[89] *Contra Faustum, loc. cit.*

[90] *Epistle* 138, sec. 9, in Schaff, Vol. 1, p. 483.

the fact of war is not by itself a breach of faith:

> when faith is pledged, it is to be kept even with the enemy against whom the war is waged, how much more with the friend for whom the battle is fought! Peace should be the object of your desire; war should be waged only as a necessity, and waged only that God may by it deliver men from the necessity and preserve them in peace. For peace is not sought in order to the kindling of war, but war is waged in order that peace may be obtained. Therefore, even in waging war, cherish the spirit of a peace maker.[91]

A severe ethical difficulty stems from the fact that the necessity of the war is based not on the judgment of the soldier (or, by extension, the governed) but on the judgment of the king (or the governor). If, as we have seen, Augustine is unwilling to verbalize precise limits to God's power and purpose in leading individuals, the question of when an individual soldier (or citizen) is justified in disobeying becomes moot. He may be justified in the sight of God while being unjustified by all standards of earthly legitimacy. Perhaps nothing can resolve this ethical dilemma short of a perfect society, or a society in which individual purposes and social purposes are completely harmonious. But why military relationships should carry with them special obligations requires more attention than Augustine gives the subject. For the sake of temporal peace the Christian soldier is morally bound to kill if so commanded, even when it offends his conscience. In other human relationships, however, Augustine does not approve of the overriding of eternal by temporal standards. His position comes close to the "doctrine of superior orders" by which Hitler's gas-chamber attendants could claim innocence.[92]

One logical way out of this impasse—an impasse that has been chronic for all responsible men caught between autocracy and anarchy—is partial surrender of the temporal for the sake of the eternal (resignation) or, where that is impossible, total surrender (suicide). But Augustine closes the door on this way out:

> no man ought to inflict upon himself voluntary death, for this is to escape the ills of time by plunging into those of eternity . . . no man ought to do so on account of his own past sins for he has all the more need of this life that these sins may be healed by repentance . . . no man should put an end to this life to obtain that better life we look for after death, for those who die by their own hand have no better life after death.[93]

Even to prevent oneself from falling into sin is no grounds for suicide, says Augustine. He takes the prohibition as an absolute command of God similar to the command of a general to his soldier. In neither case should the recipient of the command raise questions. This seems to be Augustine at his most dogmatic. But at the same place in *De Civitate Dei* he refers to those Christian virgins who committed suicide rather than submit to barbarian rape and, though he condemned their action in general terms, he nevertheless could say, "I, for my part, do not know your hearts, and therefore make no accusation."

The excruciating quality of such choices made *in extremis* applies also to the ruler's decision to go to war in the first place. Many, if not most, wars are unnecessary and hence unjust in Augustine's meaning. But even in so-called just wars the innocent are bound to suffer. Rome provided a valuable bond of peace and a condition of unity among men "but how many great wars, how much

[91] *Epistle* 189, sec. 6, in Schaff, Vol. 1, p. 554. ". . . it is obvious that peace is the end sought for by war. For every man seeks peace by waging war, but no man seeks war by making peace. For even they who intentionally interrupt the peace in which they are living have no hatred of peace, but only wish it changed into a peace that suits them better" (*De Civitate Dei,* Bk. XIX, Ch. 12, p. 687).

[92] ". . . it may be an unrighteous command on the part of the king, while the soldier is innocent, *because* [our italics] his position makes obedience a duty" (*Contra Faustum,* Bk. XXII, sec. 75, in Schaff, Vol. 4, p. 301).

[93] *De Civitate Dei,* Bk. I, Ch. 26, pp. 31–32. Morally Augustine demands less of states than of individuals while at the same time conceding them a greater earthly durability than individuals. He is thus perhaps inconsistent in granting to states a right to suicide that he does not grant to individuals.

slaughter and bloodshed have provided this unity!" Just wars are those occasioned by powers guilty of wrongdoing and blame can be directed toward them. But this does not erase the suffering of war: "Let everyone then, who thinks with pain on all these great evils, so horrible, so ruthless, acknowledge that this is misery. And if any one either endures or thinks of them without mental pain, this is a more miserable plight still, for he thinks himself happy because he has lost human feeling."[94]

[94] *Ibid.*, Bk. XIX, Ch. 7, pp. 383–84.

CONCLUSION

We are left with the ambiguity with which we began, the ambiguity that makes the political thought of Augustine so frustrating. We are to follow God as He speaks to us in the inner promptings of conscience but also as He directs us through the orders of power-hungry rulers. Politics is the product of man's sin, man's rebellion against God, yet it is also a part of the order of nature leading all men back to God. Sin is embedded in the whole social structure and (logically) all must be saved if any are to be saved but few will be saved. Law without the Holy Spirit is empty but the spirit of *caritas is* eternal law. The natural aim of the political order and its highest good is peace and harmony but violence and crisis are necessary to bring out the best in us.[95]

In one sense Augustine took politics very seriously: he gave Christians and the Church a basis for participation in the civic order. In another sense he took politics not seriously at all: politics was entirely bound by the earthly city that would pass away without ultimate significance save as a testing place for human souls. "Why rush the discords in but that harmony might be prized."[96]

Augustine bequeathed to the medieval world and to us a grim warning and a wistful hope. The ambiguity of his unsatisfying political theory is born of the ambiguity and dissatisfaction he found in life itself. In turning from Augustine to Aquinas we turn from ambiguity to definitiveness, from illuminationism to common sense, from spirituality to rationality. We turn from haphazard political theory to architectonic political theory. But whether the grandeur of Thomistic system-building can equal the rolling voice of the Bishop of Hippo in portraying the drama of life is doubtful indeed.

[95] See Edgar H. Brookes, *The City of God and the Politics of Crisis* (London: Oxford Univ. Press, 1960).

[96] *Epistle* 138. Quoted by Figgis, p. 40.

6

AQUINAS

One cannot approach the subject of Thomas Aquinas without being somewhat awed by two considerations: first, the sheer magnitude, the intellectual weight, of the *Summa theologica* gives one pause. Whoever we are, we must approach it from one of the many specialized disciplines that characterize twentieth-century learning. We realize that the inclusion of the full range of human knowledge within the framework of one theoretical system is not possible for us and is unlikely to be possible in what future we can foresee. Hence we scarcely know how to come to grips with a work of Thomas' dimensions.

Second, we cannot be unmindful of the overwhelming number of man-hours of scholarly labor expended on the exegesis of Thomas, especially intensive since the bestowal of an official and special blessing on his philosophy by Pope Leo XIII in *Aeterni Patris* (1879).[1] Are not some of the refined extrapolations more significant than the parent thought? And is it not likely that part of what has come to be known as Thomism is alien to Thomas himself? As a prophylaxis against either spurious influence or irrelevant rebuttal we shall in this chapter largely concentrate on what Thomas himself said.

LIFE

Thomas[2] was born in 1225 at the family castle of Roccasecca near the town of Aquino, not

[1] "Let carefully selected teachers endeavor to implant the doctrine of Thomas Aquinas in the minds of students, and set forth clearly his solidity and excellence over others" (quoted in Foreword to Thomas Aquinas, *Opera Omnia,* Vernon J. Bourke, ed. [New York: Musurgia, 1948], Vol. 1, p. v). Pope Leo XIII here designated the doctrine of Thomas as "Christian Philosophy." Canon 1366, issued under the authority of Pope Benedict XV in 1917, seemed to go further: philosophy and theology "must be accurately" taught by professors "according to the arguments, doctrine, and principles of S. Thomas which they are inviolately to hold" (quoted in Thomas Aquinas, *Summa theologica,* English Dominican trans. [New York: Benziger, 1947], Vol. 1, p. xvi. Subsequent page references are to this edition unless otherwise indicated.)

[2] Brief biographical accounts may be found in G. K. Chesterton, *St. Thomas Aquinas* (Garden City, N.Y.: Doubleday, Image, 1936); Reginald M. Coffey, *The Man from Rocca Sicca* (Milwaukee: Bruce, 1944); M. C. D'Arcy, *Saint Thomas Aquinas,* 2nd ed. (Westminster, Md.: Newman Press, 1955), Ch. 1; and Jacques Maritain, *St. Thomas Aquinas* (New York: World, Meridian, 1958), Ch. 1. The most thorough English biography is that of R. B. Vaughn, *The Life and Labours of St. Thomas Aquin* (London: Longmans, Green, 1871–72) but it is rambling and inaccurate.

far from Naples. He was the seventh son of a distinguished family. His mother, Theodora of Theate, was Norman and his father, Landulf, the Count of Aquino, was a Lombard nobleman and the nephew of Frederick Barbarossa. At the age of five Thomas was sent to nearby Monte Cassino for schooling with the Benedictines but, when he was fourteen or fifteen, his father withdrew him because the monastery had been under attack by the forces of Frederick II.

Thomas was thereupon sent to the University of Naples, where he studied mathematics, astronomy, music, dialectic, and certain classical writers—primarily Caesar, Cicero, and Seneca. In 1244, apparently unaware of the storm he would create within his family, Thomas joined the Order of Preachers, or Dominicans, in Naples. The Dominicans had only recently set up a house of study there and were affiliated with the University. Their mendicant ways and striking white-and-black apparel irritated traditionalists, most notably Thomas' proud family. They had become resigned to his becoming a monk but not in a new, low-status order that would bring no honor to the family.

Intense pressure was brought to bear to change Thomas' mind. Even Pope Innocent IV was induced to intervene, with the odd result that Thomas was offered the abbacy of Monte Cassino with the right of continuing to wear the Dominican habit. His parents apparently thought that the young man had been dazzled by clothes alone. But Thomas was adamant. When the Dominican master general decided on a trip to Paris and took Thomas and three other friars along, the family (his father had by this time died) somehow heard of the trip and two of Thomas' brothers waylaid the party on a road north of Rome and carried Thomas off by force to Roccasecca. Thomas was kept prisoner in the family castle for over a year and was subjected to every stratagem imaginable to obtain his renunciation of the Dominicans. On one occasion his brothers slipped a seductive female in alluring attire into his chamber to see what she could accomplish. Not much, it turned out: Thomas seized a firebrand and chased the terrified woman out of the room, marking the sign of the cross on the door after she had fled. Finally, after long conversations with his mother and his sisters —one of whom he helped lead into a nun's life—his mother helped him escape. Thomas went to Naples, then Paris, then Cologne, where he had followed his teacher, Albert the Great, the leading Aristotelian of his day.

Thomas' quietness and his willingness to be taken in by practical jokes earned for him an ironic appellation from his fellow students: "the Dumb Ox." On one occasion a student joker called Thomas to the window to see a flying ox. He came and was greeted with guffaws. Asked how he could be taken in by such an absurd claim, he answered that he would rather believe it possible for an ox to fly than for a friar to lie. His teaching career began in 1252 in Paris and carried him to Rome, back to Paris again, and finally to Naples. He was admitted as a Master of Theology by the faculty at Paris at the age of thirty-one. This was earlier than the university statutes permitted: a special dispensation from the pope was required, a procedure that aroused some hostility from the more conservative clerics.

Thomas Aquinas was a tall, heavy man with an imposing head. Despite his peaceful demeanor, he seemed to exude power. He worked hard, slept very little, seemed bored by meals. For exercise he liked to walk at great speed. He talked little and rarely mixed with crowds, frequently using his work as an excuse to avoid going to court. Once, it is said, when he was at a dinner in the court of King St. Louis—where he had gone only because he was bound under obedience—he became aroused by a theological argument and, pounding the table, shouted, "Now, that settles the Manicheans!" The King, rather than being offended, sent for scribes to take down Thomas' argument. Some of the stories about Thomas have the ring of the fictional saint: "He never busied himself with temporal affairs, and he had been accustomed from youth upwards abruptly to quit any conversation of which the theme was not the things of God."[3]

Thomas' writing began rather inauspiciously with a commentary on the *Sentences* (1254–56) of Peter Lombard and expositions on the venerable texts of Boethius and the Pseudo-Dionysius as well as the Scriptures. But soon the treatise *De ente et essentia* (On *Being and Essence,* c. 1257), the disputation *De veritate* (*On Truth,* 1259), and the start of the *Summa contra Gentiles* (four books, 1258–60),[4] which was addressed to Moslems and Jews, indicated the greatness that soon would be celebrated. In 1259 Thomas was called to the papal court at Rome. While there, new texts of Aristotle provided by Thomas' Flemish friend William of Moerbeke gave Thomas a great stimulus. He wrote commentaries on Aristotle's *De anima, Metaphysics,* and *Physics,* completed the *Summa contra Gentiles,* and began the *Summa theologica.*

Returning to Paris in 1269, Thomas was plunged into the controversy over Averroism, especially the contention over such doctrines as those claiming that intelligence was not personal to individual men and that matter was not part of divine creation. It is generally conceded that he routed the Averroists by means of such works as *De unitate intellectus contra Averroistas Parisienses.* He did so with his right hand, so to speak, while holding off with his left hand the conservative theologians who, suspicious of Aristotle's influence, were accusing him of materialism, profanity, and dangerous novelty. (Indeed, three years after Thomas' death the Bishop of Paris censured him. Some twenty Thomistic propositions were condemned. It was not until 1325, two years after Thomas' canonization, that the Bishop of Paris at that time withdrew the censures.) In this period Thomas also wrote *De malo* and the commentaries on Aristotle's *Politics* (three books, 1266–68) and *Ethics* (ten books, 1266–69) and continued work on the *Summa theologica.*

[3] Maritain, p. 54.

[4] Scholars are not agreed on these dates.

When Thomas returned to Naples in 1272, he organized a new school, preached in the vernacular, composed the *Compendium theologiae,* and, in general, worked too hard. In 1273 he experienced some kind of trance or loss of consciousness and upon recovering declared that all his writing was but chaff. He continued working but in a changed, subdued way. The very next year, on his way to the Council of Lyons where he was going at the request of Pope Gregory X, he fell ill. After lingering for months at the monastery of Fossanuova he died, a man only forty-eight or forty-nine years old.

After Thomas' escape from his family, his life had little of the drama of Augustine's. But it is well to remind ourselves that his intellectual position put him into the heart of the crucial intellectual struggles of his time and on the side of innovation rather than reaction: "Whatever its reputation some centuries later Aristoteleanism [*sic*] stood in the thirteenth century for a free and impenitent spirit of rationalism and unfettered investigation, a strong sense of the truth here and now, a dialectic of control, not of escape from the present world."[5]

Works

Paradoxical though it sounds, it is easier to deal bit by bit with Thomas' political thought than with Augustine's because Thomas is so much more systematic. Augustine's political thought is a pungent wisp of fragrance emitted by his herculean laboring after God. By itself it is uncontainable and evaporative. Thomas' political thought is a piece with squared corners that may be lifted out of the grand cosmic puzzle, examined, then put back again.

The sources of Thomas' political thought are found chiefly in two works: *De regimine principum sive de regno* (*Of the Governance of Princes or of Rulership*),[6] written about

[5] Thomas Gilby, Introduction to *Saint Thomas Aquinas, Philosophical Texts* (New York: Oxford, 1960), p. XVII.

[6] The work is sometimes cited as *De regimine principum* and sometimes as *De regno.* The most frequent English translation is *The Rule of Princes.*

1266–67, and two sections from the great *Summa theologica* written between 1267 and 1273. *De regimine principum* was written for the king of Cyprus, who died in 1267, before Thomas had finished the work. It was left unfinished and later completed—not well—by Thomas' pupil, Bartholemew of Lucca. Only Book I and through half of Chapter 4 in Book II are authentic Thomas. The fact that Thomas abandoned the work as he did suggests that it may not have been of great importance to him. The first of the two sections of the *Summa* referred to above is sometimes published separately as the "Treatise on Law." It consists of Questions 90–108 of the *Prima secundae,* the first part of the Second Part of the *Summa.* The second section contains certain questions on prudence, right, justice, and related topics—Questions 47–64 of the *Secunda secundae,* the second part of the Second Part.[7] Certain scattered passages in the *Summa contra Gentiles* also relate to politics. In addition, Thomas wrote commentaries on all the major works of Aristotle, among which those on the *Ethics* and the *Politics* have, of course, political significance.

DE REGIMINE PRINCIPUM

Natural Government Is by One

De regimine principum is less original than the "Treatise on Law." In fact, the former follows Aristotle almost slavishly at times. But it can be taken as a statement of certain basic political convictions even if it does not provide the most rigorous defense of them. The first book of the work deals with four subjects: the necessity of government, the forms of government, the motives and justifications of rulers, and the nature and duties of rulership. The second book takes up the several duties of rulers in detail but it breaks off before completing the problem of founding a city or kingdom.

In its short scope *De regimine principum* manages to set forth six political tenets characteristic of Thomist thought:

(1) Man is naturally social.

(2) The state is a natural institution.

(3) In all things there is a single governing principle (unity must precede multiplicity) from which, in its political aspect, it follows that:

(4) Monarchy is the best form of government.

(5) The virtuous life for all is the proper aim of government.

(6) As the spiritual is superior to the temporal, the Church is superior to the state.

Let us take up *De regimine principum* chapter by chapter to see how these tenets are stated and defended.

Man is a political animal, Thomas tells us at the outset, for he must live in a group, not merely to survive physically but to learn how to think. God intends that man develop "natural knowledge," which is the capacity of reasoning from "universal principles" to "what in particular concerns his well-being."[8] But an individual's reason is inadequate to reach these matters without the help of a political community. Like any other entity, a

[7] Citations to the *Summa theologica* are apt to confuse the novice but they do have a rationale. There are the equivalent of five parts to the *Summa: Pars prima, Pars prima secundae, Pars secunda secundae, Pars tertia,* and *Supplementum* (compiled after Thomas' death by Reginald of Piperno). In footnotes these are referred to, respectively, as I, I–II (sometimes Ia–IIae), II–II (sometimes IIa–IIae), III, and *Suppl.* In the manner of *Quaestio disputata,* the public debates of the Scholastics, each of these is divided into a number of Questions and each Question is divided into a number of Articles. The form of each Article is the same: the statement of a question; three, four, or five erroneous answers to the question; Thomas' *sed contra* ("But on the contrary"), in which he usually quotes another authority; his own main answer, the *respondeo;* and specific objections to each of the false answers. Hence a footnote reading I–II, 90, 3, ad 1., is to be translated *Pars prima secundae,* Question 90, Article 3, reply to Objection 1 (*ad primum discendum*). The order of the *Summa theologica* as a whole is based on the first chapter of *Genesis.*

[8] *On Princely Government,* Bk. I, Ch. 1, trans. by J. G. Dawson, in Aquinas, *Selected Political Writings,* ed. by A. P. D'Entreves (New York: Barnes & Noble, 1959), p. 5. Subsequent page references are to this edition. Compare *The Governance of Rulers,* trans. by Gerald B. Phelan (New York: Sheed & Ward, 1938).

political group has a regulative principle by which it can and should be (Thomas said must be) guided to its proper (*convenientum*) end. The guiding in this case should be done by a governor motivated solely by interest in the public good. If a government is "directed in the particular interest of the ruler and not for the common good, this is a perversion of government and no longer just. Such rulers were warned by God."

Thomas ends the chapter by outlining the six forms of government Aristotle discussed in the *Politics:* the good and bad forms of the governments of the one, the few, and the many. Thomas accepts these as given, as he accepts so much from Aristotle, but he asks at the outset of Chapter 2 whether it is better to be ruled by one man or many. The aim of rulership, Thomas reminds us once more, is unity and peace. This goal is categorical: a ruler cannot equivocate—he cannot even deliberate—about it and still be a ruler, any more than a physician can deliberate about whether he shall cure a patient. His job is to decide how to cure, not whether to cure. The ruler's job is to decide how to achieve unity and peace, not whether to achieve them. We have encountered this analogy before, in the pages of Plato, and we have seen how deceptive it can be. But Thomas does not question it: "All plurality derives from unity. . . . It follows of necessity that the best form of government in human society is that which is exercised by one person."

The difficulty of rule by several men, Thomas argues, is that they are likely to disagree and when they do the cardinal goal of unity is threatened:

> That is best which most nearly approaches a natural process, since nature always works in the best way. But in nature, government is always by one. Among members of the body there is one which moves all the rest, namely, the heart: in the soul there is one faculty which is pre-eminent, namely reason. The bees have one king, and in the whole universe there is one God, Creator, and Lord of all. And this is quite according to reason.[9]

[9] *Ibid.*, Ch. 2, pp. 11–13.

Tyranny

In Chapter 3 Thomas, like Aristotle, tells us that among the unjust governments democracy is more tolerable than tyranny because, while evil, democracy is a weak and divided evil, a conclusion of Aristotle now graced with theological overtones:

> The same conclusions are apparent from a study of the order of divine providence, which disposes of all things in the most admirable manner. For goodness arises in things out of one perfect cause, everything being so arrranged as to assist in the production of goodness; but evil arises out of singularity and individual defect. There is no beauty in a body unless all its members are harmoniously disposed one to another: but there is ugliness as soon as one member is ill-fitting. So ugliness may occur in many ways and for a diversity of reasons; but of beauty there is only one and perfect cause. This happens in every case where good and bad are contrasted; as though it were the providence of God that good, proceeding from a single cause should be the stronger; while evil, proceeding from a diversity of reasons should be the weaker.[10]

One is struck, however, by the recurring gap between theory and example in Thomas. Democracy, we have seen, is better than tyranny because it is a weak and divided form of evil, yet division itself is evil compared to unity. Again, Thomas points out—citing, as he so often does, scriptural condemnations of tyranny—that tyrants usually forbid the assemblage of citizens at weddings, banquets, and other events the tyrant cannot control because such gatherings breed a spirit that is a threat to him. Thomas' point is that in such groups familiarity and confidence enable virtue to develop and virtue in its singularity is a threat to the discord a tyrant prefers. Tyrants have in fact made such prohibitions and there is, of course, truth in Thomas' particular way of explaining this. But one could also explain it by flipping the coin over, so to speak, and arguing that the diversity of social groups is a threat to the political unity a tyrant naturally prefers.

[10] *Ibid.*, Ch. 3, pp. 15–17.

Thomas could see that there were occasions when a tyranny of more than one man could be fairly efficient and he could also concede a measure of advantage to divided government: when joint rulers realize that "there is no one person with power over the common interest, they go about the corporate task as though it were their own business." Thomas even quotes Sallust, the Roman historian, to show at least the short-run benefits of divided authority in Rome after monarchy was abandoned. A hard realism not often associated with Thomas emerges in his statement that great burdens are often accepted rather easily when levied by the whole community, whereas small exactions by kings may be protested as personal hurts. But in this way a popular state can also bankrupt itself, as when Rome began to pay wages for military service simply because it won the favor of many. This led to internal dissensions that wore everyone out and let tyranny back in.

Chapter 4's conclusion recognizes political realities: "From one side and from another, therefore, there is danger: whether from fear of tyranny the best benefits of monarchy are lost, or whether in the hope of achieving true kingship the government degenerates into evil tyranny."[11] Despite the ever present danger of tyranny arising out of excessive respect for the ruler, Thomas believes that once a tyrant gains power individual subjects have no alternative to obedience. Even a tyrant can usually maintain peace and order better than a multiple-headed government. His outrages will hurt single individuals, but they will usually stop short of provoking the whole populace to rebellion. The government of many rarely has enough internal cohesion and discipline to stop short once it is set on an unjust course. Thomas offers no historical examples of this but simply concludes that "it is more expedient to live under a monarchy than under a pluralistic government."

In Chapter 6 Thomas takes up the promising subject of how to remove the opportunity for tyrannizing from the occupant of the throne. From the standpoint of our twentieth-century democratic biases, the promise is not fulfilled. We cannot object to the basic device suggested but find it of limited helpfulness: the king, says Thomas, must be of high character. If this device fails, however, and by poor fortune a people find themselves with a king of low character, they should do nothing unless there is truly "an excess of tyranny," for should a revolt against a cruel monarch fail, greater cruelties shall certainly follow. And should it succeed, the new ruler is most often worse than his predecessor. As evidence for the latter proposition Thomas cites the experience only of a certain "old woman" of Syracuse mentioned in the writings of Valerius Maximus.

Thomas acknowledges the Old Testament examples of tyrannicide, but says that this opinion is not in accord with apostolic teaching. Martyrs, able to bear death for Christ, are admirable in a way killers of kings can never be. If, however, tyranny becomes unbearable, to move against it is an action to be undertaken by "public authority" rather than "the private judgement of individuals." This possibility was not wholly academic in Thomas' thinking, for he cited with approval the experience of Rome removing Tarquin and his sons. If the whole multitude sets up a king, the whole multitude can remove him. But Thomas' sense of hierarchy was such that he felt appeal should always be carried to a higher authority, where possible to a superior and presumably neighboring king. When legitimate political recourses failed, then "recourse must be had to God." Thomas seems to have had relatively great confidence in God's promise in the Old Testament to "free His people from tyrants."[12]

[11] Thomas' occasional realism stands in marked contrast with the perfectionist and even utopian tendencies in some of his twentieth-century disciples: "The good ruler, then, strives to gain the love of his people by first loving them. A leader who would not love his people and strive to gain their love should not be appointed to the ruling office, an office calling for universal love and friendship" (Gerald J. Lyman, *The Good Political Ruler According to St. Thomas Aquinas* [Washington: Catholic Univ. Press, Catholic University Philosophy Series No. 144, 1953], p. 15).

[12] John Locke may later have drawn on this phrase when he referred to revolution against a tyrant as an

Rewards for Ruling

In Chapter 7 there is a shift of concern from the interests of the ruled to the interests of the ruler. Thomas asks the question: what are the proper rewards for ruling? Many say honor and glory, but they are wrong, for these goods are too "fragile." Moreover, the desire for glory is hurtful because it "destroys . . . liberty of spirit." It breeds hypocrisy, presumption, and immoderation in war. In trying to please men rather than God the ruler "becomes a slave to each one." There is paradox in the earthly manifestations of glory: ". . . while glory follows virtuous action, there is virtue in despising glory. Thus, by holding glory in contempt, a man becomes the more renowned."

Many subjects, of course, think it quite appropriate for a king to seek glory. They even encourage him in this quest, for the glory seems to them infinitely superior to what happens when kings pursue wealth and pleasure. Glory has at least a trace of virtue in it. Augustine defined glory as "no more than the judgement of those who think well of their fellows."[13] Perhaps, says Thomas, glory is the best earthly good men can seek. It is a useful restraint "that men fear the disapproval of right-thinking men." But it is not enough. The good king will look to God for his reward and he will not be disappointed. If God gives wicked kings

> victory over their enemies, the subjection of kingdoms to their arms, and much plunder to carry off; what will be His reward for the good rulers who, with pious intention, minister to the people of God and oppose their enemies. To such He promises not an earthly, but a heavenly reward; one which is to be found in God alone.[14]

We seem to have left the realm of the natural for the realm of the supernatural, the realm of the temporal for the realm of the eternal, for Thomas is talking about eternal and not material rewards. But Thomas is also an Aristotelian, so immediately he proceeds:

> This conclusion can also be demonstrated by reason. For there is a firm conviction in the minds of all who think rationally that blessedness [*beatitudo*] is the reward of virtue. Virtue in anything can, in fact, be described as that which perfects its possessor and renders action beneficent. But every one, when acting rightly, strives to achieve that which he most desires; that is, to be happy [*felicem*]; for no one can desire otherwise than this. Consequently, one can rightly conclude that the reward of virtue is to make man happy.[15]

Here we find a shadow of the famous Thomistic synthesis—but is this synthesis a compound or a mixture? *Virtu* perhaps produces what all men want: the kind of happiness that is the end of universal good. But in Aristotle it was a kind of happiness (*eudaemonia*) more in tune with the good of this world. And if it was not, strictly speaking, a mortal ideal, it was certainly a political ideal, for it could not be realized by an individual outside a *polis*. Thomas pushes Aristotle beyond the boundary of mortality and into a different kind of *eudaemonia:* "There is nothing on earth . . . which could make a man blessed; nor, in consequence, is there any earthly reward sufficient for a king."[16] Again Thomas quotes Augustine: "Christian rulers we say are happy, now in hope, afterwards in very fact" (Phelan translation).

There is also a contrast between Thomas and Augustine: Augustine would have agreed

---

"appeal to heaven." It is well to remember once again that, if Thomas seems a bit complacent about the dangers of tyranny, it may have been because he was addressing the whole work to a living king. Indeed, this fact makes his strictures against tyranny seem quite forthright.

[13] Quoted by Thomas from *De Civitate Dei,* Bk. V, Ch. 12.

[14] *Ibid.*, p. 43.

[15] *Ibid.*, pp. 43–45.

[16] Thomas believed that the soul separates from the body at the time of death. For Aristotle the soul (*psyche*) was but the form of the body and not the same as the immortal intellect or mind (*nous*), which merged with the universal mind after death. To speak of rewards to a person after death in the way that Thomas does would probably have been meaningless to Aristotle. For a discussion of Thomistic-Aristotelian disjunctions as they apply to the *Nicomachean Ethics,* see Harry V. Jaffa, *Thomism and Aristotelianism* (Chicago: Univ. of Chicago Press, 1952).

that earthly rewards are futile but he would have said, therefore, let us not expect too much of the rulers of this life. Thomas seems to assume that the heavenly standards not only can be a norm but can become normal for earthly rulers. Augustine is always bordering on despair, though acknowledging repeated gracious triumphs over despair. Thomas does not seem capable of despair, which may be one reason why Augustine has a kind of direct relevance to the twentieth century that Thomas lacks.

In Chapter 9 Thomas declares that the virtue of good kings brings a higher degree of beatitude than almost any other occupation. With a surprisingly quantitative note he says that the more persons ruled, the greater the ruler's virtue, for it is "natural" that those who direct others are obliged to be superior. This is not true of all occupations; thus to teach is greater than to learn, to be an architect is greater than to be a bricklayer, and to be a general is greater than to be a private. There is a conspicuous lack of New Testament citations at this point in Thomas' account and one cannot help but wonder what has happened to "the last shall be first," "unless you be as a child," and "the least among you shall be greatest." Instead we are told that "a king merits greater reward for ruling his subjects justly than does one of his subjects for acting aright under his government."

Obligations of Rulers

Yet, as we have seen, Thomas cannot be said to gloss over the evils of tyranny. Nor is he unrealistic about the temptations of rulers. It is rather that he puts a terrible burden of moral obligation on rulers' shoulders. If ordinary men are to be praised for helping the needy, settling disputes, rescuing one who is oppressed,

> How much more, then, does he deserve praise of men and reward of God who gladdens a whole country with peace, restrains the violent, preserves righteousness, and orders the actions of men by his laws and precepts?
>
> The greatness of kingly virtue becomes further apparent from another fact; that is from a king's singular likeness to God; since a king does in his kingdom what God does in the universe.[17]

It is because of these obligations heaped on legitimate rulers that tyrants are held to be guilty not only for their own sins, but also for the sins they encourage in their subjects.

Thomas does not quite argue that one is either a wholly virtuous ruler or a tyrant. He grants special allowances to well-meaning but bungling kings: The "very difficulty which confronts princes in acting aright makes them worthy of a higher reward. And if, on occasion, they should err through frailty they are the more excusable before men and more easily obtain pardon from God"—provided, that is, they are humble and they pray.

This general mood of optimism is sustained in Chapter 10, where Thomas explains how much love and friendship can influence even a tyrant. Nevertheless, tyrants are characterized by being unable to establish a true bond of friendship with their subjects and hence their rule is less stable than that of good kings. (Julius Caesar and Octavian are cited as examples of the latter.) The deliberate use of fear made necessary by the policies of tyrants becomes a threat to the very regime that uses it. Hence, though God permits tyrants to rule in order to punish the sins of the subjects, He does not allow them to rule for very long. Thomas' optimism seems to overreach itself here and even more so as he continues: ". . . we see from experience that kings gain greater riches through justice than do tyrants by rapacity." Nor is it altogether convincing to assert that the memory of the just perseveres, while "the name of the wicked shall rot"—either because it vanishes or "remains with its stench." Perhaps because of his royal audience, Thomas perseveres in his attempt to make a case for the likelihood of temporal rewards to the virtuous ruler, even though the reward that matters is a nontemporal one. Thomas seems con-

[17] *On Princely Government,* p. 51.

cerned with being holy and practical at the same time, with justifying rule itself and good rule with interlocking arguments:

it is, then, evident, that stability in government, riches, and honour and glory, are all more surely attained by kings than by tyrants; and that a prince who would gain these ends by dishonest means risks becoming a tyrant. No one will leave the path of justice if he is kept to it by the hope of some gain. But, furthermore, a tyrant is deprived of that supreme blessedness which is the reward of a good king; and, what is worse, brings down upon himself the most terrible penalties.[18]

There is a touch of irony in Thomas' assertion that material rewards come to those kings who do not want them, the good kings, and are lost to those kings who do want them, the tyrants. This is a more subtle notion than the bald proposition that virtue always brings material rewards. But even subtle notions may be false, as this one seems to be. This seems especially to be the case if we remember that when Thomas is talking about the good king he is not talking simply about the able politician who keeps the ship of state on a more or less even keel and plunders no one conspicuously. He is talking about a ruler whose motivations are directed to God and the service of his fellows. This makes it all the more surprising when Thomas calls the regime of this paragon "patterned after the regime of nature." "The regime of nature" turns out not to be what the kings of the historical past have done but rather how God Himself acts and would have His creatures act:

Just as the divine control is exercised over all created bodies and over all spiritual powers, so does the control of reason extend over the members of the body and the other faculties of the soul: so, in a certain sense, reason is to man what God is to the universe. But because, as we have shown above, man is by nature a social animal living in community, this similarity with divine rule is found among men, not only in the sense that a man is directed by his reason, but also in the fact that a community is ruled by one man's intelligence; for this is essentially the king's duty.[19]

What training can equip a mere mortal to serve in a role analogous to that of God in the universe? Plato wrestled with this issue with a supreme intellectual effort in the *Republic*. Thomas was capable of a supreme intellectual effort but he did not expend it on this issue. He is more political than Augustine in the sense that he made politics a part of nature. But he neglects the all-important problem of civic education, including the education of rulers—a problem no student of politics since Plato is entitled to overlook. How is an ordinary mortal to become a virtuous king?

If he thinks attentively upon this point he will, on the one hand, be fired with zeal for justice, seeing himself appointed to administer justice throughout his realm in the name of God, and, on the other hand, he will grow in mildness and clemency, looking upon the persons subject to his government, as the members of his own body.[20]

If a king can be made to recognize, to reflect seriously, and to contemplate, he will gain beatitude and will be a good king. Surely this is a big "if." Thomas is somewhat more specific about this point in Chapter 13: "We must now consider what God does in the universe, and thus we shall see what a king should do." Thomas compares God's creation of the world with a king's selection of a site for a new city, his determination of where farms, camps, schools, businesses, law courts, etc., ought to go. But there is no real "analogy with the creation of the world" as Thomas promises. The discussion is a purely abstract statement of the duty of a king to consider such factors.

Of course, few rulers are called upon to found new states, so Thomas turns to the everyday governance of states based upon the divine paradigm. Here again, however, we are destined to be disappointed, for, in Chap-

[18] *Ibid.*, Ch. 11, p. 63.

[19] *Ibid.*, Ch. 12, p. 67.

[20] *Ibid.*

ter 14, Thomas slips rather casually into a discussion of how the idea of governing is related to the steering of a ship: the good pilot must have a port and know how to get there with his cargo undamaged. So, too, the governor must have an end outside the state itself toward which he guides the ship of state: "the object of human society is a virtuous life." Obviously it is not enough simply for men to come together and live for transient satisfactions: "If men consorted together for bare existence, both animals and slaves would have a part in civil society." But virtue is only the penultimate end of the state. The ultimate end is "not merely to live in virtue, but rather through virtuous life to attain to the enjoyment of God."[21]

Rulers and Priests

Thomas now turns to the relationship of Church and state. Kings, he asserts, have full authority over their subjects but are not themselves autonomous. In order to prevent confusion of the spiritual and the earthly, the spiritual kingdom has been entrusted to priests and especially to "the High Priest, the successor of Peter and Vicar of Christ, the Roman Pontiff; to whom all kings in Christendom should be subject, as to the Lord Jesus Christ Himself." This division between the spiritual and temporal spheres is necessary because priests are those who have within their care the ultimate end of man and this end must not be subordinated to the intermediate end of earthly preservation, which is in the care of kings. In the Old Testament priests were properly subject to kings because the whole worship was directed toward "temporal benefits . . . promised to the people. . . . But under the New Law there is a higher priesthood through which men are led to a heavenly reward: and under Christ's Law, kings must be subject to priests."

Despite this asserted superiority of the priesthood, the exalted role of the king remains quite intact as Book I ends. In the individual there is a natural unity, "but the unity of a community, which is peace, must be brought into being by the skill of the ruler." Moreover, while an individual can live for but a brief time, a society, once established, should be "perpetual."

Thomas ends the book with a brief glance at the three most pressing problems for a king, namely that (1) men are not constant in their capacity and ability, (2) men are perverse and lazy, and (3) wars from beyond one's borders are a never ending threat. The wise king will therefore attend carefully to the appointment of new men to office, restrain and encourage men by the proper system of rewards and punishments, and finally look to a sound military defense.

Book II

What little we have of Book II is of fairly transient worth, referring as it does to such factors as climate, food supply, the draining of marshes, and the charm of scenery in the founding of cities. What is striking is the rigorous adherence to Aristotle's doctrine of the mean: merchants are, unfortunately, necessary, but there should not be too many of them; recreation should not be neglected, for "in human intercourse it is proper to have a moderate share of pleasure . . . as a 'spice of life,' so to speak" (Phelan translation). And like Aristotle—or simply because at this point Thomas is merely a channel through which the politics of Aristotle flows—Thomas says that foreign trade is bad and contact with foreigners is to be avoided if the state is to be self-sufficient. This is, we remember, the overriding goal of the Greek *polis.*

THE *SUMMA THEOLOGICA*

Politics is incidental to the *Summa theologica;* where it is the subject matter, it is treated as an aspect of Thomas' theology. But the

[21] "To attain to the enjoyment of God" does not mean to *earn* the enjoyment of God. Thomas does not abandon the Augustinian conception of grace.

basic political tenets found in *De regimine principum* and listed above carry over with remarkable consistency to the *Summa.* Thus it seems wisest to sacrifice some political themes in the *Summa* in order to concentrate on the most important one: the idea of natural law.

Law and Nature

The "Treatise on Law" covers the definition of law, the four types of law (eternal, divine, natural, and human), the powers and functions of law, the relationship of law to change and custom, the Old Law of the Old Testament (including its "moral," "ceremonial," and "judicial" precepts), and the New Law of the gospels. Although commentators on Thomas' political theory of necessity concentrate on the more political, less scriptural first part of the "Treatise," it may be indicative of Thomas' interest and perspective that even within this short section devoted to the law the political references consume only one-third of the pages and the law of the Old and New Testaments the rest. We shall, however, need to examine those few political pages with considerable care.

The essence of law

In Question 90, entitled "The Essence of Law," Thomas states in general terms a good many of what later will be presented as conclusions to sometimes elaborate arguments. Article 1 sketches the relationship of law to reason. This relationship is described as such a close one that we may at times have trouble telling the two apart:

> Law is a rule and measure of acts whereby man is induced to act or is restrained from acting: for *lex* (law) is derived from *ligare* (to bind), because it binds one to act. Now the rule and measure of human acts is the reason, which is the first principle of human acts. . . . Since it belongs to the reason to direct to the end, which is the first principle in all matters of action, according to the Philosopher. . . . Since law is a kind of rule and measure, it may be in something in two ways. First as in that which measures and rules . . . Secondly as in that which is measured and ruled . . . so that any inclination arising from a law may be called a law, not essentially, but by participation, as it were.[22]

This distinction between *essential law,* or the measuring power of reason, and *participatory law,* or the particular judgment or act of will ruled by reason, reaffirms a distinction vital to the natural law tradition. Without this distinction disagreement over particular applications of a general norm of reason would seriously affect the validity of such a norm. In practice it means that an erroneous decree of a governor, a decree that fails to participate in reason, is not a bad law but simply no law at all. This solves one problem only by raising another, which we shall have to look at in a moment.

The concept of two-dimensional law, measuring and measured, parallels in a rough way the distinction between speculative reason and practical reason: speculative reason works with propositions in an effort to arrive at abstract conclusions; practical reason applies these conclusions to operations by means of syllogistic logic. Speculative reason, if it is to "stand firm" (We still say, "it stands to reason"), must travel back toward first principles. Practical reason, to stand firm, must travel forward toward the last end, which, in this case, is "the common good." Thomas, of course, assumes that the good of the first principle and the good of the last end are ultimately the same and here too a problem arises.

A third problem is that of will: how can reason be said to command anything, since command seems to be a relationship of the will? Thomas' answer, at this point, is:

> Reason has its power of moving from the will . . for it is due to the fact that one wills the end, that the reason issues its commands as regards things ordained to the end. But in order that the volition of what is commanded may have the nature of law, it needs to be in accord with some rule of reason. And in this sense is to be understood the saying that the will of the sovereign has the force of law; otherwise the

[22] *Summa theologica,* Vol. 1, p. 993.

sovereign's will would savor of lawlessness rather than of law.[23]

The fourth problem, namely whether the reason of any man is competent to make laws, is perhaps of the greatest interest to modern democrats. Thomas' answer is negative:

A law, properly speaking, regards first and foremost the order of the common good. Now to order anything to the common good belongs either to the whole people, or to someone who is the vice regent of the whole people. And therefore the making of a law belongs either to the whole people or to a public personage who has care of the whole people: since in all other matters the directing of anything to the end concerns him to whom the end belongs.[24]

"The whole people" should not be made too much of in this passage. This term is no doubt a concession to the model of Greek polity included in the Aristotelian typology. From *De regimine principum* we should know that Thomas would not seriously entertain the vision of a popular democracy. "The whole people" means the community taken as an entity. Private persons can of course reason, but a private person cannot be a lawmaker, for "A private person cannot lead another to virtue efficaciously: for he can only advise, and if his advice be not taken, it has no coercive power, such as the law should have, in order to prove an efficacious inducement to virtue."

Thomas' ostensible resolution of the issues raised by Question 90 permits him to end the Question with a definition of law: "Thus from the four preceding articles the definition of law may be gathered; and it is nothing else than an ordinance of reason for the common good, made by him who has care of the community, and promulgated."

The problem of natural law

Let us look at the difficulties raised by Question 90, for they are symptomatic of the whole problem of natural law. On the one hand, law is seen as an ordinance of reason, as a measuring principle; on the other hand, it is seen as a command of the will measured by reason. On the one hand, law is directed toward indemonstrable first principles; on the other hand, it is directed toward the common good of concrete human communities. On the one hand, an unreasonable sovereign's will is no law at all; on the other hand, the reason of a private person is not law, for it has no "coercive power."

Our empiricist minds immediately leap to a concrete situation: "Well," we say, "what if the sovereign is a pretty unreasonable fellow, as sovereigns often are? If his will is thereby rendered unlawful and if everyone else is legally impotent, who or what fills the vacuum? Isn't this an open invitation to political chaos?" The answer is that chaos was an improbable, even outlandish, notion to Thomas. As we have seen, he could contemplate tyranny and orderly procedures for coping with it but, he would say, if we properly understand it, we will see that God's universe is inherently orderly. Most rulers are where they ought to be, doing what they ought to do, and certainly an ordinance of reason could not violate the common good of an established community, or vice versa; the universe is not built to permit it. In all that he was doing, we must remember, Thomas was seeking to understand the very structure of the universe rather than to chronicle the peculiar difficulties of specific historical communities.

That goodness and orderliness are of the very essence of things is nowhere more starkly stated than in that section of the First Part of the *Summa theologica* called the "Treatise on the Divine Government." In Question 103, "Of the Government of Things in General," Thomas says: ". . . we observe that in nature things happen always or nearly always for the best; which would not be the case unless some sort of providence directed nature towards good as an end; which is to govern. . . . The unfailing order we observe in things is a sign of their being governed." Political government is but an aspect of this universal government. Because we moderns

[23] *Ibid.*, 1, p. 994. Some of the same difficulties arise in the relationship of habitual behavior to reason. The propositions of the practical intellect, says Thomas, are sometimes "retained in the reason by means of habit" and still possess the nature of law.

[24] *Ibid.*, 3, p. 995.

tend not to identify politics with order—indeed, we may identify it with disorder—we almost inevitably underestimate the extent to which medieval writers assumed the utter dependence of the individual subject on his ruler and likewise the utter dependence of the individual churchman on his clergy. The more formal *Summa* does not reveal this so clearly as Thomas' "Sermon on the Feast of All-Saints":

The whole merit of the saints depends on their ruler. It is a wretched and degrading and dreadful thing for a man to be subjected to one who is beneath him or base, and the Lord issues threats through His prophet, saying: *I will deliver Egypt into the hands of cruel lords.* He who serves one who is worthy, is blessed, and we read in Ecclesiasticus: *Blessed is he that hath not served such as are unworthy of him. . . .*

You may say, *Are we not subject to God?* It is true that we are, but only indirectly. That is, by means of the angels, prelates, and pedagogues, who keep us in the way we ought to come to blessedness.[25]

Earthly rule is an aspect of God's rule and is for the good, however much we suffer in the short run. We should keep this assumption in mind as we look at the more detailed treatment of eternal, natural, divine, and human law in Questions 93–95 of the "Treatise on Law."

Eternal law is "Divine Wisdom . . . moving all things to their due end." It is "Eternal Reason." It is the mind of God. As such it is the basis of all true law but it is unknowable (in more than an indeterminable degree) by the mind of man.

Natural law is the "participation of the eternal law in the rational creature." It is what man can know of God's mind unaided by special revelation. As such it is available to all men, whatever their religious faith, for, says Thomas, men are by definition rational creatures. Men vary, however, in the degree of their rationality and hence in the degree of the eternal law's participation in them. As a resolute opponent of the Averroists' contention that intelligence is uniform, universal, and residing in men without being affected by the individuality of particular men, Thomas had to admit this much indeterminacy in men's rationality.

Thomas also calls natural law "the first principles of human action." It is not easy to reconcile what we might call the participatory and the constitutive meanings of natural law. One might be regarded as subjective, the other as objective; one would seem to be normative in an internal, spiritual, and dynamic way; the other normative in an external, static, abstractly descriptive way. We have already encountered this duality both in parallel statements about law as that which measures and that which is measured and in the distinction between the judgments of the speculative reason moving toward first principles and the judgments of practical reason moving toward operations. We shall encounter this duality again and again and thus continually face the question of how reason, which is in so many respects dual, can also be one. This same question applies perhaps even more fundamentally to nature. The premise of unity in Thomas seems to drive even reason and will together in a higher concept of nature:

Every act of reason and will in us is based on that which is according to nature . . . for every act of reasoning is based on principles that are known naturally, and every act of appetite in respect of the means is derived from the natural appetite in respect of the last end. Accordingly the first direction of our acts to their last end must needs be in virtue of the natural law.[26]

Being and Goodness

Nature apparently includes everything—the push of will as well as the pull of reason, the "is" of being as well as the "ought" of goodness. If not everything imaginable, at least states of being and states of goodness are united in the concept of nature: "All those things to which man has a natural inclination

[25] *Selected Writings,* ed. by M. C. D'Arcy, English Dominican trans. (London: Dent, Everyman's, 1950), pp. 16–17.

[26] *Summa theologica,* 91, 2, ad 2, p. 997.

are naturally apprehended by reason as being good . . . [their] contraries as evil."

Self-evidence and demonstration

Thomas seems aware that there is a problem here as he raises the question (94, 2) of whether the natural law contains several precepts or only one. Despite the unity of reason, he says, the natural law, which is derived from it, contains several precepts. Thomas "proves" this by resorting characteristically to analogy and "self-evident" principles: "The precepts of the natural law in man stand in relation to practical matters as the first principles to matters of demonstration. But there are several first indemonstrable principles. *Therefore,* there are also several precepts of the natural law." If the "therefore" is meant to assert logical necessity by analogy the conclusion would be unwarranted, for a valid analogy depends on the right selection on other grounds of the terms being compared. Analogy is basically illustrative. That first principles are like the precepts of natural law in some respects would be no proof that they are alike in every respect. What Thomas presumably meant to convey here was not simply that self-evident first principles and the precepts of natural law are analogous but rather that they are identical. As examples of propositions that are self-evident in themselves, that is, propositions that contain a predicate in the notion of the subject, Thomas cites two "universally known" propositions taken from Boethius: "Every whole is greater than its parts" and "Things equal to one and the same are equal to one another." But, Thomas continues, there are other propositions that are equally self-evident but are known only by the learned because only they are familiar with the terms. Such is the statement that because an angel has no body "an angel is not circumscriptively in a place."

These are all statements dealing with the speculative reason—necessary things, things that cannot be other, things that "contain the truth without fail." (Later we shall note the difficulty Thomas worked himself into as these necessitarian assumptions came into conflict with the assumption that God is not bound by necessity.) Practical reason, however, deals with contingent matters, contingent because they are mixed with human actions:

consequently, although there is necessity in the general principles, the more we descend to matters of detail, the more frequently we encounter defects. Accordingly then in speculative matters truth is the same in all men, both as to principles and as to conclusions: although the truth is not known to all as regards the conclusions, but only as regards the principles which are called common notions. But in matters of action, truth or practical rectitude is not the same for all as to matters of detail but only as to the general principles: and where there is the same rectitude in matters of detail, it is not equally known to all.[27]

To act, then, is to "descend" in Platonic fashion from a realm of pure truth to one of muddy contingency. But for those few who see the principles of truth clearly enough and are impeccable in deducing their practical consequences, right action is knowable.

Is and ought

Thomas treats truth and rectitude as virtually identical terms—there is no separation of ought and is, such as we find in modern scientific thought.[28] The idea of the good, upon which the teleological ethics of Aristotle and Thomas are based, is related first to the prior notion of being, which is "in all things whatsoever a man apprehends. . . . Where-

[27] *Ibid.*, 4, p. 1011.

[28] It should be said, however, that even John Locke, the guiding light of British empiricism, expounds the view that moral propositions and geometric propositions may be justified by the same operation. There is a striking similarity between Thomas and Locke in this respect: as the example of a geometric proposition they both use the fact that the three angles of a triangle must add up to 180 degrees and they both (with variations) use as a parallel moral truth the concept that property must belong to its rightful owner. But Thomas seems to concede greater variation and uncertainty of application of the latter than Locke, who was at the time speaking on behalf of a science of morality. See Locke's *Essay Concerning Human Understanding,* Bk. IV, Ch. 3, sec. 18 (Chicago: Regnery, Gateway, 1956), pp. 246–47.

fore the first indemonstrable principle is that *the same thing cannot be affirmed and denied at the same time,* which is based on the notion of being and not-being."

This notion of being is basic to all others and arises simply out of apprehension. The first thing that falls under the apprehension of practical reason (which is directed to action) is the notion of the good. The first principle of the practical reason, then, is as follows: ". . . *good is that which all things seek after.* Hence this is the first precept of law, that *good is to be done and pursued, and evil is to be avoided.* All other precepts of the natural law are based upon this."

Contemporary critics of natural law in general and Thomas in particular have tended to focus too much on the practical difficulties of Thomistic ethics. They say that the injunction to "do good and avoid evil" is too general to be useful and note that deductions from it have in fact put advocates of natural law on the opposite sides of many issues. The critics are probably right but their criticism is often superficial. Thomists will readily acknowledge that believers in natural law will almost inevitably differ on many practical matters; Thomas acknowledges this from the beginning. Disagreement in practical matters, the Thomists rightly say, in no way denies the validity of the primary standard, for (1) the difficulty of applying a standard is not the measure of its worth and (2) the apparent difficulty of application may only reflect the unequal reasoning ability and dedication of will of those invoking natural law.

A more fundamental criticism focuses on the assertion that man "naturally" seeks the good. Two basic criticisms can be levied against this assertion. First, it can be argued that there is no logical way to get from what men naturally—and presumably actually—do to what they ought to do. This criticism attacks what a modern critic would call the naturalistic fallacy, the idea that what is can produce an ought. Second, it can be argued that, while a logical connection exists between the standard being sought and the seeking, it is a formal, tautological, empty connection and is therefore ethically useless: what you seek is the good; therefore, seek the good.

In each case we may say at least something in Thomas' defense. Like Plato and Aristotle, Thomas believed that knowledge of what is good is an aspect of the knowledge of what is real. The belief that there is an absolute dichotomy between value statements and factual statements is a modern innovation, perhaps most influentially expounded by David Hume in *A Treatise of Human Nature* (1739). Some recent students of symbolic logic have suggested that a quirk in the English language may have made the logical barrier between is and ought seem higher than it is.[29] As a matter of grammar and traditional logic it is impossible to derive the value statement "John ought—or ought not—to smoke" from factual statements such as "John is smoking" or "Smoking causes lung cancer." But if we drop the "ought" as a verb and use the indicative of "to be," it may be easier to derive the value statement "John is obligated to quit smoking cigarettes" from the factual statements: (1) "Cigarette smoking causes fatal diseases," (2) "Suicide is contrary to the nature of man," and (3) "John is a man." It is in some such sense that Thomas derives moral injunctions from descriptions of nature. Of course the factuality or meaningfulness of (2) would be challenged by many modern thinkers, as would other assertions Thomas uses as his descriptive base—for example, that God is perfect, that man has some reliable knowledge of this perfection, that man is naturally inclined to seek this perfection, and so forth. Hence, even if we could claim to settle the value-fact controversy on these grounds, we would not thereby have settled the natural-law controversy.

In the second case, that is, with reference

[29] See Roger T. Simonds, "The Natural Law Controversy: Three Basic Logical Issues," *Natural Law Forum,* Vol. 5 (1960), pp. 132–38. Those in the positivist tradition would discount most utterances pertaining to obligation by holding that only declarative sentences free of ambiguous words may be counted as statements and only logical propositions or empirically verifiable propositions can be nonambiguous. See Willard V. Quine, *Elementary Logic,* rev. ed. (New York: Harper & Row, 1965), p. 5.

to the charge of tautology, it is not correct to assume that Thomas used the term "good" in an undifferentiated manner, although it is correct to charge him with failing to keep all his differentiations clear. Though Thomas attributed objective reality to the good and believed that humans universally sought it, he did not, as we have seen, deny that men perceive it differently and pursue it unevenly. He explicitly distinguishes between the good and what may *appear* to be the good. In saying all men seek the good, Thomas meant that all men are *inclined* to seek the good in their various imperfect ways. Having granted the imperfections, he nevertheless believed that the supreme good is more than a far-off guide. Without a supreme good to impell them, he felt, men would have neither reason *nor* desire. Thomas distinguished between human acts (*actus humani*) and the acts of men (*actus hominis*). The latter include all sorts of passionate and reflexive acts that men share with lower animals. The former proceed from deliberate choice and are therefore moral acts. They are also, however, free acts, which means the deliberation does not crowd out entirely the element of will. While a human act is "formally" an act of reason, "materially" it is an act of will.[30] Images (*phantasma*) are the necessary mediators between sensory data and the universal concepts of reason. Thus the ethical injunction "Seek the good" when addressed to humans is equivalent neither to "Do what you already do" (which would include much beyond human—we might say humane—acts) nor to "Become God" (which would be to live without *phantasma*). It is closer to "Act in a rational manner."

Thomas failed, as perhaps all moralists have, to give us adequate objective tests for distinguishing between the good and the apparent good. He was more obligated to produce such objective tests than Augustine because, unlike Augustine, he held that reason could grasp a part of the good even apart from revelation. Reason is somehow in nature and nature's hierarchy of essences has an objective status that makes it visible to any rational man. The plurality of men's visions of the good in the face of this assumed objectivity does therefore tend to undermine Thomas' aspiration toward an underlying unity of all things. For struggling, impetuous, or resigned humanity the good as that which all things seek becomes superfluous. An alternative for Thomas consistent with his belief in reason and unity would have been a thoroughgoing determinism similar to Spinoza's, but this was inconsistent with the Christian concept of free will, which Thomas could hardly have abandoned.

What is necessary?

The premise of unity that was revealed again and again in the *De regimine principum* and the "Treatise on Law" was the skeleton of the whole Thomistic corpus; yet it clashed with other strains in Thomas' thought. The idea of the great chain of being—built upon Plato's notion of the reality of ideal forms and Aristotle's ideas of actuality and potentiality, form and matter—was not unique to Thomas but was the idea of an age, if not a civilization. Lovejoy makes brilliantly clear the reach of that idea. He shows how much Scholastic thought owed to Plato in its belief that nothing that exists is contingent and, as a corollary, that evil is nonbeing. He gives the name principle of plenitude to the notion that the sum of all possible essences is of necessity the object of divine will and shows how this notion and the whole cluster of emanationist ideas came into conflict with the view that God was free to create at will. Lovejoy examines the dilemma in Thomas, "the greatest of schoolmen," and documents "the embarrassment which this internal strain in the traditional doctrine caused him, and the ingenious but futile logical shifts to which it compelled him to resort."[31]

[30] On the intricate question of whether reason creates moral obligation see Mark R. MacGuignan, "St. Thomas and Legal Obligation," *The New Scholasticism*, Vol. 35 (1961), pp. 281–310. Along the way, MacGuignan effectively shows the error of Jacques Maritain's claim that for Thomas natural law is coextensive with all moral philosophy.

[31] Arthur O. Lovejoy, *Great Chain of Being, A Study*

The line of argument that seems most explicit and frequent in Thomas seems to fit in with his innate optimism: God's will is free in the exercise of its creative powers and the apparent multiplicity of things in the world is good. Hence in the *Summa theologica* Thomas argues that God is able to will things other than Himself (I, 19, 2), that He does not will of necessity (I, 19, 3), and yet that He is still the cause of all things (I, 19, 4). Similarly, Thomas tries to demonstrate that "distinction and multitude" in the universe is from God (I, 47, 1), that inequality in the universe is from God (I, 47, 2), and that all corporeal things are made on account of God's goodness (I, 65, 2). This last raises the age-old question of theodicy—how an omnipotent and good God can permit evil in the world. Thomas gives a fairly typical answer to this problem in *Summa contra Gentiles:*

> it does not pertain to divine goodness entirely to exclude from things the power of falling from the good. But evil is the consequence of this power, because what is able to fall does fall at times. And this defection of the good is evil. . . . if evil were totally excluded from the whole of things by divine providence, a multitude of good things would have to be sacrificed. And this is as it should be, for the good is stronger in its goodness than evil is in its malice.[32]

All this would seem to suggest that things cannot be better than they are. Indeed Thomas virtually says so in the *Summa theologica:* "If God could have made better things than He has done but was not willing so to do, He would have been envious. But envy is far removed from God." Yet Thomas draws back from the necessitarian implications of such a statement, for he adds, almost in contradiction, "Yet, God could make other things or add something to the present creation; and then there would be another and a better universe." God could not make our universe better, but He could make better universes.

Lovejoy relies mainly on several passages from the *Summa contra gentiles* to document the necessitarian strain in Thomas.[33] But there is also a rather equivocal necessitarianism present in the very passages of the *Summa theologica* where Thomas argues against necessitarianism. In Part I, Question 19, Article 3, for example, the subject is whether God wills of necessity and the answer is negative. But there is a category of absolute necessity that God of necessity wills, namely when a predicate is part of the definition of a subject. That man is an animal and that numbers are either odd or even are Thomas' examples. Thus God "wills something of absolute necessity, but this is not true of all that he wills. . . . The divine will has a necessary relation to the divine goodness, since that is its proper object. Hence God wills his own goodness necessarily, even as we will our own happiness [*beatitudo*] necessarily." Since God may adopt different means to this necessary end, "his willing things apart from himself is not absolutely necessary, yet it can be necessary by supposition, for supposing that he wills a thing, then he is not able not to will it, as his will cannot change."[34]

The political relevance of this unfamiliar theological terminology, although it may seem obscure, is this: Thomas' innate optimism—which Lovejoy thinks had a direct influence on certain thinkers of the eight-

---

of the History of an Idea (New York: Harper & Row, Torchbooks, 1960), p. 73.

[32] *On the Truth of the Catholic Faith, Summa Contra Gentiles,* Bk. III, Ch. 71, trans. by Vernon J. Bourke (Garden City, N.Y.: Doubleday, 1956), Bk. III, Part I, pp. 238–40. Thomas continues: "If evil were removed from some parts of the universe much perfection would perish from the universe." Without the evil of sickness, the good of health would not be known or appreciated, he says. While having to limp is called an evil, it is in fact a consequence of motion, which is good, with a crooked leg, which is evil, and the combination is more good than evil. See also *Summa theologica,* I, 19, 9.

[33] Lovejoy, pp. 74–79. See also *Summa contra Gentiles,* Bk. I, Chs. 75 and 81; Bk. II, Ch. 45.

[34] A thoroughgoing necessitarian position is arrived at only by piecing together "God wills his own goodness necessarily" in this passage with "all things in a certain manner pre-exist in God by their types. God, therefore, in willing himself wills other things," found in *Summa contra gentiles,* Bk. I, Ch. 75, cited by Lovejoy, p. 74. But perhaps it is unfair to try to make two statements made at different times into one. The least we can say is that Thomas was inconsistent.

eenth-century Enlightenment—was inconsistent with the undercurrent of necessitarianism born of Thomas' premise of unity. But this has been a "fruitful inconsistency" insofar as it has enabled Thomism to be this-worldly and monistic at the same time, to give us the assurance that all things work to the good and yet not to abandon the variety of the world by means of mystical rejection. This embracing of the either/or is illustrated clearly in Thomas' and the Thomists' handling of the relation of human law to natural law and divine law, which we shall take up shortly.

The concept of nature: a criticism

Though reason and rationality are closely identified with the natural and form the basis of natural law, Thomas did not hold that only reason is natural or that the operations of reason in men could not be obstructed by passions characteristic of the human animal. In Article 2 of Question 94 in the "Treatise on Law" he lists three quite different meanings of *nature:* (1) the tendency of all substances to seek the preservation of their own being; (2) those things that pertain to the preservation of man as an earthly creature, including sexual intercourse and the education of offspring; and (3) the inclination of man's reason, which includes the desire to know God and to live in human society. It seems surprising that such a range of instincts, drives, desires, and inclinations should be identified with the natural law, for our experience tells us that sexual, paternal, and social impulses may frequently come into conflict with each other.

Even more troublesome, consequently, is the implication in Article 6 of the same Question that some organic passions and some social customs may "blot out" the workings of natural law in men, though always only temporarily and provisionally. The general precepts are correctly held, "concupiscence evil) cannot be blotted out. They are, says Thomas quoting Augustine, "written in the hearts of men, which iniquity itself effaces not." But the secondary precepts, the

> conclusions following closely from first principles . . . can be blotted out from the human heart, either by evil persuasions, just as in speculative matters errors occur in respect of necessary conclusions, or by vicious customs and corrupt habits, as among some men, theft and even unnatural vices, as the Apostle states (Romans 1), were not esteemed sinful.[35]

At still a third level—the level of particular action—even when primary and secondary precepts are correctly held, "concupiscence or some other passion" can interfere with the application of natural law. Natural law includes biological and gregarious instincts as well as general rational precepts (found in the heart) and precepts derived therefrom. The general precepts cannot be obliterated but the derivative precepts can be obliterated by the tendencies of certain biological and gregarious instincts. Clearly, there is a problem here: until Thomas can tell us exactly which passions are sanctified by nature and which are enemies of nature, we are lost. Thomas was no Stoic and in specific contexts it is evident that he values positively the emotions of pity or compassion and values negatively the emotions of fear or hatred. But why the former should be regarded as natural and as an aspect of being and the latter as unnatural and as an aspect of nonbeing is not so evident. By means of such emotions as fear the species is preserved—and this was one of Thomas' criteria of the natural.

Human Law

Two forms of positive law in the Thomistic hierarchy of law are divine law and human law. "Divine law" is a more or less technical term meaning that part of the eternal law found in the Scriptures. It is "twofold, namely the Old Law and the New Law," that is, the laws of the Old and New Testaments. Human law is, of course, manmade law. It may take the form of either the decrees of sovereigns or the customary laws of a particular community.

In Question 91 Thomas anticipates a plau-

[35] *Summa theologica,* p. 1013.

sible query: why, if natural law is available to all men and is itself a manifestation of eternal law, is divine law necessary? It is necessary, he says, for four reasons: (1) it can help man to his ordained end of eternal happiness where such an end is "inproportionate to man's natural faculty." Apparently this means that God assists men in general and certain men in particular who may have deficiencies of reason to advance beyond their unaided grasp of natural law. (2) Human judgment, even though adequate to grasp the general tenets of the natural law, tends to be defective on contingent matters about which divine law may be very specific: "Thou shalt not commit adultery." (3) Through the device of human law men are able to supervise exterior movements but cannot judge or direct interior movements, to which divine law directs itself, though not exclusively. Thomas does not explain how this aspect of divine law differs from natural law, which by virtue of the concept of participation is also interior. (4) Human law as a matter of expediency cannot forbid all evil acts, whereas divine law can. Human law can legislate against certain consequences of sin; divine law can and does speak against sin itself. This seems very similar to Thomas' third point.

In Question 95 Thomas confronts the problem of the relationship between natural law and human law. If natural law is implanted in all men, why is human law necessary? We have already seen how faulty Thomas thought most men were in applying this naturally implanted law. Here he suggests that, while there is in every man a "natural aptitude for virtue," such virtue can be acquired only "by means of some kind of training." Human law, then, in a very Aristotelian way, is above all an educational device. If all men have reason, "man can use his reason to devise means of satisfying his lusts and evil passions, which other animals are unable to do." In such a passage Thomas treats reason as a purely instrumental faculty—a servant of passion as surely as the reason described by Hume. In the great variety of senses in which Thomas uses the term "reason" it is hard to believe that he was simply confused or careless. But at the least he was certainly not helpful in keeping the various usages distinct.

It is better to let human laws be framed by a few men, says Thomas, than to leave the job to many men who are obliged to improvise to meet diverse situations. This is true for three reasons: (1) wise men are few in number. Thomas does not enlighten us on how we assure that the few who are wise are the same few who make the laws and so he repeats the lapse of educational theory we saw in *De regimine principum*. (2) It is necessary that human laws be formulated in an atmosphere of reflection rather than in an atmosphere of pressure and haste. (3) Abstract formulations of the law are better than too large a number of highly specific formulations because in the latter concrete passions interfere and the "judgment [is] perverted." The difficulty of this formulation is that, though the avoidance of specificity is a well-tested way of avoiding passion, it is also a well-tested way of avoiding decisions. And, curiously, we saw that one of Thomas' arguments for divine law was the need for specificity.

The derivation of human law

In Article 2, however, Thomas firmly grasps a nettle: why, if human law is derived from natural law, do human laws vary from place to place and even contradict one another? He states his position in what seems an unequivocal way, with the result that great quantities of what passes for law turn out not to be true law: "The force of a law depends on the extent of its justice . . . every human law has just so much of the nature of law, as it is derived from the law of nature. But if *in any point* [our italics] it deflects from the law of nature, it is no longer a law but a perversion of law."

But then with characteristic ingenuity Thomas ungrasps the nettle by propounding a subtle distinction that makes possible the inclusion of considerable diversity within the supposedly ironclad fold of the law:

> But it must be noted that something may be derived from the natural law in two ways: first as a conclusion [*conclusiones*] from premises, secondly by way of determination [*determinationes*] of certain generalities. The first way is like to that by which, in sciences, demonstrated conclusions are drawn from the principles: while the second mode is likened to that whereby in the arts, general forms are particularized as to details: thus the craftsman needs to determine the general form of a house to some particular shape. Some things are therefore derived from the general principles of the natural law by way of conclusions; e.g., that *one must not kill* may be derived as a conclusion from the principle that *one should do harm to no man:* while some are derived therefrom by way of determination; e.g., the law of nature has it that the evil-doer should be punished; but that he be punished in this way or that way is a determination of the law of nature.[36]

Conclusions are one but determinations are many.

> Accordingly, both modes of derivation are found in the human law. But those things which are derived in the first way are contained in the human law, not as emanating therefrom exclusively, but have some force from the natural law also. But those things which are derived in the second way have no other force than that of human law.[37]

Presumably, however, even law that had "no other force than that of human law" would have to be consistent with natural law in order to be law at all. Were this not the case, the first paragraph quoted from Article 2 above ("if in any point it deflects") would flatly contradict the second two paragraphs quoted. But if consistent with natural law, why does it not "have some force from the natural law"? If a determination from the natural law is not a deflection from it, why is a determination denied the full authority of natural law? In any case, generations of legal scholars found it useful to identify the *jus gentium* with *conclusiones* and the *jus civile* with *determinationes,* as did Thomas himself. And many jurists used the authority of the natural law to dignify specific determinations of human law.

Law and custom

Since for Thomas all law must be conformable to reason and since the rational character of custom is not always manifest, the relationship between law and custom was a problem to Thomas—as, indeed, it still is to us. The problem as he states it is satisfactorily resolved in the "Treatise on Law" but by the light of twentieth-century assumptions, it is not well stated.

The first form in which Thomas deals with this problem is a defense of the consistency of Isidore of Seville, a bishop of the early seventh century, who, being an encyclopedist rather than a theorist, was not much concerned with consistency. At one place in his *Etymologies* Isidore says that three conditions essential to the nature of law are that it "foster religion," be "helpful to discipline," and "further the common weal." But at another place he says that law should be "according to the custom of the country" and "suitable to place and time." But, asks Thomas, are these various requirements of law always compatible? In Question 95, Article 3, Thomas puts forth the rather modest claim that law cannot be helpful to discipline unless it is conformable to the customs of the country and suitable to place and time. The one implies the other: the discipline of law is a social discipline and man, whatever his condition, cannot live without society.

The argument comes from common sense, defends an authority who needs no defense, and assumes the virtue—if not the religion-fostering qualities—of the hypothetical local custom. In an unusual departure for the standard seriated replies to initial objections, Thomas ends the article with but one reply—that summarized above—for all four objec-

[36] *Ibid.*, pp. 1014–15. Some have translated *determinationes* as "specifications."

[37] *Ibid.*, p. 1014.

tions. "This suffices," he says, "for the replies to the objections"—even though it does not.

In Question 96, Article 2, and Question 97, Article 3, Thomas comes to grips with the more difficult side of the problem: granted that law and custom are in a practical sense usually intermingled, should custom as such have the force of law and, if not, when not? In the former section Thomas notes that it is impractical for human law to try to repress all vices; human law will therefore always represent something less than the complete virtue of natural law and eternal law. Since it is designed to be understood by men not yet complete in virtue, it must take account of their imperfections in a manner analogous to the way adults take account of the limited capacities of children: ". . . the purpose of human law is to lead men to virtue, not suddenly but gradually." Although the human law does not and cannot prescribe all acts of every virtue, it should prescribe some acts under the heading of every major virtue.

If law should put an excessive burden of virtue on men, they would simply rebel, "would break out into yet greater evils." The law should adapt to custom in the spirit of adapting to human imperfection for the sake of leading men to perfection. Change merely for its own sake is, of course, bad. Change should always be justified as a deliberate movement toward perfection. But whereas change is bad, repetition appears to be good. In fact, with a curious logic, Thomas draws an analogy between the working of reason in individual man and the growth of custom in a community. The repetition of actions builds up a force and a solidity in the will and in reason, "for when a thing is done again and again, *it seems* [our italics] to proceed from a deliberate judgment of reason. Accordingly, custom has the force of law." Apparently, then, custom has the force of law only through what seems rather than what is.

All this suggests that custom, in general, is useful even though it falls short of perfection. But what of specific customs that are not simply deficient in virtue but are actually evil? In that case, "evil customs should be eradicated by law and reason." But whose law and whose reason? Quite apart from the practical problem ("it is not easy to set aside the custom of a whole people") there are some basic ambiguities in Thomas' discussion at this point. Presumably the positive law of the sovereign should eradicate evil customs. But the sovereign's judgment of what is evil is not conclusive. For one thing, some customs have unimpeachable status. Quoting Augustine, Thomas says, "The customs of God's people . . . are to be considered as laws." Moreover, if we are talking about a free people, "the consent of the whole people expressed by a custom counts for more in favor of a particular observance, than does the authority of the sovereign, who has not the power to frame laws, except as representing the people." Although not explicit at this point, it becomes clear elsewhere that the clergy has, for Thomas, a crucial role in determining which customs are sufficiently evil to warrant eradication by governmental authority. We shall look at the problem of Church-state relations in a moment.

Law and conscience

The problem of what to do about evil customs is not unrelated to the problem of conflicts between individual conscience and human law, even though the latter is probably more of a practical and theoretical problem to us than to Thomas. He says rather tersely that, if the law is just, of course it binds the conscience and, if it is not just, it is not truly a law and hence cannot bind the conscience. We are likely to conclude from this that we need not obey the unjust would-be law. That, however, would be an erroneous conclusion. Even though our conscience is not bound by the command of, for example, a tyrant, still we obey it "in order to avoid scandal or disturbance" on the authority of Matthew 5:40, in which we are admonished to give up our cloak also when our coat is taken and to walk two miles when forced to walk one. If in good conscience we endure wrongful suffering, we are to thank God for the opportunity to serve as a witness to his charitable spirit. Once again, Thomas cites the ubiquitous Romans 13:1, which abjures resistance to the established powers, as authority. Of course, if the sovereign's command is not simply unjust but is contrary to God's commandment, then a man should disobey, provided—even here—that he can "avoid giving scandal or inflicting a more grievous hurt." More than Plato or Aristotle, Thomas believed that individual virtue and the common good are in harmony.

Such was Thomas' confidence in the orderly construction of the universe that he believed no custom could prevail for long in disharmony with the common good and no ruler could rule for long in defiance of the common good. That the individual might serve a good in conflict with or not related to the common good was unthinkable: "There is no virtue whose act is not ordainable to the common good . . . either mediately or immediately."

This confidence in the normal harmony of human laws with higher laws still characterizes Thomistic thought. Few commentators on Thomas are as sophisticated, cautious, or sensitive to alternative points of view as Copleston. Yet on this point he is blandly reassuring: "If a human positive law is incompatible with the natural law, says St. Thomas, it will be a perversion of law rather than a true law. It will be an unjust law, and it will not bind in conscience. *That, of course, is an extreme case* [our italics]."[38]

Quite apart from the question of whether natural-law postulates are valid is the question of whether discrepancies between those postulates and positive laws constitute extreme cases. The answer would require a subtle and monumental survey of statutes, ordinances, judicial decisions, rulings by attorneys general, and sentences by police courts. But one need not be a cynic to question the sanguine character of Father Copleston's conclusion or to note that, despite the universality of its statement the positive law he knows best is that of one nation among many, namely, Britain. The work of appellate courts everywhere is taken up with cases where such reasonable, moral, and generally acceptable tenets as "a man shall be informed of the nature of the charge made against him," "cruel and unusual punishment is forbidden," and "a man's property should not be taken away without due process of law," have been violated by legal actions. How much more so, then, the even more general precepts of natural law? To argue in reply that positive law is not established as law until all appeals procedures are exhausted would be no way out, for until a positive law is overturned on appeal, it is enforced as the law and for every enforcement that produces a court review there are many that do not.

[38] Frederick Copleston, *Medieval Philosophy* (New York: Harper & Row, Torchbooks, 1961), p. 97.

Church and State

Part of Thomas' confidence in the normal compatibility of custom with law, the ruler's judgment with custom, and the individual's good with community good stemmed from the fact of an institutional Church equipped and practiced in interpreting the meaning of virtue in its various dimensions. The power of that institution and its agents was—as we have seen and as every introductory world-history course teaches—the basis for a political balance of power which, at times, became an almost constitutional division of powers.

On the one hand, Thomas had no desire to undermine the authority of human law and hence accepted as legal and rightful the governments of infidel rulers, which, then as now, abound in the world. On the other hand, since the ultimate purpose of law is to lead men to virtue, the Church cannot, he argued, look with indulgence on rulers who become heretics or apostates nor upon infidels who establish a new dominion over Christian subjects. "This ought by no means to be allowed."[39] He wrote:

> unbelief, in itself, is not inconsistent with dominion, since dominion is a device of the law

[39] See also Jane E. Ruby, "The Ambivalence of St. Thomas Aquinas' View of the Relationship of Divine Law to Human Law," *Harvard Theological Review*, Vol. 48 (1955), pp. 101–28.

of nations, which is a human law. . . . Now it is not within the competency of the Church to punish unbelief in those who have never received the faith, according to the saying of the Apostle (I Cor. 5:12): *What have I to do to judge them that are without* [Thomas' italics]? She can, however, pass sentence of punishment on the unbelief of those who have received the faith: and it is fitting that they should be punished by being deprived of the allegiance of their subjects: for this same allegiance might conduce to great corruption of the faith.[40]

So much for infidel rulers; what of infidel subjects? Faith is internal and therefore cannot be compelled by external force. When Christian soldiers capture unbelievers, therefore, "they should still leave them free to believe if they will." The spiritual factor in their political restraint is not wholly absent, however, for they may be incarcerated "in order to prevent them from hindering the faith of Christ." Moreover, there appears a curious and important limitation on the nice distinction between internal belief and external actions and consequently on the freedom to believe. There is a significant difference for Thomas between what is permitted to those who have never been Christians and to those unbelievers who once were Christians. Backsliding appears to be correctable by force: ". . . there are unbelievers who at some time have accepted the faith and professed it, such as heretics and apostates: such should be submitted even to bodily compulsion that they may fulfill what they have promised, and hold what they at one time received." There is little question but that Thomas means that secular government may properly be employed to effect this compulsion.

The consequences of such doctrines for Thomists attempting to relate Thomism to twentieth-century politics are by no means settled, as the far-reaching debate in Vatican Council II on the issue of religious liberty indicated. In practice the Roman Catholic Church in Barcelona, Spain, will not likely agree on the role of the state with the Roman Catholic Church in St. Louis, Missouri. American Catholic scholars will differ in emphasis. One distinguished Jesuit notes that where a majority is not Catholic, as in the United States, the separation of Church and state is "the best working arrangement under these circumstances." But "If all men were Catholics, then there would be an identity of membership between these two societies [Church and state] and the secular power would be closely integrated with and subordinate to the spiritual authority. St. Thomas speaks of the secular power being related to the spiritual as the body is to the soul."[41] A thoughtful Catholic lay scholar chooses to emphasize Thomas' contribution to constitutionalism and tolerance. Noting the parallel Thomas drew between the operation of the law of reason over man's appetitive parts (which retain a natural liberty to resist) and the operation of rulers over subjects (who retain "a certain right of opposition"), McCoy concludes, "this doctrine of tolerance has its roots in St. Thomas' jurisprudence."[42] And whereas Father Bourke makes almost no mention of democracy in his chapter on political ethics, Father Murray has tried to show the close connection between natural law and the assumptions behind American democracy.[43]

Extended comments on the various dilemmas of Church-state relationships characteristic of the twentieth century would be out of place here. But perhaps we may be justified

[40] *Summa theologica,* 12, 2, p. 1229.

[41] Vernon J. Bourke, S.J., *Ethics* (New York: Macmillan, 1951), p. 435.

[42] Charles N. R. McCoy, *The Structure of Political Theory* (New York: McGraw-Hill, 1963), pp. 121–22.

[43] John Courtney Murray, *We Hold These Truths* (New York: Sheed & Ward, 1960). Yves R. Simon, on Thomistic grounds, allies himself with the "democratic spirit" rather than the "conservative spirit" in his *Philosophy of Democratic Government* (Chicago: Univ. of Chicago Press, 1951). See also Thomas E. Davitt, S.J., *The Nature of Law* (St. Louis: Herder, 1951); Joseph V. Dolan, S.J., *Natural Law and Modern Jurisprudence* (Quebec: Librairie Philosophique M. Doyon, 1958); Thomas Gilby, *Between Community and Society* (London: Longmans, Green, 1953); Jacques Maritain, *Man and the State* (Chicago: Univ. of Chicago Press, 1952); and Gerald F. Yates, S.J., ed., *Papal Thought on the State* (New York: Appleton-Century-Crofts, 1958).

in asking present-day secularists to concede that the secular political regimes of the twentieth century have attempted to coerce belief in the interests of nationalism and have even attempted with some success to enlist the Church's aid in this effort, using a degree and kind of coercion not easily compared with that of other ages but of serious proportions nevertheless. That done, we should also ask twentieth-century religionists to concede that the formulas of the thirteenth century cannot be applied to the twentieth without the most imaginative kind of reinterpretation. Humility ought to induce us to honor even the old verities we doubt but also to criticize even the old verities we do not doubt enough.

Property

In the 1920s an eminent Catholic historian said that for Thomas individual property holding was a natural right.[44] But the citations from the *Summa theologica* he offered in support of the claim do not bear him out. In the 1930s one writer found support for the New Deal in Thomas' writings on property.[45] That, too, probably stretched a point. Thomas on property—as on a good many other practical subjects—may be regarded as codified common sense—molded, naturally enough, somewhat in the shape of the economic institutions of the thirteenth century.

Thomas regarded the private ownership and management of property as generally best for three reasons: (1) people are more careful and conscientious with their own goods than with goods owned in common; (2) there is less confusion when decisions affecting property are decentralized; (3) private ownership provides fewer occasions to quarrel and hence is conducive to a more peaceful society. There is nothing absolute about this arrangement, however, and government has a moral obligation to regulate possessions so that the common good is maintained. "In the business affairs of men, there is no such thing as demonstrative and infallible proof, and we must be content with a certain conjectural probability." He also wrote:

> if a particular piece of land be considered absolutely, it contains no reason why it should belong to one man more than to another, but if it be considered in respect of its adaptability to cultivation, and the unmolested use of the land, it has a certain commensuration to be the property of one and not of another man.[46]

The rich man is apt to forget how contingent his title to land is and Thomas reproves him "for deeming external things to belong to him principally as though he had not received them from another, namely God." But all this is not, of course, to say that the division of lands may be arbitrary or is divorced from reason altogether: ". . . the division of possessions is not according to the natural law, but rather arose from human agreement which belongs to positive law. . . . Hence the ownership of possessions is not contrary to the natural law, but an addition thereto devised by human reason."

To Thomas it seemed rational that one would have a right to that property that was necessary for the sustenance of his family and himself but no right beyond that. The misuse of property invalidates the claim to property. In believing this Thomas was following a venerable tradition that included Ambrose, Augustine, and Gregory I.

CONCLUSION

Thomas Aquinas on war, Thomas Aquinas on slavery, Thomas Aquinas on usury—on and on we could go. But as we implied at the beginning, one cannot do justice to the range of Thomas' thought nor to the range of comment on his thought in a single chapter. That limitation can perhaps be better accepted with

44 Maurice deWulf, *Medieval Philosophy* (Cambridge, Mass.: Harvard Univ. Press, 1922), Vol. 2, p. 29.

45 Clare Riedl, "The Social Theory of St. Thomas," *Proceedings of the American Catholic Philosophical Association,* Vol. 9 (1933), p. 19.

46 *Summa theologica,* II–II, 57, 3, *ibid.,* Vol. 2, p. 1433. Thomas cites here Aristotle's *Politics,* Bk. II.

equanimity if we take to heart what the more sophisticated Thomists have been telling us for some time—that Thomas' system was in fact not the closed system that it is often taken to be and has often been made to be. It was not closed in the sense of pretending to have final answers to all problems. It was a taxonomy of the universe as it appeared to Thomas with an element of indeterminacy built into it by virtue of the limited penetration of man's reason into the reaches of eternal law.

There is a second sense in which the system is not closed—or, rather, in which it is not logically self-contained, for it may be psychologically closed to those without enough faith of a certain kind to respond to it as a testament of faith. A Catholic existentialist like D'Arcy[47] can say that for Thomas existence precedes essence because Thomas' intellectual construction of categories of being did not represent—as they are so often portrayed as representing—a synthesis of Aristotelianism with Christian faith but what we might better call a reconciliation of these two systems. Faith is the starting place rather than the conclusion—despite certain rationalistic excesses, such as the five proofs of God's existence. God existed for Thomas *before* he tried to prove it. For Aristotle, as for Plato, happiness is philosophic contemplation. For Thomas, happiness is the enjoyment of God.

There is an irony buried in the appeal of Thomism: natural law is offered as dispassionate reason but Thomism offers not primarily the guidance of reason (symbolic logic and analytical philosophy can also claim to represent reason) but the reassurance of a certain positive spirit. There is a charm and a terror about the Middle Ages—the charm of childish innocence and the terror of childish nightmares—best symbolized, perhaps, by the Children's Crusades. To say this is not simply to be patronizing. Our age, if such comparisons can be made, may have by contrast less charm and more terror. But surely part of Thomas' appeal is the basic charm of simple faith that unites men rather than divides them and that sees man as a servant of nature rather than as her conqueror.

The great family of the Church is partly responsible for this medieval charm—the Church that receives her own with warm affection, chastens them reluctantly but well when they err, and manages with impressive tenacity to remain in the world but not of it. Let us overlook for the moment the Church's occasionally harsh treatment of those outside the fold. The point here is that the charm of Thomas' simple yet profound faith is an important aspect of this continuing familial warmth. Thomas combined a complex and subtle mind with childlike qualities of faith. Not without reason is he called the Angelic Doctor. After investing a lifetime of study in the monumental *Summa* he could call it "chaff."

A show-business writer once called Jesus a "throw-away prophet," one who gave his hearers more than they could understand. Thomas was likewise a "throw-away scholar" who, without pretension and claiming nothing for himself, gave out more than his immediate readers could understand. Yet through all the *Quaestiones* and *Sed Contras* came a simple message: God's in His heaven and, if all is not well with the world, its movement is of necessity from imperfection to perfection. This movement very much included the state. The state was not for Thomas what it was for Augustine, a hospital for the sick. It was an essential embodiment of God's order. This kind of political order was not alien to the most fundamental theological categories, for God's will itself was given the name eternal *law*. Moreover, by regarding the Church as the chief custodian of natural law, Thomas bound secular and spiritual power tightly together.

This basic confidence in the orderliness of God's universe is what gives a system-like quality to what Thomas himself regarded as a mere compendium of the truths found by others. And it is perhaps this faith in order more than the *Summa*'s supraorderliness that provokes frustration in many moderns as they

[47] See M. C. D'Arcy, *Thomas Aquinas* (Westminster, Md.: Newman Press, 1955).

attempt to read it. The experience can often seem like an attempt to master a vast hydraulic network with all sorts of buttons and levers marked *God, Nature, Law, Justice, The Good, The Common Good, Reason, Happiness,* and *First Principles.* Press one button in and the others move out; pull out one lever and the others retract. We can never quite isolate any of these terms from any of the others and hence have immense difficulty analyzing them. If its attractions lead us to want to analyze the *Summa theologica,* its difficulty of analysis keeps us at the task over the centuries.

7

SOME MEDIEVAL LEGACIES

The fall of the Roman Empire meant the end of centralized government in the West and a shattering break in the diffusion of Greco-Roman culture. The tribal customs of the Germanic invaders dissolved the ties of legal obligation for which Rome was famous. In the absence of cohesive political power, the Christian Church filled the vacuum. This provided, says Morrall,

> for the first time in history the somewhat paradoxical spectacle of a society trying to organize itself politically on the basis of a spiritual framework. . . . By so doing, western European thought about politics was propelled along lines which were to be sharply different from those of any other human society.[1]

THE POLITICAL AND SPIRITUAL IN THE MIDDLE AGES

A good many anthropologists would question whether medieval society was as unique as the foregoing quotation suggests. Perhaps modern secularism is what is unique. Moreover, one of the primary metaphors of Christian faith—the kingdom of heaven—was political and not even Augustine's antipolitical bias could prevent his reliance on another semipolitical symbol, the City of God. What we can say is that, for men of Europe who lived during the long stretch of time between the fifth and sixteenth centuries, salvation, fulfillment, or whatever term best identifies the hopes of ordinary men was largely divorced from the claims of civil power. Both classical man and modern man put more confidence in civil governors and civil laws than did medieval man. Or, at least the former put more confidence in politics broadly conceived than in organized religion. Even here, we are on rough terrain, however, for who is to say with any degree of certainty what the common man of ancient Athens or of thirteenth-century Paris felt? Moreover, the government in most societies, including our own, performs through its ceremonies, rituals, rewards, and incantations some of the functions of a church. The Church in medieval society, however, performed many of the functions of a government. This observation is at the heart of our present discussion.

[1] John B. Morrall, *Political Thought in Medieval Times* (New York: Harper & Row, 1962), p. 10. Morrall points out that, though the Byzantine Empire was nominally Christian, Christianity did not provide the framework for organizing society but was used by rulers as a device for sanctifying existing political forms.

The role of the Church in the Middle Ages was peculiarly political and the role of centralized civil government was correspondingly altered—even to the point of being confined within one unifying theme:

> The core of mediaeval political thought [is] . . . the conception of a single universal society, living under one principle of life, which is expounded in the last resort by a single authority. The principle is divine: the authority is a divine representative; that is why we may speak of a theocracy. The Church, enthroning itself over Christian society, makes a great and gallant attempt to unify all life, in all its reaches—political, social, economic, intellectual—under the control of Christian principle. Politically, it attempts to rebuke and correct kings for internal misgovernment, as when they falsify coinage, and for external misdoing, as when they break treaties; socially, it controls the life of the family by the law of marriage which it administers, and the life of the individual by its system of penance; economically, it seeks to regulate commerce and industry by enforcing just prices and prohibiting interest, as it seeks to control the economic motive in general by its conception of property as a trust held for the general benefit and by its inculcation of charity; intellectually, it develops a single culture in the universities, and in the last resort it enforces that culture by the persecution of heresy. It is a magnificent attempt at synthesis of the whole of life by a sovereign wisdom.[2]

As Barker points out, the hope of unity was more plausible in that simpler society than in our own but the gap between the theory of a unified social order and the highly diversified practice was nonetheless tremendous.

The widely accepted traditional view of how Church authority was related to regal authority went back to the age of the Church Fathers. Just before the end of the fifth century Pope Gelasius I wrote to the emperor in Constantinople and propounded the doctrine of the two swords, as it came to be called. Christendom was a single community but existed for two different ends—one spiritual, one temporal. Thus there were two holy swords to be wielded by two authorities—one sacerdotal, one imperial. Both swords came from God. The two authorities were interdependent, equal to each other in jurisdiction, and obliged to be mutually helpful to each other. (The Church was, however, regarded by Gelasius as superior in dignity and the maintenance of its independence required that the clergy be controlled solely by ecclesiastical courts.)

Though religious and political authorities never ceased to give lip service to the two-swords doctrine, it was challenged in fact—and, as we shall see, sometimes in theory—by a number of popes from the eleventh to the fourteenth centuries who sought a higher status than the doctrine accorded them. Reverence for Gelasius, however, seemed unaffected by disregard for his doctrine. We have already seen the degree to which a mind like Thomas', with a talent for abstract synthesizing, could harmonize apparently uncongenial theories; this talent was encouraged by the Scholastic indifference to problems of empirical verification in explaining the complex interrelationships of historical events. For example, "The idea of law as the rational reflection of the divine order in a natural society of men was more closely in harmony with the traditional folk-law conception of the Germanic tribes than the Augustinian belief in secular rule as a remedy for sin."[3] Perhaps the most striking disjunction between theory and practice is revealed by the fact that of the many theoretical works on Church, state, and Empire produced in the later Middle Ages virtually none dealt with the actual character of those feudal relationships that formed the structure and substance of medieval politics. Perhaps those writers were justified in assuming knowledge of these relationships, but we, by contrast, must ask what feudalism was.

[2] Ernest Barker, "Mediaeval Political Thought," in F. J. C. Hearnshaw, ed., *The Social and Political Ideas of Some Great Mediaeval Thinkers* (New York: Barnes & Noble, 1950), p. 15.

[3] Charles Vereker, *The Development of Political Theory* (New York: Harper & Row, 1965), p. 75.

FEUDALISM

"Feudalism," we need to remember, was not a term used in the Middle Ages. It was used by historians of the eighteenth century to describe some distinctive political-economic arrangements they observed in medieval society. The label comes from the Latin *feudum,* which in English becomes "fief." The venerable team of Pollack and Maitland were led to comment,

> *feudalism* is an unfortunate word. In the first place it draws our attention to but one element in a complex state of society and that element is not the most distinctive: it draws our attention only to the prevalence of dependent and derivative land tenure. This however may well exist in an age which can not be called feudal in any tolerable sense. What is characteristic of "the feudal period" is not the relationship between letter and hirer, or lender and borrower of land, but the relationship between lord and vassal, or rather it is the union of these two relationships. Were we free to invent new terms, we might find *feudo-vassalism* more serviceable than *feudalism.*[4]

The *fief* was an estate of land granted by a lord. It developed as an institution around the middle of the eighth century because land was the only significant source of wealth and a king could reward his nobles for services rendered with grants of land in lieu of salaries. In this way land held *alodially,* or held as one's own property without being subject to rent or other obligation to a superior, gradually disappeared and most fiefs became hereditary. *Vassalage* is the name given to the legal tie that bound the *vassal,* or the man accepting a fief, to his lord.

The time lag between form and reality is an especially difficult problem in isolating the phenomenon called feudalism. As late as the seventeenth century in England and France the forms of vassalage remained but the king's actual relationship with nobles who were technically his vassals was very different from what it was in, say, the thirteenth century. And the hierarchical pattern of the thirteenth century was in turn very different from Charlemagne's relationship with his vassals a few centuries earlier. Charlemagne, overcoming great obstacles of geography, culture, and language, was often able to assert successfully his direct authority over local landholdings. Nevertheless, what is most significant for our political understanding is the awareness that lordship over a fief came to involve rights of government and not simply—as might be true with economic power in our day—influence over government: "The possessor of a great estate must defend it, police it, maintain roads and bridges, and hold court for his tenants. Thus lordship has both economic and political aspects; it is less than sovereignty, but more than private property."[5]

Early feudalism in, say, eleventh-century France tended to be characterized by small feudal states dominated by local lords of varying titles (duke, earl, count, or marquis) who directed a group of trained soldiers loyal to them and held certain fortified positions. Their vassals performed tasks of local government in their fiefs, generally following local custom but departing from it according to each lord's wishes, if he had enough power. The ethos of some of these establishments differed very little from that of familial outlaw gangs. Later feudalism—for example, in the thirteenth century, the period most written about—was more formalized and hierarchical and rights and duties became more explicit. It became possible to appeal from a local lord to his superior and circuit courts, as in the case of the English assizes at the end of the twelfth century, were dispatched by the king with jurisdiction over vassals and local lords.

Feudalism as a social system—though

[4] *History of English Law,* 2nd ed. (Cambridge, Eng.: Cambridge Univ. Press, 1923), Vol. 1, p. 66. Quoted in Joseph R. Strayer, "Feudalism in Western Europe," in Rushton Coulborn, ed., *Feudalism in History* (Princeton: Princeton Univ. Press, 1956), p. 15. The Coulborn volume has the great advantage of dealing with feudalism in the non-Western as well as the Western world. See also F. L. Ganshof, *Feudalism,* trans. by Philip Grierson (London: Longmans, Green, 1952).

[5] *Ibid.,* p. 17.

some scholars object to calling it a system—involved conceptions of property and authority in lordship that deserve brief mention before we proceed to the more obviously political subjects of law and kingship.

The Roman conception of property had been essentially individualistic: one who owned property had rights of use and disposal that could not be infringed and that required no sharing of rights with nonowners. Ownership, in other words, was indivisible. The conception of property in the Germanic tribes was different: ownership tended to reside not in the individual but in the family or clan; at best an individual could enjoy the fruits of property but not the right of disposal. Ownership therefore did not absorb the proprietary object but consisted of rights attached to it.[6] Through the mutual relationships of lordship and vassalage, feudalism made normal what in Roman law had been exceptional. The contractual agreements relating to the use of land and the payment of revenues were indeterminate in time and gradually became hereditary as each vassal passed his rights and obligations on to his son and each lord did likewise. These rights and obligations therefore resided both in property and in persons. Quite apart from his right of gaining physical property, a free man could be commended to the protection of a superior and would thereby become his man, with a right of protection and an obligation of service: the word "homage" in fact comes from *homo*. The act of homage would customarily require the vassal to kneel, place his hands between the hands of the lord, and by oath pledge fealty to his superior. The ceremony would conclude with an act of investiture in which the lord would give the vassal some token to identify him as the lord's man. The feudal lord was a mixture of tribal chieftain and aristocratic ruler. The government was *in* him and he ruled alone within his limited domain; yet he also ruled surrounded by the restraints of custom.

[6] See Ewart Lewis, ed., *Medieval Political Ideas* (London: Routledge and Kegan Paul, 1954), Vol. 1, pp. 88–91. See also Morrall, pp. 15–17, and G. O. Sayles, *The Medieval Foundations of England* (New York: Barnes & Noble, 1961), pp. 199–211.

LAW AND KINGSHIP

Logically, it was difficult to reconcile not only Roman and Germanic laws of property but Stoic and Teutonic conceptions of law in general. The former, we recall, reflected a timeless reason derived from God and expressed in tenets of universal validity. The latter grew out of the customs of particular peoples and its validity was limited to members of a particular clan. The result was that as people moved about they carried their own law with them. In the often quoted words of the ninth-century Bishop Agobard of Lyons, "It often happened that five men were present or sitting together, and not one of them had the same law as another."[7] The resultant need for some uniform law helped to preserve Roman law, although often its original form was scarcely recognizable in the new law. Whereas, for example, custom was regarded as the lowest form of law in Roman times, feudal writers tried insofar as possible to make it a higher law. Of course the very name of Rome still carried an aura of imperial majesty without which not only Roman law but the whole idea of the Holy Roman Empire would no doubt have evaporated.

The most significant revival of Roman law occurred in the twelfth and thirteenth centuries, when the vassals' services to the lord depreciated in value due to the growth of a money economy and when the protection of the vassal by the lord became less vital due to a period of relative peace. Wider travel and more extensive economic exchange led to conflicts of laws. The *civilists*—or civilians, as they were usually called to distinguish them from the *canonists,* or writers on Church laws—were scholars and jurists

[7] Morrall, p. 17. See also Edward Jenks, *Law and Politics in the Middle Ages* (New York: Holt, Rinehart and Winston, 1898), pp. 7–21 and Ch. 5.

who attempted to adapt Roman law and legal Latin to its new environment. The recovery of the complete text of Justinian's *Corpus juris civilis* in the twelfth century greatly spurred this scholarly activity and the University of Bologna became an important center for the study of Roman law. The *Decretum* (c. 1148) of Gratian, a Bolognese monk, was the most important compilation of canon-law precedents in that century. Gratian attempted to reconcile canon law, civil law, and natural law. He clearly subordinated custom to natural law. A later figure, Bartolus of Sassoferrato,[8] is described by Ullmann as "perhaps the greatest of all the medieval lawyers who expounded Roman law."[9] The civilians had first distinguished between two kinds of ownership—direct lordship (*dominium directum*) and the vassals' lordship of use (*dominium utile*)—but Bartolus in *De regimine civitatis* went further and argued that there could be as many lordships of use as there were uses of a thing. These distinctions were important for politics because they provided a framework in which somewhat different but comparable relations between the lordship of a king and the citizenship of his subjects could be discussed. Because lordship over things and lordship over persons were never sharply separated in the Middle Ages, interpretation and adaptation of the classical distinction between property relations and governmental relations were necessary to make this medieval distinction intelligible to the medieval mind.[10]

We must be careful, however, not to describe the medieval king as simply a feudal lord: "It is one of the chief defects of current expositions on medieval kingship to speak of 'the king' without realizing that the medieval king embodied both the functions of a theocratic Ruler and of a feudal overlord."[11] Especially in the early Middle Ages, kings ruled by what Ullmann calls the "theocratic-descending thesis of government," that is kings ruled as direct agents of God. Ullmann attributes the prevalence of this conception in large part to the fact that for centuries the one book known to literate persons was the Latin Bible. Lombard kings in the sixth century began to call themselves *rex Dei gratia* (king by the grace of God) and Anglo-Saxon kings of the seventh century had similar locutions. Whereas kings had originally been elected,[12] they now claimed their authority stemmed directly from God, admitted responsibility to no one but God, and made such claims without consulting the papacy.

The theocratic authority of medieval kings was abetted by a rich mythological tradition and by the notorious superstitiousness of the Dark Ages. Kings were widely regarded as having magical powers, including the power to cure diseases. Since kings were consecrated by the holy laying-on of hands, their touch was precious. Edward the Confessor in eleventh-century England blessed rings that were then supposed to cure epilepsy. Scrofula was called the king's evil because the king's touch was supposed to cure it: Philip of Valois, fourteenth-century nephew of Philip the Fair of France, is supposed to have touched fifteen hundred persons at one sitting.

The sun, giver of light and life, was a symbol of kingship and so were the lion, "king of the beasts," and the uraeus, an early Middle-Eastern symbol of various sun-gods.

[8] Bartolus taught at Perugia, where he died in 1352.

[9] Walter Ullmann, *A History of Political Thought: The Middle Ages* (Baltimore: Penguin Books, 1965), p. 214. See also Ewart Lewis, *loc. cit.* and Vol. 1, pp. 1–31; R. W. and A. J. Carlyle, *A History of Medieval Political Theory in the West* (Edinburgh: Blackwood, 1903–36), Vol. 6, pp. 76–82; and C. Sidney Woolf, *Bartolus de Sassoferrato* (Cambridge, Eng.: Cambridge Univ. Press, 1913).

[10] In modern capitalist nations the separation of property and government is, at least in theory, clear cut. But in doctrines such as eminent domain there stand reminders of the medieval roots of our law.

[11] Ullmann, p. 146.

[12] The word "king" came from the Old English *cyning,* meaning member of the kindred. A member of a particular family was chosen to rule over it as a chieftain. Originally not the king as a person but the whole family was regarded as divine, for many families, even after the coming of Christianity, claimed to trace their ancestry back to divine origins. See Morrall, p. 13, and Fritz Kern, *Kingship and Law in the Middle Ages,* trans. by S. B. Chrimes (Oxford: Blackwell, 1939), Part I.

Like the eagle, king of birds, and gold, king of metals, the lion symbolized regal power to thousands who had never actually seen a lion in the flesh. But it was a dual symbol, representing no doubt the ambivalence all feel toward those in whose hands one's fate rests: the lion meant goodness and light when seen as the Lion of Judah and when used to represent Christ but it also meant the power of destruction when seen as the beast that devours the lamb.[13]

As early as the ninth century, however, factors of feudal lordship were mixed with the mythological and the theocratic elements in kingship and to speak of feudalism is to speak of property. In the ninth century Haimo of Halberstadt wrote, "the king is a minister of God; that is, he has been established by God for your benefit, by terror and assistance to guard and protect you, lest you be killed by your enemy and lest others snatch away your property."[14] In the same century the Frankish king Charles the Bald argued that bishops, though separate in their spiritual functions, were nevertheless subject to kings in all matters affecting royal interests, including the administration of lands they had received in fief. These assertions of regal powers cannot be called assertions of "sovereignty" as the term was used by later writers: "For the Franks, sovereignty—and thus the resolution of dualistic tensions—was inconceivable: the burden of their thought was that there was no sovereign except the direct government of God."[15] The elaborate liturgy of royal coronations symbolized the element of divinity in kingship. Bishops poured holy oil on the head of the king that he might become the Lord's anointed. Until the twelfth century this act of unction was regarded as a holy sacrament. The king became his majesty as a mark of awe and superiority and citizens became subjects as marks of subordination and inferiority.[16]

With the stabilization of law in the later Middle Ages the theocratic elements declined and the constitutional possibilities of feudal arrangements became more evident as theorists like Henry Bracton, a thirteenth-century justice of the English king, were able to point out that the lord-vassal and king-citizen relationships were both contractual ones and, being contractual, were binding in two directions.

JOHN OF SALISBURY

The important themes of medieval political thought concern the nature of kingship and law, the right relationship between ecclesiastical and temporal authority, the dream of a universal empire of peace and order, and the character of communities—religious and secular—and how they do and should relate to legislation—canonical and civil. We have already seen how Aquinas, the greatest of the Scholastics, dealt with some of these themes. Since our space is limited, let us choose four medieval theorists whose reflections on the foregoing issues most scholars regard as being of major significance. The four are John of Salisbury, Dante Alighieri, Marsilio of Padua, and Nicholas of Cusa.

Between the time of Augustine and that

[13] See H. Flander Dunbar, *Symbolism in Medieval Thought and Its Consummation in the Divine Comedy* (New York: Russell and Russell, 1961), pp. 161–62. On symbols of sun and rulership see Joseph Campbell, *The Hero with a Thousand Faces* (Cleveland: World, Meridian, 1956), *passim*, and Mircea Eliade, *Patterns in Comparative Religion*, trans. by Rosemary Sheed (Cleveland: World, Meridian, 1963), Ch. 3. When King Henry I died in 1135, young John of Salisbury wrote that "the Lion of Justice" had departed this life. See Clement C. J. Webb, *John of Salisbury* (London: Methuen, 1932), p. 4.

[14] Quoted in Karl Frederick Morrison, *The Two Kingdoms; Ecclesiology in Carolingian Political Thought* (Princeton: Princeton Univ. Press, 1964), p. 121.

[15] *Ibid.*, p. 17. See also pp. 242–46; Ernst H. Kantorowicz, *The King's Two Bodies: A Study in Medieval Political Theory* (Princeton: Princeton Univ. Press, 1957); Peter N. Reisenberg, *The Inalienability of Sovereignty in Medieval Political Thought* (New York: Columbia Univ. Press, 1956); and J. M. Wallace-Hadrill, "The *Via Regia* of the Carolingian Age," Ch. 2 in Beryl Smalley, ed., *Trends in Medieval Political Thought* (Oxford: Blackwell. 1965).

[16] Ullmann, pp. 85–91.

of John of Salisbury (c. 1120–80), a stretch of almost seven hundred years, there were a few important compendia, such as that of Isidore of Seville, and there were some influential philosophic essays, such as those of Boethius, Anselm, and Bernard of Clairvaux, but no systematic work of Western political thought appeared until John of Salisbury published the *Policraticus* (*Statesman's Book*) in 1159.[17] The paucity of nourishing political speculation before the twelfth century is indicated by the degree to which John leaned on the few classical sources available to him. And even his nonpolitical philosophical sources were limited to Boethius, who came out of the dim past, and Anselm and Bernard, who were almost contemporary with John.

Life

Born in Salisbury, England, John[18] went to France in 1136 to study with the greatest minds of his day, beginning with Peter Abelard, who taught at Mont St. Geneviève, the original left bank in Paris. Abelard, the vigorous master of nominalist dialectics, was a daring opponent of Bernard of Clairvaux's intuitionist mysticism. John then studied at Chartres, headquarters for the new humanist movement, before returning to Paris to study with Gilbert de la Porrée, another of Bernard's opponents. Despite his mentors, John was recommended to the Archbishop of Canterbury by Bernard and he returned to England in 1144 to serve as secretary to two successive Archbishops of Canterbury, Theobald and Thomas à Becket. He traveled widely on diplomatic missions for his employers, served at the papal court in Rome for a time, went with Becket when he was exiled, and was with him when he was murdered by Henry II's hired assassins. In 1176 John was made Bishop of Chartres, where he served until he died in 1180.

The *Policraticus*

John of Salisbury was a leading figure in the twelfth-century renaissance of classical learning. He wrote a history of Greek and Roman philosophy, a work on education (*Metalogicon*), poetry, the lives of Anselm and Thomas à Becket, and a fragmentary *Historia pontificalis*. *Policraticus* was a made-up word—some later medievalists thought it was the name of the author—usually translated *The Statesman's Book*.[19] John's subtitle —*De nugis curialium et vestigiis philosophorum* (*On the Playthings of Courtiers and the Vestiges of Philosophers*)—suggests both the daring spirit and the felicitous Latin style that contemporary humanists found exemplary. "The theme of the *Policraticus* is man's alienation from his true self by the ways of life found in the higher ranks of society."[20]

The first part of the subtitle, "the playthings of courtiers," designates the contents of Books I–VI, which deal with court life and the ruling classes and suggest that they are the prime examples of the perversity of

[17] If we interpret "Western" as referring to the tradition begun by Plato and Aristotle, Alfarabi's *Political Regime* might be an exception to this generalization. Alfarabi (Abū Nasr Muhammad al-Fārābī, c. 870–950) of Baghdad, Aleppo, and Damascus was called by Islamic philosophers the second master—that is, the first after Aristotle. He wrote a trilogy called *Philosophy of Plato and Aristotle* and attempted to outline the basic structure of all knowledge. His *Political Regime*, a speculation on the best state and forms of degeneration from it, was translated from Arabic into Hebrew in the thirteenth century. For excerpts from the political thought of Alfarabi see Ralph Lerner and Muhsin Mahdi, eds., *Medieval Political Philosophy: A Sourcebook* (New York: Free Press, 1963), pp. 22–94. See also Mahdi's commentary on Alfarabi in Leo Strauss and Joseph Cropsey, eds., *A History of Political Philosophy* (Chicago: Rand McNally, 1963), pp. 160–80.

[18] The biographical data comes from Maurice Demimuid, *Jean de Salisbury* (Paris: Thorin, 1873); Hans Liebeschütz, *Medieval Humanism in the Life and Writings of John Salisbury* (London: Warburg Institute, Univ. of London, 1950); and Clement C. J. Webb, *op. cit.*

[19] See *The Statesman's Book of John of Salisbury*, trans. and ed. by John Dickinson (New York: Knopf, 1927). This edition contains only Books IV–VI and parts of Books VII and VIII, but it is the only published English translation. Subsequent quotations are from this edition.

[20] Liebeschütz, p. 23.

the day. Books I–III deal with the private activities of the governing class and Books IV–VI with their public activities. The second part, on the "vestiges of philosophers" (Books VII–VIII), is over one-third of the total length.

The whole work is addressed to Thomas à Becket, who was then King Henry II's chancellor and was with him at the siege of Toulouse. It should be read in light of John's hope to inspire in Thomas, and through him the whole royal court, a way of life more austere and righteous than that suggested by the court's reputation. John, indeed, disapproved of Thomas' service to the king and hoped he would return to his duties as archdeacon of Canterbury.[21]

Organicism

John retains the Roman words *res publica* (commonwealth) to describe the political community, even though, as we have noted, the political-economic realities of feudalism scarcely fit the Roman model. The concept of the Church as the body of Christ may have had more to do with John's seeing the body politic in terms of physical metaphors than anything else. In his chapter on "What a Commonwealth Is" John says,

> The place of the head in the body of the commonwealth is filled by the prince, who is subject only to God and to those who exercise His office and represent Him on earth, even as in the human body the head is quickened and governed by the soul. The place of the heart is filled by the Senate, from which proceeds the initiation of good works and ill. The duties of eyes, ears, and tongue are claimed by the judges and governors of provinces. Officials and soldiers correspond to the hands. Those who always attend upon the prince are likened to the sides. Financial officers and keepers (I speak now not of those who are in charge of the prisons, but of those who are keepers of the privy chest) may be compared with the stomach and intestines, which, if they become congested through excessive avidity, and retain too tenaciously their accumulations, generate innumerable and incurable diseases, so that through their ailment the whole body is threatened with destruction. The husbandmen correspond to the feet, which always cleave to the soil, and need the more especially the care and foresight of the head, since while they walk upon the earth doing service with their bodies, they meet the more often with stones of stumbling, and therefore deserve aid and protection all the more justly since it is they who raise, sustain, and move forward the weight of the entire body.[22]

Organic analogies were not new to the Middle Ages but in John they came to full flower. It is easy to make fun of analogies carried to this extreme—to ask which knight is the gall bladder and is he responsible for stones—but we must remember that John was using language that fit the level of sophistication of his day and was using it quite skillfully. There is more of the prophetic and less of the legal textbook in the *Policraticus* than many commentators have recognized. If a provincial governor—note the Roman terminology—is the eyes, ears, and tongue of a king, this means that he sees, hears, and speaks the justice without which the body politic dies. He is like a physician who tries to keep a human being alive: death may come no matter what he does but a physician cannot be charged with responsibility for the death unless he is ignorant in areas where he should have knowledge or unless, knowing the right remedy, he fails to apply it. A rough analogy, perhaps, but not without value for drawing a line between a responsible and an irresponsible ruler.

The integrity of office

John was passionately devoted to the cause of responsible office-holding. He was intent upon imposing clear and firm moral

[21] Liebeschütz argues that Dickinson, in the Introduction to his edition of *The Statesman's Book*, exaggerates the significance of John's logical contradictions and the vagueness of his conception of a commonwealth precisely because Dickinson fails to take into account the practical moral problems to which the work was addressed and the persuasive rhetoric used in dealing with them. See Liebeschütz, pp. 5–6, 16–22.

[22] John is expounding on Plutarch here—hence the reference to the Senate—but the analogy is his own.

standards on secular rulers. One who holds the office of governor should be bound by his oath to keep the laws, should be given adequate enforcement powers, and should scrupulously avoid receiving gifts: "I cannot easily say which is worse, the seller or the buyer of justice, although the seller colors his wickedness with a more deceitful dye." With evenhanded scholarship, John bolsters his high standards for avoiding corrupt practices by references to Cicero and Luke.

John cannot be called complacent about the goodness of rulers, as Aquinas might be. John is a moralist, frankly outraged by governmental corruption. Even more than the rulers, their courtiers arouse his ire. They are, he says quoting Juvenal, like rotten grapes in the same bunch, spoiling one another. He also says,

> But why should I complain that among the court officials all things are for sale when even things which are not, namely omissions and inactions, are also matters of venality? Not merely is there no act, no word, to be had without payment, but they will not even keep silent unless paid a price; silence itself is a thing for sale.[23]

John gives judicial procedure quite systematic attention but treats it with almost the same degree of moral fervor. He castigates judicial sophistry and clever lawyers' tricks by which the guilty go free and the innocent are punished. He cites with approval the Code of Justinian on oaths to assure truth-telling by those who are "calumniators," "prevaricators," and "tergiversators." He deplores malicious litigation and trials that are unduly prolonged by delaying tactics. Above all, he feels that "a judge should not be intimidated by the influence or personal importance of the litigants."

There is no easy optimism in John's critique, no simple remedies for reform: ". . . it is almost impossible for a man to retain his innocence among courtiers. Who is there whose virtue would not be destroyed by the follies of the courtiers? Who is so strong, so firm, that he cannot be corrupted? . . . if virtue is to be preserved intact, the only way is to flee from the life of the court." To become a philosopher is a personal answer but philosophy is not easily come by and one who tries to be both a courtier and a philosopher will surely fail: he will become a monstrous mixed creature, a man-woman, "who, while he affects to be both, is neither." There is, however, hope in a wise and strong prince who can sweep out the Augean stables, set his house in order, and "compose all things under him to reason."

Virtue in lawful princes

Book IV of the *Policraticus* is a veritable catalog of virtues to which the dutiful prince should aspire. He should be chaste, generous, humble, learned, and as patient as Job. He should value the counsel of scholars. He should know how to temper justice with mercy. Though unaware of Aristotle's *Ethics,* John puts moderation at the center of correct behavior; a virtue pursued to excess becomes a vice. This is "inclining to the right hand." "Inclining to the left hand" is yielding directly to vices. In a prince this means being vengeful and too ready to punish subjects. "Both roads lead away from the true path; but that which inclines toward the left is more harmful."[24] This emphasis on moderation would not seem to characterize Henry II and perhaps precisely for this reason John goes out of his way to praise him in excessively lavish terms and to compare him favorably with his grandfather, Henry I, the Lion of Justice. The comparison no doubt aimed to inspire as well as flatter, for Henry admired his grandfather.

John finds horrendous evil in ambition and hints that ambition may transform a prince into a tyrant (a topic discussed more fully later). Nevertheless, a single headship for a commonwealth is a pattern necessary by nature, which may be confirmed by so

[23] *The Statesman's Book,* Ch. 10, p. 116.

[24] But moderation does not seem to mean cautious conservatism. Princes should be lovers of liberty, which means not only the love of virtue (from which "true liberty" springs) but the support of outspokenness in subjects, a surprisingly modern interpretation of "liberty."

humble an example as the "civil life" of the bees. (Part of this pattern of nature, however, is that virtue reside in the headship.) Consequently princes are due great respect and unswerving fealty from their subjects, for, as an injury to the head affects all parts of the body, so all are affected by injury to a prince. That is why the crime of *lèse-majesté* is regarded as a crime against the whole community, "a crime of the greatest gravity and nearest to sacrilege; for as the latter is an attempt against God, so the former is an attack upon the prince, who is admitted to be, as it were, the likeness of deity upon earth."

The modern mind is troubled by the apparent discrepancy between calling a prince "the likeness of deity upon earth" in one chapter and advocating the killing of a bad prince in another chapter. We must realize that a tyrant is far worse than a bad prince. He is no prince at all. The very magnitude of the authority of a prince makes its abuse that much more terrible. And we must not forget the implication of the analogy between a medieval lord and the head of a body. The feet of the body politic, says John, are husbandmen, weavers, craftsmen, and artisans so numerous that the number of feet in a commonwealth exceeds those of the centipede. These men are "inferiors" who "owe it to their superiors to provide them with service." But the superiors are just as fully obligated to protect their charges and God will punish anyone who persecutes the poor. The commonwealth is all for one and one for all.[25]

Above all, the prince is conceived of as a servant of the law and the law he serves is not just the law of a human group—it is divine law: "Princes should not deem that it detracts from their princely dignity to believe that the enactments of their own justice are not to be preferred to the justice of God, whose justice is an everlasting justice, and His law is equity." Here the acute problem of Church-state authority enters and here John shows his hand.

Church and state

The Church, we recall, is for John the soul of the body and not a separate entity. There is one Christian community with separate spiritual and temporal aspects. Such a position raises questions about the relevance of the two-swords doctrine; in Book IV John explicitly lays this doctrine aside. The Church *gives* the sword to the prince:

> This sword, then, the prince receives from the hand of the Church, although she herself has no sword of blood at all. Nevertheless she has this sword, but she uses it by the hand of the prince, upon whom she confers the power of bodily coercion, retaining to herself authority over spiritual things in the person of the pontiffs. The prince is, then, as it were, a minister of the priestly power, and one who exercises that side of the sacred offices which seems unworthy in the hands of the priesthood. For every office existing under, and concerned with the execution of, the sacred laws is really a religious office, but that is inferior which consists in punishing crimes, and which therefore seems to be typified in the person of the hangman.[26]

This passage is sometimes compared to the famous letter of Pope Gregory VII to Bishop Hermann of Metz in 1081 in which he said,

> Is not a sovereignty invented by men of this world who were ignorant of God subject to that which the providence of Almighty God established for his own glory and graciously bestowed upon the world? . . .
>
> Who does not know that kings and princes derive their origin from men ignorant of God who raised themselves above their fellows by pride, plunder, treachery, murder. . . .
>
> Does anyone doubt that the priests of Christ are to be considered as fathers and masters of kings and princes of all believers?[27]

The comparison is not altogether apt. John

[25] John supports Plutarch in saying, "that course is to be pursued in all things which is of advantage to the humbler classes, that is to say the multitude; for small numbers always yield to great." This sounds very democratic but we should not make too much of it.

[26] *The Statesman's Book*, Ch. 3, p. 9.

[27] Brian Tierney, *The Crisis of Church and State, 1050–1300, with Selected Documents* (Englewood Cliffs, N. J.: Prentice-Hall, 1964), pp. 68 and 69.

is not only more temperate in his language but he does not make the inferior status of princes depend on their own special pride. Nevertheless, John's rationale for ecclesiastical superiority is comparable to Gregory's.

Augustine provided a precedent for seeing the origin of secular government in human sin. But Augustine was using the argument to bolster the power of secular rulers, not to undercut it. After the notorious investiture controversies of the eleventh century, a different kind of battle line was drawn. John was steeped in the history of the investiture controversies and he knew where the bodies were buried. The history of the investiture struggles is long and tangled. Until the eleventh century it is probably accurate to say that the emperor dominated the pope more often than the reverse. But the papacy became exceptionally decadent in the tenth century and sees were widely bought and sold. (Benedict IX, made pope at the age of twelve as the result of an incident in petty Roman politics, was so debauched he was driven out. Returning later, he sold the papacy to his successor, Gregory VI.) Reform movements—such as the drive against *simony,* or the selling of ecclesiastical offices, by the monasteries under the Abbot of Cluny—were already beginning in the tenth century. Some popes began reform, too, but the most vigorous was Gregory VII, who became pope in 1073. In his drive against simony and the widespread marriage of the clergy, in 1075 he prohibited the lay investiture of clergy. Emperor Henry IV, fighting to preserve the hundred-year-old prerogative of appointing abbots and bishops, tried to depose Gregory; Gregory then excommunicated Henry and Henry in turn set up an antipope. The practical, if not the theoretical, issues were more or less settled by their successors in the Concordat of Worms (1122), when John of Salisbury was a young child.[28]

It seems likely that the greater power and efficiency of secular governments in the twelfth century were at least in part a delayed reaction to Gregory's challenge in the eleventh century. For his part, John strongly objected to the exploitation of clergy by secular rulers in conferring burdensome civil posts upon them; but John also had certain anti-bureaucratic feelings that were directed against the Church as well as against secular government. The weight of John's discourse, however, was to make the Church impregnable to secular attack: soldiers are not only bound to secular rulers but "bound to the Church by a solemn oath" and, if they do not actually swear such an oath, they are still "in fact under an obligation to the Church by virtue of a tacit oath if not an express one." A soldier should be loyal to his prince, to be sure, but he must be enjoined to "keep inviolate the faith which he owes first to God and afterwards to the prince and to the commonwealth." Moreover, if a soldier takes up the sword without proper auspices, "he is rightly called not a soldier but an assassin."

The Church is to be protected at all times against injuries to clergy or holy places by strict enforcement of the death penalty for such sacrilege:

> The nature of these privileges of churches and holy places and ministers is made clearly known by the law both divine and human, although it is now obvious from usage that they can only be determined before ecclesiastical judges; and if anyone lays violent hands on one of the clergy, he is to be punished by anathema which none save the Roman pontiff has power to absolve.[29]

Tyranny

John of Salisbury is best known for his defense of tyrannicide:[30] "Between a tyrant

[28] For important documents on this dispute, see Tierney, Part 2. George Sabine has a good discussion of it in his *History of Political Theory,* 3rd ed. (New York: Holt, Rinehart and Winston, 1961), Ch. 12. For extended treatment of theoretical writings of the period, see Carlyle and Carlyle, Vol. 4, Parts 2 and 3, and K. J. Leyser, "The Polemics of the Papal Revolution," Ch. 3 in Smalley.

[29] *The Statesman's Book,* Bk. V, Ch. 5, pp. 81–82.

[30] An important predecessor of John in this respect was Manegold of Lautenbach, an eleventh-century supporter of Gregory VII who defended tyrannicide on the basis of a simple contract theory: if a king becomes a

and a prince there is a simple or chief difference, that the latter obeys the law and rules the people by its dictates, accounting himself as but their servant." Later, talking about the evils of ambition, John shows its worst fruit to be tyranny. Vain and wicked men may be "tolerable so long as the point is not reached where the conduct of public business is subverted by ambition."

There are certain laws that "absolutely cannot be broken with impunity." By breaking them even kings become outlaws. Military discipline is necessary but even a soldier should not be expected to give unreasoning obedience. Some orders are "so detestable that no command will possibly justify them or render them permissible." Military decisions must be accepted by soldiers as matters morally indifferent but commands to murder innocents without military justification, to commit sacrilege, even commands "found to be expressly hostile to the safety of the commonwealth," may, John implies, be resisted.

The duties and virtues of a prince are many, says John, whereas it is easier with fewer words to describe a tyrant—though the chapter in which he does so is one of the longest in the whole *Policraticus:* "A tyrant, then, as the philosophers have described him, is one who oppresses the people by rulership based upon force, while he who rules in accordance with the laws is a prince." And what is *law?* "Law is the gift of god, the model of equity, a standard of justice, a likeness of the divine will, the guardian of well-being, a bond of union and solidarity between peoples, a rule defining duties, a barrier against the vices and the destroyer thereof, a punishment of violence and all wrong-doing." It follows that a prince is "a kind of likeness of divinity," and a tyrant is a likeness of the Devil, "even of the wickedness of Lucifer."

John grants that ecclesiastical leaders may be tyrants, too: there are "heretical, schismatic, and sacrilegious priests" who use religion as a pretext to wage war on God. They are more easily restrained by their superiors than princes, however. The long critique of ecclesiastical tyrants in Chapter 17 of Book VIII ends, significantly, with a tribute to "blessed Gregory," who "spoke nought save truth and sweetness" yet who somehow also "lashed these offenses far more bitterly."

From John's general indictment of tyranny it follows that it is "a lawful and glorious act" to slay a public tyrant, provided one is not bound to him by an oath of fealty; does the deed without violating justice, religion, and honor; and does not use poison. John is ambiguous about exactly who is entitled to declare a tyrant fair game. Yet, even if men fail to punish tyrants for their iniquity, God will do so. On this point John gives the reader many examples from history so that he may "see more clearly than the light of day that all tyrants are miserable."

John's work gave ideological support to the strong popes of the following century, of whom Innocent III was foremost. According to the French historian Janet, John had some influence on the Catholic *Liguers* of sixteenth-century France,[31] although in their use of his doctrine of tyrannicide they neglected his indictment of the tyranny of priests. This is an unfortunate oversight, for John's willingness to criticize his own brethren is one of those attributes that makes the *Policraticus* more than a piece of polemics. John was a participant in a lively political struggle but his positive vision of a single Christian community, harmoniously governed, gave perspective and moral justification to his negative attacks on tyranny. He sought to raise the position of the Church and to lower the position of the secular power but he did so not simply to justify a complacent Church. We should be grateful for his contribution to

---

tyrant, that is, if he "has begun . . . to exercise most cruelly against his subjects the tyranny which he ought to repel, is it not clear that he deservedly falls from the dignity entrusted to him and that the people stand free of his lordship and subjection, when he has been evidently the first to break the compact for whose sake he was appointed?" (*Ad Gebhardum Liber* [c. 1085], in Lewis, Vol. 1, p. 165.) See also Carlyle and Carlyle, Vol. 3, p. 164.

[31] See p. 253 below. See also E. F. Jacob, "John of Salisbury," in Hearnshaw, p. 81.

the autonomy of churches and universities within a political order; but perhaps John's most important contribution to political thought is his sympathetic use of the limited classical materials available to him—sympathetic even to the point of praising Cicero's metaphysical skepticism. His was an honorable and sensible search for the best vision possible in his own time of what human society ought to be.

THE THIRTEENTH CENTURY

In the hundred and thirty years between the death of John of Salisbury and the publication of Dante's *De monarchia* great changes occurred in the intellectual and political life of Europe. Through the Arabs Avicenna and Averroes the bulk of Aristotle's works had been reintroduced and were being studied in the newly formed (or coalesced) universities. From 1250 to 1300 the University of Paris was the dominant center of Aristotelian studies.[32] Aristotle's logical categories had been known before and were almost universally accepted, but reactions to his metaphysics were quite varied: St. Bonaventure, upholding a kind of Augustinian illuminationism, led a group of conservative critics. Robert Grosseteste and his pupil Roger Bacon shared the conservative response except for their attraction to Aristotle's natural science. We have already examined Thomas' grand synthesis of Aristotle but our special examination of it should not be allowed to suggest that it went unchallenged. In addition to the official strictures against some of the Thomistic doctrines, we find the very subtle criticisms of John Duns Scotus. Scotus shared with Thomas the view that all knowledge derives from experience and may be objectively known—special divine illumination is not necessary. He differed from Thomas in holding that the mind as well as the senses may have direct and not merely indirect apprehension of individual things.[33]

The thirteenth century also witnessed the high point of papal power that began with the accession of Innocent III in 1198. A shrewd administrator and a brilliant innovator, Innocent had motives that are still a matter of dispute. His assertions of inherent papal authority over secular matters were sweeping but, when he actually intervened in imperial elections or feudal disputes—which he did with greater frequency and success than any other pope—he always managed to find justifications that were less controversial than his theoretical utterances.[34] The century ended with the able but ailing and arrogant Boniface VIII trying but failing to do what Innocent III had done. His protracted disputes with the ruthless Philip IV (the Fair) of France are significant because they represent probably the first major struggle over a question of national sovereignty per se.

The first issue was whether a king could tax the clergy of his land. The traditional view had been that he could, as long as the purpose was to finance a just war. But in 1296 England and France were fighting and the English king was taxing his clergy and the French king was taxing his clergy—both, of course, to finance a "just war." A second dispute arose when Philip deliberately arrested and tried a bishop, who was convicted of heresy, in a civil court. In protest, Boniface summoned all French bishops to Rome, whereupon Philip forbade them to go. Less than half showed up. A few days later Boniface wrote *Unam sanctum* (1302), the most famous medieval bull on Church and state. Referring to the traditional two-swords doctrine, Boniface says,

> the one is exercised for the church, the other by the church, the one by the hand of the priest, the other by the hand of kings and soldiers,

[32] See pp. 131–32 above. See also F. C. Copleston, *Medieval Philosophy* (New York: Harper & Row, 1961), Ch. 5; Jean Dunbabin, "Aristotle in the Schools," Ch. 4 in Smalley; and Paul Vignaux, *Philosophy in the Middle Ages: An Introduction,* trans. by E. C. Hall (Cleveland: World, Meridian, 1959), Chs. 3 and 4.

[33] See Copleston, Ch. 8.

[34] See Tierney, Part 3, Ch. 4.

> though at the will and sufferance of the priest. One sword ought to be under the other and the temporal authority subject to the spiritual power. For while the apostle says "There is no power but from God and those that are ordained of God" (Romans 13:1), they would not be ordained unless one sword was under the other and, being inferior, was led by the other to the highest things. . . .
>
> Therefore, if the earthly power errs, it shall be judged by the spiritual power, if a lesser spiritual power errs it shall be judged by its superior, but if the supreme spiritual power errs it can be judged only by God not by man. . . . Whoever therefore resists this power so ordained by God resists the ordinance of God unless, like the Manicheans, he imagines that there are two beginnings, which we judge to be false and heretical.[35]

Philip was properly incensed but, in fact, except for Boniface's ingenious labeling of those who said spiritual power was not material power as Manicheans—Augustine's old enemies—the whole bull was largely a cut-and-paste job put together out of previous papal and Scholastic sources. (The closing words were borrowed from Aquinas.) Although no other pope had been quite so blunt, Boniface was not much different from several of his predecessors in his theoretical position. Without going into the details of the dispute, we can say that on the essential points—whether the king is subordinate to the pope in temporal matters outside his realm and whether royal jurisdiction may be superceded by Church authority within the king's realm—Philip and the emerging nation-state won.

The violent struggles of Boniface and Philip spawned some skillfully written tracts by both sides. One of the most extreme but systematic of Boniface's defenders was Giles of Rome (Aegidius Romanus, c. 1247–1316), one-time tutor of young Philip the Fair. In his *De ecclesiastica potestate* (1302) he disagreed with Aquinas and Aristotle that the political community is natural. Assuming the intrinsic superiority of spiritual to material things, he expounded a peculiar concept of rightful lordship (*dominium*) in which legitimacy is tied wholly to Church membership. The unbaptized cannot even legitimately own property: ". . . we wish . . . to show that no one can with justice hold lordship of anything unless he has been reborn through the church. . . . whoever is bound by the church, or excommunicated by her, can call nothing his own—or, if he can, it will be only by the indulgence of the church."[36]

The Dominican John of Paris (1269–1306) was a defender of Philip. His *De potestate regia et papali* (*On Kingly and Papal Power,* 1302) was an answer to Giles in which, with impressive dispassionateness, he defended the Aristotelian idea of the political community as the highest form of natural society, a society that could be perfected outside the sanctification of the Church. The *regnum* does not require the *sacerdotum,* even though the latter is morally superior, for the two pertain to different levels of existence:

> If the priest is superior to the ruler in dignity and absolutely speaking, nevertheless it is not necessary that he be superior to him in all things. The lower secular power is not so related to the higher spiritual power that it has its origin in, or derives from, it in the same way that the power of a proconsul is related to the emperor, who is superior in all things, inasmuch as the power of the former derives from him. Rather the relation is similar to that of the father's power to that of the general of the army: neither of these powers derives from the other; rather they both derive from some higher power.[37]

Though John's tone was that of a mediator,

[35] Quoted in Tierney, p. 189. For the whole dispute, see Tierney, Part 3, Chs. 3 and 4; Walter Ullmann, *The Growth of Papal Government in the Middle Ages,* 2nd ed. (London: Methuen, 1962); and T. S. R. Boase, *Boniface VIII* (London: Constable, 1933).

[36] Bk. II, Chs. 7 and 12, in Lewis, Vol. 1, pp. 112 and 114. Lewis also includes extracts from Giles' *De regimine principum* (1285), which follows a very different line from that of *De ecclesiastica potestate.* The former closely follows Thomas' *De regimine principum* and Aristotle's *Politics.* For other excerpts of Giles, see Carlyle and Carlyle, Vol. 5, pp. 402–09, Lerner and Mahdi, pp. 391–401, and Tierney, pp. 198–203.

[37] Ch. 5, in Lerner and Mahdi, pp. 413–14. See also Carlyle and Carlyle, Vol. 5, pp. 422–37, Lewis, Vol. 1, pp. 115–17, Morrall, pp. 90–92, and Tierney, pp. 206–10.

he dared to move beyond a tradition almost a thousand years old when he declared that the two-swords doctrine was merely an allegory and not useful as evidence. And in his discussion of the Church he almost incidentally introduced a notion of corporate authority in which some would find roots of popular sovereignty. Going back to the decretalists,[38] he argued that the authority of the Church was not concentrated in the person of the pope but was suffused throughout all its members.

With the rise in power of national kings representative institutions developed to give the king, first, information, then money, and much later, laws. One of the first such assemblies was called not by a king, however, but by Innocent III in 1200. The summons went to proctors from six cities under the temporal jurisdiction of the papacy who had full power (*plena potestas*) to speak for their cities. The phrase had been used in canon law in the twelfth century but this was probably its first political usage. Emperor Frederick II summoned proctors from different Italian cities with full authority (*auctoritas*) as representatives. Simon de Montfort's parliament of 1265 and Edward I's Model Parliament of 1295 are important events in English history. Philip the Fair called the states-general into existence. By the end of the century representative assemblies on a national basis were known in the Spanish kingdoms as well.[39]

If national kingship, especially in France, was becoming more stable by the end of the thirteenth century, the Holy Roman Empire had virtually collapsed. Emperor Frederick II was outmaneuvered and deposed by Pope Innocent IV and, after his heir Conradin was beheaded by the French Charles of Anjou in Naples in 1268, the Holy Roman Empire became a ghostly entity. The chaos of Germans, Italians, Frenchmen, and Spaniards—ostensibly fighting for and against the Empire but actually pursuing parochial interests—aroused Dante, as it would Machiavelli two centuries later, to seek an answer in a single, unifying ruler.

DANTE

Compared to thinkers like Aquinas or John of Paris, Dante might seem to be a throwback to an earlier age when the dream of universal monarchy seemed less visionary. Machiavelli, however, who also looked back to ancient Rome as a model, is often called the first modern political theorist. The fact is that Dante is something of a paradox: the poet-politician, the escapist-realist, the backward-looking, forward-looking visionary.

Life

Dante Alighieri was born in Florence in 1265 of a venerable but impoverished family. He was probably educated to some degree in the Dominican schools of that city but was mainly self-educated. The early flowering of his poetic talents admitted him to the cultured circles of Florence but exactly how he earned his living is not known. He fell in love with a young lady named Beatrice who died at the age of twenty-four but who provided Dante with a lifetime of inspiration

[38] The decretalists were those commentators on canon law who specialized in the canonical materials of the period after Gratian's *Decretum* in the mid-twelfth century. Those specializing in the interpretation of the *Decretum* itself were called decretists. Both groups were canonists.

[39] On secular medieval representation see Otto Gierke, *Political Theories of the Middle Ages,* trans. by F. W. Maitland (Boston: Beacon Press, 1958), Ch. 7; George L. Haskins, *The Growth of English Representative Government* (New York: Barnes & Noble, 1960); Morrall, Ch. 5; A. F. Pollard, *The Evolution of Parliament* (London: Longmans, Green, 1920); Gaines Post, "Plena Potestas and Consent in Medieval Assemblies (1150–1325)," *Traditio,* Vol. 1 (1943), pp. 355–408; Riesenberg, Ch. 8; Sayles, Ch. 27; and Ullmann, *A History of Political Thought,* pp. 195–214. We should not confuse the convening of a parliament (from the French *parler,* to speak) with popular representation, let alone law-making power: "Though between 1258 and 1286 nearly fifty parliaments were convoked, the commons were summoned to less than half-a-dozen" (Sayles, p. 456).

for romantic poetry in the style of the times and who became for him a theological symbol of remarkable versatility.[40] The *Vita nuova* (*New Life*), written after Beatrice's death in the early 1290s, was the first work to use her name.

In 1295 Dante entered political life and in 1300 was one of six elected to the Florence Priory, or municipal council. He allied himself with the Ghibelline faction against the Guelphs, who were loyal to Pope Boniface VIII. The two major contending groups of the city were, however, subfactions within the Guelphs—the Bianchi (Whites) and the Neri (Blacks). Dante had friends in the Bianchi and in-laws in the Neri. The Priory, to bring order, banished the leaders of both subfactions. Boniface, eager to control Florence, backed the Neri.

In 1301, while Dante was away from the city, the Neri engineered a coup and Dante was one of those banished from the city and condemned to be burned alive should they return. The same sentence was to be imposed on his two sons when they reached the age of fourteen. From this time to his death in Ravenna in 1321, Dante wandered from city to city, staying with friends, never returning to Florence.

Though cut off from his home, Dante championed both local culture and traditional philosophy. He defended the use of the vernacular in *De vulgari eloquentia* (*On the Eloquence of Common Speech*). He began but never finished *Convivio* (*The Banquet*), a catchall tribute to Dame Philosophy that became a vernacular encyclopedia. We do not know exactly when he wrote *De monarchia* (*On Monarchy*). It may have been during the time that Henry VII, the new emperor, entered Italy and eventually laid siege to Florence. Dante hailed him as a savior but when Henry died of fever in 1313 not only was the feeble Holy Roman Empire set back further but Dante was denied his last chance to return home. The last years of his life were devoted to his masterpiece, the *Divina commedia* (*Divine Comedy*).

[40] For an interpretation of Beatrice see Étienne Gilson, *Dante the Philosopher,* trans. by David Moore (London: Sheed & Ward, 1948), Ch. 1. A different interpretation will be found in Dorothy L. Sayers, *Introductory Papers on Dante* (New York: Harper & Row, 1954), pp. 108–24 and 190–98, and in Charles Williams, *The Figure of Beatrice* (London: Faber and Faber, 1943). On Dante's biography see Michele Barbi, *Life of Dante,* trans. by P. Ruggiers (Berkeley: Univ. of California Press, 1960), and Henry Sedgwick, *Dante* (New Haven: Yale Univ. Press, 1918).

The *Divina Commedia*

Dante's *Commedia* (the *Divina* was added by later generations) contains very little overt politics but offers a good many covert political nuggets. The *Divina commedia* is a grand tour through hell, purgatory, and paradise. The poet goes through nine circles of hell, observing the fitting punishment of every kind of sinner from glutton to traitor. He wanders along terraces of purgation where negligent rulers wait with the unabsolved and the excommunicated. He ascends through the ten heavens where various holy spirits enjoy nonlife in accordance with their respective virtues.

D'Entreves argues that it is a mistake to make Dante a thoroughgoing cosmopolitan on the basis of his plea for world government in *De monarchia.* Dante's political philosophy is thoroughly civic, argues D'Entreves. Dante is and remains a proud Florentine and *città* (city) is a key word in the *Divina commedia.* Dante's cosmopolitanism is "an aspiration, a cloak to conceal his scars."[41]

In Canto 15 of the *Paradiso* Dante celebrates his ancestor who dwelt in Florence:

Florence within her old enclosure stood
  whence tierce and nones she still hears daily tolled,
  and dwelt in peace, sober and chaste and good.

He also celebrates his own life in Florence among his friends:

Me to a life so lovely, so serene,
  of fellowship with citizens so staid,
  a hostelry so good to sojourn in,

[41] Alessandro Passerin d'Entreves, "Civitas," in John Freccero, ed., *Dante* (Englewood Cliffs, N. J.: Prentice-Hall, 1965), p. 142. See also D'Entreves, *Dante as a Political Thinker* (London: Oxford Univ. Press, 1952).

Did Mary give, when loudly called to aid;
and, in your ancient Baptistry, there
was I both Christ's and Cacciaguida made.[42]

Count Cacciaguida was Dante's Florentine ancestor who in most human fashion could gossip about his townsmen but who was also an allegorical symbol for family affection and patriotism.[43] The *Paradiso* was dedicated to Can Grande della Scala, the noble ruler of Verona with whom Dante lived around 1316. Though interpretations vary, some think that, after the death of Emperor Henry VII, Can Grande symbolized Dante's political hopes the way Beatrice symbolized his spiritual hopes.

Similarly, Virgil, Dante's guide through hell, is a surrogate of both the spirit of the Roman Empire and the necessary discipline of human government, as Beatrice is a surrogate of divine love. The Dark Wood is a frequently used symbol of the political maze of Florence and of the bewilderment of man when he is cut off from orderly government. Proper discipline of the individual depends upon government but the reverse is also true:

> The root of the current political confusion, in regard to which Dante has seen the truth in Mercury, lay in the misuse of individual free will. Human will, undisciplined by theology and philosophy, could no more escape annihilation through conflict with natural law, than could Guelph policies escape eclipse through conflict with Ghibelline when ungoverned by the ideals of true empire and true church in their mutual autonomies. The individual came before the state, not vice versa.[44]

Dante's use of astrology and his dualistic pairing of opposites were all part of his struggle to find a pattern of meaning in a world of conflict.

Dante distinguishes between the corruption of the Church and the state by individual men and the divine goodness that still resides in the institutions themselves. As we will see in *De monarchia,* Rome takes on crucial importance for Dante and he describes the pope and the emperor as the two suns of Rome who owe each other mutual recognition and respect. But he unmercifully flays Boniface VIII as a person in the *Divina commedia:* in the third pouch of the eighth circle of hell he finds Boniface upside down in a hole with the rest of the simoniacs, their feet aflame. In paradise he hears Peter denounce Boniface as one who has made of his sepulcher "a sewer of fetid filth and blood" to placate the Devil. In the same way, however, Dante condemns Philip the Fair for the bodily assault by his henchmen on the aging Boniface at Alagna and even finds in this act a symbol of Christ's crucifixion.

Dante's hell can be seen as an allegory of the travail of the human soul but also as an alegory of the travail of the human community:

> The City of Dis remains always the image of the City—of the Empire, of community, of man-in-society—the perverted image of that heavenly Rome which spreads its gyres so wide in the Empyrean. . . .
>
> The City of Dis is extended in time and space. She is simultaneously present at every moment of time, from her respectable suburbs (never more respected than today) inward to that withdrawn and secluded centre where . . . at the end of the descent is the "great Worm" which devours and is never satisfied.[45]

De Monarchia

The corruption of politics and the redemption of the spirit is most evident in the *Divina commedia;* the possibility of redemption within the sphere of politics appears more directly in *De monarchia.* Dante affirms that no one before him has attempted to justify a single ruler of the whole earth and he knows how incredibly ambitious this seems. To prove one more theorem of Euclid or to

[42] *Paradiso,* Canto 15, ll. 97–99 and 130–35, in *The Divine Comedy,* trans. by Geoffrey L. Bickersteth (Cambridge, Mass.: Harvard Univ. Press, 1965), pp. 627 and 629. Bickersteth's translation, a dual language edition, seeks to duplicate in English the Italian meter. Subsequent quotations are from this edition.

[43] See Sayers, pp. 7 and 52–53, and Dunbar, pp. 64–66.

[44] Dunbar, p. 55. Mercury is, variously, a symbol of incarnation, duty, and personal function.

[45] Sayers, p. 131.

follow Aristotle through the analysis of happiness once more, says Dante, is "tiresome" and "superfluous." But knowledge of the temporal government of the world, because it is not of immediate use,

> has been neglected by all. I therefore propose to drag it from its hiding place, in order that my alertness may be useful to the world and may bring me the glory of being the first to win this great prize. It is a difficult task I attempt and beyond my powers, but I rely not on my own ability; I trust in that giver of light who gives abundantly to all and reproaches none.[46]

The work sets forth three theses in three books: (1) the world should be united under one government; (2) this government should be Roman; (3) this government should not depend on the papacy. The first argument begins in a rather formalistic way. If the essence of man (his "basic capacity" in the Schneider translation) is "to be sensitive to intellectual growth," the achievement of this state should be the aim of temporal life and peace is the necessary means to this end, a conclusion approved by both Aristotle and the Scriptures. Moreover, God is "absolute world government" and, since "In the intention of God every creature exists to represent the divine likeness in so far as its nature makes this possible," mankind should strive to be, like God, a unity. Man should be under a single authority because, as Aristotle says, "a plurality of authorities is disorder."

Not content with these proofs, Dante also rather unconvincingly supports the thesis with a compound syllogism: Dante says that world government is most likely to produce freedom, that is, men capable of choosing according to judgment unprejudiced by appetite. These men, as Aristotle described them, exist for themselves and not for others. A government that is worldwide is most apt to be reasonable. The reasons Dante gives for these claims are more logical than compelling and seem in the end to boil down to the Aristotelian and Pythagorean—and, though Dante does not acknowledge it, probably the more Platonic—view that "places unity on the side of good and plurality on the side of evil." None of these forebears of Dante, however, argued for world government.

Why should Rome be the agency of this unification? "The Roman people were ordained by nature for rule." Dante sees the Roman past in a rosy hue: the Roman people were the noblest of all time and their rule was for the common good. He catalogs the famous Roman heroes and martyrs as if they were typical. The Augustan age was an age of peace and also the time of Christ: ". . . this happiest of ages was called by Paul the 'fullness of time.'" Dante admits that he once thought of Rome's imperial expansion as merely the result of force but now he sees that it was the working of divine Providence. Though "divine judgment in human affairs is sometimes revealed, sometimes hidden," the fact that the Romans won worldwide athletic contests—where rules of fair play prevail—may be taken as a mark of superiority with divine blessing. Moreover, in military contests waged out of neither hatred or love nor for money but "only out of a zeal for justice . . . are not the fruits of combat acquired *de jure?*"

Both the birth and death of Jesus also show that Rome ruled by divine authority: "Christ, as his scribe Luke testifies, willed to be born of the Virgin Mary under an edict of Roman authority in order that he, the Son of God made man, might register in that extraordinary register of mankind as a man; thus he recognized its legality." True, Christ was crucified under Roman authority but this, too, is a confirmation of the point: ". . . a penalty inflicted by an unqualified judge is not punishment but rather an injury." "Had the Roman Empire not existed *de jure,* Adam's sins would not have been punished in Christ."

In Book III Dante attempts to show that the authority of imperial rule comes directly from God and not through the papacy. (He was well aware that his doctrine would offend the Roman pont'ff. The work was con-

[46] *De monarchia,* Bk. I, Ch. 1, in *On World Government,* 2nd rev. ed., trans. by Herbert W. Schneider (New York: Liberal Arts Press, 1957), pp. 3–4. Subsequent quotations are from this edition.

demned by Pope John XXII in 1329 and put on the Index of Forbidden Books in 1559, not to be removed until the nineteenth century.) Dante's first task is to discredit the view that the authority of the Church rests on tradition. The reverse is true, he says: the authority of tradition comes from the authority of the Church, which comes from the authority of Christ, and Christ was not always a respecter of traditions. Dante criticizes the decretalists, who labor so hard at preserving the canon law that they forget the Scriptures. He challenges the common analogies that the Church is to the state as the architect is to the workman or the sun to the moon. With careful scriptural exegesis he questions both the applicability of the analogies and—not too consistently—the errors in interpreting them. He rejects the view that Christ's grant to Peter to "bind and loose" all things (Matthew 16:19) and Peter's reference to "two swords" (Luke 22:38) conveyed temporal jurisdiction to the Church.

Dante examines the argument based on the Donation of Constantine[47] and finds it wanting. Constantine could not have divided the Empire in the manner propapalists suggested: ". . . since all temporal jurisdiction is finite, and any finite quantity can be used up by finite subtractions, it would follow that the original jurisdiction could be annihilated, which is absurd." Dante seems to be arguing from a theory of indivisible sovereignty, although he does not label it as such, but he is also relying on the more obvious fact that the Empire existed and functioned well before the Church had even come into existence. The essence of Dante's syllogistic and historical arguments seems to be that "to be a man is one thing and to be a pope is another, and to be emperor is still another, just as to be a man, father, or lord are different kinds of being."

The conclusion of *De monarchia* is abrupt and disappointing. A host of questions are left not only unanswered but unasked. In the final paragraph Dante says that his conclusion that temporal power comes directly from God and not from the pope "must not be interpreted so strictly as to imply that the Roman government is in no way subject to the Roman pontificate." But he does not tell us how else it should be interpreted. Earlier he says that his proposal for a world government would not mean that "every little regulation for every city would come directly from the world government." But he does not explain what he would consider little. Gilson surely exaggerates when he says,

> If he had not read Aristotle, Dante's political passions would have been neither less compelling nor less violent, but they would have lacked what they needed in order to found themselves in reason, to define themselves in doctrine and above all to discover the remedy for the evils which had been their cause.[48]

The position Dante defends is of heroic proportions but the defense is formalistic and arid. The first-rate poet is a second-rate philosopher. His knowledge of Aristotle seems only to interrupt his fluid style as he stops to insert a superfluous syllogism. And somewhat under Thomas' shadow, he confuses Aristotle's freedom with Paul's freedom and Aristotle's ethics with Jesus' ethics.

Yet we must not condemn Dante the philosopher for a work that was only incidentally philosophic. In *De monarchia* Dante aimed neither at developing a full-scale philosophy of government nor at working out a program of governmental action. He aimed to support the idea of the Holy Roman Empire—and presumably the cause of Henry VII—and to steer the papacy away from power politics and back toward sacerdotalism. Thomas was a superior philosopher but, unlike Dante, he did not even acknowledge the Holy Roman Empire, writing always of "princes." We must also remember that *De monarchia* was not Dante's final work. The sharpness of his division between

[47] Constantine, supposedly cured of leprosy by Pope Sylvester I (314–15), donated to the Church the city of Rome together with other dignities of empire. According to the clever forgeries of the ninth century, later called the False Decretals, Sylvester received from Constantine secular authority over all of Western Europe.

[48] Gilson, p. 109.

the realm of reason and the realm of faith, the apparent dualism between the justice of Rome and the justice of the Church were modified in the *Divina commedia.*

Book II of *De monarchia* is what bothers us most. Dante believes in the nobility, rationality, and beauty of the ancient Romans with an ingenuousness that is almost embarrassing in the light of more reliable historical knowledge. But it may help to remember that Dante's world, the world he gave the Romans to rule, was much smaller than our own and that it is hard for us to grasp the extent to which the Romans were a legendary symbol.[49] Rule by Rome may well have meant to Dante essentially rule by Roman law.

Finally, can we lightly fault the basic argument of Book I? Six hundred and sixty years later, can we comfortably deny that peace requires some kind of rational authority capable of unifying the world?

MARSILIO OF PADUA

Marsilio's Padua was quite similar to Dante's Florence: both were Italian city-states struggling to gain liberty from papal power. Like Dante, Marsilio became involved in local politics and later withdrew to the secluded life of a writer. Both men were partisans of Can Grande della Scala of Verona; both were committed supporters of the Holy Roman Empire and assumed the role of reformers in its defense.

Nevertheless, despite all these parallels the thought of the two men diverged sharply, possibly because of the temperamental difference that led Dante to philosophy and poetry and Marsilio to science and medicine.[50] Dante gave us an idealized goal of universal government; Marsilio gave us a defense of government based on the natural desires of men as biological organisms.

Life

The details of Marsilio's life are uncertain. The son of Bonmatteo dei Maindardini, a notary to the University of Padua, he was born somewhere between 1275 and 1280 and died around 1342.[51] Marsilio was a student at the University of Padua during a time when Aristotelian teachings dominated. He studied medicine as well as philosophy and some time later became Rector of the University of Paris, where his masterwork, *Defensor pacis* (*The Defender of Peace,* 1324), was published. The work touched off a papal inquisition and in 1326 Marsilio and his Averroist colleague John of Jandun were declared heretics. They fled to the imperial court of Louis of Bavaria for protection. Marsilio was with Louis during his bizarre Italian expedition of 1327 when Louis had himself crowned as Emperor and set up an antipope. Pope John XXII, in exile in Avignon, thundered his condemnation of the whole procedure and excommunicated Marsilio. Unreliable rumors had it that during the time in 1328 when Louis had named Marsilio a vicar, the latter was cruel in his treatment of priests loyal to the pope. Like the eminent philosopher William of Ockham[52] Marsilio was required for personal security to spend most of the rest of his life within the protective entourage of Louis of Bavaria.

[49] See C. T. Davis, *Dante and the Idea of Rome* (London: Oxford Univ. Press, 1957), and Nancy Lenkeith, *Dante and the Legend of Rome* (London: Warburg Institute, Univ. of London, 1952).

[50] See Marjorie Reeves, "Marsilio of Padua and Dante Alighieri," in Smalley, Ch. 5.

[51] The Paduan's name is also frequently spelled "Marsiglio" or "Marsilius." On his life see C. K. Brampton, "Marsiglio of Padua, Life," *English Historical Review,* Vol. 37 (1922), pp. 501–15, and *Marsilius of Padua, The Defender of Peace,* Vol. 1, *Marsilius of Padua and Medieval Political Philosophy,* ed. and trans. by Alan Gewirth (New York: Columbia Univ. Press, 1951), pp. 20–23.

[52] William of Ockham (c. 1290–1349) was an English Franciscan and Oxford master, a leading nominalist, intuitionist, and experientialist whose name is well known in logic for Ockham's razor, or the principle of economy: every explanation should be as simple as possible, plurality should be postulated only when unavoidable. In his political thought Ockham found the basis

Defensor Pacis

The *Defensor pacis,* says its foremost contemporary translator, makes its author ". . . one of the few truly revolutionary figures in the history of political philosophy."[53] Another authority says, "It certainly is difficult, in the twentieth century, to appreciate adequately the veritable reversal in political thinking which the Marsilian ideas effected. . . . Marsiglio performed a surgical operation in which he excised from political doctrine Christian elements as irrelevant."[54] These assessments are based on Marsilio's positivistic separation of law and morals, his establishment of civil power on nontranscendent grounds, and his deposit of political authority in the people as a whole. The argument that these positions represent a revolution in political thought, however, has been challenged, as we shall shortly see.

At the outset Marsilio announces that his purpose is to refute the pope's claim that his *plenitudo potestatis* is superior to civil power, a theme developed most fully in Discourse II of the work. What is immediately striking is Marsilio's down-to-earth, naturalistic quality. He quotes the Scriptures, to be sure, but Aristotle's *Politics, Ethics,* and even *Parts of Animals,* are conspicuous. His method aims to appeal to the intellect alone "so that this book may stand by itself, needing no external proof."[55] In Chapter 2 Marsilio, using an analogy to biological health, broadens the meaning of "state" (*regnum*) to encompass the many varieties of governance by which tranquility—which he takes as the end of the state—can be achieved. "The state," he says citing Aristotle, "is like an animate nature or animal." Before Marsilio it would have been misleading to translate *regnum* as "state" in the modern sense, for then it usually meant only royal monarchy; but no longer.

By Chapter 4 of Discourse I it appears that the general aim of tranquility for the state—asserted earlier with abundant Scriptural quotations—is mainly an instrumental aim, for the final end of the state is asserted to be—in good Aristotelian fashion—"living and living well." Marsilio specifically states that he means living well in the "temporal or earthly" sense and not in the "eternal or heavenly" sense. The latter is not denigrated but is set apart from political concerns. Here is a significant secularization of politics. Marsilio treats with some sympathy even the views of "the philosophers, including Hesiod, Pythagoras, and several others of the ancients" in their justification of religion solely for its sociological effect in inducing popular behavior useful to the state. Through religion "the peace or tranquility of states and the sufficient life of men for the status of the present world were preserved with less difficulty; which was the end intended by these wise men in laying down such laws or religions." Marsilio was probably more utilitarian than Aristotle without quite realizing it.

Positive law

In Chapter 10 of Discourse I Marsilio defines four aspects of the word *law* (*lex*): (1) "a natural sensitive inclination to some action or passion"; (2) "every form, existing in the mind, of a producible thing"; (3) "the standard containing admonitions for voluntary human acts according as these are ordered toward glory or punishment in the future world"; and (4) "the science or doctrine or universal judgment of matters of civil justice and benefit, and of their opposites." Law in this fourth sense is *civil law,* that is, law divorced from religion and dependent upon the will and power of an earthly ruler. To that extent it is "positive"

of natural law in God's will, which could be arbitrary by all man's standards, rather than in immutable rational categories. For Ockham all law is based on will. His influence weakened the tight linkage between reason and law forged by the thirteenth-century Aristotelians. But his emphasis on law discovered in the Scriptures and through direct revelation was not used to bolster the power of the papacy: his *Breviloquium* was an attack on papal power in both secular and ecclesiastical spheres.

53 Gewirth, Vol. 1, p. IX.

54 Ullmann, *A History of Political Thought,* p. 213.

55 *Marsilius of Padua, The Defender of the Peace,* Vol. 2, *The Defensor pacis* (New York: Columbia Univ. Press, 1956), Disc. I, Ch. 1, sec. 8, p. 7. Subsequent page references are to this volume of this edition.

law. This civil law is further subdivided according to whether it is considered as just or unjust in itself (this pertains to the doctrine of right, or *juris*) or as "a command coercive through punishment or reward to be distributed in the present world." Marsilio says that "considered in this way it most properly is called and is, a law (*lex*)."

This almost Hobbesian or Augustinian conception of law as command with coercion is part of what leading scholars of Marsilio[56] point to when they claim him to be a revolutionary thinker. But perhaps they make too much of a casual distinction and see Marsilio as more unique than he really was:

> Marsiglio's definition of "law in the fourth sense" has been assumed to be his own invention, with some help from Aristotle. But a presumable source for it is to be found in Azo's well known and highly respected *Summa Institutionum,* to which, rather than to a *Summa Theologiae,* Marsiglio would naturally have gone for definitions of legal terms.[57]

That Marsilio accepts coercion as *a* basis of law does not mean that he makes it *the* basis of law. Aquinas also saw coercion as a factor in positive law and Marsilio also sees morality as a factor in positive law. By separating spiritual and secular bases of law he does, to be sure, open the door for later generations who wish to absorb the spiritual into the secular. But it is not clear that this is Marsilio's intention. In a related context Mrs. Lewis succinctly explains the basis of confusion over Marsilio:

> Like the author of the *Social Contract,* the author of the *Defensor pacis* proceeds with brilliant assurance to draw startling conclusions from startling premises never critically examined or quite clearly conceived . . . an apparently firm structure of tightly-articulated logic only half-conceals an ultimate vagueness and inconsistency which continually baffle interpreters and set them quarrelling."[58]

Perhaps ambiguity of intention is the fuel for scholarly disputes but in any case Marsilio's conception of law is not the only basis for controversy over his originality. Morrall, for example, agrees with Mrs. Lewis that Marsilio's view of law was not so novel as many have thought. But Morrall does see Marsilio as "the first political sociologist of the Middle Ages," one who paid uncommon attention to practical matters.[59] This is not to say, of course, that Marsilio was an empiricist. The bulk of the long Discourse II used logic, the Scriptures, and ancient authorities as a basis for attacking papal power. Marsilio offers a detailed critique of canonical statements that justified the exercise of coercive authority by priests, bishops, and popes; he attempts to show why priests must be subject to secular judges; he defends ecclesiastical poverty; he condemns the abuse of ecclesiastical benefices, abuses that "must be corrected by the human legislator"; and he gives "only to the authority of the faithful human legislator which lacks a superior" the right to call a general council of the Church.[60]

When Marsilio uses historical data, he does so with polemical force and for polemical effect:

> Their insatiable appetite for temporal things causing them to be discontented with the things which rulers have granted to them, the bishops

56 Including D'Entreves, *The Medieval Contribution to Political Thought* (Oxford: Oxford Univ. Press, 1939), Chs. 3–4; Georges de Lagarde, *Marsile de Padoue* (Saint-Paul-Trois-Chateaux, Wien: Editions Beatrice, 1934); C. W. Previte-Orton, editor of the definitive Latin edition of the *Defensor pacis* (Cambridge, Eng.: Cambridge Univ. Press, 1928); and Gewirth, who writes, "Marsilius thus is a legal positivist, in contrast to the predominantly rationalist and normative tradition of the middle ages" (Vol. 1, pp. 134–35).

57 Ewart Lewis, "The 'Positivism' of Marsiglio of Padua," *Speculum,* Vol. 38 (1963), p. 546. The legal definitions of Azo (d. 1230) are, in turn, similar to those of Cicero in *De legibus,* Bk. I, Chs. 4–6 and 12.

58 Lewis, *Medieval Political Ideas,* Vol. 1, p. 71.

59 Morrall, p. 107.

60 The latter phrase is presumably intended to support the Holy Roman Emperor but Marsilio is not explicit on the point.

William of Ockham argues in his *Dialogus* (Part I, Bk. VI, Ch. 84) that in an emergency a general council of the Church could meet without being summoned by the pope. William, however, did not attack the monarchic structure of the Church in general and hence was more acceptable to the moderates than Marsilio. See Lewis, *Medieval Political Ideas,* Vol. 2, pp. 398–402.

have made many seizures of the temporalities of provinces belonging to the empire, such as the cities of Romagna, Ferrara, Bologna, and many others, as well as estates and other possessions lying under imperial jurisdiction, especially during vacancies of the imperial seat. And what is the worst of all civil evils, they have set themselves up as rulers and legislators, in order to reduce kings and people to intolerable and disgraceful slavery to themselves.[61]

Marsilio's loyalty to Louis of Bavaria is never in question:

a certain modern so-called Roman pope, who through the above mentioned false assumptions is the most recent entrant upon the path of error and iniquity, is now striving with might and main to hinder and prevent the peaceful accession of the noble Ludwig, duke of Bavaria, elected king of the Romans, to the imperial throne.[62]

One heated appeal to patriotism against those who would devastate "this father and mother land" has sometimes been compared to the famous last chapter of Machiavelli's *The Prince*. Discourse I is the locus of recent theoretical interest but Discourse II set off the fourteenth-century fireworks.

The people

We have already encountered Marsilio's peculiar phrase "the human legislator" (*legislator humanus*), which apparently referred not simply to secular authority as distinguished from sacerdotal authority but to that sovereign authority which is located in the community as a whole. The ruling part (*pars principans*) is the government, the agent of this human legislator. A more problematic concept is the *valentior pars,* a term never defined by Marsilio and argued over endlessly by scholars. It is usually translated as the "weightier part" but the controversy centers on how much the weight is quantitative and how much qualitative. If the former is emphasized, Marsilio is invariably credited with being a forerunner of majoritarian theories. Marsilio says, in fact,

By the "weightier part" I mean to take into consideration the quantity and the quality of the persons in the community over which the law is made. The aforesaid whole body of citizens or the weightier part thereof is the legislator regardless of whether it makes the law directly by itself or entrusts the making of it to some person or persons, who are not and cannot be the legislator in some absolute sense, but only in the relative sense and for a particular time and in accordance with the authority of the primary legislator.[63]

The majoritarian interpretation of this passage had for years been enhanced by the inadvertent deletion of *et qualitate* in later manuscripts. The discovery in earlier manuscripts of the missing phrase has changed the interpretations.[64]

The *valentior pars* is not identified with any particular class structure. From other references it may be inferred that Marsilio preferred an elective monarchy and an elected legislature. Beyond that, Allen is correct in saying,

the *Defensor* contains no plea for what we call parliamentary government or for any particular form of government at all. Nor can I trace any connexion between its thought and the republicanism of Italian cities. Padua itself can hardly be said to have been a republic in 1324; but no doubt a republican tradition existed there and may have been dear to Marsilio. If so, the fact does not appear in the *Defensor*.[65]

In context, it seems clear that Marsilio was setting out in this chapter not to prescribe but to describe at a fairly high level of abstraction. His announced aim was to "discuss that efficient cause of law which is capable of demonstration." This meant not God's law, not the Mosaic law, but "only those laws

[61] *Defensor pacis,* Disc. II, Ch. 25, sec. 14, p. 340.

[62] *Ibid.,* Ch. 26, sec. 11, p. 350.

[63] *Ibid.,* Disc. I, Ch. 12, sec. 3, p. 45.

[64] See Gewirth, Vol. 1, pp. 182–99, and C. W. Previte-Orton, "Marsiglio of Padua, Doctrines," *English Historical Review,* Vol. 38 (1923), pp. 1–21. Gewirth points out that Marsilio includes a similar qualitative criterion in his discussion in *Defensor pacis* of elections to general councils and that he criticizes democracy as being not "according to proper proportion."

[65] J. W. Allen, "Marsilio of Padua," in Hearnshaw, p. 183.

of governments which emerge immediately from the decisions of the human mind."

The above interpretation varies markedly from Gierke's:

> Decisively republican . . . is the system of Marsilius of Padua. With all the consistency of democratic Radicalism it erects an abstract scheme dividing power between the *universitatus civium* and the *pars principans*. . . . With him the "Legislator" must be the Sovereign; but the People is always and necessarily the "Legislator," by the People being meant the Whole Body or a majority of those citizens who are entitled to vote.[66]

Scholars brought to the Middle Ages, as to anything else, their own axes to grind. Gierke saw Marsilio as an atomistic disrupter of medieval organicism. De Legarde saw him as a precursor of totalitarianism.[67] Gewirth sees him as a precursor of democracy. The abstractness of Marsilio's formulations in Discourse I makes it easy to apply his terms to a variety of situations and difficult to assess his originality. He was certainly not aware of all the implications that later commentators would read into his work and it is equally certain that there are nuances and ironies missed even by those commentators most skilled in medieval Latin.

Marsilio would have reason to conceal republican sympathies from his imperial patron, yet he says one man cannot be a valid law-maker:

> for through ignorance or malice or both, this one man could make a bad law, looking more to his own private benefit than to that of the community, so that the law would be tyrannical. For the same reason, the authority to make laws cannot belong to a few; for they too could sin, as above, in making the law for the benefit of a certain few and not for the common benefit, as can be seen in oligarchies. The authority to make the laws belongs, therefore, to the whole body of citizens or to the weightier part thereof.[68]

We can see with hindsight how Marsilio's conclusion may be fitted to a democratic mold. For he argues, as did Rousseau, that the whole body of citizens can be trusted more than any part because no one knowingly does injustice to himself. A bit earlier he offered an equivalent of what Lindsay was to call the "shoe-pinching" argument for democracy: that those who "wear" a policy are the best judges of its fittingness.[69] This positive justification for participation in government, however undeveloped, is very different in tone from, say, William of Ockham's position, which would restrict the temporal powers of the papacy by making a formal distinction between the temporal and spiritual spheres and leave it at that.[70] Marsilio, finally, extends the idea of the interests of the whole to the Church. The "most fitting" conception of the Church, he says, is that of "the whole body of the faithful who believe in and invoke the name of Christ, and all the parts of this whole body in any community, even the household."[71] Other critics of the papacy, such as William of Ockham or John of Paris, accepted this conception but did not use it as Marsilio did to undercut the entire hierarchic structure of the Church. The whole body of the Church (the *universitas fidelium*)

[66] Gierke, p. 46.

[67] Gierke saw Marsilio as a rebel against *Genossenschaftsrecht*, the notion of the law's corporate personality, which Gierke found embedded in medieval thought but vitiated by modern individualism. See De Lagarde. This is Volume 2 of his six-volume *La naissance de l'esprit laique au declin du moyen age*. See Gewirth, Vol. 1, pp. 303–17. Gewirth gives a more balanced interpretation than either of the other two.

[68] *Defensor pacis*, Disc. I, Ch. 12, sec. 8, pp. 48–49.

[69] See Gewirth, Vol. 1, p. 223, and A. D. Lindsay, *The Modern Democratic State* (New York: Oxford Univ. Press, 1962), p. 269.

[70] ". . . we conclude that the papal principate does not regularly include the power to abolish or disturb the rights and liberties of others, especially those of emperors, kings, princes and other laymen, since rights and liberties of this sort are in most cases reckoned among secular matters, to which the papal principate, as we have shown, by no means regularly extends" (*De imperatorum et pontificum potestate*, Ch. 4. Quoted in Lewis, *Medieval Political Ideas*, Vol. 2, pp. 608–09).

[71] See Gewirth, Vol. 1, pp. 260–65. Ironically, Marsilio is able to quote Aristotle in support of his position because *ecclesia* in Greek means "assembly," while *ecclesia* in Latin means "church." Marsilio, who did not know Greek, was relying on a faulty translation of Aristotle that confused the two terms.

should have authority over excommunication, the election of priests, the definition of articles of faith, the election of the pope (head bishop), and, as we have seen, the calling of councils.[72]

We shall look more closely at the conciliar movement in the next section. For now we may conclude that Marsilio is both a fascinating and enigmatic figure whose full intention is lost to us. He defended secular power but went beyond secularization to see man in biological terms, as many moderns would. Yet the issues that gave vitality to his whole work were highly topical in the year 1324. He was at once a pioneering Aristotelian and a simple-minded one. Like Averroes and the Averroists Marsilio associated with in Paris, he elevated Aristotle to a position of authority beyond challenge. But in fact he departed significantly from Aristotle's idea of nature: "The 'natural' as he [Marsilio] conceives it is always the primitive not the perfected; it consists in man's material endowment, physical and biological, not in his rational powers or virtues."[73]

Marsilio can be called a latent democrat, but he was too pessimistic to be a genuine democrat, even if he were to be set down in a different age. We need law, he said, because "men for the most part seem to be vicious and stupid. 'The number of the stupid is infinite' as it is said in the first chapter of Ecclesiastes." He supported in all his efforts the Holy Roman Empire but, unlike Dante, he had no use for world government and even justified war by saying it reduced the surplus population. Perhaps we must let Marsilio remain a symbol for the many other scholars who stand partly hidden in the shadows of the past.

THE CONCILIAR MOVEMENT

The Great Schism began in 1378, when a group of cardinals attempted to invalidate the election of Pope Urban VI, elected in his stead Clement VII, and took Clement to Avignon, France, where, in Babylonian captivity under the French king, popes had resided earlier in the fourteenth century. Thereafter one pope sat in Rome, another in Avignon. Hoping to resolve this embarrassment, a Church council in Pisa in 1409 made matters worse by electing a new pope without sufficient support from the Church at large, thereby creating a third pope. The schism was not primarily caused by political factors but it soon took on great political significance as France and her satellites—Scotland, Castile, Aragon, and Naples—sided with Avignon, and England, the Holy Roman Empire, and Portugal sided with Rome. (Comparison with the Moscow-Peking schism in the Communist Party in the 1960s seems inescapable.)

Since none of the rivals were willing to surrender or compromise, the Council of Constance ended the schism in 1417 by deposing John XXIII, the successor to the pope elected by the Council of Pisa, and Benedict XIII, the Avignon Pope, accepting the resignation of Gregory XII, and electing Martin V as the undisputed pope. It also condemned John Huss as a heretic and in the historic decree *Sacrosancta* asserted its own superiority over the pope: "The ecumenical council assembled at Constance represents the whole Church. It derives authority immediately from Christ. Everyone, even the Pope, owes obedience to it in all that concerns the faith, the unity of the Church and the reform of both head and members."[74]

[72] These are but a few of the 240 positions condemned by Pope Clement VI, who declared the *Defensor pacis* to be the most heretical work he had ever read. Marsilio favored the election of laymen to councils and, perhaps worst of all, he challenged on historical grounds the Church's claim to being founded on Peter in Rome. The difference in style of Discourse II led many to say that Marsilio's associate, John of Jandun, wrote at least part of it. But the most recent scholarship attributes sole authorship to Marsilio. See Alan Gewirth, "John of Jandun and the *Defensor Pacis*," *Speculum,* Vol. 23 (1948), pp. 267–72.

[73] Gewirth, Vol. 1, p. 55. See also Charles N. R. McCoy, *The Structure of Political Thought* (New York: McGraw-Hill, 1963), pp. 126–31.

[74] Quoted in Hubert Jedin, *Ecumenical Councils of*

This was the high point of the so-called conciliar movement, whose date of origin is still a matter of scholarly dispute. There had been fifteen or more councils before Constance, dating back to the Council of Nicaea in 325, but self-conscious theorizing about council superiority over the pope was another matter. The leading conciliar theorists—cardinals Pierre D'Ailly and Francis Zabarella, the German Dietrich of Niem, and the Frenchman Jean Gerson—were at Constance.[75] They drew their ideas most heavily from William of Ockham and Marsilio of Padua and perhaps from the legal theories of Bartolus. They hoped for a reformed, constitutional Church order, but their hopes were ultimately to be disappointed.

Like so many institutions, the Church at this point confronted the hard choice of unity or reform. The price of unity at Constance was the postponement of reform. The conflict between the pope's authority and the conciliarists' hopes reached a height in the interminable council that began at Basel in 1431 and lasted amid dissolutions, reestablishments, and changes of location until 1449. It was as delegate to Basel that Nicholas of Cusa wrote his great defense of the conciliar position. The conciliarists won short-term victories; however, papal power ultimately triumphed, and "Conciliarism was abandoned by its own advocates. By the mid-fifteenth century hardly any of the reputable conciliarist theoreticians were left; one by one they had drifted back to the traditional papal-monarchic point of view."[76] Had things been otherwise, it is tempting to speculate, the Second Vatican Council in the twentieth century might not have to be doing what the fifteenth century failed to do.

In his notable lecture on the conciliar movement Figgis portrayed the *Sacrosancta* of Constance as generating immense political hope and the failure to sustain its position leading to immense political tragedy:

> Probably the most revolutionary official document in the history of the world is the decree of the Council of Constance asserting its superiority to the Pope, and striving to turn into a tepid constitutionalism the Divine authority of a thousand years. It forms the watershed between the medieval and the modern world. . . . the fate of the efforts of the Councils of Pisa and Constance and Basel and the triumph of vested interests over principle would seem to show that all hope of constitutional reform of the Church was vain, and that Luther was justified in appealing to the laity to wield, in her spiritual welfare, that temporal sword with which traditional theory entrusted kings and princes, for her material defense.[77]

Without disputing the significance of this failure of the Church, later scholars have tended to question Figgis' emphasis on its political significance:

> If Figgis is right in seeing a connection between the failure of what he regards as a constitution in the Church and the growth of autocracy at this time, the connection is less simple than he thought, for political autocracy grew largely at the expense of centralized autocracy in the Church. Popes no less than popular or aristocratic assemblies lost ground to kings.[78]

Parker, the author of this quotation, argues that by the late Middle Ages, after the introduction of Aristotle's writings had forced men to consider the possibility of "natural" pagan states, people separated Church and

the Catholic Church, An Historical Outline, trans. by Ernest Graf (New York: Herder & Herder, 1960), p. 116. See also John H. Mundy and Kennerly Woody, eds., *The Council of Constance,* documents trans. by Louise R. Loomis (New York: Columbia Univ. Press, 1961). Beginning in 1352 the cardinals choosing a new pope made electoral pacts, whereby all agreed to follow certain policies if elected pope. But the pacts did not work, for once elected the pope would declare himself unbound by oaths taken as a cardinal and assert his "plenitude of power." See Ullmann, *A History of Political Thought,* pp. 219–20.

[75] Gerson, Chancellor of the University of Paris, led the movement to seek an ending of the Great Schism by means of a general council. He was a powerful tract-writer for this cause.

[76] Ullmann, *A History of Political Thought,* p. 223.

[77] J. N. Figgis, *Political Thought from Gerson to Grotius: 1414–1625* (New York: Harper & Row, Torchbooks, 1960), pp. 41 and 42.

[78] T. M. Parker, "The Conciliar Movement," in Smalley, p. 129.

state conceptually, even though conscious of their own simultaneous membership in both. Sharpened awareness of the separateness of the two sides of Christendom, civil and ecclesiastical, may have made the political consequences of conciliar action less formidable than Figgis assumed. In the heavily law-oriented Italian universities in particular there was a long tradition of compartmentalization between canon law and civil law. In fact, the origins of the theory of conciliar superiority have recently been shown to have earlier roots than was heretofore thought, roots that is, earlier than either the Great Schism or the rise of modern national monarchies.[79] Moreover, scholars are not fully agreed on what the term "conciliarism" should properly include. Gewirth is aware of earlier theories of council supremacy but he argues that more than papal-council relations may be involved: "Marsilius is the founder of conciliarism because he provides for the dependence not only of the Pope upon a general council, but also of the council upon the laity and hence upon the whole 'church.' "[80] But Marsilio was not typical even of conciliarists and it would be a mistake to read too easily our democratic presuppositions into any sector of fifteenth-century society. We must not forget the degree to which reverence for kingship, the acceptance of the privileges of nobility, and the ethos of chivalry pervaded the whole society.[81]

NICHOLAS OF CUSA

Our final thinker in this chapter is generally conceded to be the greatest of the conciliar thinkers. We may profitably search in his thought for the political significance of the conciliar movement.

[79] See Brian Tierney, *Foundations of the Conciliar Theory* (New York: Cambridge Univ. Press, 1955).

[80] *Marsilius of Padua,* Vol. 1, p. 286.

[81] Johann Huizinga's admirable *The Waning of the Middle Ages* (Garden City, N.Y.: Doubleday, Anchor, 1954), especially Chapters 3 and 4, helps us remember.

Life

Nicholas[82] was born in 1401 in Cues, opposite Berncastel on the Moselle River between Trier and Coblenz. He matriculated at the University of Heidelberg a year after the Council of Constance issued its famous decree. In 1423 he received a doctorate in canon law at Padua, after which he studied philosophy and theology at Cologne. As secretary to the Archbishop of Trier he was present in Rome in 1427 and was later dean of a church in Coblenz. Through his scholarly activities he maintained contact with Italian humanists. He was a man of some reputation when he went to the Council of Basel in 1432 to plead the case of a disputed archbishopric election. In 1433, after Pope Eugenius IV issued a bull of dissolution to the Council of Basel, young Nicholas submitted to the council his major work of political theory, *De concordantia catholica* (*On Universal Concord*). It offered, as we shall see, both a philosophic rationale and a program of action. But Nicholas did not remain on the antipapal side for long. He reacted against the French radicals, who he felt were trying to take over the whole machinery of the Church. The extreme and often petty methods of their leader, Cardinal Aleman, alienated Nicholas. In the minority on a crucial council vote in 1436, Nicholas resigned from the Commission of Faith, which had been charged with preparing articles against the pope. As delegate of the papalist minority, Nicholas then went to Constantinople to urge that an Italian city rather than Avignon be

[82] Good brief biographies may be found in John Patrick Dolan's Introduction to his *Nicholas de Cusa, Unity and Reform; Selected Writings* (Notre Dame: Univ. of Notre Dame Press, 1962), E. F. Jacob, "Nicolas of Cusa," in F. J. C. Hearnshaw, ed., *The Social and Political Ideas of Some Great Thinkers of the Renaissance and the Reformation* (London: Harrap, 1925), and Paul E. Sigmund, *Nicholas of Cusa and Medieval Political Thought* (Cambridge, Mass.: Harvard Univ. Press, 1963). Henry Bett, *Nicholas of Cusa* (London: Methuen, 1932) is a short biographical treatment. Dolan's collection, unfortunately, includes nothing from *De concordantia catholica,* which has not been translated into English. Sigmund's careful, comprehensive study is indispensable.

selected as the site of the forthcoming council seeking union between the Greek and Latin arms of the Church.[83]

In his quest for harmony, Nicholas now suported Pope Eugenius IV and his councils at Ferrara and Florence. Nicholas' *Dialogue* was written against the supporters of the antipope Felix V, set up by the Council of Basel. His energetic work to gain German support for Rome led to his being made a cardinal in 1447. He was sent by the pope as legate to Germany "to establish social peace, redress doctrinal error, and correct moral abuses."[84] As Bishop of Brixen in the Tyrol after 1452 he tried, often in vain, to reform the practices of monasteries and was engaged in bitter struggles with Archduke Sigismund of Tyrol, whose political ambitions against the pope had become a test case. Nicholas was even physically assaulted by the archduke's troops. The dispute was not settled until after Nicholas' death in 1464.

Philosophy

Despite the turbulence of his later life, Nicholas was somehow able to write significant treatises in mathematics, philosophy, and devotional literature. *De docta ignorantia* (*On Learned Ignorance,* 1440) shows the profound Platonic influence in Nicholas and has been called a precursor to the works of both Kant and Hegel. Learning is required, Nicholas argued, to know the limits of learning: the effort to understand God is required to know that God transcends understanding. Nicholas denies the validity of the principle of contradiction; at least he denies its validity for intuitive vision (*intellectus videns*), though not for discursive reason (*ratio discurrens*). Every being contains a special "contradiction" that relates it to all other created beings. The harmony of the universe grows as these disjunctive elements are united in God, who is infinite being and ultimate reality but who cannot be known directly through reason as commonly understood.[85]

Nicholas simply by-passed much of traditional Scholastic theology. Some think that by failing to support hierarchical notions of the cosmos, by denying the notion of fixed points in the universe, by making everything but God finite in equal measure, and by implying the relativity even of man's rational judgments, Nicholas opened the way to the astronomy of Galileo, Kepler, and Copernicus and to modern science: "Only when it was believed that everything outside of God was of the same limited and finite value could the shift from quality to quantity, from evaluation to measurement, which characterizes modern science, take place."[86]

In 1450 Nicholas wrote two important works: four dialogues called *Idiota* (*The Illiterate*) and a treatise called *De sapientia* (*On Wisdom*). And in 1453 he produced two other major works. The first, *De visione Dei* (*The Vision of God*), represented a "shift from what has been called the 'theological and objective mysticism' of the first centuries to the 'psychological and subjective mysticism' that has developed since the Middle Ages."[87] The second, *De pace fidei* (*On the Peace of Faith*), was his notable treatise on religious toleration. The last-named work is an imaginative dialogue in which, after the distressing fall of Constantinople to the Turks (which had in fact just occurred), God is prevailed upon to convene in Jerusalem under angelic auspices a motley collection of faiths and nationalities—a Greek, an Indian, a Jew, a

[83] Scholarly disputes still flourish over Nicholas' abandonment of the Council of Basel to support the pope: was it opportunism or conviction? See Jacob, in *Great Thinkers of the Renaissance,* pp. 49–50, and Sigmund, pp. 222–31, where the two positions are summarized.

[84] Jacob, in *Great Thinkers of the Renaissance,* p. 51.

[85] Dolan's selections from *De docta ignorantia* are at pp. 55–98. An English translation by Germain Heron, *On Learned Ignorance,* has been published by Routledge and Kegan Paul (London, 1954). See also Martin Buber, *Between Man and Man* (Boston: Beacon Press, 1955), p. 130, and Frederick C. Copleston, *Medieval Philosophy* (Harper & Row, Torchbooks, 1961), pp. 157–65.

[86] Sigmund, p. 256. Sigmund does, however, qualify the exaggerated importance Ernst Cassirer gives to Nicholas. See Cassirer, *Individual and the Cosmos in Renaissance Philosophy* (New York: Harper & Row, Torchbooks, 1963).

[87] Dolan, p. 132.

Persian, a Spaniard, a Turk, a Syrian, a German, etc.—to "try to reduce all diversity of religion to one." When the Greek points to the difficulties, the Word answers: "You will find that it is not another faith but the very same faith which is everywhere presupposed."[88]

This unity in diversity is possibly related to Nicholas' political thought. He frequently uses the analogy of an organic body with many interdependent parts when referring to both organized society and the community of faith. While freed from Scholastic narrowness in what he took to be essential, he was nevertheless thoroughly medieval in believing that the unification of all faiths on earth was a practicable possibility. He assumed that the human mind naturally seeks truth and the truth to which it would eventually and inevitably be led was the truth of Christ, the Trinity, and the universal Church.

The number three is, as Dolan calls it, a leitmotif throughout the philosophy and theology of Nicholas. The elements of faith are, as we have seen, three. The Church has three dimensions: *triumphans* (triumphant), *dormiens* (suffering), and *militans* (militant). Man is threefold: *spiritus* (spirit), *anima* (mind), and *corpus* (body). Nicholas sees, as Hegel will do later, the universe as an intricate balance of opposites that finds an ultimate resolution in an unscrutable God.[89] But God does appear in the world: the world is a "contraction" of the divine. God's unity "unfolds" in the multiplicity of the world and finite nature is potentially infinite. These tenets all "implied that nature is a worthy and fit object of study for its own sake. It was philosophies like that of Nicholas of Cusa, rather than philosophies like that of William of Ockham, which actually formed the mental background of the age in which the great scientists of the Renaissance lived and worked."[90]

De Concordantia Catholica

Nicholas was one of the few active conciliarists to write specifically on political subjects and his efforts in this direction are largely confined to this one work. The very term *De concordantia catholica,* however, appears ambiguous to our modern understanding of Church and state as wholly separate institutions. Book I of the work dealt with the Church, meaning the whole union of believers and the spirit of that whole. Book II was on the priesthood (*sacerdotium*), or "soul," of the Church. Book III treated the empire (*sacrum imperium*), as the "body" of the Church. Hence the political was subsumed under the religious—and in triadic form once again.[91]

Nicholas' political speculation was, says Sigmund, "an attempt to combine the hierarchical theories of Christian Neo-Platonism concerning the origin and structure of authority with the more equalitarian corporatist theories of consent and representation derived from Roman and canon law."[92] Sigmund notes that the widely used political-theory surveys of the Carlyle brothers, Coker, and Sabine tended to follow Figgis' pioneering work on Nicholas and deal with the second aspect only. Attention to the hierarchy-authority side of Nicholas, argues Sigmund, not only gives a more rounded picture of his thought but makes more explicable his shift from the conciliar to the papal side four years after writing *De concordantia catholica.*[93]

Book I of the *Concordantia* begins with a discussion of the hierarchical and triadic character of the universe: "From the one

[88] *Ibid.,* p. 200. Looking at the Enlightenment's acceptance of the infinite variety of religious belief, Cassirer comments: "The Enlightenment thus revives the principle which Nicholas of Cusa had formulated three centuries earlier" (*The Philosophy of the Enlightenment,* trans. by Fritz Koelln and James Pettergrove (Boston: Beacon Press, 1955), p. 165.

[89] Dolan, p. 31. See also Bett, p. 44.

[90] Copleston, pp. 164–65.

[91] It is significant that, for all the theologizing in the Middle Ages, developed theories on the nature of the Church were rare. Aquinas had no section on the *ecclesia* in his *Summa.* James of Viterbo produced what some call the first systematic theory of the Church in *De regimine Christiano,* 1301–02.

[92] Sigmund, p. 8.

[93] *Ibd.,* pp. 3 and 10.

peaceful King of infinite concordance flows a sweet and spiritual harmony in different grades and series to all subordinate members united with Him."[94] Despite the double series of nine ranks in the hierarchical order that Nicholas elucidates, in finding all bishops to be on a plane of equality he follows—without mentioning—earlier conciliar theory. The Church is a fraternity bound together in common consent. But, then, other institutions are also bound together by means of the strange chemistry that transforms private persons into public persons, that creates a sense of group unity through individual feelings of agency. Nicholas speaks of how an army captain,

> bearing in himself the consent of all, becomes one presidential, public person: so also the bishop is constituted president. . . . Thus even as a republic is a common thing of the people, and a common thing is a thing of the state, and the state is a multitude of men brought to a kind of bond of concord, as Augustine writes . . . so he who presides in the pastoral court corresponds to him to whom a republic is entrusted. Whence all who are under a court are understood to be united in him who presides as if he were one soul and they the body which the soul has to animate. Whence such a people, thus united with their pastor, constitute a church.[95]

We hardly know how to classify such remarks. Are they political psychology or religious sociology? The distinctions would be meaningless to Nicholas, who saw the common religious element in all human associations more vividly than we are able to.

In describing—and prescribing—the organization of the Church, Nicholas establishes a double hierarchy—a spiritual hierarchy with all bishops at the top and an administrative hierarchy with the pope at the top. The famed *plenitudo potestatis* claimed by the popes is not simply brushed aside: no assembly is rightfully called a general council unless it includes the pope or his legate. If a pope subsequently dissociates himself from a council he has summoned, the council may proceed, following a discreet interval, but may not decide questions of faith without the pope. The pope, then, is something like a rector of a university who cannot legislate apart from his faculty senate. Or perhaps he is like a *primus inter pares* in setting policy, the way a British prime minister is supposed to be. Nicholas is not without prudence: he is careful to criticize Marsilio for saying that doctrines of the Church need not be accepted unless they can be based on the Bible. He also carefully distinguishes between different kinds of councils: the *concilium universale patriarchale,* in which the pope sits as a patriarch with delegates subordinate to him, is different from the *perfectissima synodus,* which represents the whole body of the Church and is above the pope.[96] Nicholas is not an advocate of rampant popular sovereignty but of a carefully articulated system of checks and balances.

Book II contains the defense of consent that Figgis and others made so much of. The idea of consent had long played a role in medieval legal theory, even as the ideal of the rule of one man—the wise prince—dominated political theory. Nicholas, trained in canon law as well as steeped in conciliarist arguments, is able to combine the differing elements:

> Therefore since all men are by nature free, then every rulership whether it is by written law or by living law through a prince, which restrains the subjects from evil and directs their freedom to good through fear of punishment can only come from the agreement and consent of the subjects. For if, by nature, men are equally powerful and equally free, a true and properly ordered authority of one common ruler who is equal in power can only be naturally constituted by the election and consent of the others.[97]

[94] *De concordantia catholica,* Book I, Ch. 1, in Sigmund, p. 126. Sigmund uses the Latin text from the edition of Gerhard Kallen, Book I (Leipzig, 1939), Book II (Leipzig, 1941), and Book III (Hamburg, 1959). All three books were published as part of Nicolai de Cusa, *Opera omnia* (Leipzig and Hamburg: Heidelberger Akademie der Wissenschaften, 1932–59). Sigmund helpfully gives the Latin original in footnotes to each English quotation in the text.

[95] *Ibid.,* Bk. I, Ch. 6, in Lewis, *Medieval Political Ideas,* Vol. 2, p. 416. See also Jacob, in *Great Thinkers of the Renaissance,* pp. 41–42.

[96] *Ibid.,* Chs. 7 and 17; also Chs. 2, 13, and 18.

[97] *Ibid.,* Bk. II, Ch. 14, in Sigmund, p. 140.

The defense of both the rule of wisdom and the need for consent was based on an appeal to natural law but natural law shorn of the complicated network of distinctions given to it by Aquinas. Natural law and divine law tended to merge in Nicholas and consent was seen as a common factor in uniting Christ and his Church as well as the prince and his people. Sigmund points out that the Latin *consensus* is the word usually translated "consent," whereas the direct transliteration "consensus" may often be closer to what Nicholas meant.[98] It is significant that Nicholas took the unanimity of a general council to be a sign that the Holy Spirit was present.[99]

Sometimes Nicholas seems almost to contradict himself. In Book III, discussing the Empire, he follows Marsilio in saying, "Legislation ought to be adopted by all or a majority of those who are bound by it. . . . What touches all ought to be approved by all." Yet four chapters later he asserts that laws should be made by the rationally superior to whom lesser intellects will consent "by a natural instinct."[100] But, along with some scathing criticisms of dereliction of duty in the Church, there are in Book II certain institutional proposals for Church government that have political interest: priests should be elected by congregations, bishops should be elected by priests with the consent of congregations, bishops should elect metropolitans, and metropolitans should elect cardinals. Nicholas also proposed that a permanent advisory council from each of the various provinces be formed to assist the pope and the general council on local problems. Yet for all these institutional arrangements—which we are apt too quickly to relate to our own systems of checks and balances—Nicholas' interest was far more aimed at a spiritual harmony that could unite the whole.

While bearing the marks of extensive research, Book III of *De concordantia catholica* was the most hastily written. It proceeded on the assumption that an elective monarchy was the best form of civil government and that its structure should be articulated in hierarchical sequence on a pattern very similar to that of the Church. The Holy Roman Emperor, the King of Romans, is superior to other kings in the same way that the pope is superior to his patriarchs. Dukes correspond to archbishops, counts to bishops, and so on. The role of each part is explained by means of an elaborate physiological metaphor: conciliar degrees are veins, imperial laws are nerves from the brain, the national fatherland is the bones. The emperor's privy council, like teeth, chew on a policy until it is masticated and send it along to the great council, the stomach, which digests it, separating the pure from the impure.[101]

Reading Aristotle largely through the pages of Marsilio, Nicholas tries to make Aristotle support his theory of consent and elective monarchy and distorts the Greek master rather badly in the process. Nicholas proposes a number of reforms in the secular realm: he would suppress gambling, usury, and excess in clothing; he would stop the flow of appeals from secular authorities to the Roman curia; he proposed an annual diet to meet at Frankfort, various judicial reforms, and a panel of three judges (representing the nobility, the clergy, and the bourgeoisie) in each of the twelve districts in the Holy Roman Empire to revise taxes and laws. ". . . no final decision should be made except by the common deliberation of all three, who in difficult cases require the advice of the most expert. If, however, they disagree, the opinion of the majority should be decisive."[102] The emperor and the secular arm would carry out decisions thus reached.

[98] Sigmund, pp. 145–46. Our democratic sensibilities are bruised in reading that the "stupid and ignorant" are fixed by God in a "natural servitude" to the more intelligent. See *De concordantia catholica,* Bk. III, Preface, in Sigmund, p. 132.

[99] *De concordantia catholica,* Bk. II, Ch. 3. See Jacob, p. 44, and Sigmund, p. 175.

[100] *Ibid.,* Bk. III, Preface and Ch. 4, in Sigmund, pp. 151–52.

[101] *Ibid.,* Chs. 25 and 41, in Sigmund, pp. 133–36. See also the excerpts in Lewis, Vol. 1, pp. 314–20.

[102] *Ibid.,* Ch. 33, in Lewis, Vol. 1, p. 317. The reforms mentioned earlier are discussed in Bk. III, Chs. 35, 37 and 40.

In showing that the pope did not have dominant authority over the emperor, Nicholas becomes the first writer to discredit the Donation of Constantine by reference to historical records. Because the emperor had by law to be a Christian, he was not exempt from charges of heresy by the pope. However, the pope could only declare the emperor a heretic; it was his electors who would actually depose him. After a lengthy survey of the geography of the Empire, Nicholas concluded that, although the Roman Empire did not cover half the land area of the world, it did cover a majority of the population at that time. As legal heir to that Empire the Holy Roman Emperor could properly be called *dominus mundi.* Why, we wonder, should the emperor have to be considered ruler of the world by such an unworldly straining of the literal facts? The emperor needs a universal role, in Nicholas' view, to enforce religious laws—with coercion, if necessary. He alone among laymen is allowed to participate in Church councils. The Empire and the *sacerdotium,* we are led to see, are really but two specialized agencies serving the common end of leading men to salvation.[103]

The social, political, and religious ills Nicholas sees are faulty and inefficient taxation, administrative confusion, dereliction of duty, warfare for selfish interests, and general lack of concord. Reform is needed: "And the basic reform is the institution of annual general councils, which should start in this holy Council of Basel, and be established as a rule for the future."[104]

De concordantia catholica, said Jacob, was "a monument to the ideal of an organically harmonious Christendom, multiple in function, one in spirit. The treatise towers above the ambitions and antagonisms which it was powerless to reconcile."[105] The note of wistfulness here implies a "might have been" perhaps best captured in Durant's benedictory aphorism, "Had there been more such Nicholases there might have been no Luther."[106] The feeling that had the conciliar movement succeeded there would have been no need for a Reformation is an understandable one, as is Figgis' view that absolute monarchy might have been checked by a more vigorous conciliarism. We invest the past as well as the future with our hopes. It is Sigmund's great contribution to remind us that neither the fifteenth century nor Nicholas was as simple as that. The complexity of the fifteenth century did not make the Reformation or absolute monarchy inevitable; it only widened the range of problematic human choices we must take into account in trying to find out how we got where we are. Nicholas' complexity, his range of action, and his breadth of scientific and philosophical interests simply draw us to him as the last of the medieval and the first of the Renaissance thinkers.

CONCLUSION

We have discussed in this chapter some of the characteristics of an age too often viewed in simplistic terms. We discovered an uneven movement from theocratic toward constitutional arrangements in the vigorous struggles of popes and kings. We found John of Salisbury's organicism to be a sensitive method of distinguishing different kinds of political responsibilities, propounded by a man who shrewdly perceived the destructive effects of political corruption. In Dante we saw the hope of universal redemption and political order given both poetic and governmental expression. In Marsilio we saw autonomous civil power at last find its champion. And in Nicholas we were confronted by an interdependent theology of incarnation and politics of consensus.

The feudal socialists of nineteenth-century

[103] *Ibid.,* Chs. 15, 17 and 18. See Sigmund, pp. 205–10. Sigmund shows that the model of an ideal relation between pope and emperor was, for Nicholas, the time of Emperor Otto II. These were his good old days.

[104] *Ibid.,* Ch. 32, in Sigmund, p. 216.

[105] "Nicholas of Cusa," in *Great Thinkers of the Renaissance,* p. 49.

[106] Will Durant, *The Reformation* (New York: Simon and Schuster, 1957), p. 257.

England sought a return to some of the communal values the medieval world had possessed and their own individualist-technological society had lost. We cannot return either to their ideal world or to the world of medieval reality. But perhaps we of the twentieth century are in an even better position than nineteenth-century men to appreciate medieval values, or at least the particular unity-in-diversity characterizing that charming, warmly familial, terror-filled, death-haunted age. Certainly we are in a better position to appreciate medieval values than was the Renaissance man, whom we shall next examine. He vaulted all the way back to classical norms.

Each human child and each age, it seems, looks for instruments by which parental ties can be cut and an independent selfhood asserted. And each tends to find these instruments in the ideas, feelings, and memories of grandparents and the grandparental age.

SELECTED READINGS

Chapter 1 INTRODUCTION

BARKER, ERNEST. *Principles of Social and Political Theory.* London: Oxford Univ. Press (Galaxy Books), 1961.

BENN, S. J., AND R. S. PETERS. *Principles of Political Thought.* New York: Free Press, 1959.

BOWLE, JOHN. *Western Political Thought; An Historical Introduction from the Origins to Rousseau.* New York: Barnes & Noble (University Paperbacks), 1961.

EBENSTEIN, WILLIAM, ed. *Great Political Thinkers.* 3rd ed. New York: Holt, Rinehart and Winston, 1960. Selections from leading political theorists with prefatory statements. Good bibliography, pp. 869–974.

ELIADE, MIRCEA. *Myths, Dreams and Mysteries; The Encounter Between Contemporary Faiths and Archaic Realities.* New York: Harper & Row, 1960.

D'ENTREVES, ALEXANDER PASSERIN. *The Notion of the State: An Introduction to Political Theory.* New York: Oxford Univ. Press, 1967.

SABINE, GEORGE H. *A History of Political Theory.* 3rd ed. New York: Holt, Rinehart and Winston, 1961.

STRAUSS, LEO. *What Is Political Philosophy?* New York: Free Press, 1960.

———, AND JOSEPH CROPSEY, eds. *History of Political Philosophy.* Chicago: Rand McNally, 1964.

VEREKER, CHARLES. *The Development of Political Theory.* New York: Harper & Row (Colophon Books), 1965.

VOEGELIN, ERIC. *Order and History.* Vol. 1, *Israel and Revelation.* Baton Rouge: Louisiana State Univ. Press, 1956.

WOLIN, SHELDON S. *Politics and Vision; Continuity and Innovation in Western Political Thought.* Boston: Little, Brown, 1960.

Chapter 2 PLATO

Works by Plato

Collected Dialogues. Ed. by Edith Hamilton and Huntington Cairns. New York: Pantheon, 1961. The only one-volume edition in English.

Dialogues. Tr. by Benjamin Jowett. 4th ed. London: Oxford Univ. Press, 1953. 4 vols.

Euthyphro, Apology and Crito, and the Death Scene from Phaedo. Tr. by F. J. Church. 2nd rev. ed. New York: Liberal Arts Press, 1956.

Gorgias. Tr. by W. Hamilton. Baltimore: Penguin Books, 1960.

The Laws. Tr. by A. E. Taylor. London: Dent (Everyman's), 1960.

Parmenides, Theaitetos, Sophist, Statesman. Tr. by John Warrington. London: Dent (Everyman's), 1961.

The Republic. Tr. by F. M. Cornford. New York: Oxford Univ. Press, 1958.

The Republic. In Greek with Eng. tr. by Paul Shorey. Cambridge, Mass.: Harvard Univ. Press (Loeb Classical Library), 1953, 1956. 2 vols.

Statesman. Tr. by J. B. Skemp. New York: Liberal Arts Press, 1957.

Secondary Works

BARKER, ERNEST. *Greek Political Theory; Plato and His Predecessors.* New York: Barnes & Noble (University Paperbacks), 1960.

BOSANQUET, BERNARD. *A Companion to Plato's Republic.* New York: Macmillan, 1895.

CROSSMAN, R. H. S. *Plato Today.* Rev. ed. New York: Oxford Univ. Press, 1959.

FOSTER, MICHAEL B. *The Political Philosophies of Plato and Hegel.* Oxford: Clarendon Press, 1935.

GOULDNER, ALVIN W. *Enter Plato; Classical Greece and the Origins of Social Theory.* New York: Basic Books, 1965.

GRENE, DAVID. *Greek Political Theory; The Image of Man in Thucydides and Plato.* Chicago: Univ. of Chicago Press (Phoenix Books), 1965.

GRUBE, G. M. A. *Plato's Thought.* Boston: Beacon Press, 1958.

NETTLESHIP, RICHARD LEWIS. *Lectures on the Republic of Plato.* 2nd ed. London: Macmillan, 1901.

POPPER, KARL R. *The Open Society and Its Enemies.* Vol. 1, *The Spell of Plato.* 3rd ed. rev. London: Routledge & Kegan Paul, 1957.

TAYLOR, A. E. *Plato, The Man and His Work.* New York: World (Meridian Books), 1956.

———. *Socrates.* Garden City, N.Y.: Doubleday (Anchor Books), 1960.

THORSON, THOMAS L., ed. *Plato: Totalitarian or Democrat.* Englewood Cliffs, N.J.: Prentice-Hall (Spectrum Books), 1963.

VOEGELIN, ERIC. *Order and History.* Vol. 3, *Plato and Aristotle.* Baton Rouge: Louisiana State Univ. Press, 1957.

WILD, JOHN D. *Plato's Theory of Man; An Introduction to the Realistic Philosophy of Culture.* Cambridge, Mass.: Harvard Univ. Press, 1946.

Chapter 3 ARISTOTLE

Works by Aristotle

The Ethics of Aristotle. Tr. by J. A. K. Thomson. Baltimore: Penguin Books, 1958.

The Nicomachean Ethics. Tr. by D. P. Chase. New York: Dutton (Everyman's Library), 1915.

The Politics of Aristotle. Ed. and tr. by William L. Newman. Oxford: Clarendon Press, 1887–1902. 4 vols. Vol. 1 is Newman's introduction.

Politics and the Athenian Constitution. Tr. by John Warrington. New York: Dutton (Everyman's Library), 1961.

The Politics of Aristotle. Tr. by Ernest Barker. New York: Oxford Univ. Press, 1958.

The Works of Aristotle Translated into English. Ed. by W. D. Ross. Oxford: Clarendon Press, 1908–31. 11 vols.

Secondary Works

BARKER, ERNEST. *The Political Thought of Plato and Aristotle.* New York: Dover, 1959.

JAEGER, WERNER. *Aristotle.* 2nd ed. Tr. by Richard Robinson. New York: Oxford Univ. Press, 1962.

KAGEN, DONALD. *The Great Dialogue: A History of Greek Political Thought from Homer to Polybius.* New York: Free Press, 1964.

RANDALL, JOHN HERMAN, JR. *Aristotle.* New York: Columbia Univ. Press, 1962.

ROSS, W. D. *Aristotle.* 2nd ed. New York: World (Meridian Books), 1960.

TAYLOR, A. E. *Aristotle.* Rev. ed. New York: Dover, 1956.

WHEELWRIGHT, PHILIP. *Aristotle.* New York: Odyssey Press, 1951.

Chapter 4 THE STOICS AND ROME

Primary Works

AURELIUS ANTONINUS, MARCUS. *Communings with Himself.* Tr. by C. R. Haines. New York: Putnam's (Loeb Classical Library), 1916.

———. *Meditations* (with Epictetus, *Enchiridion*). Tr. by George Long. Chicago: Regnery (Gateway Editions), 1956.

CICERO, MARCUS TULLIUS. *De officiis.* With Eng. tr. by Walter Miller. Cambridge, Mass.: Harvard Univ. Press (Loeb Classical Library), 1951.

———. *De republica; De legibus.* With Eng. tr. by C. W. Keyes. New York: Putnam's (Loeb Classical Library), 1928.

———. *On the Commonwealth.* Tr. by George H. Sabine and Stanley B. Smith. New York: Liberal Arts Press, 1959.

EPICTETUS. *The Discourses and Fragments.* Tr. by W. A. Oldfather. New York: Putnam's (Loeb Classical Library), 1926, 1928. 2 vols. Vol. 2 reprinted by Harvard Univ. Press, 1952.

GAIUS. *The Institutes of Gaius.* Tr. by Francis de-Zulcuta. Oxford: Clarendon Press, 1946, 1953. 2 vols. Vol. 2 is commentary.

POLYBIUS. *The Histories of Polybius.* Tr. by Evelyn Shuckburgh. Bloomington: Univ. of Indiana Press, 1962. 2 vols.

Secondary Works

ARNOLD, EDWARD V. *Roman Stoicism.* London: Cambridge Univ. Press, 1911.

Carlyle, R. W., and A. J. Carlyle. *A History of Medieval Political Theory in the West.* 2nd ed. 6 vols., Vol. 1. New York: Barnes & Noble, 1927. Part 1 is on the Stoics.

Cochrane, Charles N. *Christianity and Classical Culture.* Rev. ed. New York: Oxford Univ. Press (Galaxy Books), 1957.

Fritz, Kurt von. *The Theory of the Mixed Constitution in Antiquity: A Critical Analysis of Polybius' Political Ideas.* New York: Columbia Univ. Press, 1954.

Hicks, Robert D. *Stoic and Epicurean.* New York: Russell & Russell, 1962.

Murray, Gilbert. *Stoic, Christian and Humanist.* London: Allen & Unwin, 1940.

Richards, George C. *Cicero, A Study.* Boston: Houghton Mifflin, 1935.

Walbank, F. W. *A Historical Commentary on Polybius.* Oxford: Clarendon Press, 1957.

Zeller, Eduard. *The Stoics, Epicureans and Sceptics.* Tr. by Oswald J. Reichel. New and rev. ed. New York: Russell & Russell, 1962.

Chapter 5 AUGUSTINE

Works by Augustine

An Augustine Synthesis. Ed. by Erich Przywara. New York: Sheed & Ward, 1936; Harper & Row (Torchbooks), 1958.

Basic Writings of Saint Augustine. Ed. by Whitney J. Oates. New York: Random House, 1948. 2 vols.

City of God. Tr. by Marcus Dods. New York: Random House (Modern Library), 1950.

The City of God. Tr. by John Healey (1610). New York: Dutton (Everyman's Library), 1945.

Confessions. Tr. by Rex Warner. New York: New American Library (Mentor Books), 1963.

Confessions and Enchiridion. Ed. by Albert C. Outler. (Library of Christian Classics, Vol. 7). Philadelphia: Westminster Press, 1955.

Earlier Writings. Ed. and tr. by J. H. S. Burleigh. (Library of Christian Classics, Vol. 6). Philadelphia: Westminster Press, 1953.

Later Works. Ed. and tr. by John Burnaby. (Library of Christian Classics, Vol. 8). Philadelphia: Westminster Press, 1955.

Political Writings of St. Augustine. Ed. by Henry Paolucci. Chicago: Regnery (Gateway Editions), 1962.

Works. Ed. by Marcus Dods. Edinburgh: T. & T. Clark, 1872–1934. 8 vols.

Secondary Works

Andreson, Carl, ed. *Bibliographia Augustiniana.* Darmstadt, Germany: Wissenschaftliche Buchgesellschaft, 1962.

Battenhouse, Roy, ed. *A Companion to St. Augustine.* New York: Oxford Univ. Press, 1955.

Brooks, Edgar H. *The City of God and the Politics of Crisis.* London: Oxford Univ. Press, 1960.

Combes, Gustave. *La Doctrine politique de Saint Augustin.* Paris: Librairie Plon, 1927.

Cullmann, Oscar. *The State in the New Testament.* New York: Scribner's, 1956.

D'Arcy, M. C., ed. *Saint Augustine.* New York: World (Meridian Books), 1957. A symposium.

Deane, Herbert A. *The Political and Social Ideas of Saint Augustine.* New York: Columbia Univ. Press, 1963.

Figgis, John Neville. *The Political Aspects of S. Augustine's City of God.* London: Longmans, Green, 1921.

Gilson, Étienne. *The Christian Philosophy of St. Augustine.* Tr. by L. E. M. Lynch. New York: Random House, 1960.

Pope, Hugh. *St. Augustine of Hippo.* London: Longmans, Green, 1954.

Portalié, Eugene. *A Guide to the Thought of Saint Augustine.* Tr. by Ralph J. Bastian. Chicago: Regnery, 1960.

Versfeld, Marthinus. *A Guide to the City of God.* New York: Sheed & Ward, 1958.

Chapter 6 AQUINAS

Works by Aquinas

On Kingship to the King of Cyprus. Tr. by Gerald B. Phelan. New ed., rev. by I. T. Eschmann. Toronto: Pontifical Institute of Medieval Studies, 1949. (1938 ed. titled *On the Governance of Rulers.*)

Philosophical Texts. Ed. and tr. by Thomas Gilby. New York: Oxford Univ. Press (Galaxy Books), 1960.

The Political Ideas of St. Thomas Aquinas. Ed. by Dino Bigongiari. New York: Hafner, 1953.

Selected Political Writings. Tr. by J. G. Dawson. Ed. by A. P. d'Entreves. Oxford: Blackwell & Mott, 1948.

Summa contra Gentiles. Tr. by English Dominican Fathers. London: Burns & Oates, 1928–29. 5 vols.

Summa Theologica. Tr. by English Dominican Fathers. Amer. ed. New York: Benziger, 1947–49. 3 vols.

Treatise on Law. Tr. by English Dominican Fathers. Chicago: Regnery (Gateway Editions), n.d.

Secondary Works

BRENNAN, ROBERT E., ed. *Essays in Thomism.* New York: Sheed & Ward, 1942.

CHESTERTON, G. K. *St. Thomas Aquinas.* Garden City, N.Y.: Doubleday (Image Books), 1956.

COPLESTON, FREDERICK C. *Aquinas.* Baltimore: Penguin Books (Pelican Books), 1955.

D'ARCY, MARTIN. *St. Thomas Aquinas.* Glen Rock, N.J.: Newman Press, 1955.

FARRELL, WALTER. *A Companion to the Summa.* New York: Sheed & Ward, 1939–42. 4 vols.

GILBY, THOMAS. *The Political Thought of Thomas Aquinas.* Chicago: Univ. of Chicago Press, 1958.

———. *Principality and Polity; Aquinas and the Rise of State Theory in the West.* London: Longmans, Green, 1958.

GILSON, ÉTIENNE. *The Christian Philosophy of Saint Thomas Aquinas.* Tr. by L. K. Shook. New York: Random House, 1956.

JAFFA, HARRY V. *Thomism and Aristotelianism; A Study of the Commentary by Thomas Aquinas on the Nicomachean Ethics.* Chicago: Univ. of Chicago Press, 1952.

MARITAIN, JACQUES. *St. Thomas Aquinas.* New York: World (Meridian Books), 1958.

MIHALICH, JOSEPH C. *Existentialism and Thomism.* New York: Philosophical Library, 1960.

SERTILLANGES, ANTONIN G. *Saint Thomas Aquinas and His Work.* Tr. by Godfrey Anstruther. London: Blackfriars, 1957.

Chapter 7 SOME MEDIEVAL LEGACIES

General

CARLYLE, R. W., AND A. J. CARLYLE. *A History of Medieval Political Theory in the West.* New York: Barnes & Noble, 1953. 6 vols.

COPLESTON, FREDERICK C. *Medieval Philosophy.* New York: Harper & Row (Torchbooks), 1961.

DUNNING, WILLIAM A. *A History of Political Theories: Ancient and Medieval.* New York: Macmillan, 1936.

D'ENTREVES, ALEXANDER PASSERIN. *The Medieval Contribution to Political Thought.* London: Oxford Univ. Press, 1939.

FIGGIS, JOHN NEVILLE. *The Divine Right of Kings.* 2nd ed. New York: Harper & Row (Torchbooks), 1965.

GIERKE, OTTO. *Political Theories of the Middle Age.* Tr. by F. W. Maitland. Boston: Beacon Press, 1958.

GILSON, ÉTIENNE. *A History of Christian Philosophy in the Middle Ages.* New York: Random House, 1955.

HEARNSHAW, F. J. C., ed. *The Social and Political Ideas of Some Great Medieval Thinkers.* London: Harrap, 1923.

JENKS, EDWARD. *Law and Politics in the Middle Ages.* New York: Holt, Rinehart and Winston, 1932.

KANTOROWICZ, ERNST H. *The King's Two Bodies; A Study in Medieval Political Theology.* Princeton, N.J.: Princeton Univ. Press, 1957.

KERN, FRITZ. *Kingship and Law in the Middle Ages.* Tr. by S. B. Chrimes. Oxford: Blackwell & Mott, 1939.

LERNER, RALPH, AND MUHSIN MAHDI, eds. *Medieval Political Philosophy: A Sourcebook.* New York: Free Press, 1963.

LEWIS, EWART K., ed. *Medieval Political Ideas.* London: Routledge & Kegan Paul, 1954. 2 vols.

MCILWAIN, CHARLES H. *The Growth of Political Thought in the West.* New York: Macmillan, 1932, chs. 5 and 6.

MORRALL, JOHN B. *Political Thought in Medieval Times.* Rev. ed. New York: Harper & Row (Torchbooks), 1962.

RIESENBERG, PETER N. *The Inalienability of Sovereignty in Medieval Political Thought.* New York: Columbia Univ. Press, 1956.

ROSENTHAL, ERWIN I. J. *Political Thought in Medieval Islam.* London: Cambridge Univ. Press, 1958.

TIERNEY, BRIAN. *The Crisis of Church and State, 1050–1300.* Englewood Cliffs, N.J.: Prentice-Hall (Spectrum Books), 1964. With selected documents.

ULLMAN, WALTER. *History of Political Thought: The Middle Ages.* Baltimore: Penguin Books (Pelican Books), 1965.

———. *Medieval Papalism; The Political Theories of the Medieval Canonists.* London: Methuen, 1949.

WILKS, MICHAEL J. *The Problem of Sovereignty in the Later Middle Ages.* London: Cambridge Univ. Press, 1963.

John of Salisbury

JOHN OF SALISBURY. *Early Letters.* Vol. 1, *Letters.* Ed. by W. J. Millor and H. E. Butler. Rev. by C. N. L. Brooke. London: Nelson, 1955.

———. *Policraticus.* Ed. by C. C. J. Webb. Oxford: Clarendon Press, 1909. 2 vols.

———. *The Statesman's Book of John of Salisbury.* Tr. by John Dickinson. New York: Knopf, 1927.

LIEBESCHUTZ, HANS. *Medieval Humanism in the Life and Writings of John of Salisbury.* London: Univ. of London Press (Warburg Institute), 1950.

WEBB, CLEMENT C. J. *John of Salisbury.* London: Methuen, 1932.

Dante

DANTE ALIGHIERI. *The Divine Comedy.* Italian with Eng. tr. by Geoffrey L. Bickersteth. Cambridge, Mass.: Harvard Univ. Press, 1965.

———. *De Monarchia.* Tr. by Henry Aurelia. Boston: Houghton Mifflin, 1904.

———. *On World Government.* Tr. by Herbert W. Schneider. 2nd rev. ed. New York: Liberal Arts Press, 1957.

DAVIS, CHARLES T. *Dante and the Idea of Rome.* London: Oxford Univ. Press, 1957.

D'ENTREVES, ALEXANDER PASSERIN. *Dante as a Political Thinker.* Oxford: Clarendon Press, 1952.

GILSON, ÉTIENNE. *Dante and Philosophy.* Tr. by David Moore. New York: Harper & Row (Torchbooks), 1963.

LENKEITH, NANCY. *Dante and the Legend of Rome.* London: Univ. of London Press (Warburg Institute), 1952.

ROLBIECKI, JOHN J. *The Political Philosophy of Dante Alighieri.* Washington, D.C.: Catholic Univ. of America Press, 1921.

Marsilio of Padua

ALLEN, J. W. "Marsilio of Padua and Medieval Secularism." In F. J. C. Hearnshaw, ed., *The Social and Political Ideas of Some Great Medieval Thinkers.* London: Harrap, 1923, ch. 7.

EMERTON, EPHRAIM. *The Defensor Pacis of Marsilio of Padua: A Critical Study.* Gloucester, Mass.: Peter Smith, 1951.

D'ENTREVES, ALEXANDER PASSERIN. *The Medieval Contribution to Political Thought.* London: Oxford Univ. Press, ch. 2.

MARSILIUS OF PADUA. *The Defender of Peace.* Ed. and tr. by Alan Gewirth. New York: Columbia Univ. Press, 1951. 2 vols. Vol 1 is commentary.

PREVITÉ-ORTON, C. W. *Marsilius of Padua.* London: Milford, 1935.

Nicholas of Cusa

BETT, HENRY. *Nicholas of Cusa.* London: Methuen, 1932.

MORRALL, JOHN B. *Gerson and the Great Schism.* Manchester, Eng.: Manchester Univ. Press, 1960.

NICOLAI DE CUSA. *De Concordantia Catholica.* Ed. by Gerhard Kallen. Hamburg: Meiner, 1964–65. 2 vols.

———. *Unity and Reform: Selected Writings of Nicholas de Cusa.* Ed. by John P. Dolan. Notre Dame, Ind.: Univ. of Notre Dame Press, 1962.

SIGMUND, PAUL. *Nicholas of Cusa and Medieval Political Thought.* Cambridge, Mass.: Harvard Univ. Press, 1963.

TIERNEY, BRIAN. *Foundations of the Conciliar Theory.* New York: Cambridge Univ. Press, 1955.

WATANABE, MORIMICHI. *The Political Ideas of Nicholas of Cusa.* Geneva: Libraire Droz, 1963.

Chapter 8 MACHIAVELLI

Works by Machiavelli

Chief Works and Others. Ed. and tr. by Allan H. Gilbert. Durham, N.C.: Duke Univ. Press, 1965. 3 vols.

The Discourses. Tr. by Leslie J. Walker. New Haven, Conn.: Yale Univ. Press, 1950. 2 vols.

The Historical, Political and Diplomatic Writings of Niccolo Machiavelli. Tr. by Christian E. Detmold. Boston: Houghton Mifflin, 1882–91. 4 vols.

History of Florence and of the Affairs of Italy. Intro. by Felix Gilbert. New York: Harper & Row (Torchbooks), 1960.

The Prince and The Discourses. Tr. by Luigi Ricci and Christian Detmold. New York: Random House (Modern Library), 1940.

Secondary Works

BUTTERFIELD, HERBERT. *The Statecraft of Machiavelli.* New York: Macmillan (Collier Books), 1962.

CHABOD, FREDERICO. *Machiavelli and the Renaissance.* Tr. by David Moore. Cambridge, Mass.: Harvard Univ. Press, 1958.

GILBERT, ALLAN H. *Machiavelli's Prince and Its Forerunners.* Durham, N.C.: Duke Univ. Press, 1938.

GILBERT, FELIX. *Machiavelli and Guicciardini; Politics and History in Sixteenth-Century Florence.* Princeton, N.J.: Princeton Univ. Press, 1965.

GUICCIARDINI, FRANCESCO. *Maxims and Reflections of a Renaissance Statesman.* Tr. by Mario Domandi. New York: Harper & Row (Torchbooks), 1965.

HALE, JOHN RIGBY. *Machiavelli and Renaissance Italy.* New York: Macmillan, 1960.

MEINECKE, FRIEDRICH. *Machiavellism; The Doctrine of Raison D'Etat and Its Place in Modern History.* Tr. by Douglas Scott. London: Routledge & Kegan Paul, 1957.

RIDOLFI, ROBERTO. *The Life of Niccolo Machiavelli.* Tr. by Cecil Grayson. Chicago: Univ. of Chicago Press, 1963.

STRAUSS, LEO. *Thoughts on Machiavelli.* New York: Free Press, 1958.

WHITFIELD, JOHN H. *Machiavelli.* Oxford: Blackwell & Mott, 1947.

Chapter 9 THE REFORMATION

General

ALLEN, J. W. *Political Thought in the Sixteenth Century.* Rev. ed. New York: Barnes & Noble, 1957.

AMES, RUSSELL A. *Citizen Thomas More and His Utopia.* Princeton, N.J.: Princeton Univ. Press, 1949.

BAINTON, ROLAND H. *The Reformation of the Sixteenth Century.* Boston: Beacon Press, 1952.

CHURCH, WILLIAM FARR. *Constitutional Thought in Sixteenth-Century France.* Cambridge, Mass.: Harvard Univ. Press, 1941.

DALY, LOWRIE JOHN. *The Political Theory of John Wyclif.* (Jesuit Study, No. 17.) Chicago: Loyola Univ. Press, 1962.

DODGE, GUY H. *The Political Theory of the Huguenots of the Dispersion.* New York: Columbia Univ. Press, 1947.

DUNNING, WILLIAM A. *A History of Political Theory from Luther to Montesquieu.* New York: Macmillan, 1905.

ERASMUS, DESIDERIUS. *The Education of a Christian Prince.* Tr. by Lester K. Born. New York: Columbia Univ. Press, 1936.

HAMILTON, BERNICE. *Political Thought in Sixteenth-Century Spain.* Oxford: Clarendon Press, 1963.

HARBISON, E. HARRIS. *The Age of Reformation.* Ithaca, N.Y.: Cornell Univ. Press, 1955.

KAUTSKY, KARL. *Thomas More and His Utopia.* New York: Russell & Russell, 1959.

MORE, THOMAS. *Utopia.* Tr. by H. S. V. Ogden. New York: Appleton-Century-Crofts, 1949.

MOSSE, GEORGE L. *The Holy Pretence; A Study in Christianity and Reason of State from William Perkins to John Winthrop.* Oxford: Blackwell & Mott, 1957.

MURRAY, ROBERT H. *The Political Consequences of the Reformation.* London: Benn, 1926.

REYNOLDS, E. E. *St. Thomas More.* New York: Kenedy, 1953.

SMITH, PRESERVED. *Erasmus.* New York: Harper & Row, 1923.

TAWNEY, R. H. *Religion and the Rise of Capitalism.* New York: New American Library (Mentor Books), 1958.

TROELTSCH, ERNST. *The Social Teaching of the Christian Churches.* Tr. by Olive Wyon. New York: Macmillan, 1950. 2 vols.

Vindiciae contra tyrannos. Tr. by H. J. Laski. London: Bell, 1924.

WEBER, MAX. *The Protestant Ethic and the Spirit of Capitalism.* Tr. by Talcott Parsons. New York: Scribner's, 1950.

Luther

BAINTON, ROLAND H. *Here I Stand: A Life of Martin Luther.* New York: New American Library (Mentor Books), 1955.

CRANZ, FERDINAND EDMUND. *An Essay on the Development of Luther's Thought on Justice, Law and Society.* Cambridge, Mass.: Harvard Univ. Press, 1959.

ERIKSON, ERIK H. *Young Man Luther.* New York: Norton, 1958.

FORELL, GEORGE. *Faith Active in Love: An Interpretation of Principles Underlying Luther's Social Ethics.* New York: American Peoples Press, 1954.

LUTHER, MARTIN. *Reformation Writings.* Tr. by Bertram Lee Wolf. London: Lutterworth Press, 1952, 1956. 2 vols.

———. *Selections from His Writings.* Ed. by John Dillenberger. Garden City, N.Y.: Doubleday (Anchor Books), 1961.

———. *Works.* Ed. by Jaroslav Pelikan and Helmut T. Lehman. St. Louis, Mo.: Concordia; Philadelphia: Muhlenberg Press. 1955 et sec. 55 vols.

MUELLER, WILLIAM A. *Church and State in Luther and Calvin.* Nashville, Tenn.: Abingdon, 1954.

RITTER, GERHARD. *Luther, His Life and Work.* Tr. by John Riches. New York: Harper & Row, 1963.

SCHWEIBERT, ERNEST G. *Luther and His Times.* St. Louis, Mo.: Concordia, 1950.

WARING, LUTHER H. *The Political Theories of Martin Luther.* New York: Putnam's, 1910.

Calvin

CHENEVIERE, MARC-EDOUARD. *La Pensée politique de Calvin.* Geneva: Éditions Labor, 1937.

CALVIN, JOHN. *Institutes of the Christian Religion.* Ed. by J. T. McNeill. Tr. by F. L. Battles. (Library of Christian Classics, Vols. 20, 21.) Philadelphia: Westminster Press, 1960. 2 vols.

———. *Tracts Relating to the Reformation.* Tr. by H. Beveridge. Grand Rapids, Mich.: Eerdmans, 1957. 3 vols.

HARKNESS, GEORGIA. *John Calvin: The Man and His Ethics.* Nashville, Tenn.: Abingdon (Apex Books), 1958.

MACKINNON, JAMES. *Calvin and the Reformation.* London: Longmans, Green, 1936.

MCNEILL, JOHN T. *The History and Character of Calvinism.* New York: Oxford Univ. Press, 1954.

MOSSE, GEORGE L. *Calvinism, Authoritarian or Democratic?* New York: Holt, Rinehart and Winston, 1957.

Bodin

BODIN, JEAN. *Method for the Easy Comprehension of History* (1566). Tr. by Beatrice Reynolds. New York: Columbia Univ. Press, 1945.

———. *Oeuvres philosophiques.* Tr. by Pierre Mesnard. Paris: Presses Universitaires de France, 1951, 1952. 2 vols.

———. *The Six Bookes of a Commonweale* (Eng. tr. of 1606). Ed. by Kenneth D. McRae. Cambridge, Mass.: Harvard Univ. Press, 1962.

———. *Six Bookes of the Commonwealth.* Abridged ed. Tr. by M. J. Tooley. (Blackwell's Political Texts.) New York: Macmillan, 1955.

FRANKLIN, JULIAN H. *Jean Bodin and the Sixteenth-Century Revolution in the Methodology of Law and History.* New York: Columbia Univ. Press, 1963.

REYNOLDS, BEATRICE. *Proponents of Limited Monarchy in Sixteenth-Century France: Francis Hotman and Jean Bodin.* New York: Columbia Univ. Press, 1931.

Hooker

DAVIES, E. T. *The Political Ideas of Richard Hooker.* London: Society for Promoting Christian Knowledge, 1946.

HOOKER, RICHARD. *Works.* Ed. by John Keble. 7th ed. Oxford: Clarendon Press, 1888. 3 vols.

———. *Hooker's Ecclesiastical Polity, Book VIII.* Intro. by R. Houk. New York: Columbia Univ. Press, 1931.

———. *Of the Laws of Ecclesiastical Polity.* New York: Dutton (Everyman's Library), 1907. 2 vols.

MORRIS, CHRISTOPHER. *Political Thought in England, Tyndale to Hooker.* London: Oxford Univ. Press, 1953, ch. 9.

MUNZ, PETER. *The Place of Hooker in the History of Thought.* London: Routledge & Kegan Paul, 1952.

SHIRLEY, F. J. *Richard Hooker and Contemporary Political Ideas.* London: Society for Promoting Christian Knowledge, 1949.

Chapter 10 THE SEVENTEENTH CENTURY

General

BOULENGER, JACQUES. *The Seventeenth Century.* (The National History of France, No. 3.) New York: Putnam's, 1920.

CARRÉ, MAYRICK. *Phases of Thought in England.* Oxford: Clarendon Press, 1949.

CLARK, G. N. *The Seventeenth Century.* New York: Oxford Univ. Press (Galaxy Books), 1961. An intellectual survey of Europe.

GOOCH, G. P. *Political Thought in England from Bacon to Halifax.* London: Butterworth, 1914.

STANKIEWICZ, W. J. *Politics and Religion in Seventeenth-Century France.* Berkeley: Univ. of California Press, 1960.

WILLEY, BASIL. *The Seventeenth Century Background; Studies in the Thought of the Age in Relation to Poetry and Religion.* New York: Columbia Univ. Press, 1934; Garden City, N.Y.: Doubleday (Anchor Books), 1953.

The Political Obligation of Subjects

ALLEN, J. W. *English Political Thought, 1603–1644.* London: Methuen, 1938.

BACON, FRANCIS. *Essays or Counsels Civil and Moral.* London: Dent (Everyman), 1906. A reprint of the fifth and last edition written by Bacon and published in 1625. The first edition was published in 1597.

FIGGIS, JOHN NEVILLE. *The Theory of the Divine Right of Kings.* 2nd ed. New York: Harper & Row (Torchbooks), 1960.

FILMER, ROBERT. *Patriarcha and Other Political Works.* Ed. by Peter Laslett. Oxford: Blackwell & Mott, 1949.

GROTIUS, HUGO. *De juri belli et pacis.* London: Cambridge Univ. Press, 1853. 3 vols. Latin text of 1625 with tr. by William Whewell. The *Prolegomena* is published by Liberal Arts Press, 1957.

JAMES I. *The Political Works of James I.* Ed. by Charles H. McIlwain. Cambridge, Mass.: Harvard Univ. Press, 1918.

KNIGHT, W. S. M. *The Life and Work of Hugo Grotius.* London: Sweet & Maxwell, 1925.

KRIEGER, LEONARD. *The Politics of Discretion: Pufendorf and the Acceptance of Natural Law.* Chicago: Univ. of Chicago Press, 1965.

PUFENDORF, SAMUEL. *De officio hominis et civis* (1673). (Carnegie Classics in International Law.) New York: Oxford Univ. Press, 1921. 2 vols. Vol. 2 tr. by F. G. Moore.

———. *De jure naturae et gentium* (1688). (Carnegie Classics in International Law.) Oxford: Clarendon Press, 1934. 2 vols. Vol. 2 tr. by C. H. Oldfather and W. A. Oldfather.

SPINOZA, BENEDICT DE. *Writings on Political Philosophy.* Ed. by A. G. A. Balz. New York: Appleton-Century-Crofts, 1937. Contains the *Tractatus politicus* of 1677 in full in the R. H. M. Elwes tr. of 1883.

———. *The Political Works.* Ed. and tr. by A. G. Wernham. Oxford: Clarendon Press, 1958. Contains the *Tractatus politicus* in full and the *Tractatus theologico politicus* (1670) in part.

SYKES, NORMAN. "Bossuet." In F. J. C. Hearnshaw, ed. *The Social and Political Ideas of Some Great French Thinkers of the Age of Reason.* London: Harrap, 1930, ch. 2.

VREELAND, HAMILTON. *Hugo Grotius.* New York: Oxford Univ. Press, 1917.

Restraints upon Rulers: Constitutionalism

ALTHUSIUS, JOHANNES. *Politica methodica digesta.* Ed. by Carl J. Friedrich. Cambridge, Mass.: Harvard Univ. Press, 1932.

———. *The Politics of Johannes Althusius.* Abridged ed. Tr. by Frederick S. Carney. Boston: Beacon Press, 1964.

BARKER, ARTHUR. *Milton and the Puritan Dilemma, 1641–1660.* Toronto: Univ. of Toronto Press, 1942.

BOWEN, CATHERINE DRINKER. *The Lion and the Throne; The Life and Time of Sir Edward Coke.* Boston: Little, Brown, 1956.

COKE, EDWARD. *The First Part of the Institutes of the Laws of England.* Ed. by Francis Hargrove and Charles Butler. London: Clarke, 1832.

CROMWELL, OLIVER. *The Writings and Speeches of Oliver Cromwell.* Ed. by Wilbur C. Abbott. Cambridge, Mass.: Harvard Univ. Press, 1937–47. 4 vols.

GARDINER, SAMUEL RAWSON, ed. *The Constitutional Documents of the Puritan Revolution.* Oxford: Clarendon Press, 1889.

GERBRANDY, P. S. *National and International Stability; Althusius, Grotius, Van Vollenhoven.* London: Oxford Univ. Press, 1944.

GOOCH, G. P. *English Democratic Ideas in the Seventeenth Century.* 2nd ed. New York: Harper & Row (Torchbooks), 1960.

MILLER, PERRY. *The New England Mind; The Seventeenth Century.* New York: Macmillan, 1939.

MILTON, JOHN. *Areopagitica.* New York: Dutton (Everyman's Library), 1927.

PERRY, RALPH BARTON. *Puritanism and Democracy.* New York: Vanguard, 1944.

WILLIAMS, ROGER. *Works.* Providence, R.I.: Narragansett Club, 1866. 6 vols. The standard edition.

———. *Roger Williams; His Contribution to the American Tradition.* Indianapolis, Ind.: Bobbs-Merrill, 1953.

WOODHOUSE, A. S. P., ed. *Puritanism and Liberty; Being the Army Debates (1647–1649) from the Clarke Manuscripts.* 2nd ed. Chicago: Univ. of Chicago Press, 1951.

ZAGORIN, PEREZ. *A History of Political Thought in the English Revolution.* London: Routledge & Kegan Paul, 1954.

The Ground of Political Authority: Populism

BLITZER, CHARLES. *An Immortal Commonwealth: The Political Thought of James Harrington.* New Haven: Yale Univ. Press, 1960.

FRANK, JOSEPH. *The Levellers; A History of the Writings of Three Seventeenth-Century Social Democrats: John Lilburne, Richard Overton, William Walwyn.* Cambridge, Mass.: Harvard Univ. Press, 1955.

GIBB, M. A. *John Lilburne the Leveller; A Christian Democrat.* London: Drummond, 1947.

HALLER, WILLIAM. *Liberty and Reformation in the Puritan Revolution.* New York: Columbia Univ. Press, 1955.

———, ed. *Tracts on Liberty in the Puritan Revolution, 1638–1647.* New York: Columbia Univ. Press, 1934. 3 vols.

———, AND GODFREY DAVIES, eds. *The Leveller Tracts, 1647–1653.* New York: Columbia Univ. Press, 1944.

HARRINGTON, JAMES. *Political Writings; Representative Selections.* Ed. by Charles Blitzer. New York: Liberal Arts, 1955.

HARRISON, WILFRED. *Conflict and Compromise; A History of British Political Thought, 1593–1900.* New York: Free Press, 1965.

JONES, RUFUS M. *Mysticism and Democracy in the English Commonwealth.* Cambridge, Mass.: Harvard Univ. Press, 1932.

ROBERTSON, D. B. *The Religious Foundations of Leveller Democracy.* New York: Columbia Univ. Press, 1951.

WINSTANLEY, GERRARD. *Works.* Ed. by George H. Sabine. Ithaca, N.Y.: Cornell Univ. Press, 1941.

WOLFE, DON M. *The Leveller Manifestoes of the Puritan Revolution.* Camden, N.J.: Nelson, 1944.

Natural Law, Reason of State, and Comparative Politics

D'ENTREVES, ALEXANDER PASSERIN. *Natural Law.* New York: Hillary House, 1952.

GIERKE, OTTO. *Natural Law and the Theory of Society, 1500–1800.* London: Cambridge Univ. Press, 1934. 2 vols.; 1 vol. ed., 1950; Boston: Beacon Press, 1957.

HALIFAX, LORD (George Savile). *The Complete Works of George Savile, First Marquess of Halifax.* Ed. by Walter Raleigh. Oxford: Clarendon Press, 1912.

Chapter 11 HOBBES

Works by Hobbes

The English Works of Thomas Hobbes. Ed. by William Molesworth. London: Bohn, 1839–45, 11 vols.

Behemoth, or the Long Parliament. Ed. by F. Tonnies. London: Simpkin Marshall, 1889.

De cive, or The Citizen. Ed. by Sterling P. Lamprecht. New York: Appleton-Century-Crofts, 1949.

The Elements of Law, Natural and Politic. Ed. by F. Tonnies. London: Simpkin Marshall, 1889.

Leviathan. Ed. by A. D. Lindsay. New York: Dutton (Everyman's Library), 1950.

Leviathan. Ed. by Michael Oakeshott. Oxford: Blackwell & Mott, 1946.

Selections. Ed. by Frederick J. E. Woodbridge. New York: Scribner's, 1930.

Secondary Works

BOWLE, JOHN. *Hobbes and His Critics; A Study in Seventeenth-Century Constitutionalism.* London: Cape, 1951.

BROWN, KEITH C., ed. *Hobbes Studies.* Cambridge, Mass.: Harvard Univ. Press, 1965.

GOLDSMITH, M. M. *Hobbes's Science of Politics.* New York: Columbia Univ. Press, 1966.

HOOD, F. C. *The Divine Politics of Thomas Hobbes: An Interpretation of Leviathan.* Oxford: Clarendon Press, 1964.

JESSOP, THOMAS EDMUND. *Thomas Hobbes.* London: Longmans, Green, 1960.

LAIRD, JOHN. *Hobbes.* London: Oxford Univ. Press, 1934.

MACPHERSON, C. B. *The Political Theory of Possessive Individualism: Hobbes to Locke.* New York: Oxford Univ. Press, 1962.

PETERS, RICHARD. *Hobbes.* Harmondsworth, Eng.: Penguin Books, 1956.

STEPHEN, LESLIE. *Hobbes.* New York: Macmillan, 1904.

STRAUSS, LEO. *The Political Philosophy of Hobbes.* Tr. by Elsa M. Sinclair. Chicago: Univ. of Chicago Press (Phoenix Books), 1963.

WARRENDER, J. HOWARD. *The Political Philosophy of Hobbes; His Theory of Obligation.* Oxford: Clarendon Press, 1957.

WATKINS, J. W. N. *Hobbes's System of Ideas: A Study in the Political Significance of Philosophical Theories.* London: Hutchinson, 1965.

Chapter 12 LOCKE

Works by Locke

The Correspondence of John Locke and Edward Clarke. Ed. by Benjamin Rand. London: Oxford Univ. Press, 1927.

An Essay Concerning Human Understanding (1690). Ed. by Alexander Campbell Fraser. Oxford: Clarendon Press, 1894. 2 vols. A convenient abridged ed. is Russell Kirk, ed., Chicago: Regnery (Gateway Editions), 1956.

Essays on the Law of Nature (*c.* 1670's). Ed. by Wolfgang von Leyden. Oxford: Clarendon Press, 1954. Latin with Eng. tr.

A Letter Concerning Toleration (1685). Ed. by J. W. Gough. Oxford: Blackwell & Mott, 1947. See also entry below under *Two Treatises.*

The Reasonableness of Christianity (1695). Ed. by I. T. Ramsey. (Library of Modern Religious Thought.) Stanford, Cal.: Stanford Univ. Press, 1958.

Two Tracts on Government. Ed. and tr. by Philip Abrams. New York: Cambridge Univ. Press, 1967. Two early tracts on civil power and religion.

Two Treatises of Government. Intro. and Apparatus Criticus by Peter Laslett. London: Cambridge Univ. Press, 1960. The definitive edition, incorporating for the first time Locke's final revisions. See also Thomas I. Cook, ed. New York: Hafner, 1947; *A Treatise of Civil Government and A Letter Concerning Toleration.* Ed. by Charles L. Sherman. New York: Appleton-Century-Crofts, 1937; and *Of Civil Government.* Chicago: Regnery (Gateway Editions), 1955.

The Works of John Locke. London: Tegg, 1823. 10 vols.

Secondary Works

AARON, R. I. *John Locke.* 2nd ed. New York: Oxford Univ. Press, 1955.

COX, RICHARD H. *Locke on War and Peace.* New York: Oxford Univ. Press, 1960.

CRANSTON, MAURICE. *John Locke; A Biography.* New York: Macmillan, 1957.

CZAJKOWSKI, C. J. *The Theory of Private Property in Locke's Political Philosophy.* Notre Dame, Ind.: Univ. of Notre Dame Press, 1941.

FOX-BOURNE, H. R. *The Life of John Locke.* London: King & Jarrett, 1876. 2 vols.

GOUGH, JOHN W. *John Locke's Political Philosophy; Eight Studies.* Oxford: Clarendon Press, 1950.

LAMPRECHT, STERLING P. *The Moral and Political Philosophy of John Locke.* (Archives of Philosophy, No. 1.) New York: Columbia Univ. Press, 1918.

LASLETT, PETER. Intro. to his ed. of Robert Filmer's *Patriarcha.* Oxford: Blackwell & Mott, 1949.

O'CONNOR, D. J. *John Locke.* Baltimore: Penguin Books, 1952.

POLIN, RAYMOND. *La Politique morale de John Locke.* Paris: Presses Universitaires de France, 1960.

VAUGHN, C. E. *Studies in the History of Political Philosophy Before and After Rousseau.* Manchester, Eng.: Univ. of Manchester Press, 1925. 2 vols. Vol. 1, pp. 130–204.

YOLTON, JOHN Y. *John Locke and the Way of Ideas.* London: Oxford Univ. Press, 1956. Excellent bibliography.

Chapter 13 THE EIGHTEENTH CENTURY

The Enlightenment

BECKER, CARL L. *The Heavenly City of the Eighteenth-Century Philosophers.* New Haven, Conn.: Yale Univ. Press, 1932.

CASSIRER, ERNST. *The Philosophy of the Enlightenment.* Tr. by F. C. A. Koelln and J. P. Pettegrove. Boston: Beacon Press, 1955.

COBBAN, ALFRED. *In Search of Humanity: The Role of the Enlightenment in Modern History.* New York: Braziller, 1960.

DE TOCQUEVILLE, ALEXIS. *The Old Regime and the French Revolution* (1856). Tr. by Stuart Gilbert. Garden City, N.Y.: Doubleday (Anchor Books), 1955.

FLEISHER, DAVID. *William Godwin: A Study in Liberalism.* London: Allen & Unwin, 1951.

FRANKEL, CHARLES. *The Faith of Reason; The Idea of Progress in the French Enlightenment.* New York: Columbia Univ. Press, 1948.

GAY, PETER. *The Enlightenment: An Interpretation.* New York: Knopf, 1966. The bibliographic essay, pp. 423–555, is a tour de force.

———. *Voltaire's Politics; The Poet as Realist.* Princeton, N.J.: Princeton Univ. Press, 1959.

GODWIN, WILLIAM. *An Enquiry Concerning Political Justice.* Ed. by F. E. L. Priestly. 3rd ed. Toronto: Univ. of Toronto, 1946. 2 vols.

HAZARD, PAUL. *European Thought in the Eighteenth Century; From Montesquieu to Lessing.* Tr. by J. Lewis May. New Haven, Conn.: Yale Univ. Press, 1954.

HEARNSHAW, F. J. C., ed. *Social and Political Ideas of Representative Thinkers of the Revolutionary Age.* New York: Barnes & Noble, 1950.

———, ed. *Social and Political Ideas of Some Great French Thinkers of the Age of Reason.* New York: Barnes & Noble, 1950.

KANT, IMMANUEL. *Metaphysical Elements of Justice.* Ed. by John Ladd. New York: Liberal Arts Press, 1963.

KEGAN PAUL, C. *William Godwin.* London: King & Jarrett, 1876. 2 vols.

KETTLER, DAVID. *The Social and Political Thought of Adam Ferguson.* Columbus: Ohio State Univ. Press, 1965.

LASKI, HAROLD J. *The Rise of European Liberalism.* London: Allen & Unwin, 1936.

———. *Political Thought in England; Locke to Bentham.* London: Oxford Univ. Press (Home University Library), 1920.

MARTIN, KINGSLEY. *The Rise of French Liberal Thought; A Study of Political Ideas from Bayle to Condorcet.* Ed. by J. P. Mayer. New York: New York Univ. Press, 1954.

ROBBINS, CAROLINE. *The Eighteenth-Century Commonwealthman.* Cambridge, Mass.: Harvard Univ. Press, 1959.

ROCKWOOD, RAYMOND O., ed. *Carl Becker's Heavenly City Revisited.* Ithaca, N.Y.: Cornell Univ. Press, 1958.

ROWE, CONSTANCE. *Voltaire and the State.* New York: Columbia Univ. Press, 1955.

STEPHEN, LESLIE. *History of English Thought in the Eighteenth Century.* 3rd ed. New York: Harcourt, Brace & World (Harbinger Books), 1962. 2 vols.

VOLTAIRE. *Oeuvres Complètes.* Ed. by Louis Moland. Paris: Garnier, 1883–85. 52 vols.

———. *Philosophical Dictionary.* Sel. and ed. by H. I. Woolf. New York: Knopf, 1938.

———. *Selections.* Ed. by George R. Havens. New York: Century, 1925.

VYVERBERG, HENRY. *Historical Pessimism in the French Enlightenment.* Cambridge, Mass.: Harvard Univ. Press, 1958.

WILLEY, BASIL. *The Eighteenth-Century Background; Studies on the Idea of Nature in the Thought of the Period.* London: Chatto & Windus, 1940.

Economics and Politics

BEER, MAX. *An Inquiry into Physiocracy.* New York: Macmillan, 1940.

CROPSEY, JOSEPH. *Polity and Economy; An Interpretation of the Principles of Adam Smith.* The Hague: Nijhoff, 1957.

GINZBERG, ELI. *The House of Adam Smith.* New York: Columbia Univ. Press, 1934.

HEILBRONER, ROBERT L. *The Worldly Philosophers.* New York: Simon and Schuster, 1953, chs. 1–4.

HIGGS, HENRY. *The Physiocrats.* New York: Macmillan, 1897.

POLANYI, KARL. *The Great Transformation.* Boston: Beacon Press, 1957.

SCHUMPETER, JOSEPH A. *A History of Economic Analysis.* New York: Oxford Univ. Press, 1954, Part 2.

SMITH, ADAM. *Adam Smith's Moral and Political Philosophy.* Ed. by Herbert W. Schneider. New York: Hafner, 1948.

———. *An Inquiry into the Nature and Causes of the Wealth of Nations.* Ed. by E. B. Bax. London: Bell, 1896. 2 vols.

History and Politics

ADAMS, H. P. *The Life and Writings of Giambattista Vico.* London: Allen & Unwin, 1935.

BOLINGBROKE, LORD (HENRY ST. JOHN). *A Dissertation on Parties.* 10th ed. London: Davies and Cadell, 1775 (orig. ed., 1734).

———. *The Idea of a Patriot King* (1738). Ed. by Sydney W. Jackman. New York: Liberal Arts Press, 1965.

———. *Letters on the Study and Use of History.* 2nd ed. London: Cadell, 1770 (orig. ed., 1735).

CAPONIGRI, A. R. *Time and Idea; The Theory of History in Giambattista Vico.* Chicago: Regnery, 1953.

CONDORCET, MARQUIS DE (MARIE JEAN ANTOINE NICHOLAS DE CARITAT). *Outlines of an Historical View of the Progress of the Human Mind.* Philadelphia: Carey, Rice, Orwood, Bache, and Fellows, 1796.

CROCE, BENEDETTO. *The Philosophy of Giambattista Vico.* Tr. by R. G. Collingwood. New York: Macmillan, 1913.

PETRIE, CHARLES. *Bolingbroke.* London: Collins, 1937. A critical biography.

SCHAPIRO, J. SALWYN. *Condorcet and the Rise of Liberalism.* New York: Harcourt, Brace & World, 1934.

VICO, GIAMBATTISTA. *The New Science.* Tr. by Thomas G. Bergin and Max H. Fisch. Ithaca, N.Y.: Cornell Univ. Press, 1948. From 3rd ed. of 1744.

Law and Constitutionalism

ADAMS, JOHN. "A Defense of the Constitution." In *Works.* Ed. by Charles Francis Adams. Boston: Little, Brown, 1851. Vol. 6.

BECKER, CARL. *The Declaration of Independence: A Study in the History of Political Ideas.* New York: Random House (Vintage Books), 1957.

BLACKSTONE, WILLIAM. *Commentaries on the Laws of England.* Ed. by William G. Hammond. 8th ed. San Francisco: Whitney, 1890. Also Oxford: Clarendon Press, 1765–69. 4 vols.

BOORSTIN, DANIEL J. *The Mysterious Science of the Law; An Essay on Blackstone's Commentaries.* Boston: Beacon Press, 1958.

FARRAND, MAX, ed. *The Records of the Federal Convention of 1787.* New Haven, Conn.: Yale Univ. Press, 1911. 2 vols.

The Federalist. New York: Random House (Modern Library), 1937.

FRIEDRICH, CARL J. *The Philosophy of Law in Historical Perspective.* Chicago: Univ. of Chicago Press, 1958.

GOUGH, JOHN. *Fundamental Law in English Constitutional History.* Oxford: Clarendon Press, 1955.

HANDLER, EDWARD. *America and Europe in the Political Thought of John Adams.* Cambridge, Mass.: Harvard Univ. Press, 1964.

HARTZ, LOUIS. *The Liberal Tradition in America.* New York: Harcourt, Brace & World (Harvest Books), 1955.

LOCKMILLER, DAVID A. *Sir William Blackstone.* Chapel Hill: Univ. of North Carolina Press, 1938.

OTIS, JAMES. *Rights of British Colonies Asserted and Proved.* London: Williams, 1766.

WHITE, ANDREW DICKSON. *Seven Great Statesmen in the Warfare of Humanity with Unreason.* New York: Century, 1912. Ch. 3 is on Thomasius.

WILSON, JAMES. *Works.* Ed. by J. D. Andrews. Chicago: Callaghan, 1896. 2 vols.

Theory of Revolution

ACTON, LORD (JOHN E. E. D. ACTON). *Lectures on the French Revolution.* London: Macmillan, 1910.

BEST, M. A. *Thomas Paine; Prophet and Martyr of Democracy.* New York: Harcourt, Brace & World, 1927.

BRINTON, CRANE. *The Anatomy of Revolution.* New York: Norton, 1938.

CONWAY, M. C. *The Life of Thomas Paine.* New York: Putnam's, 1892. 2 vols.

JEFFERSON, THOMAS. *Life and Selected Writings.* Ed. by Adrienne Koch and William Peden. New York: Random House (Modern Library), 1944.

———. *Political Writings.* Ed. by Edward Dumbauld. New York: Liberal Arts Press, 1955.

PAINE, THOMAS. *The Complete Writings.* Ed. by Philip Foner. New York: Citadel Press, 1945. 2 vols.

TALMON, J. L. *The Origins of Totalitarian Democracy.* New York: Praeger, 1960.

WICKWAR, W. HARDY. *Baron d'Holbach: A Prelude to the French Revolution.* London: Allen & Unwin, 1935.

Chapter 14 MONTESQUIEU

Works by Montesquieu

Cahiers, 1716–1755. Ed. by Bernard Grasset. Paris: Grasset, 1941.

Considerations on the Causes of the Grandeur and the Decadence of the Romans. Tr. by Jehu Baker. New York: Appleton-Century-Crofts, 1894.

Oeuvres complètes. Ed. by Edouard Laboulaye. Paris: Garnier, 1875–79. 7 vols.

Persian and Chinese Letters. Tr. by John Davidson. New York: Dunne, 1901.

The Spirit of the Laws. Ed. by Franz Neumann. Tr. by Thomas Nugent. New York: Hafner, 1949. Many other editions.

Secondary Works

CABEEN, DAVID C. *Montesquieu Bibliography.* New York: New York Public Library, 1947. An extended and excellent annotated bibliography.

COURTNEY, CECIL PATRICK. *Montesquieu and Burke.* Oxford: Blackwell & Mott, 1963.

DEDIEU, JOSEPH. *Montesquieu; L'Homme et l'oeuvre* (1913). Paris: Boivin, 1943.

DURKHEIM, ÉMILE. *Montesquieu et Rousseau; Precurseurs de la sociologie.* Intro. by George Davy. Paris: Rivière, 1953. (Written 1892 and 1918.)

FAGUET, ÉMILE. *La Politique comparée de Montesquieu, Rousseau, et Voltaire.* Paris: Société d'Imprimerie et de Librairie, 1902.

GRANT, A. J. "Montesquieu." In F. J. C. Hearnshaw, ed., *The Social and Political Ideas of Some Great French Thinkers in the Age of Reason.* London: Harrap, 1930.

HOLMES, OLIVER WENDELL. "Montesquieu." In *Collected Legal Papers.* New York: Appleton-Century-Crofts, 1921.

LEVIN, LAWRENCE MEYER. *The Political Doctrine of Montesquieu's Esprit des Lois; Its Classical Background.* New York: The Institute of French Studies, 1936.

SHACKLETON, ROBERT. *Montesquieu: A Critical Biography.* London: Oxford Univ. Press, 1961.

STARK, W. *Montesquieu: Pioneer of the Sociology of Knowledge.* Toronto: Univ. of Toronto Press, 1961.

TEBERT, COURTNEY. *Montesquieu.* Oxford: Clarendon Press, 1904.

VAUGHN, C. E. *Studies in the History of Political Philosophy Before and After Rousseau.* Manchester, Eng.: Univ. of Manchester Press, 1939. 2 vols. Vol. 1, pp. 253–302.

Chapter 15 ROUSSEAU

Works by Rousseau

The Confessions. Tr. by Edmund Wilson. New York: Knopf, 1923. 2 vols. Many other editions.

Émile. Tr. by Barbara Foxley. New York: Dutton (Everyman's Library), 1948.

The First and Second Discourses. Ed. by Roger D. Masters and Judith R. Masters. New York: St. Martin's Press, 1964.

Oeuvres complètes. Paris: Hachette, 1886–1911. 13 vols.

The Political Writings of Jean-Jacques Rousseau. Ed. by C. E. Vaughn. New York: Wiley, 1962 (orig. ed., 1915). 2 vols. Note Vaughn's introduction.

Rousseau; Political Writings. Tr. by Frederick W. Watkins. London: Nelson, 1953.

The Social Contract and Discourses. Tr. by G. D. H. Cole. New York: Dutton (Everyman's Library), 1950. Note Cole's introduction.

The Social Contract. Ed. by Charles Frankel. New York: Hafner, 1947. An eighteenth-century translation revised by Frankel.

Secondary Works

BABBITT, IRVING. *Rousseau and Romanticism.* Boston: Houghton Mifflin, 1919; New York: World (Meridian Books), 1955.

BROOME, J. H. *Rousseau; A Study of His Thought.* London: Arnold, 1963.

CASSIRER, ERNST. *The Question of Jean-Jacques Rousseau.* Trans., ed., and intro. by Peter Gay. New York: Columbia Univ. Press, 1954.

———. *Rousseau, Kant, and Goethe.* Princeton, N.J.: Princeton Univ. Press, 1945.

CHAPMAN, JOHN W. *Rousseau—Totalitarian or Liberal?* New York: Columbia Univ. Press, 1956.

COBBAN, ALFRED. *Rousseau and the Modern State.* Hamden, Conn.: Shoe String Press (Archon Books), 1961.

DERATHÉ, ROBERT. *Jean-Jacques Rousseau et la science politique de son temps.* Paris: Presses Universitaires de France, 1950.

———. *Le Rationalisme de Jean-Jacques Rousseau.* Paris: Presses Universitaires de France, 1948.

GREEN, F. C. *Jean-Jacques Rousseau; A Critical Study of His Life and Writings.* London: Cambridge Univ. Press, 1955.

GRIMSLEY, RONALD. *Jean-Jacques Rousseau; A Study of Self-Awareness.* Cardiff, Wales: Univ. of Wales Press, 1961.

HENDEL, CHARLES W. *Jean-Jacques Rousseau, Moralist.* London: Oxford Univ. Press, 1934. 2 vols.

HØFFDING, HARALD. *Jean-Jacques Rousseau and His Philosophy.* Tr. by William Richards and Leo Saidla. New Haven, Conn.: Yale Univ. Press, 1930.

McDONALD, JOAN. *Rousseau and the French Revolution, 1762–1791.* London: Athlone Press, 1965.

MORLEY, JOHN. *Rousseau.* London: Macmillan, 1905. 2 vols.

OSBORNE, ANNIE M. *Rousseau and Burke.* London: Oxford Univ. Press, 1940.

SCHINZ, ALBERT. *La Pensée de Jean-Jacques Rousseau.* Northampton, Mass.: Smith College, 1929.

STAROBINSKI, JEAN. *Jean-Jacques Rousseau: La Transparence et l'obstacle.* Paris: Librairie Plon, 1957.

WRIGHT, ERNEST HUNTER. *The Meaning of Rousseau.* London: Oxford Univ. Press, 1929.

Chapter 16 HUME

Works by Hume

David Hume's Political Essays. Ed. by Charles W. Hendel. New York: Liberal Arts Press, 1953. From the 1777 edition of *Essays, Moral and Political.*

Dialogues Concerning Natural Religion. Ed. by Norman Kemp Smith. 2nd ed. London: Nelson, 1947.

An Enquiry Concerning Human Understanding. Ed. by L. A. Selby-Bigge. Oxford: Clarendon Press, 1894. From the 1777 edition.

Essays and Treatises on Several Subjects. Edinburgh: Bell and Bradfate, 1800. 2 vols. Vol. 1 is *Essays, Moral, Political, and Literary.* Vol. 2 contains, among other works, *An Enquiry Concerning the Principles of Morals* and *The Natural History of Religion.*

The History of England from the Invasion of Julius Caesar to the Revolution of 1688. London: Cadell and Davies, 1802 (orig. ed., 1754–62). 8 vols.

The History of England from the Revolution to the Death of George II. Ed. by T. G. Smollett. London: Cadell and Baldwin, 1804. 5 vols.

Hume; Theory of Politics. Ed. by Frederick Watkins. Austin: Univ. of Texas, 1953. Note Watkins' introduction.

Moral and Political Philosophy. Ed. by Henry Aiken. New York: Hafner, 1948.

Treatise of Human Nature. Ed. by L. A. Selby-Bigge. Oxford: Clarendon Press, 1896.

Secondary Works

BONGIE, LAURENCE L. *David Hume: Prophet of the Counter-Revolution.* Oxford: Clarendon Press, 1965.

BRYSON, GLADYS. *Man and Society; The Scottish Inquiry of the Eighteenth Century.* Princeton, N.J.: Princeton Univ. Press, 1945.

HUXLEY, THOMAS. *Hume.* London: Macmillan, 1881.

KYDD, RACHEL M. *Reason and Conduct in Hume's Treatise.* London: Oxford Univ. Press, 1946.

LAING, B. M. *David Hume.* London: Benn, 1932.

LAIRD, JOHN. *Hume's Philosophy of Human Nature.* London: Methuen, 1932.

LETWIN, SHIRLEY R. *The Pursuit of Certainty: David Hume, Jeremy Bentham, John Stuart Mill, Beatrice Webb.* London: Cambridge Univ. Press, 1965.

MOSSNER, ERNEST C. *The Life of David Hume.* Austin: Univ. of Texas, 1954.

ROSS, WILLIAM G. *Human Nature and Utility in Hume's Social Philosophy.* Berea, Ky.: published by the author, 1942.

SMITH, NORMAN KEMP. *The Philosophy of David Hume.* London: Macmillan, 1941.

STEWART, JOHN B. *The Moral and Political Philosophy of David Hume.* New York: Columbia Univ. Press, 1963.

Chapter 17 BURKE

Works by Burke

Appeal from the New to the Old Whigs. Ed. by John M. Robson. New York: Liberal Arts Press, 1962.

Burke's Politics. Ed. by Ross Hoffman and S. J. Levack. New York: Knopf, 1949.

The Philosophy of Edmund Burke; A Selection from His Speeches and Writings. Ed. by L. I. Bredvold and R. G. Ross. Ann Arbor: Univ. of Michigan Press, 1961.

Reflections on the Revolution in France. Ed. by Russell Kirk. Chicago: Regnery, 1955.

Selected Writings of Edmund Burke. Ed. by Walter J. Bate. New York: Random House (Modern Library), 1960. *Appeal from the New to the Old Whigs* is a conspicuous omission from this collection.

Selected Writings and Speeches. Ed. by Peter J. Stanlis. Garden City, N.Y.: Doubleday (Anchor Books), 1963.

The Writings and Speeches of Edmund Burke. Boston: Little, Brown, 1901. 12 vols.

Secondary Works

CANAVAN, FRANCIS. *The Political Reason of Edmund Burke.* Durham, N.C.: Duke Univ. Press, 1960.

COBBAN, ALFRED. *Edmund Burke and the Revolt Against the Eighteenth Century.* New York: Macmillan, 1929.

COPELAND, THOMAS W. *Edmund Burke; Six Essays.* London: Cape, 1950.

HARRIS, RONALD W. *Political Ideas, 1760–1772.* London: Gollancz, 1963.

KIRK, RUSSELL. *The Conservative Mind; From Burke to Santayana.* Chicago: Regnery, 1953.

LASKI, HAROLD J. *Political Thought in England; Locke to Bentham.* London: Hutchinson, 1937, ch. 6.

MACCUNN, JOHN. *The Political Philosophy of Burke.* London: Longmans, Green, 1913.

MANSFIELD, HARVEY C., JR. *Statesmanship and Party Government; A Study of Burke and Bolingbroke.* Chicago: Univ. of Chicago Press, 1965.

MURRAY, ROBERT H. *Edmund Burke; A Biography.* Oxford, Clarendon Press, 1931.

PARKIN, CHARLES. *The Moral Basis of Burke's Political Thought; An Essay.* London: Cambridge Univ. Press, 1956.

STANLIS, PETER J. *Edmund Burke and the Natural Law.* Ann Arbor: Univ. of Michigan Press, 1958.

Chapter 18 THE NINETEENTH CENTURY

General

BARKER, ERNEST. *Political Thought in England, 1848–1914.* 2nd ed. London: Oxford Univ. Press (Home University Library), 1928.

BOWLE, JOHN. *Politics and Opinion in the Nineteenth Century.* New York: Oxford Univ. Press (Galaxy Books), 1964. See bibliography, pp. 500–02.

BRINTON, CRANE. *English Political Thought in the Nineteenth Century.* Cambridge, Mass.: Harvard Univ. Press, 1933.

FAGUET, ÉMILE. *Politiques et moralistes du dix-neuvième siècle.* Paris: Boivin, 1899. 3 vols.

HEARNSHAW, F. J. C., ed. *Essays in the Social and Political Ideas of the Age of Reaction and Reconstruction.* London: Harrap, 1932.

———, ed. *Social and Political Ideas of the Victorian Age.* London: Harrap, 1933.

KRIEGER, LEONARD. *The German Idea of Freedom.* Boston: Beacon Press, 1957. See bibliography, pp. 529–33.

LÖWITH, KARL. *From Hegel to Nietzsche.* Tr. by David E. Green. New York: Holt, Rinehart and Winston, 1964.

MAYER, J. P. *Political Thought in France from Sieyès to Sorel.* London: Faber & Faber, 1948.

MURRAY, R. H., ed. *Studies in English Social and Political Thinkers of the Nineteenth Century.* Heffer, 1929. 2 vols. Vol. 1 contains selections from Malthus, Bentham, James Mill, John Stuart Mill, Owen, Coleridge, Disraeli, Carlyle, Cobden, and Kingsley. Vol. 2 contains selections from Spencer, Maine, Ruskin, Arnold, Seeley, Bagehot, Green, Bryce, Maitland, and assorted socialists.

REISS, H. S., ed. *The Political Thought of the German Romantics, 1793–1815.* Oxford: Blackwell & Mott, 1955. Selections from Fichte, Novalis, Müller, Schleiermacher, Savigny.

RUGGIERO, GUIDO DE. *A History of European Liberalism.* Tr. by R. G. Collingwood. London: Oxford Univ. Press, 1927; Boston: Beacon Press, 1959. See bibliography.

SCHAPIRO, J. SALWYN. *Liberalism and the Challenge of Fascism; Social Forces in England and France, 1815–1870.* New York: McGraw-Hill, 1949. See bibliography, pp. 405–13.

SOLTAU, ROGER. *French Political Thought in the Nineteenth Century.* New Haven, Conn.: Yale Univ. Press, 1931.

English Utilitarianism [See also the bibliography for Chapter 19, "Bentham."]

AUSCHUTZ, R. P. *The Philosophy of John Stuart Mill.* Oxford: Clarendon Press, 1953.

AUSTIN, JOHN. *Austinian Theory of Law.* Ed. by W. Jethro Brown. London: Murray, 1906.

———. *The Province of Jurisprudence Determined; and, The Uses of the Study of Jurisprudence.* Ed. by H. L. A. Hart. London: Weidenfeld & Nicolson, 1954.

BRITTON, KARL. *John Stuart Mill.* Harmondsworth, Eng.: Penguin Books, 1953.

BULLOCK, ALAN, AND MAURICE SHOCK. *The Liberal Tradition: Fox to Keynes.* London: Oxford Univ. Press (Galaxy Books), 1967.

COWLING, MAURICE. *Mill and Liberalism.* New York: Cambridge Univ. Press, 1964.

HAMBURGER, JOSEPH. *Intellectuals in Politics: John Stuart Mill and the Philosophical Radicals.* New Haven, Conn.: Yale Univ. Press, 1965.

MILL, JAMES. *Essays on Government, Jurisprudence, Liberty of the Press, and Law of Nations.* Ed. by Philip Wheelwright. (Doran Series.) Garden City, N.Y.: Doubleday, Doran, 1935. Bound with works by Bentham and John Stuart Mill.

MILL, JOHN STUART. *Disquisitions and Discussions.* London: Longmans, Green, 1859–75. 4 vols.

———. *Essays on Politics and Culture.* Garden City, N.Y.: Doubleday, 1963.

———. *A Selection of His Works.* Ed. by John M. Robson. New York: St. Martin's Press, 1966.

———. *A System of Logic.* 8th ed. London: Longmans, Green, 1925, Book 6.

———. *Utilitarianism, Liberty, and Representative Government.* New York, Dutton (Everyman's Library), 1951. Many other editions.

Continental Liberalism

BASTID, PAUL. *Benjamin Constant et sa doctrine.* Paris: Colin, 1966. 2 vols.

CONSTANT, BENJAMIN. *Principes de politique,* in *Oeuvres.* Ed. by Alfred Roulin. Paris: Gallimard, 1957, pp. 1099–1249.

DE TOCQUEVILLE, ALEXIS. *Democracy in America.* Ed. by H. S. Commager. Tr. by Henry Reeve. London: Oxford Univ. Press, 1946. Many other editions.

———. *The Old Regime and the French Revolution.* Tr. by Stuart Gilbert. Garden City, N.Y.: Doubleday (Anchor Books), 1955. From 4th French ed. (1858).

GUIZOT, FRANÇOIS. *Democracy in France.* New York: Appleton-Century-Crofts, 1849.

HERR, RICHARD. *Tocqueville and the Old Regime.* Princeton, N.J.: Princeton Univ. Press, 1962.

LIVELY, JACK. *The Social and Political Thought of Alexis de Tocqueville.* London: Oxford Univ. Press, 1962.

MAZZINI, JOSEPH. *The Duties of Man and Other Essays.* New York: Dutton (Everyman's Library), 1929.

ROYER-COLLARD, PIERRE PAUL. *Les Fragments philosophiques.* Intro. by André Schimberg. Paris: Alcan, 1913.

SCHERMERHORN, ELIZABETH W. *Benjamin Constant.* London: Heinemann, 1924.

TALMON, J. L. *Political Messianism: The Romantic Phase.* New York: Praeger, 1961.

VON TREITSCHKE, HENRICH. *Politics.* Tr. by Blanche Dugdale and T. de Bille. New York: Macmillan, 1916. 2 vols.

Social Darwinism

BAGEHOT, WALTER. *Physics and Politics.* New York: Appleton-Century-Crofts, 1873.

DEWEY, JOHN. *The Influence of Darwin on Philosophy.* New York: Holt, Rinehart and Winston, 1910.

HOBHOUSE, LEONARD. *Social Evolution and Political Theory.* New York: Columbia Univ. Press, 1911.

HOFSTADTER, RICHARD. *Social Darwinism in American Thought.* Philadelphia: Univ. of Pennsylvania Press, 1944; Boston: Beacon, 1955. See bibliography.

RITCHIE, DAVID G. *Darwinism and Politics.* London: Sonnenschein, 1889.

RUMNEY, JUDAH. *Herbert Spencer's Sociology*. London: Williams and Norgate, 1934.

SPENCER, HERBERT. *First Principles*. New York: Appleton-Century-Crofts, 1864.

———. *The Man Versus the State*. Caldwell, Ida.: Caxton, 1940.

———. *Social Statics*. New York: Appleton-Century-Crofts, 1864.

STARR, HARRIS. *William Graham Sumner*. New York: Holt, Rinehart and Winston, 1925.

SUMNER, WILLIAM GRAHAM. *The Challenge of Facts and Other Essays*. New Haven, Conn.: Yale Univ. Press, 1914.

———. *Essays*. Ed. by A. G. Keller and M. R. Davie. New Haven, Conn.: Yale Univ. Press, 1934. 2 vols.

Conservatism [See also the bibliography for Chapter 20, "Hegel."]

BERLIN, ISAIAH. *The Hedgehog and the Fox; An Essay on Tolstoy's View of History*. New York: Simon and Schuster, 1953. Relates De Maistre to Stendahl and Tolstoy.

CAIRD, EDWARD. *The Social Philosophy and Religion of Comte*. London: Macmillan, 1885.

COMTE, AUGUSTE. *A General View of Positivism* (1848). Tr. by J. H. Bridges. Stanford, Cal.: Academic Reprints, n. d.

DE BONALD, LOUIS. *Legislation primitive*. 5th ed. Paris: Le Clere, 1857.

DEMAISTRE, JOSEPH. *The Works of Joseph deMaistre*. Ed. by Jack Lively. New York: Macmillan, 1965.

———. *On God and Society*. Tr. by Elisha Greifer. Chicago: Regnery (Gateway Editions), 1959.

FICHTE, JOHANN G. *Addresses to the German Nation*. Tr. by R. F. Jones and G. F. Turnbull. LaSalle, Ill.: Open Court, 1922.

GIANTURCO, ELIO. *Joseph de Maistre and Giambattista Vico*. Washington, D.C.: published by the author, 1937.

LASKI, HAROLD J. *Authority in the Modern State*. New Haven, Conn.: Yale Univ. Press, 1919, ch. 1.

MILL, JOHN STUART. *Auguste Comte and Positivism*. 3rd ed. London: Turner, 1882.

British Idealism

BOSANQUET, BERNARD. *Philosophical Theory of the State*. 4th ed. London: Macmillan, 1923.

BRADLEY, F. H. *Ethical Studies; Selected Studies*. Intro. by Ralph Ross. New York: Liberal Arts Press, 1951 (orig. ed., 1876).

GREEN, THOMAS HILL. *Lectures on the Principles of Political Obligation* (1879). Intro. by A. D. Lindsay. London: Longmans, Green, 1941.

———. *The Political Theory of T. H. Green*. Ed. by John R. Rodman. New York: Appleton-Century-Crofts, 1964.

HOBHOUSE, LEONARD. *The Metaphysical Theory of the State*. London: Allen & Unwin, 1918.

RICHTER, MELVIN. *The Politics of Conscience: T. H. Green and His Age*. Cambridge, Mass.: Harvard Univ. Press, 1964.

RITCHIE, DAVID G. *Natural Rights*. London: Allen & Unwin, 1894.

Elitism

CARLYLE, THOMAS. *Critical and Miscellaneous Essays*. 2nd ed. New York: Appleton-Century-Crofts, 1871.

———. *Heroes, Hero-Worship, and the Heroic in History*. New York: Burt, n. d. (orig. ed., 1841).

CASSIRER, ERNST. *The Myth of the State*. New Haven, Conn.: Yale Univ. Press, 1946, 1960. Ch. 15 is on Carlyle.

CHAMBERLAIN, HOUSTON STEWART. *The Foundations of the Nineteenth Century*. Tr. by John Lees. London: Lane, 1911. 2 vols.

DE GOBINEAU, ARTHUR. *The Inequality of Human Races*. Tr. by Adrian Collins. New York: Putnam's, 1915.

LIPPINCOTT, BENJAMIN E. *Victorian Critics of Democracy*. Minneapolis: Univ. of Minnesota Press, 1938. On Carlyle, Ruskin, Arnold, Stephen, Maine, and Lecky.

ROE, FREDERICK WILLIAM. *The Social Philosophy of Carlyle and Ruskin*. New York: Harcourt, Brace & World, 1921.

RUSKIN, JOHN. *The Seven Lamps of Architecture, Sesame and Lilies, Unto This Last*. Sterling ed. Boston: Estes, n. d.

Socialism and Anarchism [See also the bibliographies for Chapter 21, "Marx," and Chapter 24, "Lenin."]

AURICH, PAUL. *The Russian Anarchists*. Princeton, N.J.: Princeton Univ. Press, 1967.

BAKUNIN, MICHAEL. *Marxism, Freedom, and the State*. Tr. and ed. by K. J. Kenafick. London: Freedom, 1950.

———. *The Political Philosophy of Bakunin*. Ed. by G. P. Maxinoff. New York: Free Press, 1964.

BELLAMY, EDWARD. *Looking Backward* (1887). Memorial ed. Boston: Houghton Mifflin, 1898. Many other editions.

BERNERI, MARIE LOUISE. *Journey Through Utopia*. London: Routledge & Kegan Paul, 1950. See bibliography, pp. 320–29.

BRISBANE, ALBERT. *The Social Destiny of Man*. Philadelphia: Stollmeyer, 1840. By Fourier's chief American disciple.

BROGAN, DENIS W. *Proud'hon*. London: Hamilton, 1934.

BUBER, MARTIN. *Paths in Utopia*. Tr. by R. F. C. Hull. Boston: Beacon Press, 1960.

CARR, E. H. *Michael Bakunin*. London: Macmillan, 1937.

COLE, G. D. H. *A History of Socialist Thought*. London: Macmillan, 1953–60. 5 vols. A monumental work covering the period from 1789 to 1939. See the bibliographies in each volume.

———. *Robert Owen*. London: Benn, 1925.

COLE, MARGARET. *The Story of Fabian Socialism*. Stanford, Cal.: Stanford Univ. Press, 1962.

FOURIER, CHARLES. *Selections from the Works of Fourier*. Tr. by Julia Franklin. London: Swan, Sonnenschein, 1901.

GEORGE, HENRY. *Progress and Poverty* (1881). New York: Vanguard, 1929.

JAURÈS, JEAN, ed. *Histoire socialiste, 1789–1900*. Paris: Rouff, 1901–08. 4 vols.

KROPOTKIN, PETER. *Mutual Aid*. Rev. ed. London: Heinemann, 1904.

LLOYD, HENRY DEMAREST. *Wealth Against Commonwealth*. New York: Harper & Row, 1894.

MANUEL, FRANK E. *The New World of Henri Saint-Simon*. Cambridge, Mass.: Harvard Univ. Press, 1956.

———. *The Prophets of Paris: Turgot, Condorcet, Saint-Simon, Fourier, and Comte*. New York: Harper & Row (Torchbooks), 1965.

OWEN, ROBERT. *Book of the New Moral World*. London: Wilson, 1836.

———. *A New View of Society and Other Writings* (1813). New York: Dutton (Everyman's Library), 1927.

PROUDHON, PIERRE JOSEPH. *What Is Property?* Tr. by Benjamin R. Tucker. New York: Humboldt, 1876.

SAINT-SIMON, COMTE DE (CLAUDE DE ROUVROY). *Social Organization, The Science of Man, and Other Writings*. Ed. and tr. by Felix Markham. New York: Harper & Row (Torchbooks), 1966.

SCHAPIRO, J. SALWYN, ed. *Movements of Social Dissent in Modern Europe*. Princeton, N.J.: Van Nostrand (Anvil Books), 1962.

WILSON, EDMUND. *To the Finland Station; A Study on the Writing and Acting of History*. Garden City, N.Y.: Doubleday (Anchor Books), 1959, Part 2, chs. 1–4.

WOODCOCK, GEORGE. *Pierre-Joseph Proud'hon*. London: Routledge & Kegan Paul, 1956.

Chapter 19 BENTHAM

Works by Bentham

A Fragment on Government. Ed. by F. C. Montague. Oxford: Clarendon Press, 1891.

A Fragment on Government and Introduction to the Principles of Morals and Legislation. Ed. by Wilfred Harrison. Oxford: Blackwell & Mott, 1948.

Handbook of Political Fallacies. Ed. by Harold A. Larrabee. New York: Harper & Row (Torchbooks), 1962.

Introduction to the Principles of Morals and Legislation. Oxford: Clarendon Press, 1879. New ed., 1907.

Introduction to the Principles of Morals and Legislation. Ed. by Lawrence J. Lafleur. New York: Hafner, 1948.

Theory of Legislation. Ed. by C. K. Ogden. London: Routledge & Kegan Paul, 1950.

The Works of Jeremy Bentham. Ed. by John Bowring. Edinburgh: Tait, 1838–42. 22 vols.

Secondary Works

ALBEE, ERNEST. *A History of English Utilitarianism*. London: Swan, Sonnenschein, 1900.

BAUMGART, DAVID. *Bentham and the Ethics of Today*. Princeton, N.J.: Princeton Univ. Press, 1952.

DAVIDSON, WILLIAM L. *Political Thought in England; The Utilitarians from Bentham to J. S. Mill*. New York: Oxford Univ. Press, 1950.

EVERETT, CHARLES W. *The Education of Jeremy Bentham*. New York: Columbia Univ. Press, 1931.

HALÉVY, ELIE. *The Growth of Philosophic Radicalism*. Tr. by Mary Morris. Boston: Beacon Press, 1955. See bibliography, pp. 522–46.

KEETON, G. W., AND GEORGE SCHWARZENBERGER, eds. *Jeremy Bentham and the Law*. London: Stevens, 1948.

LEAVIS, F. R., ed. *Mill on Bentham and Coleridge*. London: Chatto & Windus, 1950.

MACK, MARY P. *Jeremy Bentham: An Odyssey of Ideas*. New York: Columbia Univ. Press, 1963.

OGDEN, C. K. *Bentham's Theory of Fictions.* New York: Harcourt, Brace & World, 1932.

PLAMENATZ, JOHN. *The English Utilitarians.* London: Oxford Univ. Press, 1949.

STEPHEN, LESLIE. *The English Utilitarians.* London: Duckworth, 1900. 3 vols. Vol. 1 is on Bentham.

Chapter 20 HEGEL

Works by Hegel

Early Theological Writings. Tr. by T. M. Knox. Chicago: Univ. of Chicago Press, 1948. Reprinted as *On Christianity.* New York: Harper & Row (Torchbooks), 1961. In the latter see Richard Kroner's introduction, pp. 1–66.

Hegel's Political Writings. Tr. by T. M. Knox. Intro. by Z. Pelczynski. London: Oxford Univ. Press, 1964.

Phenomenology of Mind. Tr. by J. B. Baillie. 2nd ed. rev. London: Allen & Unwin, 1961.

The Philosophy of Hegel. Ed. by Carl J. Friedrich. New York: Random House (Modern Library), 1954.

Philosophy of History. Tr. by J. Sibree. London: Bell, 1905; New York: Dover, 1955.

Philosophy of Right. Tr. by T. M. Knox. Oxford: Clarendon Press, 1942; Corrected eds., 1945, 1949, 1953.

Reason in History. Tr. by R. S. Hartman. New York: Liberal Arts Press, 1953. Contains introduction to *Philosophy of History.*

Sämtliche Werke. Vols. 1–27. ed. by G. Lasson. Vols. 28–30 ed. by J. Hoffmeister. Vols. 1–26, Leipzig, 1923–32; Vol. 27, Hamburg, n.d.; Vols. 28–30, Hamburg, 1952–58. All published by Meiner. A critical edition, the best of several collected works. 35 vols. projected.

Selections. Ed. by J. Loewenberg. Rev. ed. New York: Wiley, 1944.

Secondary Works

CAIRD, EDWARD. *Hegel.* Edinburgh: Blackwood, 1883.

CROCE, BENEDETTO. *What Is Living and What Is Dead in Hegel's Philosophy?* Tr. by D. Ainslie. London: Macmillan, 1915 (orig. Italian ed., 1906).

FINDLAY, JOHN N. *Hegel: A Re-examination.* New York: Macmillan (Collier Books), 1962.

FOSTER, MICHAEL B. *The Political Philosophies of Plato and Hegel.* Oxford: Clarendon Press, 1935.

KAUFMANN, WALTER. *Hegel: A Reinterpretation.* Garden City, N.Y.: Doubleday (Anchor Books), 1966.

LOEWENBERG, JACOB. *Hegel's Phenomenology: Dialogues on the Life of the Mind.* LaSalle, Ill.: Open Court, 1965.

MARCUSE, HERBERT. *Reason and Revolution; Hegel and the Rise of Social Theory.* Boston: Beacon Press, 1960.

MURE, G. R. G. *An Introduction to Hegel.* Oxford: Clarendon Press, 1940.

REYBURN, HUGH A. *The Ethical Theory of Hegel; A Study of the Philosophy of Right.* Oxford: Clarendon Press, 1921.

ROSENZWEIG, FRANZ. *Hegel und der Staat.* Munich: Oldenbourg, 1920. 2 vols.

STACE, W. T. *The Philosophy of Hegel.* New York: Dover, 1955.

TRAVIS, D. C., ed. *A Hegel Symposium.* Austin: Univ. of Texas Press, 1962.

WEIL, ERIC. *Hegel et l'état.* Paris: Vrin, 1950.

Chapter 21 MARX

Primary Works

ENGELS, FRIEDRICH. *Herr Eugen Dühring's Revolution in Science* [*Anti-Dühring*] (1877–78). London: Lawrence & Wishart, 1894. Three chapters of *Anti-Dühring* were published separately as *Socialism, Utopian and Scientific* in 1880 and subsequently. See Edward Aveling's tr. Chicago: Kerr, 1902.

———. *The Origin of the Family, Private Property, and the State* (1884). Tr. by Ernest Untermann. Chicago: Kerr, 1902.

Handbook of Marxism. Ed. by Emile Burns. New York: Random House, 1935.

MARX, KARL. *Capital* (1867–94). Tr. by Samuel Moore and Edward Aveling. Chicago: Kerr, 1904–09. 3 vols.

———. *The Civil War in France* (1871). Intro. by Friedrich Engels. New York: International Publishers, 1933.

———. *A Critique of the Gotha Program* (1891). Ed. by C. P. Dutt. New York: International Publishers, 1933.

———. *Critique of Political Economy* (1859). Tr. by N. I. Stone. Chicago: Kerr, 1904. From the 2nd German ed.

———. *Early Writings.* Ed. and tr. by T. B. Bottomore. New York: McGraw-Hill, 1964.

———. *The Poverty of Philosophy* (1847). Tr. by H. Quelch. Chicago: Kerr, 1920.

———, and Friedrich Engels. *Basic Writings on Politics and Philosophy*. Ed. by Lewis S. Feuer. Garden City, N.Y.: Doubleday (Anchor Books), 1959.

———. *The Communist Manifesto*. Tr. by Eden Paul and Cedar Paul. New York: International Publishers, 1930.

———. *The Communist Manifesto, with Selections from the Eighteenth Brumaire of Louis Napoleon*. Ed. by Samuel Beer. New York: Appleton-Century-Crofts, 1955. There are countless editions of the Manifesto.

———. *Selected Works of Marx and Engels*. Ed. by C. P. Dutt. New York: International Publishers, 1936. 2 vols.

Marx on Economics. Ed. by Robert Freedman. New York: Harcourt, Brace & World (Harvest Books), 1961.

Writings of the Young Marx on Philosophy and Society. Ed. and tr. by Loyd D. Easton and Kurt H. Guddat. Garden City, N.Y.: Doubleday (Anchor Books), 1967.

Secondary Works

Berlin, Isaiah. *Karl Marx; His Life and Environment*. 2nd ed. New York: Oxford Univ. Press, 1948 (Galaxy Books, 1959). See bibliography.

Böhm von Bawerk, E. *Karl Marx and the Close of His System*. Ed. by Paul M. Sweezy. New York: Kelley, 1949.

Bober, M. M. *Karl Marx's Interpretation of History*. Rev. ed. Cambridge, Mass.: Harvard Univ. Press, 1948.

Carr, E. H. *Karl Marx; A Study in Fanaticism*. London: Dent, 1935.

Croce, Benedetto. *Historical Materialism and the Economics of Karl Marx*. Tr. by C. M. Meredith. London: Allen & Unwin, 1922.

Fromm, Erich. *Marx's Concept of Man*. New York: Ungar, 1961.

Hook, Sidney. *From Hegel to Marx*. Ann Arbor: Univ. of Michigan Press, 1962.

Hunt, R. N. Carew. *The Theory and Practice of Communism*. 5th ed. New York: Macmillan, 1957.

Kautsky, Karl. *The Economic Doctrines of Karl Marx*. London: Black, 1925.

Lichtheim, George. *Marxism; An Historical and Critical Study*. New York: Praeger, 1964.

Lindsay, A. D. *Karl Marx's Capital: An Introductory Essay*. 2nd ed. London: Oxford Univ. Press, 1947 (orig. ed., 1925).

Mayo, Henry B. *Introduction to Marxist Theory*. New York: Oxford Univ. Press, 1960. Note Mayo's excellent bibliography, pp. 310–25.

Meyer, Alfred G. *Marxism*. Cambridge, Mass.: Harvard Univ. Press, 1954.

Schumpeter, Joseph A. *Capitalism, Socialism, Democracy*. 3rd ed. New York: Harper & Row, 1950, Part 2.

Tucker, Robert M. *Philosophy and Myth in Karl Marx*. London: Cambridge Univ. Press, 1961.

Wilson, Edmund. *To the Finland Station; A Study in the Writing and Acting of History*. New York: Harcourt, Brace & World, 1940; Garden City, N.Y.: Doubleday (Anchor Books), 1959.

Wolfe, Bertram D. *Marxism: One Hundred Years in the Life of a Doctrine*. New York: Dial Press, 1965.

Chapter 22 NIETZSCHE

See Herbert Reichert and Karl Schlechta, eds., *International Nietzsche Bibliography*. Chapel Hill: Univ. of North Carolina Press, 1960.

Works by Nietzsche

Beyond Good and Evil. Tr. by Helen Zimmern. New York: Boni and Liveright, 1917; tr. by Marianne Cowan. Chicago: Regnery, 1955.

The Birth of Tragedy; and The Genealogy of Morals. Tr. by Francis Golffing. Garden City, N.Y.: Doubleday (Anchor Books), 1956.

Complete Works. Tr. by Oscar Levy. New York: Macmillan, 1924. 18 vols.

The Genealogy of Morals; A Polemic. Tr. by Horace B. Samuel. New York: Macmillan, 1924.

The Joyful Wisdom. Tr. by Thomas Common. 2nd ed. London: Foulis, 1918.

The Philosophy of Nietzsche. New York: Random House (Modern Library), 1937.

The Portable Nietzsche. Ed. by W. Kaufmann. New York: Viking Press, 1954.

Thus Spake Zarathustra. Tr. by Thomas Common. New York: Macmillan, 1911; New York: Random House (Modern Library), n. d.

The Use and Abuse of History. Tr. by Adrian Collins. New York: Liberal Arts Press, 1949.

Werke. Leipzig: Naumann, 1899–1904. 15 vols.

The Will to Power. Tr. by Anthony M. Ludovici. Edinburgh: Foulis, 1910.

Secondary Works

Brinton, Crane. *Nietzsche*. Cambridge, Mass.: Harvard Univ. Press, 1941.

Danto, Arthur C. *Nietzsche as a Philosopher*. New York: Macmillan, 1965.

JASPERS, KARL. *Nietzsche: An Introduction to the Understanding of His Philosophical Activity.* Tr. by C. F. Wallraff and F. J. Schmitz. Tucson: Univ. of Arizona Press, 1965.

KAUFMANN, WALTER A. *Nietzsche; Philosopher, Psychologist, Anti-Christ.* Princeton, N.J.: Princeton Univ. Press, 1950. See bibliography, pp. 383–95.

LEA, FRANK A. *The Tragic Philosopher; A Study of Friedrich Nietzsche.* New York: Philosophical Library, 1957.

MENCKEN, H. L. *The Philosophy of Friedrich Nietzsche.* 3rd ed. Boston: Luce, 1913.

MORE, PAUL ELMER. *Nietzsche.* Boston: Houghton Mifflin, 1912.

MORGAN, GEORGE ALLEN, JR. *What Nietzsche Means.* New York: Harper & Row, 1965.

REYBURN, HUGH A. *Nietzsche; The Story of a Human Philosopher.* London: Macmillan, 1948.

Chapter 23 THE TWENTIETH CENTURY

The multiplicity of books and the uncertainty of criteria of importance make this selection even more arbitrary than the selections for other chapters. For more extended bibliographies see Christian Bay, *The Structure of Freedom* (Stanford, Cal.: Stanford Univ. Press, 1958), pp. 391–408; Arnold Brecht, *Political Theory* (Princeton, N.J.: Princeton Univ. Press, 1959), pp. 499–574; Albert R. Chandler, ed., *The Clash of Political Ideals,* 3rd ed. (New York: Appleton-Century-Crofts, 1957), pp. 334–74; Henry S. Kariel, *In Search of Authority: Twentieth-Century Political Thought* (New York: Free Press, 1964), *passim;* William Kornhauser, *The Politics of Mass Society* (New York: Free Press, 1959), pp. 239–47; and J. Roland Pennock, *Liberal Democracy* (New York: Holt, Rinehart and Winston, 1950), pp. 373–94.

Totalitarianism

ARENDT, HANNAH. *The Origins of Totalitarianism.* New York: Harcourt, Brace & World, 1951; rev. and exp. ed., New York: World (Meridian Books), 1958.

CARSTEIN, F. L. *The Rise of Fascism.* Berkeley: Univ. of California Press, 1967.

EBENSTEIN, WILLIAM. *Totalitarianism: New Perspectives.* New York: Holt, Rinehart and Winston, 1962.

FRIEDRICH, CARL J., ed. *Totalitarianism.* Cambridge, Mass.: Harvard Univ. Press, 1954.

———, AND ZBIGNIEW BRZEZINSKI. *Totalitarian Dictatorship and Autocracy.* Cambridge, Mass.: Harvard Univ. Press, 1956.

GENTILE, GIOVANNI. *The Genesis and Structure of Society.* Tr. by H. S. Harris. Urbana: Univ. of Illinois Press, 1960.

HARRIS, H. S. *The Social Philosophy of Giovanni Gentile.* Urbana: Univ. of Illinois Press, 1960.

HITLER, ADOLF. *Mein Kampf.* Tr. by Ralph Manheim. Boston: Houghton Mifflin, 1943.

HOFFER, ERIC. *The True Believer.* New York: Harper & Row, 1951.

MILOCZ, CESLAW. *The Captive Mind.* Tr. by Jane Zielonko. New York: Knopf (Vintage Books), 1953.

MUSSOLINI, BENITO. *The Political and Social Doctrine of Fascism.* Tr. by Jane Soames. London: Hogarth, 1933.

ROCCO, ALFREDO. "The Political Doctrine of Fascism." Tr. by D. Bigongiari in *International Conciliation Bulletin No. 223.* New York: Carnegie Endowment for International Peace, 1926.

SCHNEIDER, HERBERT W. *Making the Fascist State.* New York: Oxford Univ. Press, 1928.

SOREL, GEORGES. *Reflections on Violence.* Tr. by T. E. Hulme and J. Roth. New York: Free Press, 1950.

WEBER, EUGEN J. *Varieties of Fascism.* Princeton, N.J.: Van Nostrand (Anvil Books), 1964.

Liberalism-Conservatism [For Socialism, see the bibliography for Chapter 24, "Lenin."]

AUERBACH, MORTON. *The Conservative Illusion.* New York: Columbia Univ. Press, 1959.

BAY, CHRISTIAN. *The Structure of Freedom.* New York: Atheneum, 1965.

BERLIN, ISAIAH. *Two Concepts of Liberty.* Oxford: Clarendon Press, 1958.

CRANSTON, MAURICE. *Freedom; A New Analysis.* 2nd ed. London: Longmans, Green, 1954.

FRANKEL, CHARLES. *The Democratic Prospect.* New York: Harper & Row, 1962.

FRIEDMAN, MILTON. *Capitalism and Freedom.* Chicago: Univ. of Chicago Press (Phoenix Books), 1962.

GALBRAITH, JOHN KENNETH. *The Affluent Society.* Boston: Houghton Mifflin, 1958.

———. *American Capitalism.* Rev. ed. Boston: Houghton Mifflin, 1956.

———. *The New Industrial State.* Boston: Houghton Mifflin, 1967.

———. *Studies in Philosophy, Politics and Economics.* Chicago: Univ. of Chicago Press, 1967.

KENDALL, WILLMOORE. *The Conservative Affirmation.* Chicago: Regnery, 1963.

KEYNES, JOHN MAYNARD. *The Economic Consequences of the Peace.* New York: Harcourt, Brace & World, 1920.

———. *The General Theory of Employment, Interest, and Money.* London: Macmillan, 1936; New York: Harcourt, Brace & World, 1936.

LASKI, HAROLD J. *A Grammar of Politics.* London: Allen & Unwin, 1925.

———. *Liberty in the Modern State.* New York: Harper & Row, 1930.

———. *The State in Theory and Practice.* New York: Viking Press, 1935.

LIPPMANN, WALTER. *Essays in the Public Philosophy.* New York: New American Library (Mentor Books), 1957.

———. *The Essential Lippmann.* Ed. by Clinton Rossiter and James Lare. New York: Random House (Vintage Books), 1965.

———. *An Inquiry into the Principles of the Good Society.* Boston: Little, Brown, 1937.

———. *Public Opinion.* New York: Harcourt, Brace & World, 1922; Baltimore: Penguin Books, 1946.

McGOVERN, WILLIAM M., AND DAVID S. COLLIER. *Radicals and Conservatives.* Chicago: Regnery, 1957.

MEYER, FRANK S., ed. *What Is Conservatism?* New York: Holt, Rinehart and Winston, 1964.

MINOGUE, KENNETH. *The Liberal Mind.* London: Methuen, 1963.

OAKESHOTT, MICHAEL. *Rationalism in Politics.* New York: Basic Books, 1962.

ORTEGA Y GASSET, JOSÉ. *The Revolt of the Masses.* New York: Nelson, 1932.

RUSSELL, BERTRAND. *Authority and the Individual.* New York: Simon and Schuster, 1945.

VON HAYEK, FRIEDRICH A. *The Constitution of Liberty.* Chicago: Univ. of Chicago Press, 1960.

Freudianism

BIRNBACH, MARTIN. *Neo-Freudian Social Philosophy.* Stanford, Cal.: Stanford Univ. Press, 1961.

BROWN, NORMAN. *Life Against Death; The Psychoanalytic Meaning of History.* New York: Random House (Vintage Books), 1961.

FREUD, SIGMUND. *Civilization and Its Discontents* (1930). Tr. by Joan Rivière. London: Hogarth, 1939, 1951.

———. *Civilization, War, and Death.* Ed. by John Rickman. London: Hogarth, 1939. Consists of three essays written in 1915, 1929, 1933.

———. *The Future of an Illusion.* Tr. by W. D. Robson-Scott. London: Hogarth, 1928; Garden City, N.Y.: Doubleday (Anchor Books), 1957.

FROMM, ERICH. *Escape from Freedom.* New York: Holt, Rinehart and Winston, 1941.

———. *The Sane Society.* New York: Holt, Rinehart and Winston, 1955.

HORNEY, KAREN. *The Neurotic Personality of Our Time.* New York: Norton, 1937.

JOHNSON, THOMAS. *Freud and Political Thought.* New York: Citadel Press, 1965.

JUNG, CARL G. *Modern Man in Search of a Soul.* London: Kegan Paul, Trench, Trübner, 1933.

MARCUSE, HERBERT. *Eros and Civilization.* New York: Random House (Vintage Books), 1962.

NELSON, BENJAMIN, ed. *Freud and the Twentieth Century.* New York: World (Meridian Books), 1957.

PROGOFF, IRA. *Jung's Psychology and Its Social Meaning.* New York: Grove Press, 1957.

RIEFF, PHILIP. *Freud: The Mind of the Moralist.* Garden City, N.Y.: Doubleday (Anchor Books), 1961.

SCHAAR, JOHN H. *Escape from Authority; The Perspectives of Erich Fromm.* New York: Basic Books, 1961.

Existentialism

ARENDT, HANNAH. *Between Past and Future; Six Exercises in Political Thought.* New York: Viking Press, 1961.

———. *The Human Condition.* Chicago: Univ. of Chicago Press, 1958.

———. *On Revolution.* New York: Viking Press, 1963.

BARRETT, WILLIAM. *Irrational Man.* Garden City, N.Y.: Doubleday (Anchor Books), 1962.

CAMUS, ALBERT. *The Myth of Sisyphus and Other Essays.* Tr. by Justin O'Brien. New York: Knopf, 1955.

———. *The Rebel.* Tr. by Anthony Bower. London: Hamilton, 1953; New York: Random House (Vintage Books), 1959.

———. *Resistance, Rebellion, and Death.* Tr. by Justin O'Brien. New York: Knopf, 1961.

CRANSTON, MAURICE. *Jean-Paul Sartre.* New York: Grove Press, 1962.

CRUICKSHANK, JOHN. *Albert Camus and the Literature of Revolt.* New York: Oxford Univ. Press (Galaxy Books), 1960.

DESAN, WILFRED. *The Marxism of Jean-Paul Sartre.* Garden City, N.Y.: Doubleday, 1965.

DOUGLAS, KENNETH. *A Critical Bibliography of Existentialism (The Paris School).* Yale French Studies, Special Monograph No. 1, 1950.

GREENE, NORMAN N. *Jean-Paul Sartre, The Existentialist Ethic.* Ann Arbor: Univ. of Michigan Press, 1960.

GRENE, MARJORIE. *Introduction to Existentialism.* Chicago: Univ. of Chicago Press (Phoenix Books), 1959.

HEINEMANN, FREDERICK. *Existentialism and the Modern Predicament.* 2nd ed. New York: Harper & Row (Torchbooks), 1958.

JASPERS, KARL. *The Future of Mankind.* Tr. by E. B. Ashton. Chicago: Univ. of Chicago Press, 1961.

———. *Man in the Modern Age.* Tr. by Eden Paul and Cedar Paul. Garden City, N.Y.: Doubleday (Anchor Books), 1957 (orig. German ed., 1931).

SARTRE, JEAN-PAUL. *Théorie des ensembles pratiques.* Vol. 1, *Critique de la raison dialectique.* Paris: Gallimard, 1960.

———. *Existentialism and Humanism.* Tr. by Philip Mairet. London: Methuen, 1948.

———. *Literary and Philosophical Essays.* Tr. by Annette Michelson. New York: Criterion Books, 1955.

———. *Search for a Method.* Tr. by Hazel Barnes. New York: Knopf, 1963.

WILLHOITE, FRED H., JR. *Beyond Nihilism: Albert Camus's Contribution to Political Thought.* Baton Rouge: Louisiana State Univ. Press. To be published in 1968.

Chapter 24 LENIN

Useful bibliographies may be found in Henry B. Mayo, *Introduction to Marxist Theory* (New York: Oxford Univ. Press, 1960), pp. 310–25; and Harry Overstreet and Bonaro Overstreet, *What We Must Know about Communism* (New York: Norton, 1958), pp. 314–24. See also works listed below by Daniels, Haimson, Hammond, and Meyer.

Works by Lenin

Collected Works. New York: International Publishers, 1927–42. Vols. 4, 13, 18–20, 21 only are translated (badly) into English.

Essentials of Lenin. London: Lawrence & Wishart, 1947. 2 vols.

Marx-Engels-Marxism. 3rd Eng. ed. Moscow: Foreign Language Publishing House, 1947. Includes excerpts from "State and Revolution," "What Is to Be Done?" and most of the major tracts.

Selected Works. New York: International Publishers, 1935–43. 12 vols.

Selected Works. Moscow: Foreign Language Publishing House, 1946. 2 vols.

Sochineniya (Works). 5th ed. Moscow: Marx-Engels-Lenin Institute, 1958–65. 55 vols. Many of the various Lenin tracts have been published separately in English by International Publishers, New York.

The Suppressed Testament of Lenin; The Complete Original Text with Two Explanatory Articles by L. Trotsky. New York: Pioneer, 1935. Lenin's famous criticism of Stalin, not published in the Soviet Union until 1956.

Secondary Works

APTHEKER, HERBERT, ed. *Marxism and Alienation: A Symposium.* New York: Humanities Press, 1965.

BARON, SAMUEL H. *Plekhanov, The Father of Russian Marxism.* Stanford, Cal.: Stanford Univ. Press, 1963.

BUKHARIN, NIKOLAI I. *Historical Materialism.* New York: International Publishers, 1925. Author's tr. from 3rd Russian ed.

CARR, EDWARD H. *The Bolshevik Revolution, 1917–1923.* New York: Macmillan, 1954. 3 vols.

CHEN, YUNG PING. *Chinese Political Thought: Mao Tse-tung and Liu Shao-chi.* The Hague: Nijhoff, 1966.

DANIELS, ROBERT V. *The Conscience of the Revolution; Communist Opposition in Soviet Russia.* Cambridge, Mass.: Harvard Univ. Press, 1960.

FISCHER, LOUIS. *The Life of Lenin.* New York: Harper & Row, 1964.

HAIMSON, LEOPOLD H. *The Russian Marxists and the Origins of Bolshevism.* Cambridge, Mass.: Harvard Univ. Press, 1955. See bibliography, pp. 235–40.

HAMMOND, THOMAS TAYLOR. *Lenin on Trade Unions and Revolution, 1893–1917.* New York: Columbia Univ. Press, 1957. See bibliography, pp. 130–50.

HILLQUIT, MORRIS. *From Marx to Lenin.* New York: Hanford, 1921.

History of the Communist Party of the Soviet Union (Bolsheviks): Short Course. New York: International Publishers, 1939. The so-called Stalin history.

KAUTSKY, KARL. *The Economic Doctrines of Karl Marx.* Tr. by H. J. Stenning. London: Black, 1925.

———. *Terrorism and Communism; A Contribution to the Natural History of Revolution.* Tr. by W. H. Kerridge. London: Allen & Unwin, 1920.

MAO TSE-TUNG. *Mao Tse-tung: An Anthology of His Writings.* Ed. by Anne Freemantle. New York: New American Library (Mentor Books), 1962.

MEYER, ALFRED G. *Leninism.* Cambridge, Mass.: Harvard Univ. Press, 1957. See bibliography, pp. 295–98.

PLAMENATZ, JOHN. *German Marxism and Russian Communism.* New York: Harper & Row (Torchbooks), 1965.

PLEKHANOV, GEORGI. *The Development of the Monist View of History* (1895). Tr. by Andrew Rothstein. Moscow: Foreign Language Publishing House, 1956.

POSSONY, STEFAN T. *Lenin: The Compulsory Revolutionary.* Chicago: Regnery, 1963.

SCHRAM, STUART A. *The Political Thought of Mao Tse-tung.* New York: Praeger, 1963.

STALIN, JOSEPH. *Problems of Leninism.* 11th ed. Moscow: Foreign Language Publishing House, 1941. Moscow-published works by Stalin tend to be unreliable.

TREADGOLD, D. W. *Lenin and His Rivals.* New York: Praeger, 1955.

TROTSKY, LEON. *Lenin.* Author's trans. New York: Minton, Balch, 1925.

———. *My Life; An Attempt at an Autobiography.* New York: Scribner's, 1931.

———. *The Permanent Revolution.* Tr. by Max Schachtman. New York: Pioneer, 1931.

ULAM, ADAM B. *The Unfinished Revolution.* New York: Random House, 1960.

WILSON, EDMUND. *To the Finland Station; A Study in the Writing and Acting of History.* Garden City, N.Y.: Doubleday (Anchor Books), 1959.

WOLFE, BERTRAM D. *Three Who Made a Revolution.* Boston: Beacon Press, 1956.

Chapter 25 DEWEY

Works by Dewey

Democracy and Education. New York: Macmillan, 1916.

Ethics, with James H. Tufts. Rev. ed. New York: Holt, Rinehart and Winston, 1932.

Experience and Nature. LaSalle, Ill.: Open Court, 1925.

Freedom and Culture. New York: Putnam's, 1939.

German Philosophy and Politics. New York: Holt, Rinehart and Winston, 1915; Boston: Beacon Press, 1945.

Human Nature and Conduct. New York: Holt, Rinehart and Winston, 1922; New York: Random House (Modern Library), 1930.

The Influence of Darwin on Philosophy. New York: Holt, Rinehart and Winston, 1910.

Intelligence in the Modern World. Ed. by Joseph Ratner. New York: Random House (Modern Library), 1939.

John Dewey and Arthur F. Bentley: A Philosophical Correspondence, 1932–1951. Ed. by Sidney Ratner and Jules Altman. New Brunswick, N.J.: Rutgers Univ. Press, 1964.

Liberalism and Social Action. New York: Putnam's, 1935.

The Public and Its Problems. New York: Holt, Rinehart and Winston, 1927; Chicago: Regnery (Gateway Editions), 1946; Denver, Colo.: Swallow, 1957.

The Quest for Certainty. New York: Minton, Balch, 1930.

Reconstruction in Philosophy. New York: Holt, Rinehart and Winston, 1920; enl. ed. Boston: Beacon Press, 1949.

School and Society. Rev. ed. Chicago: Univ. of Chicago Press, 1915.

Secondary Works

EDMAN, IRWIN. *John Dewey; His Contribution to the American Tradition.* Indianapolis, Ind.: Bobbs-Merrill, 1955.

Essays in Honor of John Dewey on the Occasion of His Seventieth Birthday. New York: Holt, Rinehart and Winston, 1929.

FELDMAN, W. T. *The Philosophy of John Dewey.* Baltimore: Johns Hopkins Press, 1934.

GEIGER, GEORGE R. *John Dewey in Perspective.* London: Oxford Univ. Press, 1958.

HOOK, SIDNEY. *John Dewey; An Intellectual Portrait.* New York: Day, 1939.

———, ed. *John Dewey; Philosopher of Science and Freedom.* New York: Dial Press, 1950.

JOHNSON, A. H., ed. *The Wit and Wisdom of John Dewey.* Boston: Beacon Press, 1949.

LAMONT, CORLISS, ed. *Dialogue on Dewey.* New York: Horizon Press, 1959.

LEANDER, FOLKE. *The Philosophy of John Dewey.* Göteborg, Sweden: Elanders, 1939.

MOORE, EDWARD C. *American Pragmatism; Peirce, James, and Dewey.* New York: Columbia Univ. Press, 1961.

RATNER, SIDNEY, ed. *The Philosopher of the Common Man.* New York: Putnam's, 1940.

SCHILPP, PAUL, ed. *The Philosophy of John Dewey.* Evanston, Ill.: Northwestern Univ. Press, 1939.

"Symposium on John Dewey," *Journal of the History of Ideas,* Vol. 20 (1959), pp. 515–76.

WHITE, MORTON G. *The Origin of Dewey's Instrumentalism.* New York: Columbia Univ. Press, 1943.

Chapter 26 NIEBUHR

For a complete bibliography of the writings of Reinhold Niebuhr see Harry R. Davis and Robert C. Good, eds., *Reinhold Niebuhr on Politics* (New York: Scribner's, 1960), p. 359. For a listing of Niebuhr's writings to 1956 see Kegley and Bretall, *Reinhold Niebuhr* (listed below), pp. 455–78. Issues of *Christianity and Crisis* from the early 1940's on provide a record of Niebuhr's political commentary.

Works by Niebuhr

The Children of Light and the Children of Darkness. New York: Scribner's, 1944.

Christian Realism and Political Problems. New York: Scribner's, 1953.

Christianity and Power Politics. New York: Scribner's, 1940.

Faith and History. New York: Scribner's, 1949.

An Interpretation of Christian Ethics. New York: Harper & Row, 1935.

The Irony of American History. New York: Scribner's, 1952.

Man's Nature and His Communities. New York: Scribner's, 1965.

Moral Man and Immoral Society. New York: Scribner's, 1932.

The Nature and Destiny of Man. New York: Scribner's, 1941. 2 vols.

Pious and Secular America. New York: Scribner's, 1958.

Reflections on the End of an Era. New York: Scribner's, 1934.

Secondary Works

BENNETT, JOHN C. *Christians and the State.* New York: Scribner's, 1958.

BINGHAM, JUNE. *The Courage to Change; An Introduction to the Life and Thought of Reinhold Niebuhr.* New York: Scribner's, 1961.

CARTER, PAUL A. *The Decline and Revival of the Social Gospel; Social and Political Liberalism in American Protestant Churches, 1920–1940.* Ithaca, N.Y.: Cornell Univ. Press, 1954. See bibliography, pp. 251–60.

GILL, THEODORE. *Recent Protestant Political Theory.* London: Hunt, Barnard, 1953.

HARLAND, GORDON. *The Thought of Reinhold Niebuhr.* New York: Oxford Univ. Press, 1960.

HOFMAN, HANS. *The Theology of Reinhold Niebuhr.* New York: Scribner's, 1956.

HUTCHISON, JOHN A., ed. *Christian Faith and Social Action.* New York: Scribner's, 1953.

KEGLEY, CHARLES W., AND ROBERT W. BRETALL, eds. *Reinhold Niebuhr; His Religious, Social, and Political Thought.* New York: Macmillan, 1956.

MARITAIN, JACQUES. *Man and the State.* Chicago: Univ. of Chicago Press, 1951.

MEYER, DONALD. *The Protestant Search for Political Realism, 1919–1941.* Berkeley: Univ. of California Press, 1960.

ODEGARD, HOLTAN P. *Sin and Science; Reinhold Niebuhr as Political Theologian.* Yellow Springs, Ohio: Antioch Press, 1956. See bibliography, pp. 221–34.

SCHNEIDER, HERBERT W. *Religion in Twentieth-Century America.* Cambridge, Mass.: Harvard Univ. Press, 1952.

TILLICH, PAUL. *Love, Power, and Justice.* New York: Oxford Univ. Press, 1954.

WHITE, MORTON G. *Social Thought in America; The Revolt Against Formalism.* Rev. ed. Boston: Beacon Press, 1958. Epilogue contains a critique of Niebuhr.

Chapter 27 POLITICAL THEORY AND THE SCIENCE OF POLITICS

CHARLESWORTH, JAMES C. *Contemporary Political Analysis.* New York: Free Press, 1967.

COWLING, MAURICE. *The Nature and Limits of Political Science.* New York: Cambridge Univ. Press, 1963.

EASTON, DAVID, ed. *Varieties of Political Theory.* Englewood Cliffs, N.J.: Prentice-Hall, 1966.

FRIEDRICH, CARL J. *Man and His Government; An Empirical Theory of Politics.* New York: McGraw-Hill, 1963.

FROHOCK, FRED M. *The Nature of Political Inquiry.* Homewood, Ill.: Dorsey, 1967.

RUNCIMAN, W. G. *Social Science and Political Theory.* London: Cambridge Univ. Press, 1963.

INDEX

Works discussed in depth are indexed under their titles. All other works are indexed under authors and are grouped alphabetically at the end of the author entries. Pages on which the chief discussion of a topic appears are printed in bold type.

A 0
B 1
C 2
D 3
E 4
F 5
G 6
H 7
I 8
J 9